T0334376

History in Management and Organization Studies

There has in recent times been an increasing interest in history, broadly defined, among management scholars. But what specifically a historical approach or perspective can contribute to research on organizational fields, organizations, strategy, etc., and how exactly such historical research should be carried out remain questions that have been answered only partially, if at all.

Building on the authors' prior and ongoing work, *History in Management and Organization Studies: From Margin to Mainstream* is unique in presenting a comprehensive and integrated view of how history has informed management research, with a focus on organization theory and strategy. More specifically, the volume provides an overview of how the relationship between history and management scholarship has evolved from the nineteenth century until today, focusing mainly on the post–World War II period, and systematically surveys the kind of research programs within organization theory and strategy that have used historical data and/or history as a theoretical construct, while also identifying the remaining "blind spots". As a whole, it offers a kind of roadmap for management scholars and historians to situate their research and, hopefully, find new roads for others to travel.

The book is intended for anybody conducting or planning to conduct historical research within management and organization studies and aims, in particular, at becoming a standard feature of research methods courses in business schools and departments of management.

Behlül Üsdiken is Emeritus Professor of Management and Organization at Sabancı University and Adjunct Professor in the Faculty of Business at Özyeğin University, both in Istanbul, Turkey.

Matthias Kipping is Professor of Policy and the Richard E. Waugh Chair in Business History in the Schulich School of Business at York University in Toronto, Canada.

Routledge Studies in Management, Organizations and Society

This series presents innovative work grounded in new realities, addressing issues crucial to an understanding of the contemporary world. This is the world of organised societies, where boundaries between formal and informal, public and private, local and global organizations have been displaced or have vanished, along with other nineteenth century dichotomies and oppositions. Management, apart from becoming a specialized profession for a growing number of people, is an everyday activity for most members of modern societies.

Similarly, at the level of enquiry, culture and technology, and literature and economics, can no longer be conceived as isolated intellectual fields; conventional canons and established mainstreams are contested. **Management, Organizations and Society** addresses these contemporary dynamics of transformation in a manner that transcends disciplinary boundaries, with books that will appeal to researchers, students and practitioners alike.

Recent titles in this series include:

The Psychodynamics of Toxic Organizations
Howard Stein and Seth Allcorn

Organizational Reliability
Human Resources, Information Technology and Management
Agnieszka Bieńkowska, Katarzyna Tworek and Anna Zabłocka-Kluczka

Management, Organization and Fear
Causes, Consequences and Strategies
Marek Bugdol and Kazimierz Nagody-Mrozowicz

History in Management and Organization Studies
From Margin to Mainstream
Behlül Üsdiken and Matthias Kipping

For more information about this series, please visit: www.routledge.com/

History in Management and Organization Studies

From Margin to Mainstream

Behlül Üsdiken and
Matthias Kipping

Routledge
Taylor & Francis Group

NEW YORK AND LONDON

First published 2021
by Routledge
52 Vanderbilt Avenue, New York, NY 10017

and by Routledge
2 Park Square, Milton Park, Abingdon, Oxon, OX14 4RN

Routledge is an imprint of the Taylor & Francis Group, an informa business

Library of Congress Cataloging-in-Publication Data
A catalog record for this book has been requested

ISBN: 978-1-138-72091-6 (hbk)
ISBN: 978-1-315-19484-4 (ebk)

Typeset in Sabon
by Apex CoVantage, LLC

Contents

Illustrations

Figures

Tables

Acknowledgments

This book has been a long time coming, and we are both relieved to have finished it. As usual, there are many people who deserve our gratitude. First of all, there is the, perhaps surprisingly, large and growing number of scholars who have been taking history seriously in their research—knowingly and at times unknowingly. They have provided all the raw material for our work. We are conscious of the fact that we can't do justice to them all and that more publications will have already appeared by the time our book is printed and that even more will come out afterwards. We hopefully managed to provide a map for past, current and future authors to help situate their scholarship within the bigger picture and maybe some guidance for those who are looking to contribute. Then, there are our editors at Routledge: David Varley, who made the original suggestion to extend our 2014 article in the *Academy of Management Annals*; little idea did he have how long that might take. And there are Brianna Ascher and her editorial assistants, Mary Del Plato and now Naomi Round Cahalin, who patiently tried to corral us into finally delivering on our promise to do so and shepherded the manuscript through production.

We also want to thank those who helped get us here in multiple ways: Behlül's research assistant, Çağla Yılmaz, who compiled the list of journal publications in Chapter 4. The German Alexander von Humboldt Foundation, whose research award allowed Matthias to concentrate a bit more on the manuscript during a sabbatical at the Freie Universität Berlin; and the Management Department there, where his host professors, Jörg Sydow and Georg Schreyögg, and their collaborators provided a very supportive and stimulating environment. This book owes much to them and to the many other colleagues at our own institutions and at many other universities, workshops and conferences, where we presented and discussed our work and received valuable feedback and suggestions—though, as usual, the responsibility for the result is ours alone. Matthias would like to add a special recognition to Behlül for his incredible patience and diligence during this whole process. Without that, we might have never finished the book. I owe you quite a few beers in the years to come!

Last but not least, there are those who are probably most impacted by a project like this, our families. This book not being the first one, they now mostly know when they have to take a back seat during periods of intense reading and writing. Without their silent suffering and unwavering support, none of this would have been possible. Thank you! Thank you all!

1 Objective
Finding History in Management Research

Introduction

This initial chapter lays out the overall aims of the book and puts the remainder in context, namely by looking at how history has recently become of interest in general and, somewhat more surprisingly perhaps, has also found a growing number of "fans" within management and organization studies—though the one type of history they don't seem particularly interested in is the history of management, both as a practice and as an idea. In what follows, the chapter will first look at the wildly different levels of interest in history, then provide a summary of the apparent rationale—and the reality—of the growing calls for "more history" in mainstream management research and, lastly, stake out the contribution of this book to these ongoing efforts and how this contribution differs from what has been said by others, as well as the authors themselves in an earlier article (Kipping and Üsdiken 2014).

Let's Look to the Past: History Is Back, or Was It Ever Gone?

Like Hot Cakes: The Recent Popularity of History

There is no doubt that over the past decades, history—broadly understood—has been selling well. In the most commercial sense, history has actually been used increasingly to provide products, brands and companies with authenticity—and legitimacy (Suddaby, Foster and Quinn-Trank 2010, 2016; Anteby and Molnár 2012; Hatch and Schultz 2017). Many alcoholic beverage producers and distributors, for instance, are drawing on their past to project an image of such authenticity as well as craftsmanship. This has a longer tradition in the wine industry (see, e.g., Beverland 2005) but some corporately owned beer brands are also going back to their history—in part to counter the competition from the surging number of craft breweries. Thus, as Hatch and Schultz (2017) have shown in some detail, the Danish brewer Carlsberg used the Latin phrase

Semper Ardens ("always burning") that had been carved in stone above the entrance to its headquarters in 1901 first, in 1999, to name new craft beers and then, in 2010, as a motto in its identity statement.

History has also been supplying material for multiple forms of entertainment. Thus, Netflix has been serializing the lives and adventures of some iconic figures and families from the past, including Marco Polo, the Medici and the Borgia—though often taking "artistic" liberties with the historical record. Already since 1995 there has been The History Channel on cable television, renamed simply "History" in 2008. It has screened documentaries—sometimes based on a rather broad definition of history, as well as dubious science, including ones on "UFO Hunters" and "Ancient Aliens", and recently veered toward reality TV but has also produced a highly successful historical drama on "The Vikings". More historical programming can be found on the Public Broadcasting Service (PBS): Again documentaries, among others on the Medici, as well as adaptations of some best-selling history books have been brought to the screen, namely Jared Diamond's (1999) Pulitzer Prize–winning overview of human civilization *Guns, Germs and Steel* (PBS 3 January 2020) and Niall Ferguson's (2008) financial history of the world *The Ascent of Money*—a shortened version of a series produced by Channel 4 in the UK, which received an International Emmy for best documentary in 2009.

Scottish historian Niall Ferguson has possibly been the most prolific producer of historical bestsellers over the past two decades—a success that has earned him positions at some of the world's top universities, including Oxford, the London School of Economics, New York and Harvard, where he held professorships in both history and business administration. Following a loose affiliation since 2005, in 2016 Ferguson became a senior fellow at the Hoover Institution, a public policy think tank located at Stanford University. Most of his books revolve around topics and figures that have always captured public attention. Thus, he has chronicled the rise and decline of "empires"—from the British to the American and, currently, the Chinese as well as the wars they fought during the twentieth century—with one edited volume considering alternative, "counterfactual" outcomes (Ferguson 1997). He has also looked at the elements and factors that underpinned these empires—namely money and networks, including Facebook, as well as examining some of the families and individuals that built and sustained them—from the Rothschilds to Kissinger.

Major anniversaries, like the centenary of World War I, or specific current events have provided additional opportunities for historical studies and historians to reach a certain level of public visibility, if not popularity. One example is the British historian Adam Tooze, who moved to Yale in 2009 and is now at Columbia University. Originally an expert in German economic history, he subsequently wrote more wide-ranging books, including *The Deluge*, a study of the First World War and its aftermath (Tooze 2014) and, most recently, *Crashed*, which looked at "How a Decade of Financial Crises Changed the World" (Tooze 2018), i.e. a topic that seems to allow for little historical distance or archival research. The financial crisis of 2008 actually prompted both a scholarly and public interest in past parallels, with most authors focusing on the Great Depression of the 1930s. Some have gone back much further, like economists Carmen Reinhart and Ken Rogoff (2009). They looked at "eight centuries of financial folly" and concluded that people generally failed to predict or anticipate each of the recurring crises despite being aware of the previous ones, because they always tended to be driven by steadfast and optimistic beliefs that *This time is different*. Similarly, the recent COVID-19 pandemic has unearthed the Great Influenza of 1918, as well as even earlier pandemics, which hitherto had largely been forgotten by the general public—despite their staggering death tolls.

Not surprisingly, the (world) economy and key economic actors—organizations as well as individuals—were the subjects of many of these best-selling history books. More surprising—or maybe not—is a much less pronounced public interest in histories of management and managers.

Who Cares? Little Regard for Histories of Managers and Management

Just to be clear, books on business and management as well as (auto) biographies of top managers, business leaders and entrepreneurs, also sell well. While most of these publications do not satisfy scholarly standards—prompting one critic to ironically label them "Heathrow Organization Theory", referring to the location of the bookshops where they could be found (Burrell 1989: 307), they have tended to turn their authors into celebrities and "gurus"—if their actual activities had not done so yet (see, among others, Furusten 1999; Guthey, Clark and Jackson 2009). In any case, these popular management books generally look to the future rather than examining history, even if authors sometimes try to extrapolate from the present and recent past to derive their predictions and suggestions for action (e.g. Collins 2001).

There have been some doubts regarding the veracity of the evidence they have been relying on—most famously concerning *In Search of Excellence*, the very first blockbuster management book written by two McKinsey consultants (Peters and Waterman 1982), with the former apparently admitting to having "invented" some of the data (Byrne 2001). There is also the question of how good these authors are at predicting the future. Many of these "excellent" companies no longer exist, and some started faltering soon after the publication of the book. As for history, even when authors draw on their own experiences and careers, the main focus remains overwhelmingly prescriptive. And if they do dwell on the past at times, it is generally to justify or legitimize their own actions. That has also been identified as the primary objective of the corporate histories that continue to be commissioned and handed out to multiple stakeholders at the occasion of major anniversaries—although, more recently, ever fewer companies seem to survive as independent entities long enough to reach these kind of milestones (Foster and Kaplan 2001).

Neither is the history of management or the history of management thought very popular as an academic pursuit. On the contrary, while Management History (MH) was among the ten "professional divisions" that were initially formed in 1971 within the US-based Academy of Management (AoM) (see further Chapter 6, this volume), at the time of writing, it had the lowest number of members among the association's 25 divisions and interest groups (Academy of Management, 16 January 2020). And the *Journal of Management History* (JMH), established in 1995, struggled to survive from the get-go and was actually integrated into *Management Decision* in the year 2000, regaining a separate identity only in 2006 (see Chapter 6, this volume). A journal on *Management & Organizational History* (MOH), founded in 2006, has also been slow to get off the ground (see Chapter 7, this volume). Business history might be a bit more attractive and active, but is only slightly less marginal, with annual meetings of its various associations rarely exceeding 250 participants. It does have three journals, including the venerable *Business History Review*, established as the *Bulletin of the Business Historical Society* at the Harvard Business School in 1926. While impact factors are imperfect measures for many reasons, they still allow a basic comparison between journals. As Table 1.1 shows, neither of the business history journals has a high impact factor—though they are not far from the top-ranked history journal. However, they pale in comparison to management journals, including regional ones. And of the two management history journals only MOH is included in the Web of Science citation index—and that only since 2019.

Again, one has to be careful not to read too much into these numbers, since they partially reflect how authors in a given discipline report the work of others. But even leaving management and organization studies aside for a moment, within history as a whole, neither management nor business history is among the list of different schools of thought recognized by the various overviews of the discipline and its evolution (see Chapter 2, this volume). The only related approach that received some recent academic and even broader recognition is the so-called "history of capitalism", which has been looking in particular at the history of various commodity-based industries, with some books, such as Sven Beckert's (2014) *Empire of Cotton*, achieving a wider readership, while, and that is important, actually saying little about entrepreneurs, firms and managers

Table 1.1 Impact factors of selected history and management and organization journals, 2019

History	Founded	Impact factor	Management and organization	Founded	Impact factor
American Historical Review	1895	1.894	Academy of Management Journal	1958/1963[d]	7.571
Business History Review	1926/1954[a]	1.184	Organization Science	1990	2.790
Business History	1958	1.010	Organization Studies	1980	3.941
Enterprise & Society	1968/2000[b]	0.483	Strategic Management Journal	1980	5.471
Journal of Management History	1995[c]	n/a	Academy of Management Annals	2009	11.865
Management & Organizational History	2006	0.371	Baltic Journal of Management	2006	1.719

Source: Clarivate Analytics, *InCites Journal Citation Reports*; accessed 15 July 2020.

a *Bulletin of the Business Historical Society* (1926–1953).
b *Papers of the Annual Meeting of the Business History Conference* (1968); *Papers of the Business History Conference* (1969–1972); *Proceedings of the Business History Conference* (1973–1975); *Business and Economic History* (1975–1999).
c Integrated into *Management Decision* between 2000 and 2006.
d *The Journal of the Academy of Management* (1958–1962).

(see further Decker, Kipping and Wadhwani 2015; Kipping, Kurosawa and Wadhwani 2017).

But while management has figured little in publications focusing on history, both the ones that have reached a broader audience and those addressed at academics, history seems to have recently found increasing interest, as well as a number of vocal advocates, among management and organizational scholars.

Crazy About History? Management and Organization Studies

The origins of this renewed interest for history among those researching management and organizations are generally traced back to two scholars, one on each side of the Atlantic: In the US, there was Mayer N. Zald (1931–2012), a professor at the University of Michigan, who wrote a series of articles and chapters (Zald 1990, 1991, 1993) that called for a greater recourse to the humanities in general, not just history, within management and organizational research to complement and counterbalance what he referred to as the prevalent "engineering logic". And independently, in Europe Alfred Kieser, at the time professor at the University of Mannheim in Germany, argued in an article that organization theory needed "historical analyses". He provided a number of reasons for this position and some suggestions for how these analyses should be done, largely drawing on examples from his own work (Kieser 1994).

But it has only been since the beginning of the twenty-first century that calls for "taking history more seriously" (Marquis and Tilcsik 2013: 230) have become more frequent, even fashionable. These more recent developments clearly originated in Europe, with the European Group for Organizational Studies (EGOS) playing an important, one might say catalytic, role. Alfred Kieser was once again involved. Together with Behlül Üsdiken, they organized a sub-theme on "Re-discovering History in Studying Organizations" at the 2001 EGOS Colloquium in Lyon, France. They subsequently published a number of selected and revised papers that had been presented there in a special issue of *Business History* (Vol. 46, No. 3, 2004). In the introduction to that special issue, Üsdiken and Kieser (2004) presented a first attempt to classify the ways in which history had been used within management and organization studies. They identified three distinct approaches, labeled "supplementarist", "integrationist" and "reorientationist" (see further Chapter 3, this volume).

That these papers were published in *Business History* rather than EGOS's own journal *Organization Studies* is indicative of the fact that at the time "history" still remained marginal within management and organizational research. As Table 1.2 shows, this changed over time, as history-themed issues or forums appeared in top management journals, interspersed with others in history journals (for the latter, e.g., Godelier 2009; Üsdiken, Kipping and Engwall 2011; Weatherbee et al. 2012;

Table 1.2 "History" special issues in top management journals

Year	Journal	Title	Editors
2010	Journal of Management Studies	Business history	O'Sullivan and Graham
2011	Organization Studies	Organizational path dependence	Schreyögg and Sydow
2016	Academy of Management Review	History and organization studies	Godfrey, Hassard, O'Connor, Rowlinson and Ruef
2018	Organization Studies	Uses of the past in organization studies	Wadhwani, Suddaby, Mordhurst and Popp
2020	Strategic Management Journal	History-informed strategy research	Argyres, De Massis, Foss, Frattini, Jones and Silverman

Carter 2013; Mills et al. 2016; Decker et al. 2018), as well as dedicated edited volumes (see Kahl, Silverman and Cusumano 2012; Bucheli and Wadhwani 2014; McLaren, Mills and Weatherbee 2015).

In most other aspects, the main patterns prevalent in Üsdiken and Kieser's (2004) special issue have largely persisted until today in that (a) most of the attempts to bring history and management research together take place in Europe, namely within the context of EGOS, even if some more efforts are now being made on the other side of the Atlantic; (b) editors and contributors of special issues tend to be management scholars rather than historians—and almost all of the latter are based in business schools; and (c) much of what has been written is either programmatic or largely driven by theoretical concerns—though a few more empirically based articles are beginning to appear.

1. *Still ahead, barely: EGOS as the main arena with AoM on its heels*: As noted, the starting point for the surge of interest in historical analyses within management and organization studies was a sub-theme at the 2001 EGOS colloquium in Lyon. Following additional history-related sub-themes, there was a successful application to establish a so-called standing working group (SWG) on "Historical Perspectives in Organizational Studies", which ran from 2011 onward (see Kipping and Üsdiken 2015). SWGs generally represent topics that are of interest to a broader swath of EGOS membership and attract a good number of submissions at its annual colloquia, though they are limited to a maximum of six years. Even afterwards, there have been sub-themes focusing on or at least welcoming historical contributions as well as specific sub-plenaries. But there were also growing efforts at the AoM, namely through the organization of professional development workshops (PDWs) (see, e.g., Weatherbee et al. 2012; Wadhwani and Bucheli 2014)—efforts often driven by scholars from North America, particularly Canada, who are involved with EGOS. And recently, representatives from that growing group of scholars have been taking on leadership roles in the AoM's MH division to open up an even larger arena for research combining history with management and organization theory. However, the jury is still out on whether they will succeed given the marginal—and not terribly well respected—status of MH within management academia (see earlier and Chapters 6 and 7, this volume).

2. *Still in charge: Editors and authors mainly from management, not history*: Both Üsdiken and Kieser, despite their affinity with history and historical analyses, are management and organization theorists who worked at the time in business and management schools or departments. Editors for most of the special issues listed in Table 1.2 have similar profiles, with the exceptions of the 2010 special issue of the *Journal of Management Studies*, where both were employed at

business and management schools at the time but also had history credentials and a long-standing involvement with the business history community and, more recently, the 2018 issue of *Organization Studies* on "uses of the past", where three of the four editors were historians, all tied in some way to the Copenhagen Business School. In all other cases there is at best one "fig-leaf" (business) historian among the editorial team. Management scholars similarly dominate among the authors of the articles within these special issues, though those trained as historians have gradually been making inroads, first mainly as co-authors with more mainstream management scholars but more recently also as single authors or writing jointly. Still, even these historians continue to come from business/management schools and departments not from history departments—a pattern not too surprising, given the difference in tenure and promotion criteria. Geographically, historians have predominantly tended to be based at or affiliated with business schools in the UK, much less so the US, or in Scandinavia, with the Copenhagen Business School probably the single most important one.

3. *Still debating: More on what should be done than actually doing it*: The contribution to the 2004 special issue of *Business History* that garnered the most interest, measured by the number of citations, was the article by two British management scholars, Peter Clark and Michael Rowlinson (2004), who presented an emphatic call for an "historic turn" in organization studies. Possibly because of its simplicity and ambiguity, the notion of such an "historic turn" became a kind of rallying cry for those wanting to see more history in management and organizational research. The authors themselves largely used it to advocate for a narrative, linguistic or postmodern turn which had swept—and to some extent come to dominate—history as an academic discipline since the 1970s (see Chapter 2, this volume) but had yet to make major inroads into management research, especially on the other side of the Atlantic—and never really did. Rowlinson, it should be noted, also had an affinity for business history per se and had advocated for its more extensive use in organization studies in earlier articles written jointly with other authors (for details, see Chapter 3, this volume). Most importantly, many of the subsequent contributions did not focus on providing exemplary research demonstrating that historical analyses could enrich management research, but rather on debating why it was necessary and how it could and should be done. Some were more cautious, raising concerns about the difficulties inherent in bringing the two together—and how they might possibly be overcome.

But whatever the remaining constraints and imbalances, the overall trend is clear: Since the start of the twenty-first century the explicit interest among management researchers in history is growing—while, and that should also be stressed, the interest among historians for the study of management and organizations remains limited, especially if one discounts commissioned company histories. The question is what has been driving this trend.

Separated in the Past, Rejoined in the Present?

Who Kicked History Out: "Science" or Sociology?

The main argument used by most of those advocating for a greater role of history within management and organization studies revolves around the notion that the latter had become overly concerned with creating timeless general models by the increasingly predominant natural science approaches. It has probably been put forward most poignantly by Zald (1990, 1991, 1993), who suggested complementing the latter with the humanities (philosophy, literature and history). His aim was to move business school researchers and teachers from what he called an "engineering" model, preoccupied mainly with solving managerial problems, to an "enlightenment" model, focusing on "education for public and civic participation" (Zald 1993: 514). The obvious foil for this critique and the proposed solution was the "scientistic turn" that management research had taken in the US since the 1950s to further its own acceptance within academia (Augier and March 2011), a development that gradually extended to business schools around the globe (Engwall, Kipping and Üsdiken 2016, Ch. 10).

While stylized as a break with that dominant "scientistic" present, the call for more history has also been portrayed as a return to earlier times when the two were seen to have much closer connections with several authors pointing to some of the classic thinkers, and in particular Max Weber and Karl Marx, as prime examples for an integration of economic, sociological and historical perspectives and approaches. Thus, Kieser (1994: 607) started his widely cited plea for "why organization theory needs historical analysis" with reference to one of its "forefathers", Max Weber, for whom, "history and sociology were inseparable disciplines". To explain the subsequent "rejection of the past in modern organization theory", he pointed to the "professionalization of sociology", namely its increasing use of "a precise methodology analogous to that of science". Similarly, when trying to explain the gap between history and "organization studies", Greenwood and Bernardi (2014) also looked at the long term and the relationship between history and sociology. But for them the current "rift" had its origins already in the nineteenth century, when the different disciplines found their homes in modern academia, and in particular with the decision of "many universities to separate their Social Science and their Humanities faculties" (p. 925).

A somewhat different view on the separation between history and sociology was taken by Goldman (1994: 622–623) in his brief reply to Kieser's (1994) plea. He argued that social scientists are still being trained in both history and theory and that "most of us read, and force our students to read, Alfred Chandler and Charles Perrow, and we have access to the scholarship in business and economic history". Crucially, he points out that at the time of writing the vast major ity of those completing doctorates in organization studies were doing so *not* in sociology or social science departments, but in management departments, which, in his view, resulted in a narrower focus. This brings the attention back to the earlier-mentioned scientistic turn. While not explicitly mentioning it, Goldman (1994) highlighted the fact that journals in the field had become dominated by a "functionalist" paradigm leading to a "low proportion of articles using qualitative methodologies". Importantly, he also pointed to the influence of "the journal article format" itself, which "is most hospitable to work that can be presented compactly".

Business historians have also highlighted the earlier connections between history and the social sciences. They namely constructed a timeline that links the German historical school of economics of the late nineteenth century with Alfred Chandler (Kipping et al. 2017), whose 1962 book *Strategy and Structure* is still widely seen as one of the foundational texts of management as an academic discipline (e.g. Eisenhardt 1991; Bedeian and Wren 2001; Kahl et al. 2012). The founding dean of the Harvard Business School (HBS) in 1908, Edwin Francis Gay, was actually the chair of Economic History at Harvard and had done his doctorate in Berlin under the supervision of Gustav von Schmoller, one of the most prominent members of the historical school of economics, which advocated building general insights through the patient accumulation of in-depth case studies. Gay's successor, Wallace Brett Donham, created a first chair in Business History in 1927, which was eventually held by Chandler between 1970 and 1989. This account also implicitly suggests that it was that the scientistic turn which eventually cut short what seemed like a promising relationship (see also Kipping and Üsdiken 2008; Üsdiken and Kipping 2014). At the same time, this relationship persisted somewhat longer outside the US, notably in Japan, where Weber as well as Marx had a long-lasting influence on both historians and social scientists (Kipping et al. 2017).

While the timing of the schism between history and management and organization studies and its underlying causes, be they institutional, intellectual or methodological, are open to some debate, it seems clear that the scientization of management research since the 1950s played an important, if not decisive, role. It removed historical perspectives and approaches from the new mainstream, marked by that "engineering logic"—as well as confining the history of management to the margins.

The question then arises whether the desired (re)introduction of history into the mainstream is a realistic endeavor.

Can the Twain Ever Meet Again?

Not surprisingly, opinions as to whether history has a future in management and organization studies—and what kind of future—vary. Clearly, nobody advocates or realistically expects a return to what is probably a stylized and idealist past anyway. Both academic disciplines have significantly evolved since the nineteenth century and the times of Weber and Marx. In what follows, a number of the recent attempts to compare and contrast the current differences between history and management and organization studies—and what it means for their interaction—are summarized (see Table 1.3).

Table 1.3 Juxtapositions between (business) history and management and organization studies

Author(s)	Main source of differences	History	Management
Kahl et al. (2012)	"Conventions", "norms of evaluation"	Detailed narrative, contextualization, books	[Strategy:] Raw data, generalization, journal articles
Rowlinson and Hassard (2013)	Sources and methodology	Neo-institutional history: primary sources	Historical neo-institutionalism: secondary sources; formal methods
Rowlinson et al. (2014)	Epistemology	Prioritization of documentary sources, periodization, narrative	Prioritization of self-generated data, simple chronology, analysis
Wadhwani and Bucheli (2014)	Temporal perspectives	Retrospective approach; context and sequences	Timeless (cross-sectional); longitudinal
Leblebici (2014)	"Cultures of inquiry" and "types of understanding"	"Organizational history"; subjectivity, uniqueness	"historical organization theory"; objectivity, application of theory
Greenwood and Bernardi (2014)	Methodology, objectivity, relevance	"humanities"	"science"
Maclean et al. (2016)	Epistemological paradigms	"historical veracity", "narratives"	"theory development", "conceptual rigor"

Thus, there are the optimists, as one might call them, those who believe in the ability of research and publications, presumably journal articles, that combine "theory development" with "historical veracity" to achieve what they refer to as "dual integrity", i.e. fulfill the requirements of both disciplines (Maclean, Harvey and Clegg 2016: 609). To what extent the other contributions to the special topic forum of the *Academy of Management Review* on "history and organization stud ies", where their article was published, actually achieved this "dual integrity" remains an open question—especially since most of them were conceptual rather than empirical. Not surprisingly, two of the article's authors take a more cautious tone in the call for papers for a sub-theme on "Realizing the Potential of Historical Organization Studies" at the 2019 EGOS Colloquium in Edinburgh (Clegg, Maclean and Suddaby 2019). In that call, they echoed once again the legacy of the scientistic turn by pointing to the predominant focus of mainstream management research on "contemporary cross-sectional studies covering limited periods of time". Yet, importantly, they also highlighted the difficulties when attempting to incorporate "a traditionally empirically oriented discipline like history [. . .] into a traditionally theoretically oriented discipline like organization studies". One should note the hierarchy implied here, whereas the earlier publication had aimed for "equal status" (Maclean et al. 2016: 610).

Others, while equally keen on embracing and supporting a rapprochement between history and management and organization studies, have been more skeptical when examining their underlying differences. And they do struggle when considering how best to bring the two (back) together with the extent to which they consider this possible, depending on the underlying differences they identify between the two disciplines (see also Kipping and Üsdiken 2015). Among those who are nevertheless rather positive regarding the prospect of "the integration between history and, in this case specifically, strategy research" are Kahl et al. (2012) in their editorial introduction to a volume of *Advances in Strategic Management* dedicated to *History and Strategy*. Not surprisingly, they point once again to the classics, especially Chandler's (1962) *Strategy and Structure*, and more importantly, attribute the differences mainly to the "conventions" and "norms of evaluation" in each discipline, including the presentation and interpretation of data, respectively, in narrative or "raw" form or, relatedly, the publication of books vs. journal articles (p. ix-xi)—ultimately implying that it should be possible to overcome these. The volume includes a chapter that offers a "roadmap" of how history might complement strategy research that ultimately points in the direction of the quantification of historical data (Ingram, Rao and Silverman 2012). However, most other contributions in the book, whether written by historians or management scholars, actually provide examples for an empirically based, narrative interpretative approach to strategy research. The introduction to the recent special issue of the *Strategic Management Journal* (Argyres et al. 2020) strikes a similarly positive tone about the "promise" of history, and some of its contributions are narratively based—though as many, if not more, are predominantly conceptual or use quantitative methodologies.

Another example attempting to combine empirical and theoretical concerns is by Rowlinson and Hassard (2013). Focusing on one of the major research programs within organization theory, neo-institutionalism, they compare two scenarios in terms of differing primary interests and focus: on the one hand, how historians might make use of its theoretical insights, leading to what they label "neo-institutional history" and, on the other hand, how neo-institutional scholars might incorporate historical analysis, leading to "historical neo-institutionalism" (see, for the latter, also Suddaby, Foster and Mills 2014). They see the resulting differences mainly at the level of the data and methodologies used, with historians preferring primary sources and the neo-institutionalists predominantly applying "formal methods" (Rowlinson and Hassard 2013: 111). In a subsequent article, this time together with business historian Stephanie Decker, they contrast history and organization theory more broadly along three epistemological dimensions: explanation, evidence and temporality (Rowlinson, Hassard and Decker 2014). The resulting "dualisms", as they call them, lead, on the one extreme, to "narrative organizational history", which draws on verifiable documentary sources and establishes an explicit periodization, and, on the other extreme, to "historical organization theory", which combines the analysis of constructed data with a constant chronology. They then further subdivide organizational history into four kinds: corporate, analytically structured, serial and ethnographic.

A somewhat bleaker view of the ongoing efforts to combine history and organization theory is presented in the introductory chapter to the *Organizations in Time* book (Bucheli and Wadhwani 2014), which the editors characterize as "a dialogue of the deaf" (Wadhwani and Bucheli 2014). They attribute the fact "that historians and other social scientists tend to talk past one another even as they discuss the same phenomena" (p. 8) to the fundamental epistemic differences that have been highlighted in much of the relevant literature, contrasting the humanities and sciences or historical and functional social scientific research—a contrast which they believe predisposes mainstream management researchers to "discount history". Instead, they argue, it is important to understand the differences in temporal perspectives between the two: They characterize functionalist social sciences as either atemporal, namely in cross-sectional studies, or longitudinal in the form of an unfolding chronology, while they portray historians as retrospective, looking back into past actions as well their antecedents and consequences, hence their focus on both "context and sequence" (p. 9). What they suggest for integrating history into organization studies is not to use this historical reasoning across the board but for research questions about entrepreneurs, organizations and markets where such a temporal perspective promises to contribute novel insights, including regarding the "paths not taken" (for the example of entrepreneurship see Wadhwani and Jones 2014).

At least one contributor to the book (Leblebici 2014) is not convinced that even such a limited integration is feasible—or even desirable. His position is based on a broad comparison between organizational theory and business history in terms of their "cultures of inquiry" and "types of understanding". Drawing on Runciman's (1983) notions of reportage, description, explanation and evaluation, he highlights how historians tend to insist in their narratives on the uniqueness of events and their causes as well as contexts and how they see the meaning attributed by historical actors as well as current observers as subjective. By contrast, when looking at history, organizational theorists strive for objectivity and see each specific case as an application of a given theory and its basic assumptions and implied causalities. This, in his view, explains the difficulties in integrating both approaches. Instead, he suggests first of all an acceptance from both sides of the different types of understanding and their respective strengths, giving, not surprisingly, once again Chandler's work as an example for the contribution of rich historical research to organization theory. This would then, in his view, form the basis for a transdisciplinary dialogue and debate, "not on methods but on research questions that are mutually interesting and relevant", which, however, requires "publication outlets that are problem oriented rather than discipline oriented" (pp. 78–80). The example he gives, the *Journal of Industrial and Corporate Change*, demonstrates how difficult this is, since it evolved from such a broad-based, phenomena-driven publication to one focusing almost exclusively on the (micro)economics of innovation.

Probably the most critical are once again Greenwood and Bernardi (2014). After having identified the origins of "the grand historical battle between History and Sociology" (p. 912) in the institutional separation of both disciplines in the nineteenth century (see earlier), they attributed their ongoing "rift" to "differences of epistemological standpoint", which they summarize as follows, before discussing each of them in detail (pp. 915–923): "1) The social scientific need for an explicit methodology", "2) The social scientific ideal of objectivity: a science versus a humanity" and "3) The social scientific priority on practical relevance and applicability". While downplaying some of the distinctions between historians and organization studies scholars and highlighting "their large intersection of interests", they still argue that, due to the underlying "chasm of difference", the two will remain "uneasy bedfellows". Therefore, in order to realize the potential benefits both might derive from working with each other, the way forward they suggested consists of "cooperation not integration" (p. 927).

Not surprisingly, most of these comparisons summarized in Table 1.3 above point to similar origins of the "gap" they identify between history and management and organization studies, namely in terms of data, methodology and the attempted level of generalization and theorization. They nevertheless diverge substantially in terms of their perception of how sizable the actual gap is and their suggestions for closing it: from "dual integrity" to mutual respect and cooperation. While these comparisons are important and while the differences between the two disciplines are undeniable, what this book attempts to do is different. It will try to take stock, as systematically and comprehensively as possible, of the "history" that can already be found in management and organization studies. Its main argument, in a nutshell, is that there is a lot of history—and definitely "more than meets the eye" at first glance (see also Kipping and Üsdiken 2014).

Let's Have Another Look: History Is Already There, Kind of

As Stated Before: More Than Meets the Eye

As mentioned, first calls for bringing history back into management and organizational research already appeared in the 1990s. And while Zald did not provide specific examples of work that incorporated a historical dimension and/or approach, Kieser (1994) did point to extant research on the development of organizational culture, including during the Nazi period, and drew on his own work on medieval guilds. He also used accounts of the early putting-out system in Germany to (a) show how historical phenomena could be interpreted by applying different organizational theories—here labor process and new institutional economics—and (b) link the past with the present by pointing to the re-emergence of similar systems in contemporary garment production. And in the special issue of *Business History* Üsdiken and Kieser (2004) not only published additional papers combining history and organization theory but also used extant work to derive their taxonomy of the different ways in which history contributed to management research. And two of the articles mentioned earlier (Rowlinson and Hassard 2013; Leblebici 2014) identified, respectively, 55 and 102 articles in leading management journals with a historical orientation that were based on at least some empirical research. The former went back to the 1990s, whereas the latter only included publications from the first decade of the new millennium, but both surveys suggested that these types of articles had grown more significantly since the beginning of the twenty-first century (see also Chapter 4, this volume).

So, there clearly has been this kind of research out there at least since the 1990s, as the authors of the present volume have also shown in their earlier publications. Thus, in their overview of business history and management for *The Oxford Handbook of Business History*, Kipping and Üsdiken (2008) identified a number of topics where research in these two academic disciplines had overlapped or where both perspectives had been in a dialogue or, even more rarely, had been integrated to some degree in specific publications. These topics included, in particular, the evolution of big business in the US in the late nineteenth and early twentieth centuries and the Americanization of management ideas and practices in Western Europe and Japan after World War II, as well as international business more generally. However, with respect to the latter, Jones and Khanna (2006) had earlier denounced mentions of history in international business research as largely representing "lip service", while suggesting various ways in which the two could be combined more fruitfully. In a more recent publication (Üsdiken and Kipping 2014) and in a lengthy contribution to the *Academy of Management Annals* (Kipping and Üsdiken 2014), the authors had already taken a more inclusive stand toward what they considered "history" within management and organizational research by going significantly beyond what trained academic historians might be able to recognize as an historical approach—without necessarily endorsing it as "proper" historical research—and by even moving away from insisting on the use of the word "history" itself, as most other observers had done so far.

In the latter piece in particular, they argued that by taking such a broader point of view, there was more history to be found in the management and organization theory literature "than meets the eye" or, put differently, that history in some shape and form had been more prevalent in mainstream management research than most of those calling for its revival had considered or acknowledged. As the key to structuring their survey of the place history had found in the mainstream, they focused on its relationship to theory, given that the quest for theorization was a core feature of post–World War II management research. This, moreover, as others have pointed out, contrasts with "a traditionally empirically oriented discipline" like history itself (Clegg et al. 2019; see also Maclean et al. 2016)—though, as will be shown in Chapter 2 (this volume), such a view somewhat simplistically brushes over long-standing and intense debates among historians about ontology, epistemology and methodology, as well as the benefits and limits of generalization.

Nevertheless, taking "theory" as the reference point Kipping and Üsdiken (2014) distinguished between "history *to* theory" and "history *in* theory". Broadly speaking, the former involves using data from the past to address particular research questions or to illustrate, test, elaborate and modify extant theory. By contrast, the latter refers to theoretical models where history is an integral part as a driver or moderator, meaning that the past is theorized to influence in some way or other the present and the future. When structuring their survey, Kipping and Üsdiken (2014) used the level of analysis as an additional dimension, distinguishing studies that focused on individual organizations, on the one hand, and those that looked at aggregates and/or interactions of organizations such as organizational populations or fields—and consequently excluding those studies that examine the internal working of organizations or its component elements, as well as the ones that look at the very macro level such as national business or innovation systems. Based on a few exemplary publications, they also identified a way of combining the two disciplines, reminiscent of Üsdiken and Kieser's (2004) integrationist approach. Labeled "historical cognizance", it suggested making theories more contingent on the historical context from which they were derived.

Haven't We Seen This Movie Already? Opening the Package...

The present book builds on these earlier efforts, and in particular the *Annals* article (Kipping and Üsdiken 2014), continuing with a focus on the "macro" level management and organizational research (including strategy), though it extends and modifies them in multiple ways, namely by

1. *Providing a broader context*: To contextualize the systematic survey and discussion of history's evolving role in management research, the book looks at how both developed into and as academic disciplines. For history, it shows its deep roots and long traditions, as well as the richness and diversity of current research, both of which tend to be simplified, if not neglected, in most other recent attempts of bringing the two together. It also shows how historians have continued to seek a dialogue with other social scientists throughout most of the twentieth century. For management, the book recounts some of the early efforts to turn it into a science in addition to the well-known story of its more systematic scientization, starting in the US in the 1950s and then gradually expanding elsewhere. This more extended perspective casts some doubt on the widespread view blaming this scientization for what is often portrayed as a sudden and radical rupture with history (see earlier). Taken together, these more fine-grained accounts of the evolution of research in both history and management help establish a more balanced understanding of their interaction over time and show, in particular, that their separation was neither as sudden nor as profound as it generally has been made out to be. Moreover,

in addition to examining their actual trajectories, both separate and intertwined, the book looks at the joint roads not taken in the past, namely as a way to identify possibilities for bringing them (back) together going forward.

2. *Considering both history of and in management*: The 2014 *Annals* piece focused exclusively on the management literature and examined publications that used history, defined broadly as noted earlier, though within certain boundaries in terms of the levels of analysis. It did also discuss some writings by self-identified historians that were widely considered "classics" by management scholars and/or referenced extensively in that literature. This book, in addition, includes an extensive survey and discussion of the literature that looks at the history of management and management thought, which, in many ways, represents a first and kind of "natural" attempt to combine historical and management research. Though, as the contextual sections of the book will show, management history was never considered an important part of the remit of historical scholarship, despite some early points of contact through the historical school of economics, subsequent related but ultimately marginal efforts in business history often associated with the work of Alfred Chandler and a more recent interest in the history of capitalism, which remains, however, largely devoid of enterprise and managers. Within management research, an interest in history arose early, often focusing on the so-called pioneers, and management history took a prominent place among the initial building blocks of its most prominent scholarly association: AoM. And even if its early prominence was never more than a mirage, the history of management and management thought quickly became marginalized as mainstream management research increasingly became scientized. Attempts at a revival since the 1990s quickly stalled, though the recent push by a few leading management scholars to bring history back might give it a new lease on life. By including the history of management, the book not only sheds light on another way to combine the two, as marginal as it might have been within management scholarship, but also provides a contrast with history being integrated into mainstream research and opens another possible path for future developments.

3. *Rescoping the survey of the literature*: Compared to the 2014 article, this book not only adds the history *of* management, it also expands and restructures the survey of history *in* management. At the same time, and very importantly, it does maintain the original distinction between the two fundamental ways in which history and management research relate "history *to* theory" and "history *in* theory". However, while the levels of analysis which constituted

the second dimension in that original article are still relevant, based on an in-depth analysis of journal articles (reported in Chapter 4, this volume), they have been replaced by the type of data used in the research: *qualitative* and *quantitative*. As elaborated further in Chapter 4, this is more in line with the established distinction of methods within management research itself, while a more narrowly defined historical approach has traditionally relied mostly on case studies and qualitative data—though there is also a tradition of cliometrics (see Figure 4.1). Moreover, the treatment of some of the specific research programs touched upon in the earlier article, namely process studies and strategy, was also expanded to better reflect the range and richness of history-related work in these areas.

In general, and not surprisingly, the book contains more details and examples for all of these research programs than the article. However, it is important to note that the survey and review cannot be, and are not meant to be, comprehensive, since there are truly many more publications that bring together history and management than meet the eye. So, the authors apologize to all those who might feel slighted by the choices they had to make to keep the overview of the literature to a manageable size and readable. It should also be noted that at the time the book is published, the selection of publications on history *of* and *in* management will no longer be up to date given the ongoing research in all of the programs identified. But the overall structure of the survey and the basic argument should still be relevant and help make sense of the growing body of relevant literature.

. . . And Displaying Its Contents

Following this introductory chapter, the remainder of the book consists of three parts. Part I provides the necessary context by recounting in some detail the development of history and management, both separately and in interaction. Part II focuses on the history *of* management, from its inception to what could be called the classical or orthodox view and a chorus of more critical voices. And Part III dissects history *in* management research looking at both history *to* and *in* theory as defined earlier. Most of the chapters across all parts are broadly chronologically structured so as to reflect the evolution of the different disciplines and research programs discussed over time.

Within Part I, Chapter 2 traces the evolution of both history and management on their way to eventually becoming academic disciplines— suggesting that the differences and similarities in their respective origins and trajectories influenced their subsequent interaction, which was affected significantly, though not exclusively, by the efforts to turn management into a "true"—read natural—science starting in the US during the 1950s and expanding globally thereafter. Chapter 3 then shows how historians tried to maintain a dialogue with the social sciences, including the so-called "New Look" management, but how their efforts found little resonance until the 1990s, when certain frustrations among management scholars with the overly scientized approaches led to calls for a renewed engagement with either business history or the social sciences more broadly and sociology in particular. Subsequently, these calls became more frequent but also less clear about what direction(s) to pursue in what came increasingly—and somewhat ambiguously—to be referred to as an "historic turn". Chapter 4 takes a step back from these efforts and debates to look at some evidence. Following two examples mentioned earlier, it conducts a systematic quantitative survey of articles in top management journals, though extending the time frame (starting in the 1960s) and the range of journals to a total of nine. The analysis shows a noticeable increase, on the one hand, of publications covering the history of management as well as management and organization studies and, on the other, of those linking history and theory in various ways.

Going beyond the top management journals, Parts II and III then provide a systematic, though more narrative and broadly chronological, overview of these two evolving types of literatures, which are labeled, respectively, history *of* and history *in* management. Within Part II, Chapter 5 looks at early writings about the history of management and management thought, which go back to the time of initial efforts to systematize actual management activities around the turn of the twentieth century. As the chapter also shows, many of the themes evoked at the outset would reappear after World War II, when history of management started coming into its own. Initially most authors were consultants and practicing managers, but academics became more involved since the 1960s, when the first two textbooks were published, and management history became an integral part of AoM. These developments are covered in Chapter 6, which also details how the topic became increasingly marginalized as mainstream management research "scientized" in the subsequent decade, while historians of management perpetuated their limited focus on the "pioneers" and the progressive evolution of different schools of management thought—with management ideas widely seen as responding to managerial needs. Chapter 7 then summarizes a set of disparate approaches that at different times challenged what had become a kind of orthodoxy—with none of them reaching broader audiences among management scholars. Those that eventually did, like Critical Management Studies (CMS), had lost their initial connection with history.

Part III moves to examine how history has made its way into the mainstream of management research, with its first two chapters covering the research programs, which rely on historical data (history *to* theory) and the next two summarizing those that incorporated the past into their theoretical models (history *in* theory). Thus, Chapter 8 looks at studies in mainstream management research, where historical cases of one or several organizations and of organizational fields have been used for theorizing. These include, first and foremost, institutionalism, both old and new, and many of the latter's more specific research programs such as institutional entrepreneurship, work and logics, as well as process studies in organizations and strategy. Chapter 9 also reports on research where evidence is drawn from the past but where theory is developed, tested, refined or elaborated based on longitudinal quantitative data. Pioneering and still dominant among these kinds of studies is organizational ecology. It emerged in the 1980s and is still a powerful and widespread research program focusing on populations of organizations and their emergence, survival or decline and disappearance, which has recently also been drawing on insights from neo-institutional theories. The next two chapters deal with management and organization theories that include history in terms of incorporating the effects of past conditions or processes as drivers or moderators at the organizational or aggregate levels into their models. Chapter 10 looks at two of the most widely—and often loosely—used theoretical models with such historical drivers, namely "imprinting" and "path dependence". Both have been developed either independently or as part of other research programs with frequent—but not exclusive—use of historical data. This is also the case of the research programs presented in Chapter 11, which had already been discussed as examples of history *to* theory, and in particular organizational ecology, where some of the main theoretical building blocks include the past—usually as an impediment to change, like in the notion of "structural inertia". Similar mechanisms can be found in important theoretical models of the strategy literature, also discussed in this chapter.

Following the three main parts and concluding the book is Chapter 12, which very briefly summarizes the main insights and then outlines possible ways forward toward a deeper integration between history and management research—going beyond the various approaches identified throughout the book. It will point to three possibilities, outlining the contribution they might make to the overall aim of taking history more seriously, as well as evaluating—very tentatively—their likelihood to succeed in the given contexts. First, there are management, organizational and business history. With few exceptions, all of them seem reticent to embrace generalization and theorization to the extent required within the mainstream of management scholarship but will continue to provide evidence for other social science disciplines, including management. Second is a relatively recent approach, generally referred to as "uses of the past", which is deeply embedded in neo-institutional theory but focuses exclusively on history as a source of legitimacy—which ultimately will limit its broader appeal. The most promising remains what Kipping and

Üsdiken (2014) have referred to as "historical cognizance", which is not wedded to specific research programs but takes history seriously—and moves away from natural science like claims of general "laws" by contextualizing extant (or novel) theories by making them contingent on specific historically defined boundary conditions.

References

Academy of Management, http://aom.org/DIG/ (accessed 16 January 2020).

Anteby, M. and Molnár, V. (2012) "Collective memory meets organizational identity: Remembering to forget in a firm's rhetorical history," *Academy of Management Journal*, 55(3): 515–540.

Argyres, N. S., De Massis, A., Foss, N. J., Frattini, F., Jones, G. and Silverman, B. S. (2020) "History-informed strategy research: The promise of history and historical research methods in advancing strategy scholarship," *Strategic Management Journal*, 41(3): 343–368.

Augier, M. and March, J. G. (2011) *The Roots, Rituals, and Rhetorics of Change: North American Business Schools After the Second World War*, Stanford, CA: Stanford University Press.

Beckert, S. (2014) *Empire of Cotton: A Global History*, New York: Alfred A. Knopf.

Bedeian, A. G. and Wren, D. A. (2001) "Most influential management books of the 20th century," *Organizational Dynamics*, 29(3): 221–225.

Beverland, M. B. (2005) "Crafting brand authenticity: The case of luxury wines," *Journal of Management Studies*, 42(5): 1003–1029.

Bucheli, M. and Wadhwani, R. D. (eds) (2014) *Organizations in Time: History, Theory, Methods*, Oxford: Oxford University Press.

Burrell, G. (1989) "The absent centre: The neglect of philosophy in Anglo-American management theory," *Human Systems Management*, 8(4): 307–312.

Byrne, J. A. (2001) "The real confessions of Tom Peters," *Bloomberg Businessweek*, 2 December.

Carter, C. (2013) "The age of strategy: Strategy, organizations and society," *Business History*, 55(7): 1047–1057.

Chandler, A. D. Jr. (1962) *Strategy and Structure: Chapters in the History of the Industrial Enterprise*, Cambridge, MA: MIT Press.

Clark, P. and Rowlinson, M. (2004) "The treatment of history in organisation studies: Towards an 'historic turn'?" *Business History*, 46(3): 331–352.

Clegg, S., Maclean, M. and Suddaby, R. (2019) "Sub-theme 30: Realizing the potential of historical organization studies," Call for Papers, 35th EGOS Colloquium, University of Edinburgh Business School, 4–6 July, www.egosnet.org/jart/prj3/egos/main.jart?rel=de&reserve-mode=active&content-id=1539047741567&subtheme_id=1535187600357 (accessed 21 January 2020).

Collins, J. (2001) *Good to Great: Why Some Companies Make the Leap . . . and Others Don't*, New York: Harper Business.

Decker, S., Kipping, M. and Wadhwani, R. D. (2015) "New business histories! Plurality in business history research methods," *Business History*, 57(1): 30–40.

Decker, S., Üsdiken, B., Engwall, L. and Rowlinson, M. (2018) "Special issue introduction: Historical research on institutional change," *Business History*, 60(5): 613–627.

Diamond, J. M. (1999) *Guns, Germs and Steel: The Fates of Human Societies*, New York: W. W. Norton & Co.

Eisenhardt, K. M. (1991) "Better stories and better constructs: The case for rigor and comparative logic," *Academy of Management Review*, 16(3): 620–627.

Engwall, L., Kipping, M. and Üsdiken, B. (2016) *Defining Management: Business Schools, Consultants and Media*, New York: Routledge.

Ferguson, N. (ed) (1997) *Virtual History: Alternatives and Counterfactuals*, London: Picador.

Ferguson, N. (2008) *The Ascent of Money: A Financial History of the World*, New York: Penguin.

Foster, R. and Kaplan, S. (2001) *Creative Destruction: From 'Built to Last' to 'Built to Perform'*, London: FT Prentice-Hall.

Furusten, S. (1999) *Popular Management Books: How They Are Made and What They Mean for Organizations*, London: Routledge.

Godelier, E. (2009) "History, a useful 'science' for management? From polemics to controversies," *Enterprise and Society*, 10(4): 791–807.

Godfrey, P. C., Hassard, J., O'Connor, E. S., Rowlinson, M. and Ruef, M. (2016) "Introduction to special topic forum: What is organizational history? Toward a creative synthesis of history and organization studies," *Academy of Management Review*, 41(4): 590–608.

Goldman, P. (1994) "Searching for history in organizational theory: Comment on Kieser," *Organization Science*, 5(4): 621–623.

Greenwood, A. and Bernardi, A. (2014) "Understanding the rift, the (still) uneasy bedfellows of history and organization studies," *Organization*, 21(6): 907–932.

Guthey, E., Clark, T. and Jackson, B. (2009) *Demystifying Business Celebrity*, London: Routledge.

Hatch, M. J. and Schultz, M. (2017) "Toward a theory of using history authentically: Historicizing in the Carlsberg Group," *Administrative Science Quarterly*, 62(4): 657–697.

Ingram, P., Rao, H. and Silverman, B. S. (2012) "History in strategy research: What, why and how?" in S. J. Kahl, B. S. Silverman and M. A. Cusumano (eds), *History and Strategy*, Bingley, UK: Emerald, pp. 241–273.

Jones, G. and Khanna, T. (2006) "Bringing history (back) into international business," *Journal of International Business Studies*, 37(4): 453–468.

Kahl, S. J., Silverman, B. S. and Cusumano, M. A. (eds) (2012) *History and Strategy* (Advances in Strategic Management 29), Bingley, UK: Emerald.

Kieser, A. (1994) "Why organization theory needs historical analyses—And how this should be performed," *Organization Science*, 5(4): 608–620.

Kipping, M., Kurosawa, T. and Wadhwani, R. D. (2017) "A revisionist historiography of business history: A richer past for a richer future," in J. F. Wilson, S. Toms, A. de Jong and E. Buchnea (eds), *The Routledge Companion to Business History*, London: Routledge, pp. 19–35.

Kipping, M. and Üsdiken, B. (2008) "Business history and management studies," in G. Jones and J. Zeitlin (eds), *The Oxford Handbook of Business History*, Oxford: Oxford University Press, pp. 96–119.

Kipping, M. and Üsdiken, B. (2014) "History in organization and management theory: More than meets the eye," *Academy of Management Annals*, 8(1): 535–588.

Kipping, M. and Üsdiken, B. (2015) "Turning how and where? The potential for history in management and organizational studies," in P. G. McLaren, A. J.

Mills and T. G. Weatherbee (eds), *The Routledge Companion to Management and Organizational History*, London: Routledge, pp. 372–379.

Leblebici, H. (2014) "History and organization theory: Potential for a transdisciplinary convergence," in M. Bucheli and R. D. Wadhwani (eds), *Organizations in Time: History, Theory, Methods*, Oxford: Oxford University Press, pp. 56–99.

Maclean, M., Harvey, C. and Clegg, S. R. (2016) "Conceptualizing historical organization studies," *Academy of Management Review*, 41(4): 609–632.

Marquis, C. and Tilcsik, A. (2013) "Imprinting: Toward a multilevel theory," *Academy of Management Annals*, 7(1): 193–243.

McLaren, P. G., Mills, A. J. and Weatherbee, T. G. (eds) (2015) *The Routledge Companion to Management and Organizational History*, London: Routledge.

Mills, A. J., Suddaby, R., Foster, W. M. and Durepos, G. (2016) "Re-visiting the historic turn 10 years later: Current debates in management and organizational history—An introduction," *Management & Organizational History*, 11(2): 67–76.

O'Sullivan, M. and Graham, M. B. W. (2010) "Guest editors' introduction—Moving forward by looking backward: Business history and management studies," *Journal of Management Studies*, 47(5): 775–790.

PBS, www.pbs.org/gunsgermssteel/index.html and www.pbs.org/wnet/ascentofmoney/ (accessed 3 January 2020).

Peters, T. J. and Waterman, R. H. Jr. (1982) *In Search of Excellence: Lessons from America's Best-Run Companies*, New York: Harper and Row.

Reinhart, C. M. and Rogoff, K. S. (2009) *This Time Is Different: Eight Centuries of Financial Folly*, Princeton, NJ: Princeton University Press.

Rowlinson, M. and Hassard, J. (2013) "Historical neo-institutionalism or neo-institutionalist history? Historical research in management and organization studies," *Management & Organizational History*, 8(2): 111–126.

Rowlinson, M., Hassard, J. and Decker, S. (2014) "Strategies for organizational history: A dialogue between historical theory and organization theory," *Academy of Management Review*, 39(3): 250–274.

Runciman, W. G. (1983) *A Treatise on Social Theory: The Methodology of Social Theory*, Cambridge: Cambridge University Press.

Schreyögg, G. and Sydow, J. (2011) "Organizational path dependence: A process view," *Organization Studies*, 32(3): 321–335.

Suddaby, R., Foster, W. M. and Mills, A. J. (2014) "Historical institutionalism," in M. Bucheli and R. D. Wadhwani (eds), *Organizations in Time: History, Theory, Methods*, Oxford: Oxford University Press, pp. 100–123.

Suddaby, R., Foster, W. M. and Quinn-Trank, C. (2010) "Rhetorical history as a source of competitive advantage," in J. A. C. Baum and J. Lampel (eds), *Globalization of Strategy Research*, London: Emerald, pp. 147–173.

Suddaby, R., Foster, W. M. and Quinn-Trank, C. (2016) "Organizational re-membering: Rhetorical history as identity work," in M. G. Pratt, M. Schultz, B. E. Ashforth and D. Ravasi (eds), *The Oxford Handbook of Organizational Identity*, Oxford: Oxford University Press, pp. 297–316.

Tooze, A. (2014) *The Deluge: The Great War, America and the Remaking of the Global Order, 1916–1931*, London: Allen Lane.

Tooze, A. (2018) *Crashed: How a Decade of Financial Crises Changed the World*, New York: Viking.

Üsdiken, B. and Kieser, A. (2004) "Introduction: History in organization studies," *Business History*, 46(3): 321–330.

Üsdiken, B. and Kipping, M. (2014) "History and organization studies: A long-term view," in M. Bucheli and D. Wadhwani (eds), *Organizations in Time: History, Theory, Methods*, Oxford: Oxford University Press, pp. 33–55.

Üsdiken, B., Kipping, M. and Engwall, L. (2011) "Historical perspectives on organizational stability and change: Introduction to the special issue," *Management & Organizational History*, 6(1): 3–12.

Wadhwani, R. D. and Bucheli, M. (2014) "The future of the past in management and organization studies," in M. Bucheli and R. D. Wadhwani (eds), *Organizations in Time: History, Theory, Methods*, Oxford: Oxford University Press, pp. 3–30.

Wadhwani, R. D. and Jones, G. (2014) "Schumpeter's plea: Historical reasoning in entrepreneurship theory and research," in M. Bucheli and R. D. Wadhwani (eds), *Organizations in Time: History, Theory, Methods*, Oxford: Oxford University Press, pp. 192–216.

Wadhwani, R. D., Suddaby, R., Mordhurst, M. and Popp, A. (2018) "Introduction to the Special Issue—History as organizing: Uses of the past in organization studies," *Organization Studies*, 39(12): 1663–1683.

Weatherbee, T. G., Durepos, G., Mills, A. and Helms Mills, J. (2012) "Theorizing the past: Critical engagements," *Management & Organizational History*, 7(3): 193–202.

Zald, M. N. (1990) "History, theory and the sociology of organizations," in J. E. Jackson (ed) *Institutions in American Society: Essays in Market, Political and Social Organizations*, Ann Arbor, MI: University of Michigan Press, pp. 81–108.

Zald, M. N. (1991) "Sociology as a discipline: Quasi-science and quasi-humanities," *The American Sociologist*, 22(3): 165–187.

Zald, M. N. (1993) "Organization studies as a scientific and humanistic enterprise: Towards a reconceptualization of the foundation of the field," *Organization Science*, 4(4): 513–528.

Part I

2 Origins

History and Management Becoming "Sciences"

Introduction

This chapter aims to provide the necessary context for the remainder of the book by briefly tracing the struggles of both history and management to come into their own as academic disciplines. The chapter will discuss in particular how the differences and similarities in their origins and trajectories shaped their evolution and interrelations until the present day. Broadly speaking, historical writing has deep roots, going back to antiquity, whereas research and writing on management are much more recent. In their origins as "modern" academic disciplines or "sciences", however, they are only about a century apart: the early nineteenth century for history and the early twentieth century for business, within which management developed as a distinct discipline only since the 1950s. Geographically, Germany can probably be seen as some sort of "cradle" for both history and business—though some of the subsequent formative developments happened elsewhere, namely in the US.

While occurring at different times, patterns for the establishment and expansion of both history and business appear broadly similar in terms of (a) claiming their initial legitimacy within the university context by drawing on—and then differentiating themselves from—more established disciplines, as well as by developing a more or less codified methodological apparatus; (b) becoming institutionalized through the establishment of associations of researchers and academic journals; and (c) diversifying subsequently into different sub-disciplines based on topics or approaches (including different methodological, epistemological and/or ontological stances; "theories"; and ideologies)—often with their own associations, journals and handbooks (see for the establishment of new academic disciplines Engwall, Pahlberg and Persson 2018). As will be shown, despite these similar patterns overall, business and management had a somewhat different trajectory, since at the outset business was not welcome in the university environment in many parts of the world, where it consequently had to establish separate educational institutions—many of which persist today.

In what follows, the chapter first provides a summary of the deep origins of history around the world, before focusing on its establishment, starting in Germany, as a "science" (*Geschichtswissenschaft*) within universities during the nineteenth century, followed by a brief overview of its subsequent expansion and diversification. Shifting to business and management, the chapter then looks at how business, or commerce, as it was called at the time, struggled for acceptance within the university context during the nineteenth century, followed by initial and partially successful claims toward becoming a "science" during the first half of the twentieth century, mainly in Germany, before establishing itself as "New Look" business and management studies modeled on the "hard" sciences during the second half of the century, first in the US and then increasingly elsewhere.

Always There: The Ever-Present Hand of History

This section provides a succinct overview of "historiography", i.e. the "history of history", which has received quite extensive treatments elsewhere that should be consulted for more detail (see, among many others, Sreedharan 2004; Breisach 2007; Vann 2018; Woolf 2019). Three important observations need to be noted here: (a) the fundaments of "history" in terms of the ability to memorize events from long ago in the past and the urge—or whatever you want to call it—to tell and listen to "stories" are widely seen as distinctive and unique features of the human species (e.g. Woolf 2019: 1); (b) when referring to "history" almost all of the treatises on historiography refer to "written" history, though they do acknowledge a much earlier—and ongoing—tradition of oral transmission, as well as many other forms of engagement with the past (p. 2), including through artifacts; and (c) while "the West neither invented nor enjoyed a monopoly on history", the Western practice of writing history has become "hegemonic", particularly in institutionalized academic history, which includes measuring everything against Europe and, more recently, the US (pp. 4–5, 8).

The following concise, and necessarily partial, overview will first look at the geographically diverse origins of historical writing, which already raised many of the important issues, namely regarding the use of (original) sources, the relationship of the historian to their narratives and the nature of truth claims. It will then examine in some more detail the nineteenth century when history became an academic discipline, the conditions under which this happened and the claims history laid to being considered a "science". The final sub-section sketches out the subsequent, almost immediate, diversification within history as an academic discipline.

Early and Everywhere: Origins of Written Histories Around the Globe

In terms of the beginnings of historical writing, these are said to be located in ancient Egypt and in what could be called the Near East, between the Nile delta, the plains of the Euphrates and Tigris rivers and Anatolia, home to various civilizations. They mainly take the form of chronological lists of rulers but also include parts of the Hebrew Bible. The earliest identifiable and self-conscious historical writers can probably be found in ancient Greece. Among them Herodotus of Halicarnassus (c. 484—c. 420 BC) is often—though not unanimously—referred to as the "father of history", in part because he was the first to use the term "historia", which denoted his investigative approach. He was apparently also the first to introduce his own person, style and opinion into the writing, creating a tradition that over the next centuries resulted in "virtually an obligation of the historian to declare up-front his preferences, methods and biases—even his [*sic*] position with respect to previous historians" (Woolf 2019: 22).

Herodotus is often compared with Thucydides (d. c. 401 BC) in terms of the kind of history they practiced. While both focused on the recent past and ongoing events and relied almost exclusively on oral testimony, the former provided more context (including the "marvellous and unusual"), went far back in search for causes, spoke to many people and was not afraid to present different, even conflicting, views. The latter tended to have a narrower focus and considered most accurate the knowledge of immediate insiders, including himself—he had been a political and military leader, leading him to profess stronger truth claims. At the same time, possibly borrowing from Greek tragedy, he enlivened his accounts with speeches which he, admittedly, never recorded verbatim or even heard himself—and might even have invented (Woolf 2019: 23–24). While Thucydides was viewed more favorably by subsequent Greek historians, most of them widened their use of sources to inscriptions and public records (for a recent application of his work in an international relations context see Allison 2017).

Greek historians were also among the first to recount (and embrace) the rise of Rome, with Polybius (c. 200–118 BC) one of the earliest and well-known examples. He can be said to have started seeing history as a cumulative and ultimately teleological process (Woolf 2019: 26–27). This was picked up, with what appeared as even more convincing evidence, by later historians who produced multivolume histories of the geographic expansion and ultimate supremacy of the Roman Empire—a view that also influenced Christian historiography later on. Two other features became prominent among Roman historians. One linked history with rhetoric or persuasion, which prompted them to see "the praise of the virtuous and successful, and condemnation of the corrupt, wicked or weak, as a key motivation for any historian" (p. 30). The other, somewhat contradictory, was the declared need to be impartial in their writing, summarized possibly most succinctly in the oft-cited exhortation by Tacitus (c. 56–c. 117 AD) to write *sine ira et studio*, i.e. without anger and keenness—though it is not entirely evident he was able to always follow it himself (Breisach 2007: 67; Woolf 2019: 32–33). Rome also saw the origins of Jewish historiography (beyond the exegesis of the Hebrew Bible) with Flavius Josephus (c. 37–c. 100 AD), a Romanized Jew writing in Greek, in particular *Jewish Antiquities*, "a quasi-universal history with the Jews at its center" (Breisach 2007: 70; Woolf 2019: 18–20).

Starting this overview with Egypt, Greece and Rome is an illustration of historiography's inherent "Western" bias, since as Woolf (2019: 35) states very clearly in his recent overview: "No civilization in the world has consistently and continuously placed as a high a priority on the recording and understanding of its past as the Chinese". And it is no surprise that at least in the more recent accounts, Chinese historian Sima Qian (145–86 BC) is mentioned and discussed alongside Herodotus as a pioneer (Martin 2009; Woolf 2019: 39–43). Historical writing in China eventually became more central than in Greece or Rome, namely through a link with philosophy and the connections with the ruling dynasties. Chinese historians struggled with similar issues as their Western counterparts, including the nature of historical reality, but had different, more circular notions of time and addressed sources more carefully, while at the same time copying the work of earlier writers. They also used history as a moral "mirror", though often in very subtle ways. The first identifiable Chinese chronological history is the so-called "Spring and Autumn Annals", or *Chunqiu*, a history of the vassal state of Lu, supposedly revised by Confucius (551–479 BC). It is part of the five classics of Confucianism which became the dominant philosophy under the Han dynasty that ruled the country for four centuries (206 BC—220 AD).

It is in this context that Sima Qian, who had followed his father as the official grand scribe, or *taishi*, wrote his "Records of the Grand Historian", or *shiji*. It was a long and complex work in five parts containing annals; chronological tables; overviews of different branches of knowledge; essays on the leading "houses"; and biographies of statesmen, scholars and others—with most chapters followed by his comments and advice for the lessons to be learned from history. The *shiji* became a template for subsequent official histories, which would limit themselves to covering a single dynasty rather than the succession of all dynasties. Over the following centuries, Chinese history writing continued at a high level, despite an often-violent succession of various dynasties, and became institutionalized under the Tang dynasty (618–907) with the establishment of a "Bureau for the Writing of History", or *shiguan* (Woolf 2019: 64). While the bureau faded under subsequent dynasties, "history became a critical part of the Chinese educational system" with a focus on its "practical lessons" and "a useable past", for instance, in the form of encyclopedias. Importantly, some historians such as Sima Guang (1019–86) eventually started to exceed the bounds of a single dynasty (Woolf 2019: 66–67). The Chinese example (and language) also influenced emergent historical writings in Japan, which, however, since the eleventh century developed their own genre in the shape of "historical tales" (*rekishi monogatari*). While some of them were difficult to distinguish from fiction, others sought for patterns and meaning in an unstable environment (pp. 67–70).

Since the seventh century, the Islamic culture also brought forth remarkable historical writings, both in the Arabic and, somewhat later, the Persian languages, which soon went beyond an "effort to record only true statements by or about the Prophet" (Woolf 2019: 57). Islamic scholars, in their reflections upon their own craft, foreshadowed what would become the concerns of modern Western historians since the nineteenth century. These are expressed possibly most succinctly by Ibn Khaldun (1332–1406), probably the best-known Islamic historian and historiographer in the West, where he is also widely seen—not always accurately—as a precursor to "modern" social sciences (Irwin 2018). In his famous prolegomenon (*Muqaddimah*, or "Introduction to History"), he starts by highlighting that "untruth naturally afflicts historical information" and identifies the "various reasons that make this unavoidable", which include, among others, "prejudice and partisanship" and a "reliance upon transmitters". The way to deal with this, in his view, is through "critical investigation", which requires a "knowledge of the nature of civilization": "the normative method for distinguishing right from wrong in historical information on the grounds of (inherent) possibility or absurdity, is to investigate human social organization, which is identical with civilization" (Ibn Khaldun 1958).

In contrast, history writing in the West became less prolific as the Roman Empire gradually declined and took a turn toward rather circumscribed views with the officialization of Christianity (see for the following, in summary, Woolf 2019: 49–56, 71–83; in more detail, Breisach 2007: Chs. 7–10). Early Christian writing was influenced by Augustine's (354–430) distinction between the "City of God" and the "Earthly City" and constrained by "a time-line from the Creation to the Last Judgement" (Breisach 2007: 83). It also created a new genre, ecclesiastical history and, with the Crusades from the late eleventh to the early thirteenth century, had a topic to write about. The most important genre during this period—from the demise of the Roman Empire through the barbaric migrations and the eventual establishment of more stable territorial entities during the medieval period—was the so-called chronicle, an "annalistically organized text" (Woolf 2019: 91). In its pure "Christian" form the chronicle was "universal", "spanning all of time and all peoples" (Breisach 2007: 128), but following the end of the Crusades,

" 'Christendom' began to cede its centrality as an organizing concept to individual kingdoms and principalities" whose rulers "increasingly saw the utility in history" in asserting their power against competing claims, including from the Church (Woolf 2019: 77, 79). A parallel development was the increasing use of local "vernacular" languages instead of Latin.

A break with this medieval tradition of historical writing, which was very distinct from what had been done before and what was to come afterwards, arrived in two waves: the Renaissance of the fifteenth century and the Enlightenment of the eighteenth century. The former saw a renewed interest in the classic historical texts, which were unearthed, translated and, initially, served as "models of style, genre, and suitable content" (Woolf 2019: 89). More important was a gradual development of a "sense of the past", seen less as a source of examples for behavior and increasingly as a "road" to the present, a road that needed to be understood in its own context (p. 92)—an understanding that eventually turned some against the uncritical, if not "slavish [. . .] imitation of the classics (p. 97). Since the eighteenth century, within a context marked by the gradual emergence of nation-states and challenges to the political and social order in many of these, "historians were called on to mediate between the demands for change and the equally strong desire to see the continuity of the past, present, and future preserved" (Breisach 2007: 228; for details Chs. 13–16). It was in this context that history eventually morphed into a fully fledged academic discipline and "science".

Scientizing History and Historicizing Everything: The Rankean "Revolution"

The development of history as a profession and as a science has been associated with the person of Leopold von Ranke (1795–1886), a professor at the University of Berlin since 1825. His crucial contribution is widely recognized among historiographers. Thus, in his selection of writings by Western historians since Voltaire on their own discipline, Fritz Stern (1926–2016), himself an eminent scholar of German and Jewish history, called Ranke "the father as well as the master of modern historical scholarship" (Stern 1973: 54). Breisach (2007: 233) agrees that Ranke deserves to be "celebrated as the pioneer of a critical historical science", and Woolf (2019: 176) calls him "the great transformer".

Ranke stands out partially because of his own prolific scholarship, publishing 54 volumes, mainly on political history, including *Geschichten der romanischen und germanischen Völker von 1494 bis 1514* (Ranke 1824) which propelled him from a high school teacher in Frankfurt/Oder to the professorship in Berlin. But it was mainly his quest to use a wide range of sources, check each of them "for trustworthiness and its own context" and then combine them "not to pass judgement on the past but simply to report '*wie es eigentlich gewesen*' or 'as it *essentially* was' ", which is by far his most quoted phrase (Woolf 2019: 178, emphasis in original). And not only did he follow his own methods religiously by not letting "his own distaste for the French revolution or the papacy sway his findings", for instance (Breisach 2007: 233). He also established an apprenticeship-like way to teach aspiring historians the proper methods by having them go to archives and then present their findings and interpretations to a critical audience of professor(s) and other students in a seminar, first held at his home in 1833 (Sreedharan 2004: 182), which remains the centerpiece of educating history scholars to the present day.

While there should indeed be no doubt about his transformative role in the development of history into an established academic discipline, a profession and even a "science", *Geschichtswissenschaft* in German, he acted in a supportive context and could draw and build on earlier ideas and efforts (see, for the following, Woolf 2019: 131–132). Thus, since the Enlightenment, historians had become public figures and history a topic of conversation in salons, gentlemen's clubs (including the more secretive ones) and a growing number of learned societies built on the model of the *Academie française*, established in 1635. And in addition to books, periodicals became a way of disseminating and debating history—though they did have a literary rather than scholarly orientation. Probably even more important was the creation of specific professorships at universities, like the ones on "Universal History and Greek and Roman Antiquities" at the University of Edinburgh in 1719 and in modern history at both Oxford and Cambridge in 1724. In Germany, the University of Göttingen founded in 1734 became an early center for historical research, with one of its professors, Johann Christoph Gatterer (1727–1799), developing ancillary disciplines for historical research, experimenting with the seminar format (Breisach 2007: 233) and editing a short-lived *Historisches Journal* (1772–1781). But it was the university founded upon the initiative of Wilhelm von Humboldt (1767–1835) in Berlin in 1809, which eventually provided the seedbed for the institutionalization of *Geschichtswissenschaft*—separate from both philosophy and literature. This should not be surprising given Humboldt's own insistence on the combination between *Forschung und Lehre* (research and instruction) and his view that "[t]he historian's task is to present what actually happened" (quoted by Woolf 2019: 178).

And then there is Ranke himself, whose training left him uniquely positioned to become this "great transformer". He had studied classical philology and Lutheran theology in Leipzig, which subsequently helped in his development of source criticism (*Quellenkritik*). It also brought him into contact with the work of Barthold Georg Niebuhr (1776–1831) whose *Römische Geschichte*, published since 1812, is known to have significantly influenced Ranke's methodological approach: "It was Niebuhr who showed how to analyze the strata in a source [. . .] and how to discard the worthless and thereby lay bare the material from which the historical facts could be reconstructed" (Editors of Encyclopedia Britannica, 22 September 2019; on Niebuhr and his influence, see also Stern 1973: Ch. 2; Woolf 2019: 146, 176). Equally influential on Ranke's intellectual development were debates among his professorial colleagues at Berlin, namely the philosopher Georg Wilhelm Friedrich Hegel, who saw history as a unitary, all-embracing process leading toward greater rationality, and Friedrich Karl von Savigny and Karl Friedrich Eichhorn, two law professors, who maintained that "legal norms manifest themselves only in concrete historical contexts in the evolution of the spirit of a people"—a position that was very close to Ranke's own understanding of historical development (Iggers 2011: xviii; see also Breisach 2007: 230–232; Woolf 2019: 176–178).

The "Berlin revolution in historiography", as Sreedharan (2004: 169) has referred to it, quickly spread not only in Germany but elsewhere. Ranke's seminar and his lectures played an important role in this respect, since they were attended by students from around the world (Sreedharan 2004: 182–184; Woolf 2019: 178–180). These and others then emulated them in their own instruction. And despite Ranke being interpreted and assessed differently (see, e.g. for his reception in Germany and the US, Iggers 1962), what happened at the University of Berlin influenced the professionalization of history and its acceptance as an academic discipline in its own right, independent from philosophy, literature and law, in many parts of the world (Woolf 2019: 174):

> the expansion of university systems and the turning of many of them by the century's end to formal training in historical scholarship; the introduction of earned doctorates with a research component; the systematization of public record systems; the advent of new professional associations, frequently accompanied by a new style of learned, peer-reviewed periodical or journal.

Indeed, as Table 2.1. shows, the second half of the nineteenth century saw the foundation of historical journals and academic societies in numerous countries.

While the Danish *Historisk Tidsskrift*, was the first of its kind—if one discounts the short-lived *Historisches Journal* (see earlier), the *Historische Zeitschrift* became the model and reference for the many that were to follow. It was founded in 1857 by Heinrich von Sybel (1817–1895) who, in hindsight, was probably Ranke's most distinguished disciple, just after he had taken up a professorship at the University of Munich. In his first editorial von Sybel asserted that "This periodical should, above all, be a scientific one" and also made it clear that it planned to be "historical" rather than "antiquarian" or "political" (Stern 1973: 171). Another Ranke student, Ludwig Riess (1861–1928), played a crucial role in the

Table 2.1 Establishment of select historical journals and societies

Country	Journal		First Editor/Society	
	Year		Year	
Denmark	1840	*Historisk Tidsskrift*	1839	Danish Historical Society (Den danske historiske forening)
Germany	1859	*Historische Zeitschrift*		Heinrich von Sybel (1817–1895)
France	1876	*Revue historique*		Gabriel Monod (1844–1912)
Italy	1884	*Rivista Storica Italiana*		Costanzo Rinaudo (1847–1937)
UK	1886	*English Historical Review*		Mandell Creighton (1843–1901)
Japan	1889	*Shigaku(kai)-Zasshi*	1889	The Historical Society of Japan (Shigakukai)
USA	1895	*American Historical Review*	1884	American Historical Association (AHA)

Sources: Stern (1973: 170–177); Stieg (1986); Woolf (2019: 180–181); Historisk Tidsskrift 23 September 2019; Rivista storica italiana 15 October 2019; Shigakukai (The Historical Society of Japan) 9 August 2019.

introduction of modern historiography in Japan. In 1887, a couple of years after completing his doctorate at Berlin, Riess was hired by the Meiji government as part of its broader modernization efforts and became the first professor of history at Tokyo Imperial University, where he trained many Japanese historians until his departure in 1902. Already in 1889 he was instrumental in the establishment of a Department of Japanese History at Tokyo and the creation of a historical society and journal (Woolf 2019: 208–209). There was also a growing number of manuals dealing with methodology (pp. 181–182), with the ones by Bernheim (1889) and Langlois and Seignobos (1898) proving particularly influential and long-lasting.

But during the nineteenth century history not only turned into a fully fledged academic discipline in many countries around the globe, it also spread more broadly in a "Western world [that] has become intensely historical-minded" (Stern 1973: 11). Satisfying "society's growing demand for history" was facilitated by improvements in printing technology which made the expanding historical scholarship accessible to wider audiences, including as textbooks for schools. In a context of emerging and consolidating nation-states, combined with rising imperialist and colonialist tendencies, governments also showed ever more interest in—and provided funding for—historical research. As we know with hindsight, this often made it difficult for historians to retain their commitment to finding the "truth", and some of them became all too willing collaborators in biased writings and uses of history (Berger and Lorenz 2010). Others, in contrast, as the next sub-section shows, came to fundamentally question the truth claims of Ranke and his disciples.

Beyond a Single Truth: Multiplying the "Houses of History"

The belief by Ranke and his disciples that a critical analysis of the available sources would allow them to approximate the truth "as it essentially was" did not remain uncontested for long—if it ever was. Soon, divergent approaches toward historical scholarship emerged and quickly multiplied. Table 2.2 lists two recent overviews of these different approaches. Green and Troup (2016) offer possibly the most systematic explanation for what they refer to as "houses of history" by arguing "that every piece of historical writing has a theoretical basis on which evidence is selected, filtered and understood", while acknowledging that most historians do not make their underlying theories explicit, rendering their identification by others difficult (pp. 3–4). They use a broad understanding of "theory", ranging "from the identification of patterns in the historical evidence that explain historical change over long periods of time to smaller abstract concepts that define particular phenomena", with some of these concepts also constituting "the building blocks of grand theory, as in the concept of 'class' for the Marxist theory of historical materialism". As for the purpose of these concepts and theories, Green and Troup (2016: 2) point to "the process of formulating new questions and interpretations, and identifying patterns of change in the past". And in terms of their origins they mention "a wide range of disciplines in the humanities and social sciences, particularly literary criticism, linguistics, anthropology,

Table 2.2 The diversification of historical scholarship

	"Houses" of history (Green and Troup 2016)	*Since 1830 (Woolf 2019: Chs. 6 and 7)*
1.	The empiricists	Empiricism and historicism
2.	Marxist historians	Determinism (Comte, Hegel, Marx)
3.	Psychoanalysis and history	"Memory" and "History"
4.	The Annales	The Annales; Microhistory
5.	Historical sociology	History and the Social Sciences
6.	Quantitative history	History and the Social Sciences
7.	Anthropology and ethnohistorians	Cultural and Social Alternatives
8.	The question of narrative	The Linguistic Turn: Postmodernism
9.	Gender and history	From Women's History to Histories of Gender and Sexuality
10.	The challenge of poststructuralism/ postmodernism	The Linguistic Turn: Postmodernism
11.	Postcolonial perspectives	De-centering the West: Postcolonialism
12.	Public history	History from Below
13.	Oral history	History from Below; "Memory" and "History"
14.	History of emotions	History from Below Varieties of intellectual history

sociology, psychology, geography, and philosophy". [Note that management and organization theory is conspicuously absent!] In addition to the differences in these theoretical underpinnings, there are other, often geographically based distinctions. In his overview Woolf (2019), for instance, also looks at "history under dictatorships and authoritarian regimes" (pp. 239–247) and "postwar African historiography" (pp. 260–262).

What this table shows, in a nutshell, is the variety and richness of contemporary historical scholarship, which also prompted the establishment of a wide range of specialist journals (see, for early examples, Stieg 1986) and which this concise summary cannot do adequate justice. In the context of this book, three observations are important. First of all, while presented in broadly chronological order, these "houses of history" are not substituting for each other but coexist within the same "village", to stay within the same metaphor—though with varying importance over time. The Ranke-style "empiricism", for instance, continues to play a significant role today in the training of historians worldwide—intellectually as well as institutionally. Among business historians, for instance, it probably remains the predominant approach.

Second and relatedly, not all of these approaches are of equal importance, i.e. some "houses" are bigger than others—again with some changes over time in either direction. Probably the most significant development in historiography since the "empiricist" Berlin revolution was the so-called "linguistic" or "cultural turn", also referred to, at times interchangeably, as postmodernism or poststructuralism. While empiricism "is based upon the belief that it is possible to reconstruct the past based on surviving evidence", "poststructuralists argue that our understanding of the past, and our sources, are framed through structures of language and discourse, and that there is no access to an unmediated past" (Green and Troup 2016: 4). Those espousing the latter view since the 1960s drew on ideas in literary theory and philosophy developed among many others by Jean-François Lyotard, Jacques Derrida and Michel Foucault in France, as well as Walter Benjamin, Martin Heidegger and Hans-Georg Gadamer in Germany (see, for a summary, Woolf 2019: 262–267; for a more extensive treatment, Breisach 2003). Among historians an early, vocal and ultimately iconic proponent of this view was Hayden White (1928–2018). While not negating the existence of a "real" past, he saw it as no longer "reachable", not even by studying "original" sources, since "they, too, are selections from past life, mediated by *their* authors, and because they have no inherent *meaning* that is not bestowed on them by the historian's interpretation" (Woolf 2019: 264–265; emphasis in original)—ultimately blurring the boundary between history and fiction.

Third and importantly in this context, while there is reference to the social sciences, business and management history do not have a separate house of history, neither in the two examples chosen for Table 2.2 nor in any other major historiographies—probably because of their relatively limited importance within today's "village". Not even economic history apparently deserves its own house, though it is mentioned in the discussion of, among others, Marxism, the *Annales* and quantitative history by either Green and Troup (2016) or Woolf (2019) or both. This probably demonstrates the current dominance of the postmodern approach, since among the *Varieties of History* presented in Stern's (1973) book almost a half-century ago, there were chapters on both "economic history" (Ch. II.6) and "a new [i.e. quantitative] economic history" (Ch. II.14). What this means, as will be discussed in the following chapter, is a dearth of possible points of contact for those asking for a historic turn within management research.

A Bumpy Road: Developing Business and Then Management Into a "Science"

While history was welcomed into the university environment starting in the eighteenth century and became a fully fledged academic discipline in the nineteenth, this was not the case for business and business schools—or their precursors. On the contrary, both the subject itself and the schools that housed it faced resistance, even ridicule, from the more established parts of the universities, exemplified by the oft-quoted dictum by sociologist Thorstein Veblen (1918: 210) comparing colleges of commerce with departments of athletics, neither of which, in his view, "belongs in the corporation of learning". Neither did the *Rektor* (head) of the University of Würzburg think differently when he referred in 1902 to the emergent *Handelshochschulen* (commercial schools) in Germany as "pathological creations" that should not exist, as they had no science tradition (quoted in Üsdiken, Kieser and Kjaer 2004: 385). They did not receive much initial welcome from businesspeople either, wherever they were emerging (see, e.g., Léautey 1886; Kieser 2004).

Originally, all of these schools were dedicated purely to teaching, often of a vocational nature, aiming to prepare students for various tasks in "commerce". Thus, almost from the outset they had to devise ways to gain access to academia and acquire academic status for their discipline in order to increase their own reputation and the standing of their graduates. They did manage to establish themselves within higher education mainly in the first half of the twentieth century—albeit in diverse ways and forms in different parts of the world. It was within the framework of these organizational and institutional developments that claims to "business" as an academic discipline were made. These claims strengthened in the immediate post–World War II period, mainly in the US, culminating eventually in management and organization studies becoming strongly established, together with other specialisms in business, as a distinct "science".

Late, Diverse and Difficult: The Origins of "Business" Schools

Antecedents and predecessors of many of today's business schools and departments developed since the mid-nineteenth century on both sides of the Atlantic Ocean (see further, Engwall, Kipping and Üsdiken 2010, 2016). Rather lengthy processes resulted in the emergence of quite different institutional setups, contrasting the US, on the one hand, and continental Europe on the other. Thus, in the US, despite the previously mentioned resistance, schools of business became part of universities as "professional" schools, following the earlier examples of law, medicine and divinity. In continental Europe, by contrast, the study of commerce initially remained outside the university system. Emulating the example of engineering and technical schools, it took place in stand-alone institutions, often founded and funded by local business communities and associations—with the French *écoles de commerce* and German *Handelshochschulen* particularly influential for developments elsewhere in Europe as well as further afield.

Efforts to establish commercial schools within universities commenced in the US in the 1850s, but many of the first movers shut down quickly or delayed their plans. Even the Wharton School of Finance and the Economy established at the University of Pennsylvania in 1881—and now widely considered the pioneer—struggled at the beginning due to a lack of student interest (Engwall et al. 2016: 46). Demand for higher education in commerce seems to have picked up across the country at the turn of the century—leading to new foundations, with more than 60 universities offering commercial education by 1918. Some of these offerings came as evening programs, and the vast majority only provided undergraduate degrees, usually with a strong liberal arts component—reflecting the latter's domination within the US university system (Clark 1995) and thus as a way to fit into the university. The first to offer the new subject at the graduate level was the Amos Tuck School at Dartmouth College, which established its two-year Master in Commercial Science as an add-on to a bachelor's degree. But what became determinant in hindsight was the establishment of the Graduate School of Business Administration at Harvard following the models of the university's medical and, most importantly, law schools—with the latter also providing the case-based teaching method. Moreover, it was here that the now almost ubiquitous two-year Master of Business Administration (MBA) originated. It nevertheless took another half-century for the graduate degree to displace the undergraduate one in the US, and even longer for the MBA to become the global reference for what eventually came to be called management education— a period during which business schools strived to establish their professional and, increasingly, scientific credentials (Engwall et al. 2016).

As noted, in continental Europe similar efforts by business communities, in particular the chambers of commerce, failed to overcome the resistance from the universities and prompted the establishment of self-standing "schools of commerce". Most of the earliest foundations occurred in France. They accelerated during the second half of the nineteenth century, when *Écoles Supérieures de Commerce* (ESC) were set up in many of the provincial capitals. In this context, the German schools of commerce (*Handelshochschulen*) were relative latecomers. The first *Handelshochschulen* were created in Leipzig and Aachen in 1898, quickly followed by five others before the start of World War I. These schools also became the model and the suppliers of teachers and textbooks for similar efforts in, for example, the Nordic countries (Engwall et al. 2016: 49).

Despite their apparent success, the German *Handelshochschulen* were the first of these new schools to experience major changes, which made the German model of commercial or business education comparatively special. From the outset, they had tried to balance the conflicting pressures from the various stakeholders, namely the need to provide an education focused on practice with an aspiration to be accepted within a higher education system driven by "science" (*Wissenschaft*). They squared this circle by gradually developing during the first two decades of the twentieth century a new academic discipline subsequently labeled *Betriebswirtschaftslehre* (BWL), often translated into English as "business economics". In fact, this is only a partially adequate translation. The term *Betrieb*—literally "undertaking" or "establishment"—is both broader and narrower than "business"; broader, since it not necessarily has to focus only on business activities, and narrower in that it refers to a concrete organization rather than business in the abstract. Furthermore, the translation omits the term *Lehre*, which is part of the idea of "unity of research and instruction", which marked the German university, based on the ideals first established by Wilhelm von Humboldt in the early nineteenth century (see earlier).

Thirsting for Legitimacy: Early Claims to "Science"

It should not be surprising that the first fully fledged endeavor to make the teaching and the study of business "scientific" and create a separate academic discipline originated in the German *Handelshochschulen*, given the country's pioneering role in establishing the modern university system with the "unity" of research and instruction (*Forschung und Lehre*; see earlier). However, references to "science" had actually been there before BWL came into its own. The ESC in France that emerged and expanded, as mentioned earlier, in the nineteenth century were already referring to teaching *science de commerce* (see e.g., Léautey 1886)—though this term, as the German *Wissenschaft*, is more encompassing than the natural science model that eventually came to dominate management research. BWL too had its origins in *Handelswissenschaft*—i.e. the science of "commerce" which aimed to bring teaching on various commercial activities into a coherent whole (Tribe 1995). Next came a redefinition in the early 1910s as *Privatwirtschaftslehre* (PWL) or *Einzelwirtschaftslehre*—literally, the "economics" of the "private" or the "individual" enterprise, which was also meant to distinguish it from *Volkswirtschaftslehre* that examined national economies (Engwall et al. 2016: 102). By the early 1920s, it was relabeled BWL to thwart the critique by economists that PWL could not be a "science" because of its focus on private gain and ways of making a greater profit (Locke 1984; Tribe 1995).

These developments meant that the study of commercial or business activity became a subject of research first in Germany. Eugen Schmalenbach, the main figure in the development of BWL, was saying already in 1906 that "it would be essential to do research in the science of commerce. Since this subject is specific to the new colleges, it is in this area that these colleges have to prove that they are capable of conducting research" (quoted in Üsdiken et al. 2004: 385). For Schmalenbach "working towards a practical goal should not be taken 'as a reason to deny our field the character of a science' ". Although not without contest, this orientation toward bettering actual business practice prevailed, though not through "normative" principles but through some forms of "observation", which were then turned into prescriptions.

What characterized BWL as an academic discipline (or a "science") was a focus on the operation of an economic undertaking as a whole—differently, as will be seen later, from the US, where a specialized focus on separate business functions (such as accounting, marketing and finance) had already emerged during the interwar years (Schmaltz 1930). Overall, accounting constituted the core of BWL. And it was the efforts in accounting, led by Schmalenbach, which contributed to the scientization and acceptability of BWL within academic circles in Germany (Üsdiken et al. 2004; Engwall et al. 2016). Driven by the quest for gaining academic legitimacy, it was also in Germany that journals focusing specifically on business first emerged. Schmalenbach's *Zeitschrift für handelswissenschaftliche Forschung* began publication in 1906. The *Zeitschrift für Handelswissenschaft und Handelspraxis* followed in 1908 (becoming *Die Betriebswirtschaft* from 1930 onwards), as did various others after 1920 (Schmaltz 1930; Engwall et al. 2016). One could see the advance toward greater scientization in the publications in these journals too. In Schmalenbach's journal, for example, whereas most of the earlier articles were descriptions of accounting systems of individual firms, those published after World War I more often involved theoretical analyses of cost accounting and control (Üsdiken et al. 2004: 404).

With its research, books and journals BWL had by 1930 secured its position within German higher education, expedited by the incorporation of the *Handelshochschulen* in Frankfurt and Cologne into the newly founded universities in these cities in 1914 and 1919 (Meyer 1998). In Frankfurt and Cologne obtaining a doctoral degree in BWL had thus become possible—a practice extended in 1927 first to the *Handelshochschule* in Berlin and then to various others (Tribe 1995). Like the *Handelshochschulen* serving as an institutional model for commercial education in various countries, BWL, while not having any impact on the US, the UK or France, did influence Scandinavia as well as Eastern Europe, Spain, Italy, Turkey and Japan (Locke 1984), though not always with the research orientation that it embodied, but rather as content for teaching (see Üsdiken et al. 2004). Inadvertently, the Nazi purges and forced resignations of academic staff also contributed to the spread of BWL internationally (Üsdiken et al. 2004). This was to be largely eradicated, however, with the strong post–World War II surge of US influence abroad.

Until then, the impact of US commercial and business education on Europe and elsewhere had been very limited. The country also lagged behind Germany in moving toward scientization. It was not that there were no initiatives to that end. Indeed, there were, as doctoral studies were initiated and bureaus of research established. Thus, the University of Chicago started a doctoral program in 1920 (Engwall et al. 2016: 96). Harvard followed in 1922 (Khurana 2007: 171). However, the expansion of doctoral programs remained limited, and those that did exist were not actually geared toward educating researchers (Gordon and Howell 1959; Augier and March 2011). Bureaus of research did proliferate, though the "research" they produced was largely confined to contract work. Overall, therefore, advances in research remained rather limited, leading Gordon and Howell (1959), for example, to suggest in one of the so-called "foundation reports" (see later) that there needed to be a shift from descriptions of practice and case studies toward quantitative analysis.

Journals focused on business had begun to appear too. Harvard University and the University of Chicago were again at the forefront. Their respective journals, *Harvard Business Review* (HBR) and *The University Journal of Business*, as it was initially called, both began publication in 1922. HBR was oriented mainly to practitioners and increasingly more so, though it did have continued academic impact too (Engwall et al. 2016). Chicago's journal (which became the *Journal of Business of the University of Chicago* in 1928 and the *Journal of Business* from 1954 onwards until it ceased publication in 2006) had more scholarly ambitions. These two pioneering "generalist" journals—in the sense that they both carried the word "business" in their titles—were soon joined in 1926 by the *Bulletin of the Business Historical Society* (from 1954 onwards, the *Business History Review*), also published under the auspices of HBS. The period between the two world wars also saw the appearance of journals in the US that were focused, as mentioned earlier, on particular functional specializations, namely, accounting, marketing and finance, with each of them seeking recognition as distinct professions (see e.g., Agnew 1941;

Lounsbury 2002). These journals were setting a pattern that would continue subsequently—though involving greater proliferation after World War II, as academic specialization and professional claims expanded in the US. Differently from the earlier university-based generalist journals, these outlets were publications of specialized associations, which could, especially in earlier stages, include practitioners but would increasingly come under the control of academics.

The first among these journals was *The Accounting Review* which came out as early as 1926. It was initially published by the American Association of University Instructors of Accounting, which was founded in 1916 and renamed the American Accounting Association in 1935 (Scovill 1941). Next was the *Journal of Marketing*. It was founded in 1936 during the merger between the National Association of Marketing Teachers (dating originally back to 1915, though under a different name) and the American Marketing Society (dating back to 1930) to form the American Marketing Association in 1937. Both of the predecessor associations had their respective publications, *National Marketing Review* (beginning in 1935) and the *American Marketing Journal* (beginning in 1934), which were then replaced in 1936 by the *Journal of Marketing* (Agnew 1941). And, finally, the *Journal of Finance* was a publication of the American Finance Association, which had been formally established in 1940. The journal was initially called *American Finance*, published annually in 1942 and 1943, followed by a break due to World War II and resuming publication as the *Journal of Finance* in 1946 (Keenan 1991). Although all these journals voiced "scientific" aspirations, until well after World War II they published articles that were descriptive and geared mainly toward practitioner audiences (Lounsbury 2002; Engwall et al. 2016).

"Management" turned out to be a latecomer in achieving recognition as a distinct academic specialty. An American Management Association was formed in 1923, but unlike others mentioned earlier focused exclusively on practitioners (Wren and Bedeian 2018: 208; see also Chapter 5, this volume). Potentially more promising perhaps was the creation of the Academy of Management (AoM)—today the largest organization for management academics (see also Chapter 6, this volume). Founded informally in 1936 and then formally in 1941, it was initially "conceived" as "a permanent organization for teachers of management" (Wrege 1986: 78). Nevertheless, already in 1941, the objectives set for the organization made reference to the "sound application of the scientific method to the solution of managerial problems" (Wren and Bedeian 2018: 285). However, the annual conferences remained very small, as debates continued as to whether this would be an organization for the "elite", true to the name "Academy", or ought to be more encompassing and whether practitioners should be included or not (Wrege 1986). Dormant from 1942 to 1946 due to World War II, the organization was resurrected in 1947 but continued to remain small until the late 1960s, when membership reached around 800 (Myrick, Mills and Mills 2013: 360). And its first journal, *The Journal of the Academy of Management*, as it was called at the time, only began publication in 1958. Moreover, the early articles, like in the other disciplines mentioned earlier, only provided discussions on issues such as developing a "general theory of management" and business education or, in case of the empirical ones, descriptions of practice (Goodrick 2002).

Getting There—And Globally: Turning Management Into a "True" Science

The 1950s saw the creation of two journals in the US related in some way to "management" which for the first time ever carried the word "science" in their titles: *Management Science* in 1954 and the *Administrative Science Quarterly* (ASQ) in 1956. These two journals epitomized the shift toward the scientization of the study and teaching of business and management, led, as it was, by the US. They were at one in turning "management" or "administration" into a "science"—in the sense of emulating the natural sciences—though different in the way they aimed to do this, both then and since.

In fact, operations researchers had already made the first move, heartened, it seems, by what they had been able to do during World War II. The Operations Research Society of America (ORSA) had launched in 1952, right after it was founded, the journal *Operations Research*—the flagship of scientization, or what Locke (1989) referred to as the "new paradigm". A split within ORSA pertaining to the extent of attention to be devoted to issues concerning management led to the establishment in 1953 of an alternative association, The Institute of Management Sciences (TIMS)—hence the new journal, *Management Science* in 1954 (Horner 2017). As the founding editor C. West Churchman (1954: 96) put it, the "objective" of the journal was "to identify, extend, and unify scientific knowledge that contributes to the understanding and practice of management", and the articles they sought would be expected to "further the aim of developing a unified science of management"—statements which clearly demonstrated the aspirations of the time. The journal also had an eye on practitioners, as indicated in Churchman's (1954: 96) additional statements in terms of being "accessible to persons in managerial positions". Moreover, the very first article in the inaugural issue was written by two practitioners who endorsed the journal's aims by saying that the "Science of Managing is, like all *true* sciences, creating an expanding universe of concepts and principles" (Smiddy and Naum 1954: 31; capitalization in original, emphasis added).

ASQ was not different in terms of the espoused aims; the unsigned editorial (1956: 1) in the first issue, for example, proclaimed that the journal "expresses a belief in the possibility of developing an administrative science and a conviction that progress is being made and will continue". The founding editor, James D. Thompson (1956: 103), in a companion article in the same issue took this further by saying that "testable hypotheses which will link abstract notions with empirical data are urgently needed". This was coupled with the warning that "the focus of attention on results with immediate utility limits thought and perception and thereby reduces the ultimate contributions of the research to administrative science" (p. 110). While the foregoing editorial statements point to the commonalities in intent, the two journals also differed in significant ways, contributing to the development of distinct disciplines. *Management Science* represented the "new paradigmatic" form of the engineering tradition that dated back to Taylor and prioritized advances in mathematical modeling (Denizel, Üsdiken and Tunçalp 2003). An "administrative science" and its journal ASQ would, as Thompson (1956: 103) put it, stand "approximately in relation to the basic social sciences as engineering stands with respect to the physical sciences, or as medicine to the biological".

Thus, of the two, ASQ served as the initial platform in the scientization of "management" and its concurrent development of a separate disciplinary identity—often considered together with "organization". *Management Science*, together with *Operations Research*, did the same for what came to be known as the operations research/management science (OR/MS) field (see Denizel et al. 2003). In achieving this science shift, not only these two but also the other business disciplines such as marketing or finance benefited extensively from the massive financial support provided in the 1950s and the 1960s by the Ford Foundation to US business schools (see further Engwall et al. 2016: Ch. 10). The findings and recommendations of the so-called "foundation reports" by Gordon and Howell (1959) and Pierson (1959), sponsored, respectively, by the Ford Foundation and the Carnegie Corporation, served as a further impetus for Ford Foundation support in the dissemination of what in foundation circles was dubbed the "New Look" for US business schools (Khurana 2007). Moreover, these initiatives for creating a "science of managing" (Smiddy and Naum 1954) or administration were taking place at a time when science was enjoying a prominent status, again especially in the US context, not least as an aftereffect of World War II. Social sciences at large were also deemed to be holding strong potential for dealing with human problems (Augier, March and Sullivan 2005). Indeed, not only the normative setting provided by such widespread conceptions but also the material environment was highly favorable for US business schools, not least with respect to student as well as financial resources (Augier et al. 2005).

In fact, the scientization drive had begun even before the Ford Foundation intervened, as demonstrated by the founding of the three journals mentioned earlier. Boulding (1958), for example, in a comparison of the first and the second volumes of ASQ, showed the immediate outcomes that were obtained. Not only did "research papers" constitute most of the articles in the second volume but there were also twice as many as in the first. Studying the articles published in the same journal over the period 1959–1979, Daft (1980) found that whereas most of the earlier papers were qualitative case studies, later on a majority were using some form of quantitative methodology and statistical analyses. Goodrick (2002) demonstrated that a similar kind of shift had been happening in the *Academy of Management Journal* (AMJ) during the same period. This pattern was further confirmed and strengthened when the AoM decided to launch a second journal—the *Academy of Management Review* (AMR)—so that the AMJ could only publish empirical research articles (see also Chapter 6, this volume).

In the meantime, "management" was gaining a separate identity as a discipline in its own right, aided by the publication platforms that had emerged, as well as the expansion of AoM in the US. Its ten "professional divisions" created in 1971 in response to growth reaffirmed that management had become a distinct discipline, since, among various other business disciplines, only "operational analysis" was granted a division status (Wrege 1986). Moreover, the establishment of these divisions within AoM attested to the diversification and specialization that had been emerging within management studies. Now, "organization and management theory" (OMT) became a sub-discipline itself, encompassing the "macro" side of organizational analysis, as distinct from, for example, "organizational behavior" and "organizational policy and planning" (nowadays, "strategic management") (Wrege 1986).

Within management at large, this tendency toward diversification continued particularly throughout the 1970s and the 1980s, as indicated by the increase of professional divisions in AoM. By 1990, there were 19 divisions and two "interest groups". Among the new additions were "careers", "entrepreneurship", "managerial consultation", "research methods" and "women in management" (Academy of Management, 1990). By the end of 2019, divisions and interest groups numbered 25, with "critical management studies" and "management spirituality and religion" among the new ones created since 1990 (Academy of Management, 14 October 2019). The trend toward greater diversification could also be observed in the creation of specialist journals within management from the 1960s onward in sub-disciplines such as human resources, organizational behavior, international business, entrepreneurship, organization theory, strategic management and business ethics (see further Engwall et al. 2016: 202–203 and 265).

While scientization progressed in the US during the 1960s and the 1970s, occasional dissenting voices appeared. Concerns were expressed that prioritization of theoretical questions was leading to a disengagement from practical managerial problems (see e.g., Koontz 1980). Such opposition had little effect, however, and management and its sub-disciplines, such as OMT, became more and more firmly settled on the scientization route. Already by the mid-1970s, publishing in refereed journals had become almost as important as teaching in promotion and tenure decisions in US business schools (e.g., Stark and Miller 1976). The same period also saw the expansion of the US influence internationally, not least due to various forms of aid provided within the Cold War context—though this aid was geared more toward building capacity for business education rather than research (Engwall et al. 2016: Ch. 10). Nevertheless, US-led scientization and the diversification of business studies into functional specialisms and further sub-disciplines began to spread after the 1980s as business schools also expanded to other parts of the world. It was then when management as well as other specialisms, such as marketing or finance, started to gain a disciplinary identity more globally (see Üsdiken 2014).

Yet in the meantime another challenge emerged after the late 1970s, concerned not with the question of whether links to practice were severed (although this was to re-emerge later too), but rather with scientism itself as a way of generating knowledge on management and organizations. Van Maanen (1979: 521–522), for instance, in the preface to a special issue of ASQ, referred to increasing concerns about the "almost monopolistic grip" of quantitative methods in studies of organizations and pointed to a "renewed interest and a felt need for qualitative research". Alternative approaches—interpretive, critical and postmodernist—were also emerging, more so from Europe and in particular the UK, which in one way or another stood in opposition to the scientistic orientation dominant in the US (see Üsdiken 2010). That such a schism had taken shape by the early 1990s between research coming out of the US and Europe was shown empirically (Üsdiken and Pasadeos 1995). It was also apparent when, for instance, DeNisi (1995: 942), then editor of AMJ, wrote that

> while we accept papers based on alternative methodologies and approaches we do have clear standards that we will not compromise. European authors will have to adapt to our conventions and models if they want to publish in our journals just as we would have to adapt to theirs to publish in their journals.

Nevertheless, "alternative methodologies and approaches", in particular qualitative research, did gain more legitimacy, also leading—then and later—to calls for greater engagement with history (see Chapter 3, this volume).

Conclusion

Comparing the development of history, on the one hand, and management and organization studies, on the other, the roots of the former go back many thousand years when one looks at historical writings and even longer, possibly to the origins of humanity itself, when oral traditions are included. Moreover, history has been told and discussed critically in most cultures. In contrast, studies—rather than practices—of management and organizations are much more recent, two centuries at best, and they are largely confined to the North Atlantic economies. When it comes to their establishment as academic disciplines, however, they were less than a hundred years apart, with history in its empiricist—"how it essentially was"—variety being established as a "science", or *Wissenschaft* in Germany, more specifically at the newly founded University of Berlin in the first half of the nineteenth century and then spreading around the globe. That same process also underpinned the diversification of historical research into multiple "houses", with differences in their subjects, methodologies and epistemologies.

Attempts to establish management and organization studies as a "science" go back to the turn of the twentieth century, when some of those teaching management at the growing number of commerce or business schools in the industrial and industrializing economies aspired to also conduct research. This process eventually came to fruition after World War II in the US, where the business schools experienced significant growth and where management as an academic discipline became firmly established by drawing on adjacent disciplines and borrowing methodologies and epistemologies from the natural sciences—a model that spread around the world subsequently. As will be discussed in detail in the following chapter, this "scientization" made it increasingly difficult for historians to find common ground with management scholars—though some of them did keep trying. As the next chapter will also show, it was a growing dissatisfaction with the prevailing "hard" science model that eventually led certain researchers in management and organization studies to take a more qualitative orientation and eventually prompted calls for "more history" and even a "historic turn".

References

Academy of Management (1990) *Academy of Management Journal*, 33(4): 653.

Academy of Management, http://aom.org/DIG/ (accessed 14 October 2019).

Agnew, H. E. (1941) "The history of the American Marketing Association," *Journal of Marketing*, 5(4): 374–379.

Allison, G. (2017) *Destined for War: Can America and China Escape Thucydides's Trap?* Boston: Houghton Mifflin Harcourt.

Augier, M. and March, J. G. (2011) *The Roots, Rituals, and Rhetorics of Change: North American Business Schools After the Second World War*, Stanford, CA: Stanford University Press.

Augier, M., March, J. G. and Sullivan, B. N. (2005) "Notes on the evolution of a research community: Organization studies in Anglophone North America, 1945–2000," *Organization Science*, 16(1): 85–95.

Berger, S. and Lorenz, C. (eds) (2010) *Nationalizing the Past: Historians as Nation Builders in Modern Europe*, Basingstoke: Palgrave Macmillan.

Bernheim, E. (1889) *Lehrbuch der Historischen Methode*, Leipzig: Duncker & Humblot.

Boulding, K. E. (1958) "Evidences for an administrative science: A review of the *Administrative Science Quarterly*, volumes 1 and 2," *Administrative Science Quarterly*, 3(1): 1–22.

Breisach, E. (2003) *On the Future of History: The Postmodernist Challenge and Its Aftermath*, Chicago, IL: The University of Chicago Press.

Breisach, E. (2007) *Historiography: Ancient, Medieval, and Modern*, 3rd edn, Chicago, IL: The University of Chicago Press.

Churchman, C. W. (1954) "Policy statement for *Management Science*," *Management Science*, 1(1): 96.

Clark, B. R. (1995) *Places of Inquiry: Research and Education in Modern Universities*, Berkeley, CA: University of California Press.

Daft, R. L. (1980) "The evolution of organization analysis in ASQ, 1959–1979," *Administrative Science Quarterly*, 25(4): 623–636.

DeNisi, A. (1995) "From the editor," *Academy of Management Journal*, 38(4): 941–942.

Denizel, M., Üsdiken, B. and Tunçalp, D. (2003) "Drift or shift? Continuity, change and international variation in knowledge production in OR/MS," *Operations Research*, 51(5): 711–720.

Editors of Encyclopedia Britannica, www.britannica.com/biography/Barthold-Georg-Niebuhr (accessed 22 September 2019).

Engwall, L., Kipping, M. and Üsdiken, B. (2010) "Public science systems, higher education, and the trajectory of academic disciplines: Business studies in the United States and Europe," in R. Whitley, J. Glaser and L. Engwall (eds), *Reconfiguring Knowledge Production: Changing Authority Relationships in the Sciences and Their Consequences for Intellectual Innovation*, Oxford: Oxford University Press, pp. 325–353.

Engwall, L., Kipping, M. and Üsdiken, B. (2016) *Defining Management: Business Schools, Consultants and Media*, New York: Routledge.

Engwall, L., Pahlberg, C. and Persson, O. (2018) "The development of IB as a scientific field," *International Business Review*, 27(5): 1080–1088.

Goodrick, E. (2002) "From management as a vocation to management as a scientific activity: An institutional account of a paradigm shift," *Journal of Management*, 28(5): 649–668.

Gordon, R. A. and Howell, J. E. (1959) *Higher Education for Business*, New York: Columbia University Press.

Green, A. and Troup, K. (eds) (2016) *The Houses of History: A Critical Reader in History and Theory*, 2nd edn, Manchester: Manchester University Press.

Historisk Tidsskrift, www.dendanskehistoriskeforening.dk/ (accessed 23 September 2019).

Horner, P. (2017) "History lesson: The evolution of INFORMS," *ORMS Today*, 44(1), https://pubsonline.informs.org/magazine/orms-today/loi (accessed 17 September 2019).

Ibn Khaldun (1958) *The Muqaddimah* (translated by Franz Rosenthal), www.muslimphilosophy.com/ik/Muqaddimah/ (accessed 21 September 2019).

Iggers, G. G. (1962) "The image of Ranke in American and German historical thought," *History and Theory*, 2(1): 17–40.

Iggers, G. G. (ed) (2011) *The Theory and Practice of History* by Leopold von Ranke, London: Routledge.

Irwin, R. (2018) *Ibn Khaldun: An Intellectual Biography*, Princeton, NJ: Princeton University Press.

Keenan, M. (1991) "Fifty years of the American Finance Association," *The Journal of Finance*, 46(3): 1113–1156.

Khurana, R. (2007) *From Higher Aims to Hired Hands: The Social Transformation of American Business Schools and the Unfulfilled Promise of Management as a Profession*, Princeton, NJ: Princeton University Press.

Kieser, A. (2004) "The Americanization of academic management education in Germany," *Journal of Management Inquiry*, 13(2): 90–97.

Koontz, H. (1980) "The management theory jungle revisited," *Academy of Management Review*, 5(2): 175–187.

Langlois, C.-V. and Seignobos, C. (1898) *Introduction aux Études Historiques*, Paris: Hachette.

Léautey, E. (1886) *L'enseignement Commercial et les Écoles de Commerce en France et Dans le Monde Entiere*, Paris: Libraire Comptable et Administrative.

Locke, R. R. (1984) *The End of the Practical Man: Entrepreneurship and Higher Education in Germany, France and Great Britain, 1880–1940*, Greenwich, CT: JAI Press.

Locke, R. R. (1989) *Management and Higher Education Since 1940: The Influence of America and Japan on West Germany, Great Britain, and France*, Cambridge: Cambridge University Press.

Lounsbury, M. (2002) "Institutional transformation and status mobility: The professionalization of the field of finance," *Academy of Management Journal*, 45(1): 255–266.

Martin, T. R. (2009) *Herodotus and Sima Qian: The First Great Historians of Greece and China: A Brief History with Documents*, Boston: Bedford/St. Martin's.

Meyer, H.-D. (1998) "The German Handelshochschulen, 1898–1933: A new departure in management education and why it failed," in L. Engwall and V. Zamagni (eds), *Management Education in Historical Perspective*, Manchester: Manchester University Press, pp. 19–33.

Myrick, K., Mills, J. H. and Mills, A. J. (2013) "History-making and the Academy of Management: An ANTi-History perspective," *Management & Organizational History*, 8(4): 345–370.

Pierson, F. C. (1959) *The Education of American Businessmen: A Study of University-College Programs in Business Administration*, New York: McGraw-Hill.

Ranke, L. V. (1824/1884) *Geschichten der romanischen und germanischen Völker von 1494 bis 1514*, 3rd Aufl, Leipzig: Duncker & Humblot.

Rivista storica italiana, www.edizioniesi.it/rivistastoricaitaliana/index.php?id=la-rivista (accessed 15 October 2019).

Schmaltz, K. (1930) "The business periodicals of Germany," *The Accounting Review*, 5(3): 231–234.

Scovill, H. T. (1941) "Reflections of twenty-five years in the American Accounting Association," *Accounting Review*, 16(2): 167–175.

Shigakukai (The Historical Society of Japan), www.shigakukai.or.jp/english/about/ (accessed 9 August 2019).

Smiddy, H. F. and Naum, L. (1954) "Evolution of 'science of managing' in America," *Management Science*, 1(1): 3–31.

Sreedharan, E. (2004) *A Textbook of Historiography, 500 BC to AD 2000*, Hyderabad: Orient Blackswan.

Stark, B. J. and Miller, T. R. (1976) "Selected personnel practices relating to research and publication among management faculty," *Academy of Management Journal*, 19(3): 502–505.

Stern, F. (ed) (1973) *The Varieties of History: From Voltaire to the Present*, 2nd edn, New York: Vintage.

Stieg, M. F. (1986) *The Origin and Development of Scholarly Historical Periodicals*, Tuscaloosa, AL: University of Alabama Press.

Thompson, J. D. (1956) "On building an administrative science," *Administrative Science Quarterly*, 1(1): 102–111.

Tribe, K. (1995) *Strategies of Economic Order: German Economic Discourse, 1750–1950*, Cambridge: Cambridge University Press.

Üsdiken, B. (2010) "Between contending perspectives and logics: Organizational studies in Europe," *Organization Studies*, 31(6): 715–735.

Üsdiken, B. (2014) "Centres and peripheries: Research styles and publication Patterns in 'top' US journals and their European alternatives, 1960–2010," *Journal of Management Studies*, 51(5): 764–789.

Üsdiken, B., Kieser, A. and Kjaer, P. (2004) "Academy, economy and polity: *Betriebswirtschaftslehre* in Germany, Denmark and Turkey," *Business History*, 46(3): 381–406.

Üsdiken, B. and Pasadeos, Y. (1995) "Organizational analysis in North America and Europe: A comparison of co-citation networks," *Organization Studies*, 16(3): 503–526.

Van Maanen, J. (1979) "Reclaiming qualitative methods for organizational research: A preface," *Administrative Science Quarterly*, 24(4): 520–526.

Vann, R. T. (2018) "Historiography," Encyclopedia Britannica Online, www.britannica.com/topic/historiography (accessed 6 July 2018).

Veblen, T. (1918) *The Higher Learning in America: A Memorandum on the Conduct of Universities by Business men*, New York: B. W. Huebsch.

White, H. V. (1966) "The burden of history," *History and Theory*, 5(2): 111–134.

Woolf, D. R. (2019) *A Concise History of History: Global Historiography from Antiquity to the Present*, Cambridge: Cambridge University Press.

Wrege, C. D. (1986) "The inception, early struggles, and growth of the Academy of Management," *Academy of Management Proceedings*, 78–88.

Wren, D. A. and Bedeian, A. G. (2018) *The Evolution of Management Thought*, 7th edn, Hoboken, NJ: Wiley.

3 Aspirations
Bringing History and Management Studies (Back) Together

Introduction

As the preceding chapter has shown, history and management experienced their elevation to a "science" almost a century apart—and what it meant to be a science was rather different in the nineteenth and the second half of the twentieth century. However, while history became fully integrated into the extant (and new) universities around the globe, in many countries, business and then management were initially offered within stand-alone institutions of higher education rather than university-based schools or departments—a pattern that persists today in many of these places. What the preceding chapter has also shown is that both history and management soon after—and partially even before—their fully fledged acceptance as academic disciplines embarked on a process of diversification into various "houses", or sub-disciplines, often with their own associations and, most importantly, scholarly journals.

The different understandings of "science" resulting from these processes made a possible collaboration, and even communication, between the two disciplines difficult—and this despite the multiplication of sub-disciplines, which might have offered possible points of contact. This left historians with a difficult choice among three basic roles, which are summarized succinctly by one of the discipline's eminent historiographers (Breisach 2007: 1): (a) the "traditional historians", who aimed "to observe 'how things had gradually come to be' "—put differently, far from the concerns of mainstream management scholars; (b) historians confined to an auxiliary role, "content with unearthing the raw materials for the social scientists who alone explain [. . .] human life in a 'scientific manner' "; and (c) those who recognized the futility of reconstructing "the past in its actuality—even imperfectly" and therefore saw "history as a special type of literature" to be analyzed through the application of "literary criticism and theory"—the latter a clear reference to postmodernism which, since the 1960s, had prompted the most significant shift in historical research since the "Rankean revolution" of the nineteenth century.

As the next section will discuss, historians did try to maintain a dialogue, definitely with the social sciences as a whole and, later on, also with the scientized "New Look" management scholarship—though the latter fell to a rather marginal and ultimately smallish group of (business) historians, whose origins can be traced back to the (German) historical school of economics rather than to history itself. Overall, these efforts were limited to a few intellectual and institutional points of contact and, as will be elaborated in the subsequent section, initially found little resonance among management scholars who, in their vast majority, remained indifferent to the absence of history in their discipline. This, as the chapter will elaborate then, only changed gradually, following attempts since the 1980s to broaden the basis of management research beyond its foundational focus on the "hard" sciences—a focus which clearly motivated some of the advocates for "more history". These pioneers were eventually followed by those calling—more ambitiously—for a "historic turn". Many of its proponents already had or sought contact with business history and incorporated some notions of the earlier postmodern "cultural turn" in both history and management studies—though what such a historic turn actually entailed and where it would lead remained subject to debate.

Anybody Out There? Contacts Between Historical and Business and Management Research

This section outlines some points of contact between the various "houses of history" that emerged since the late nineteenth century (Green and Troup 2016) and business, then management research, pinpointing a number of paths available but not taken. It then focuses on the post–World War II period and the increasingly limited interactions between the two disciplines after the "scientization" of management and organization studies (Chapter 2, this volume).

Roads to Nowhere: Missed Opportunities

As briefly noted in the previous chapter, historians of different persuasions, or "houses", did show interest in economic issues. Among them were, not surprisingly, Marxist historians, though they focused on the working class more than on other parts of society—not entirely surprising either, given that at the time of Marx's own writing "managers" and "management" had not really entered the fray yet. James Burnham's (1941) book on *The Managerial Revolution* could have provided a contact point, but did not for a variety of reasons, including its timing, the subsequent turn of its author toward the political right and the absence of a more elaborate historical dimension. Another opportunity within the Marxist context arose in the 1970s with the so-called Labor Process

Theory based on a book by Harry Braverman (1974). But while Braverman's work looked at the history of management, namely Taylorism, most of those subsequently developing his ideas were not historians or historically inclined. So, the historical dimension waned and eventually vanished (see Chapter 7, this volume, for some more detail).

There was also economic history which, in its early research, did form an important foundation for business history (see later for the connection between the two). But similar to the "scientization" of management research, "old" economic history gradually gave way to a "new" version based largely on quantification. And this new cliometric economic history subsequently became subsumed both intellectually and institutionally into neoclassical, mainstream economics, i.e. evolved in directions more and more remote from the concerns of both history (Boldizzoni 2011) and management and organization studies. The largely French-based *Annales* school (Green and Troup 2016: Ch. 5) also looked at economic systems over the long run, but both its levels of analysis (either very local or macro, e.g. trade in the Mediterranean) and its predominant focus on periods further in the past (mainly the medieval and early modern times) were of little interest to management scholars—even before the arrival of the "New Look".

In the US, historians did manage to maintain an institutional connection with the social sciences through the Social Science Research Council, which had been established in 1923 and was formally incorporated the following year. In addition to history, it brought together the American associations and societies representing anthropology, economics, political science, psychology, sociology and statistics, but not management. (The Academy of Management was founded only later, but never joined anyway.) From the history-related publications by the council it becomes clear that historians had to work hard to establish their legitimacy within this context—and how challenging these efforts actually were for both sides. The efforts began in 1942 with a meeting of the Committee on Problems and Policy of the Council with a small group of historians. A subset of the latter eventually constituted the Committee on Historiography and was tasked with "preparing a manual to clarify thought about history and to aid historians in teaching and writing it". Apparently, "the committee encountered a great many problems with its labors", starting with agreeing on a common terminology (Curti 1946: vii). And while the committee did not "claim to having 'settled' any of the issues" (p. ix), it eventually published a report entitled *Theory and Practice in Historical Study* (Anon. 1946), consisting of separate contributions by some committee members and a "selective reading list on historiography and the philosophy of history".

Dealing with "theory" was, not surprisingly, the biggest issue and constituted a core topic of subsequent reports by the committee. Entitled *The Social Sciences in Historical Study*, the next report (Anon. 1954) was jointly authored by the whole committee, now chaired by Thomas C. Cochran, an "old-style" economic historian though open to new approaches. His work on American business in its social and cultural context, starting with a pioneering book on *The Age of Enterprise* (Cochran and Miller 1942), and his keen interest in the social sciences (see also Stern 1973: Ch. II.3) could have been foundational for business history and an excellent point of contact, but was neither (see later)—and still isn't. The report tried to promote interdisciplinarity once again by making concepts and methods on both sides explicit, concluding with a chapter on what was seen both as the core of historical analysis and as a "problem": the "narrative synthesis" and its limitations (Anon. 1954: Ch. 7). The third report (Gottschalk 1963) was even more explicit about the core issue already in its title: *Generalization in the Writing of History*. In his foreword, the editor distinguished "two groups" of historians: the "descriptive historians" and the "theoretical historians" who "try to find in their subject matter a basis for comparison, classification, interpretation, or generalization" (p. v). He then stated that the report—and hence the committee, tellingly renamed "Committee on Historical Analysis"— was only concerned with the latter group.

There does seem to have been some interest in theory among historians at the time. Thus, 1960 saw the founding of a journal entitled *History and Theory*—though the subtitle, *Studies in the Philosophy of History*, already indicated an internal and reflective rather than an external, interdisciplinary focus. Moreover, in the opening essay—which was, it should be noted, not an official statement of purpose—the philosopher and historian of ideas Isaiah Berlin clearly stated that "to say of history that it should approximate to the condition of a [hard] science is to ask it to contradict its essence" (Berlin 1960: 31). In any case, the vast majority of historians—with the exception of those espousing cliometrics (see earlier)—seems to have belonged to the "descriptive" group, leading Hayden White (1966: 111) to the following ironic characterization:

> [W]hen criticized by social scientists for the softness of his [*sic*] method, the crudity of his organizing metaphors, or the ambiguity of his sociological and psychological presuppositions, the historian responds that history has never claimed the status of a pure science, that it depends as much upon intuitive as upon analytical methods, and that historical judgments should not therefore be evaluated by critical standards properly applied only in the mathematical and experimental disciplines. All of which suggests that *history is a kind of art* (emphasis added).

White, as we know, went on to become one of the pioneers of the postmodern "cultural" or "linguistic" turn by arguing that history should actually be closer to the literary arts (see also Chapter 2, this volume.)

While these opportunities and efforts toward a sustained dialogue between history and the social sciences had a limited impact, contacts and even some collaboration did eventually take place. But they involved only a rather small, even somewhat marginal, group of historians, though they were connected to a highly visible and central institution: the Harvard Business School (HBS).

Lonely Hearts: Business Historians and "New Look" Management Studies

The most developed, fruitful interactions between management and history concern a sub-discipline that does not have its own "house" and is not even mentioned in most historiographical overviews: business history (see Chapter 2, this volume). Its development is complex and varied—more so than even most business historians themselves, let alone outsiders would be aware of—but does offer multiple contact points with management research along the way. This becomes especially clear when going beyond the established accounts that tend to situate the origins of business history at HBS during the interwar period and its fully fledged development with Alfred D. Chandler Jr. (1918–2007), whose work is often listed among the early classics of management (see for the following in detail Kipping, Kurosawa and Wadhwani 2017).

However, the origins of business history, both intellectually and institutionally, actually go back to the historical school of economics in Germany and, to a lesser extent, the UK in the mid-to-late nineteenth century. Its proponents, led by Gustav von Schmoller (1838–1917), opposed both the abstract and highly theoretical approach of (neo)classical economics and the deterministic (and materialistic) views of Hegel and Marx. Instead, they were concerned with human agency, the role of organizations and institutions and their historical development, paving the way for the likes of Max Weber (1864–1920) and the somewhat less well-known Werner Sombart (1863–1941). Methodologically, the research of the historical school tended to be inductive, comparative and, ultimately, cumulative, taking both time and place seriously. This approach led to a very public spat, the so-called *Methodenstreit*, with the deductive, assumption-based Austrian school of economics, represented by Carl Menger (1840–1921) (see, among others, a special issue of the *Journal of Institutional and Theoretical Economics* at the occasion of Schmoller's 150th birthday, coordinated by Richter 1988; and, more recently, Louzek 2011).

The historical school of economics also spread to many other countries, once again—like in the case of Ranke's Berlin revolution—mainly through the international mobility of scholars. Thus, the founding dean of HBS in 1908, Edwin F. Gay, did his doctorate with Schmoller and then took a position as professor of economic history at Harvard. And his student N. S. B. Gras became the first Isidor Straus professor in business history at HBS in 1927. Among others, many Japanese scholars also studied historical economics in Germany and, upon their return, shaped the economics departments and their research focus at the universities in Tokyo and Kyoto—albeit in competition with Marxist approaches. And while Weberian and Marxist approaches persisted in Japan and many European countries well into the post–World War II period (for more details, see Kipping et al. 2017), the emergence of the "New Look" management research made this more challenging in the US, though it looked initially as if HBS might remain an exception. Thus, at a panel discussion on approaches to business history held there in 1962 (with contributions published in the *Business History Review*), at least one of the participants saw the increasing scientization of business schools as an opportunity, since it allowed business historians to "provide an enormous deposit of fact against which a myriad hypotheses can be tested" (quoted by Kipping et al. 2017: 24).

That same year, Alfred D. Chandler Jr. published his book on the multidivisional organizational structure, or M-form (Chandler 1962), which is still considered one of the early "classics" of management research (see Chapter 12, this volume). His work also prompted a large-scale, comparative research program at HBS examining the origins and propagation of the M-form in a range of countries—often in the shape of doctoral dissertations, co-supervised by Bruce Scott and Chandler, who had been appointed to the business history professorship at HBS in 1970. In addition, the M-form became the subject of a large number of quantitative studies, once the transaction cost economist Olivier Williamson had converted Chandler's ideas into a testable hypothesis (for a critical overview of this research, see Kipping and Westerhuis 2012; for a later extension of the original HBS studies, Whittington and Mayer 2000). But what looked promising ultimately remained limited (for details Kipping and Üsdiken 2008; Üsdiken and Kipping 2014), as business history turned increasingly inward, developing its own "organizational synthesis" (for details, Kipping et al. 2017), all the while stressing its importance for teaching (future) managers (e.g. Kantraw 1986). Most importantly, as the following section will show, the little outreach there was met largely with indifference from management and organization scholars—until the 1990s, when internal dissatisfaction with the overly scientistic nature of management research eventually prompted some of the latter to look toward history, among others.

Unrequited Love: Management Indifference From the 1960s Through the 1980s

During the first decades after the advent of scientization in US management research, few seemed to pay attention to or care, let alone complain about the absence of history—and suggestions regarding a need for "more history" were even fewer. Among those who took note early on was Boddewyn (1965: 261) as part of an effort to advocate a "comparative approach" for "business administration" with a particular emphasis on bringing in an international dimension. In his view, one reason for the slow development of such comparative and international research within US academia was "a fairly widespread disinterest in business history". Still, Boddewyn (1965: 265) located the comparative method within the scientization project and was careful to note that the comparison he proposed was different from the historical approach, as it aimed to identify patterns of similarities and differences, treating the "unique" only as a "residual".

Going somewhat further in pinpointing the absence of history, particularly in organizational research, was Mouzelis (1967: 174–175) when he observed that "present organization theory is not only ethnocentric but ahistorical as well" and that "organization studies seem to exist in a timeless dimension", which meant scholars at the time had also moved away from the historical perspective of the classical writers such as Weber and Marx. This was exemplified, Mouzelis (1967) thought, by contemporary authors who provided a critique of Weberian bureaucracy focusing on the organizational level, while neglecting the influence of the historical context, and who were primarily oriented toward developing hypotheses and generalizations. With these arguments, Mouzelis (1967) was echoing Delany (1963: 459), who had earlier said that "sociology and the sociological study of administration have tended to become predominantly ethnocentric, nonhistorical, and microcosmic in orientation". Interestingly enough, this was the same Delany (1960: 449) who a few years back had suggested that history should not be the first priority in organizational research (see Kipping and Üsdiken 2008: 100).

As quantitative comparative studies expanded, further reactions to the ahistoricism of organizational research appeared, albeit intermittently. Benson (1977: 1 and 6–7), for instance, noted that the study of organizations was "guided by a succession of rational and functional theories and by positivist methodology" and that "actual historical research" was "rare". As an alternative to this predominant orientation, he proposed a Marxian or a "dialectical approach". Such a dialectical view, Benson (1977) argued, should be mainly concerned with the processes of the social production and reproduction of organizational patterns and would draw upon historical evidence in developing explanatory accounts. Likewise, Frost (1980: 502), proposing a critical or a "radical" approach to organization theory, identified as one of the weaknesses of current practice that it was "preoccupied with snapshots and short time-frame perspectives [. . .] which amount to essentially ahistorical perspectives [. . .] and little attention is given to the evolution of organizational forms".

From a different angle, McNeil (1978) lamented that sociological studies of organizations had not given adequate attention to issues of organizational power raised by Weber. And he criticized the lack of attention to history in contemporary research: "While sociologists claim to be following Weber, the mainstream of sociological research is not. The search is now for ahistorical theoretical generalizations, not causal explanations of unique historical patterns" (McNeil 1978: 78). Similarly, Meyer and Brown (1977) argued that research at the time had sidetracked Weber's central concern with the development of bureaucracies. For them, a "factor limiting the usefulness of most [. . .] studies [was] that they present data from one point only and thus overlook the possible effects of history" (Meyer and Brown 1977: 365).

This was also the time when earlier comparative studies of organizational sociologists were evolving, together with the advent of the open-systems view, toward the so-called "contingency approach" in the management and organizations literature. Research pursuing this approach focused primarily on organizational structures and was typically based on cross-sectional empirical studies. Reacting to this prevalent orientation, Ranson, Hinings and Greenwood (1980) pointed to the "ahistorical" nature of the research that looked for such patterns in structural arrangements, as well as to a more general lack of attention to the temporal element in studies on structural change. The theoretical approach they proposed to remedy these deficiencies was directed toward processes of structuring and aimed to explain the historical development of organizational structures. Their framework, the authors claimed, could serve this purpose because it brought together not only phenomenological and structural-contingency perspectives but also views that attended to the broader historical contexts (Ranson et al. 1980: 14).

Somewhat more comprehensively, Hage (1978) explicitly searched for integration between sociological and historical approaches with reference to organization theory by focusing on the concept of organizational environments. For him, while organizational sociology and history differed with respect to the emphasis on the general vs. the specific, there still existed possibilities for integrating these two traditions. Hage's emphasis was on expanding the range of general variables to describe organizational environments. The synthesis he called for involved using these general variables to identify the historically specific conditions that organizations confront. The various ways he thought that this could be done included, for example, attending to processes of contextual change either by tracing environmental variables, singularly or in combination, over time or by studying how the relationships among organizational variables differed in distinct historical stages.

These intermittent observations about the ahistoricism of organizational analysis and the few calls for greater attention to history were later supplemented by occasional papers that advocated the use of history as a tool for research on management and organizations. Lawrence (1984: 307), for example, distinguished between "historical research" and a "historical perspective". The latter did not involve an interest in the past per se, but rather the use of knowledge of the past for a better understanding of the present. For Lawrence (1984) taking a historical perspective would hence, on the one hand, help to set time limits for the generalizability of theory and findings and, on the other, aid in generating new research questions or readdressing old ones. Similarly, Fombrun (1989: 441), also pointing to the predominant "static" and "ahistorical" nature of prior studies, spoke of the "necessity" to "supplement traditional empirical research with both *historical* and *interpretive* data" (emphasis in the original). Equally, Pettigrew (1990: 269), another advocate of historical research (see also Chapter 8, this volume), pointed out that the earlier literature on organizational change had been "ahistorical, aprocessual, and acontextual in character". Likewise, Goodman and Kruger (1988) considered the utility of historical research for studying management. For them, primacy had to remain with quantitative methodologies, as they allowed for testing hypothesized relationships. But in their view, historical research could be of use as a supplement in the research process, particularly in the selection of variables and the development of theory and hypotheses.

A few empirical papers using history also appeared at this time. Kieser (1987) provided a narrative account of the process of "rationalization" that medieval Catholic monasteries and monks went through, which led to tensions between asceticism and the generation of wealth, not dissimilar to the constraints later imposed by bureaucratization on employees. He was explicit in the value of historical analysis as the best way for understanding and explaining how "organization building" was reciprocally influenced by "societal belief systems, institutions, and individuals' motivations" (Kieser 1987: 119–120). In a companion piece on how medieval guilds in Germany were replaced by putting-out systems and factories, Kieser (1989: 540–541) not only joined some of the previously mentioned authors by observing that "most organization theories [were] ahistoric" but also argued that a "theoretical frame" based on "historical analysis" could "explain the genesis and further historical development of formal organizations" (see also Chapter 11, this volume). Kieser was also among those who would subsequently issue more explicit calls to resurrect the use of history in management and organization studies, as detailed in the subsequent section.

Feeling Nostalgic: Growing Calls for "More History" Since the 1990s

Calls for greater engagement with history in studying management and organizations began to increase in the 1990s. These early calls were framed in two different ways, each associated with a different connection to history that was believed to have existed in the past. One set of these calls saw possibilities in reinvigorating previous links with business history, while the second was associated with injecting history more broadly into the ways that the study of organizations and management was conventionally understood and implemented.

The first stream was exemplified by the early work of Rowlinson and his colleagues (e.g. Rowlinson and Hassard 1993; Rowlinson 1995; Rowlinson and Procter 1999)—with Rowlinson (1988) having come in touch with business history through a research project on Cadbury. Although there was reference to organization studies being "ahistorical" more generally (Rowlinson and Hassard 1993: 299), the particular focus in this work was on organizational culture, a popular concept at the time both in academic and practitioner circles. These authors viewed culture as providing a possible bridge for relinking business history and organization studies. This was because organizational culture was widely acknowledged as being "historically based" (Rowlinson and Procter 1999: 369). Thus, the study of culture offered possibilities both for organizational researchers and for business historians to provide a historical perspective. Rowlinson and his colleagues surmised that neither of these opportunities was actually taken up. The predominant managerial, symbolism or postmodern approaches to culture were not amenable to engagement with history, due not least to their preferred methodologies. Neither did business historians, despite an interest, actively engage with the study of organizational culture because of the affinity of business history to economics and the equally strong norms of objectivity. Nevertheless, for Rowlinson and his colleagues, the potential for a historical approach to organizational culture was still there. It needed to entail, however, a deconstructionist approach to disciplinary conventions and the ways in which corporate histories were constructed by businesses (see e.g., Rowlinson and Hassard 1993).

The second stream of calls made no specific reference to business history. Rather, they were situated within the framework of the relations between history and sociology, which were seen to have been much closer at the outset, in particular, through the work of Max Weber. So, for Zald (1990) and Kieser (1994), who were the first to explicitly put forward a broader call for rapprochement with history, the ahistoricism of organization theory was part of a similar development in social sciences at large. Indeed, Zald (1993) later located his appeal for greater engagement with history in organization studies within a bid for reaching out to the humanities, as he had already done for sociology (Zald 1991). For him, the social sciences, including organizational studies, were "not only sciences, but humanities" (Zald 1993: 514).

With respect to history more specifically, Zald (1990: 82) opined that the newer approaches of the 1970s and the 1980s in organizational analysis "continue the nomothetic, ahistorical cast of organizational theory, and for that matter, most of social science". "Models are developed and propositions stated", Zald (1990: 82) noted, "as if they apply to all organizations in all societies, over an indefinite time span". Instead, he proposed a "historically nested, comparative approach" which would enable locating "general propositions in [a] historical and societal context" (Zald 1990: 83, 87). Invoking Weber, he believed that bringing in history would be useful in addressing what was largely missed in current theorizing—the exploration of how organizational arrangements were influenced by broader politico-economic structures and processes (see also Zald 1991). Taking a historical and comparative approach would also enhance the contribution that organization theory could make to policy by revealing experiences in different societal contexts, the institutional alternatives that were available and the choices that had been made in the past.

According to Zald (1990: 102), the main question was "how one goes about *combining* history, theory and the study of organizations" (emphasis added). Zald (1990) believed that this could be done in different ways. Although he acknowledged that there could be a "history-for-itself approach", he suggested that in such instances too the selection and use of cases could be geared toward addressing more general issues and offering generalizations (Zald 1990: 103). The other approaches he suggested involved (a) using history as a "testing ground for nomothetic propositions", (b) "developing historical theories of organizations" or (c) using "historical data" to account for how particular organizational forms become shaped and how they undergo significant transformations. Although Zald (1990) did point out that these suggestions were put tentatively, what he proposed was to reappear in a later work that in some way linked history with management and organization studies, as will be shown in the remainder of this chapter as well as the chapters in Part III (this volume).

Although developed separately, Kieser's (1994) views on "why organization theory needs historical analyses" were also framed with recourse to the historical perspectives of Weber and Marx and around the tensions between history and sociology—and, for that matter, organizational sociology. Kieser (1994) did argue, though, that history and organization studies were not necessarily incommensurable and that a two-way relationship could be re-established, i.e. on the one hand, organization theory could benefit from historical analyses and, on the other, historical phenomena could be examined using organization theory. Achieving the former was possible by (a) bringing a historical dimension into internationally comparative research, (b) contrasting present-day concepts and practices with similar ones in history, (c) studying past developments to account for present-day organizational arrangements and (d) putting current theories to test in historical contexts. Applying organization theory to history, on the other hand, might involve (a) using theory to identify ideal types and contrasting historical cases with ideal typical formulations or among themselves or (b) developing generalizations while attempting to explain singular or multiple historical phenomena. All in all, though, much like Zald (1990), Kieser (1994: 619) believed that "historical analyses do not replace existing organization theory; they enrich our understanding of present-day organizations".

While all these calls contributed toward drawing attention to the ahistoricism of management and organization studies, they were at the same time sowing the seeds of fissures within what on the surface appeared to be a project of bringing about greater engagement with history. As Rowlinson and Carter (2002: 528) realized, "an historical perspective" was being "advocated from a variety of standpoints".

Whole Lotta Love: Increasing Diversity as History Attracts Greater Attention

That calls for closer links with history represented separate viewpoints was captured by Üsdiken and Kieser (2004: 322) who identified three distinct positions, which they labeled "supplementarist", "integrationist" and "reorientationist". As exemplified by Lawrence (1984) and Goodman and Kruger (1988) mentioned earlier, as well as Goldman's (1994) rejoinder to Kieser (1994), the supplementarists saw the utility of history as a testing ground for general theory or as a methodological aid in selecting variables and developing hypotheses for quantitative analysis. The integrationist approach envisioned, as Zald (1990) and Kieser (1994) did, a rapprochement, where historical research could serve as a basis for generalization or where history featured as an explanatory factor in management and organization theories. Different from both these approaches, the reorientationist position viewed an historical perspective as a way for moving away from the science aspirations of organization studies (Carter, McKinlay and Rowlinson 2002). As highlighted by Clark and Rowlinson (2004), such an "historic turn" would in addition involve not only turning toward history but also engaging with debates on historical theory, epistemology and method—with the "factual" approach to history deemed particularly problematic (see also Rowlinson 2004). It was this version of the call for an historic turn that served as the foundation for the creation of the journal *Management & Organizational History* (see Booth and Rowlinson 2006; and Chapter 7, this volume).

The diversity in approaches notwithstanding, the kind of calls mentioned earlier did fuel greater attention to the potential for a stronger relationship between history and management and organization studies. Focused sub-themes and sessions were held at various conferences; more articles started to appear, both in special editions of journals and separately, and so did (hand)book chapters and complete edited volumes (see, for details Chapter 1, this volume). As a result, the literature on combining management and organization studies with history expanded significantly since the late 1990s (Leblebici 2014). Due to these publication opportunities and a broader momentum, linked in part to organization theories with an eye to longitudinal analyses, there was a parallel growth in actual research that incorporated history in one way or another. As interest in history grew, elaborations of the extent and the kinds of connections to history in management and organizational research expanded, promulgating varied ways in which this could be done. Slightly rewording the way Kipping and Üsdiken (2015) put it, positions differed with respect to the "where and how" of the turn they advocated. In fact, the term "historic turn"—initially mentioned by Zald (1996: 252) for the social sciences at large in combination with reference to an ongoing literary-linguistic turn, and then reframed by Clark and Rowlinson (2004) specifically with respect to organization studies (see earlier)—began to gain different meanings. The expanding literature also led to new ways of classifying the various proposals for interaction with history.

Turning Where? Business History, History or Postmodern History

Echoing in part the early calls mentioned in the previous section, different positions emerged as to what exactly management and organization studies should be turning to (see also Decker 2015). Three predominant answers can be distinguished with respect to what discipline or literature could serve as a source for making the study of management and organizations more historical: (a) business history, (b) history more broadly and (c) the postmodern or cultural turn within history (see, for the latter also Chapter 2, this volume).

In some writings, possibilities of greater interaction were considered largely within the confines of business history. Kipping and Üsdiken (2008), in an early piece, for example, constructed a chronological narrative starting out with the close relationship until the 1960s between business history and business administration, particularly in the US. After recounting the distancing that later happened between the two disciplines, they pointed to various contributions to management studies made by business historians, seeing a greater potential for impact in view of the calls for more history from within the former. Similarly, in a forum centered on Godelier's (2009) assessment of the French literature, for both the article itself and all the responses (Kobrak 2009; Popp 2009; Tiffany 2009), it was business history that constituted the main frame of reference. The central question was whether business history could be useful for management thinking and practice, though Popp (2009), in his response, did warn against the dangers a rapprochement in those terms could entail for business history. Leblebici (2014), too, saw the issue as one of building connections between business historians and organization theorists, making reference to history at large only in his comparison to the social sciences more broadly.

A second stream of literature, while starting out with or making occasional references to business history, went beyond this focus and extended its view to history more broadly (Decker 2015). Wadhwani and Bucheli (2014: 5), for example, begin with a call for a "deeper dialogue between management scholars and business historians" and provide an overview of the more recent developments in both disciplines to suggest that the time is ripe for an extended conversation. Although they do return later to a discussion of the institutional separation between these two academic communities, the main body of the text is devoted to the promises of "historical perspective and reasoning" and "historical research" for management and organization studies, which are set against the dominant "functional" approaches. Similarly, in their article on history in strategy Vaara and Lamberg (2016) at times referred to business history. They do demonstrate their broader stance, however, by explicitly stating that the historical approaches they consider are "not limited to business history" (Vaara and Lamberg 2016: 637). Kipping and Üsdiken (2014: 537), in a more recent piece, followed very much the same path by formulating their main concern as exploring the ways in which history "has actually been employed in organization and management theory". Some of these authors made no reference to the historic turn, and those who did interpreted the term in a more comprehensive manner, taking it to mean the incorporation of history into the study of organizations (e.g. Wadhwani and Bucheli 2014).

Finally, for a third group of authors the turn was to be neither to business history nor to history more broadly. This does not mean connections to business history were not considered at all. Suddaby (2016: 47), for example, started out by positing that the main task was to "bridge the gap between business history and management". Likewise, Rowlinson and Hassard (2014: 148) spoke about seeking a "rapprochement" with business history as a "neighboring field". Yet these authors concur that this could not be with the business history as typically understood and practiced. Indeed, Clark and Rowlinson (2004: 331) explicitly stated that the historic turn or historical reorientation in management and organization studies should not necessarily be toward business history. This was because business history and research were seen as "integrationist" (Rowlinson, Jacques and Booth 2009: 289) and, consequently, deemed not only as empirically objectivist but also atheoretical in the sense of lacking engagement with historical theory and philosophy. Debates within history itself arising from the entry of poststructuralist and postmodernist views (see Chapter 2, this text) were seen to have been excluded in business history (Weatherbee 2012). Business historians as well as historians at large were viewed as shunning reflection on their methods, particularly by not addressing debates around representations of the past (Rowlinson and Hassard 2014; Suddaby, Foster and Mills 2014).

Thus, for making such a rapprochement possible, recourse to the post-modern "cultural turn" in history was necessary, which entailed reflexivity about methodological proclivities (Rowlinson and Delahaye 2009). Indeed, it was suggested that the purported division between business history and organization studies was "superficial" (Coraiola, Foster and Suddaby 2015: 217). If it were not for the "functionalists" in the two disciplines, as Suddaby (2016: 50) put it, the "gap" would look much smaller and links could be more readily established. So, the main problem these authors had was with what they considered the "modernist" or "realist" view of history and its conflation with the past (Suddaby et al. 2014). The cultural turn in history instead recognized that there were alternatives to this modernist or "reconstructionist" approach. On offer were also "constructionist" positions, where social science concepts are brought into historical writing, as well as "deconstructionist" ones, where historical narratives are only seen as texts open to questioning and critique (Rowlinson and Hassard 2014; Coraiola et al. 2015). Hence, the historic turn needed to be toward the latter in order to advance an historical reorientation in organization studies (Weatherbee 2012).

Turning How? Searching for Some Form of "Synthesis"

The expanding programmatic literature on bringing history and the study of organizations (back) together led to different interpretations of what the various views that were offered amounted to. In Decker's (2016: 364) view, for example, "the very term 'historic turn' (Clark and Rowlinson 2004), originally considered by Üsdiken and Kieser as *reorientationist*, has become a more encompassing term that now refers to bringing history into OS". She further suggested that although "supplementarist" and "reorientationist" positions still existed, the dominant orientation since Üsdiken and Kieser's (2004) formulation had been toward an "integrationist" position, which she broadly paints as seeking "to make sense of how history can contribute to organizational research" (Decker 2016: 364), while acknowledging that it might be interpreted in different ways. Indeed, Maclean, Harvey and Clegg (2016: 611), in proclaiming their position as integrationist, stated that it was "predicated on a union between organization theory and historical analysis"—a union sought within the framework of the "social scientific tradition". In contrast, Decker's (2016: 370) typology also included work that called for a turn to cultural history, such as Coraiola et al. (2015)—a position skeptical about adhering to a social scientific orientation and, at times, even calling for a reorientation (e.g., Rowlinson et al. 2009; Rowlinson and Hassard 2014) rather than an integration as understood by Maclean et al. (2016) or Üsdiken and Kieser (2004).

While based on markedly different interpretations of what an integrationist position means, these two viewpoints can both be considered as being geared toward addressing the question of *how* with respect to a purported historic turn. Nevertheless, they are also indicative of two distinctive approaches as to how the turn to history is to be achieved, namely, through "historical organization studies" or through "organizational history" (see also Rowlinson and Hassard 2013; Leblebici 2014; Rowlinson, Hassard and Decker 2014).

Looking back, it must have been Zald (1990) who for the first time aired the idea of "historical theories of organizations" (see earlier). In the way he defined it, "historical theories make time dependent events or processes critical to explaining later stages and events of organizations" (Zald 1990: 103). One could then find the same notion in an article by Leblebici and Shah (2004: 358) who also argued for an "historical organization theory" in which "temporality is combined with event sequences and narrative explanations". Leblebici (2014) developed this idea to propose a dichotomy, similar to the one suggested earlier, where he distinguished between "historical organization theory" and "organizational history". In Leblebici's (2014: 73) definition, historical organization theory is "based on universal history" and "subscribes to an understanding of history that implicitly claims the existence of a temporally dynamic but holistic social system moving through objective time". Rowlinson, Hassard, et al. (2014: 259–260), too, referred to "historical—or 'historically informed'—organization theory" to provide a contrast with "narrative—or 'theoretically informed'—organizational history". For these authors, historical organization theory was associated with "analysis of relationships between concepts", "data constructed from a specified replicable procedure" and "chronology of predefined occurrences" (Rowlinson, Hassard, et al. 2014: 260). In addition, they identified four historical research strategies labeled corporate, analytically structured, ethnographic and serial history. In their view, serial history represented historical organization theory and was the most frequently used method. It was also distinct from the other three as the only one that focused not on individual organizations, but on organizational fields or populations.

Subsequent work extended and modified these ideas. Thus, while not specifically using the term "historical organization theory", Kipping and Üsdiken (2014: 536) developed the companion notion of "history *in* theory", "where history or the past are part of the theoretical model itself as a driver or moderator". This was in contrast to "history *to* theory", where history is used as a source of data or evidence with the purpose of illustrating, testing or elaborating theory. Echoing some of Zald's earlier suggestions, they added the notion of "historical cognizance", which referred to theorizing that considered historical and contextual conditionality. Most notably, Kipping and Üsdiken (2014), not constrained by a focus on business history, explicitly pointed out that history could feature in theory and analyses not only at the organizational level but also at more macro levels such as industries, fields and populations (see also Wadhwani and Bucheli 2014). Maclean et al. (2016: 609) extended these ideas further toward what they labeled "historical organizational studies". This was defined as

> organizational research that draws extensively on historical data, methods, and knowledge, embedding organizing and organizations in their sociohistorical context to generate historically informed theoretical narratives attentive to both disciplines—alert to changing interpretations of meaning over time and the residue or sedimentation of prior templates.

Like Kipping and Üsdiken (2014), Maclean and her colleagues (2016) see a wide range of research programs in organization studies at various levels of analysis as involving links to history. Following on this view, they took the additional step of formulating a typology of the ways in which such links have been established—a typology based on two dimensions: the "purpose of incorporating history" ("exposition" vs. "interpretation") and the "mode of inquiry" ("social scientific" vs "narrative"). The combination of these two dimensions resulted in four different integrationist "conceptions" of the relationship between history and theory: (a) "evaluating" (testing/refining theory), (b) "explicating" (applying/developing theory), (c) "conceptualizing" (generating theory) and (d) "narrating" (explaining origins of current phenomena) (Maclean et al. 2016: 612). In addition, these authors proposed a range of principles that research along any of these conceptions should follow, framed overall by what they referred to as "dual integrity", taken to mean, like Leblebici (2014), adherence to the scholarly requirements of the two disciplines by entailing both "historical veracity and conceptual rigor" (Maclean et al. 2016: 617).

The second approach as to how history and organization theory could be brought together put the emphasis on the creation of a new sub-field, typically labeled "organizational history". The origins of this idea go back to Carroll's (2002) introduction to a special issue of the *Journal of Organizational Change Management* on the "strategic use of the past and the future in organizations", as well as Booth and Rowlinson's (2006) inaugural statement for *Management & Organizational History*. From the outset, organizational history was put forth as an alternative to business history, due to a disappointment with the latter because of its purported lack of attention to questions of ontology and epistemology. In these early stages, what exactly organizational history was meant to involve was put forth rather vaguely. Reference was made, in particular, to organizational memory, identity and the strategic uses of the past (Carroll 2002), as well as to some work in management history of a critical revisionist or counter-historical nature (Booth and Rowlinson 2006; see Chapter 7, this volume, for examples). While Leblebici (2014) who had distinguished organizational history from historical organization theory did not see the former as a separate (sub-)field, others have recently made more pronounced attempts to further elaborate the idea and flesh out the distinctive features of organizational history. Godfrey et al. (2016: 592), for example, in their "loose" formulation define "organizational history" as "research and writing combining history and organizational theorizing". In their view, the "theory" requirement makes organizational history distinct from both business history and management history, which are, so the argument goes, not "explicitly theorized" (Godfrey et al. 2016: 592)—with theorization taken to mean methodological reflexivity, engagement with historiographical debates and the use of theoretical perspectives from organization studies. Godfrey et al. (2016) do acknowledge, however, that boundaries may become blurred when some form of theory is employed in research on business and management history.

That organizational history as an emergent sub-field should be characterized by an organizational level of analysis has been made particularly explicit by Rowlinson, Hassard, et al. (2014: 250), when they say in their definition "we mean the history of organizations as such, with a focus on individual organizations rather than fields or populations". As mentioned earlier, among the research strategies that these authors identified, serial history stood out, as it was more likely to be used in studying more macro levels, which located it within historical organization theory rather than organizational history. Accompanying the call for organizational history as a sub-field is a preference and encouragement for the use of organizational archives, the mainstay of historical research. This would be possible for corporate, analytically structured and ethnographic histories, while it would be much less likely, even largely impossible in serial history.

In all then, these two approaches to the question of *how* a synthesis could be achieved tend to differ in four main ways. First, although both sets of views refer to theory, what is implied by theory differs. Whereas theory is understood in historical organization studies in the social scientific sense, in the case of organizational history, it carries a somewhat different meaning in that it relates both to historical and historiographical theory and to perspectives within organizational analysis, which stand in opposition to a social science orientation. Second, while historical organization studies are more comprehensive in the sense of incorporating organizational research at various levels of analysis such as fields and populations, organizational history tends to focus on the level of individual organizations. In some of the writings, this focus is accompanied by an attempt to carve out an intellectual space for organizational history as a sub-field, which would be distinct from business history and management history. Third, the two approaches differ in their ontological assumptions. While authors aiming to advance an historical organization theory see the truthful representation of the past as a core principle of historical work, those calling for organizational history problematize the relationship between the past and history, claiming that the latter can only be subjective. And finally, there are differences with respect to methodological proclivities. Historical organization theory is more open to the use of secondary sources in research. Those aiming to develop organizational history as a new field, in contrast, give primacy to organizational archives or extant historical narratives on organizations.

Above and Beyond: Extending the Historic Turn in Organization Studies to Other Domains

Various authors associated with each of these approaches also considered the possible impact of their preferred way of how the turn toward history in organization studies should be achieved on other research domains. A prime target has been business history, or even more broadly, history. O'Sullivan and Graham (2010), for example, thought that business history could benefit from greater interaction with organization theory, as it could serve to counter the tendency in the former to refrain from generalization and theory. Maclean, Harvey and Clegg (2017) took a step further and approached the possibilities of a rapprochement entirely from the perspective of business history. Indeed, they suggested that forging links with organization theory could be an answer to the "marginalization" of business history in management research. They also argued that business history research was not necessarily atheoretical, and therefore the potential for a beneficial dialogue with organization theory was already there. Notably, though, like Popp (2009), O'Sullivan and Graham (2010) also pointed to the skepticism on the part of some business historians about a closer engagement with theory as it would jeopardize the distinctiveness of business history as a scholarly activity.

Rowlinson and Hassard (2013: 121) also saw benefits in "exporting theory to history". Projecting the distinction between historical organization theory and organizational history into the neo-institutional perspective in organization studies, they distinguished between what they referred to as "historical neo-institutionalism" and "neo-institutionalist history". Historical neo-institutionalism was defined as "the use of historical research to illustrate or advance neo-institutionalist theory", whereas neo-institutionalist history referred to "the use of neo-institutionalist theory in historical research to illuminate historiographical debate" (Rowlinson and Hassard 2013: 121). Going beyond the neo-institutional framework, the broader argument in this line of thinking has been that the benefits to be gained by business history can be fulfilled if and when business historians are willing to engage with organization studies by drawing upon the cultural turn in history (Rowlinson and Delahaye 2009; Rowlinson and Hassard 2014). Thus, these views are markedly different from what O'Sullivan and Graham (2010) or Maclean et al. (2017) proposed as a prospective contribution to business history of an engagement with organization theory, which both considered as encouraging a movement toward generalization and theorizing. Indeed, Rowlinson and Hassard (2014) have been particularly critical of these kinds of proposals in that they saw them as indicative of the constructionist approach referred to earlier, which eschews addressing epistemological issues in carrying out historical research. For Rowlinson and Hassard (2014: 154), to attend to these issues critically requires a "deconstructionist culturalist" approach, which should involve archival research.

Authors who advocate linking organization theory with history under the banner of organizational history have also seen this as an opportunity for reinvigorating a historical perspective in Critical Management Studies (CMS). Rowlinson et al. (2009), for example, acknowledged that the predecessor of CMS, namely, labor process theory, was historical, though in a manner that in their view was constructionist history (see earlier). In any case, when CMS took shape as a separate sub-field, the link to history was lost (see Chapter 7, this volume; also Weatherbee 2012). Thus, for Rowlinson et al. (2009), the historic turn, or the reorientation in organization studies that they advocated, could and needed to be linked with CMS (see also Godfrey et al. 2016). From a CMS perspective, too, the historic turn should involve a deconstructionist approach to history.

Conclusion

While historians, depending on where they were based, maintained a more or less intensive interaction and dialogue with the social sciences more broadly, the scientistic turn in management and organization studies in the US since the late 1950s had made research largely ahistorical. Some points of contact remained. They were mainly located at HBS and linked with business history and its widely recognized doyen, Alfred D. Chandler Jr., whose early work is considered a "classic" of management even today. Among the majority of "New Look" management scholars, however, the ahistorical nature of their research was noted, at least initially, by few and lamented by even fewer. It was only since the early 1990s that some voices arose, belonging initially to Mayer N. Zald and Alfred Kieser, asking for "more history" in management research or, as they portrayed it, a "return" to what appeared like the earlier unity of the two, embodied namely by Max Weber. They were soon joined by others who called, somewhat grandiosely, for a "historic turn" in management and organization studies and then started deliberating and debating where this turn was meant to be leading and how it should be carried out.

Within this fast-growing, largely programmatic rather than empirical literature authors identified and usually coalesced around one of two poles, which eventually came to be called historical organization studies/theory, on the one hand, and organizational history, on the other. These two approaches differed in terms of their understanding of theory, their levels of analysis, their ontological positions and the sources and methods used. Equally, if not more importantly, they also differed with respect to their intended audiences and their broader agendas, with some authors wishing to make business history more open to both generalizations and postmodern ideas, while others were hoping to crack a chink in the armor of the scientistic paradigm in management research and yet others aiming for both. But while ultimately united in their calls for "more history", of whatever kind, few of these authors checked how much history—again, broadly defined—there actually was within mainstream management publications. This will be the aim of the subsequent chapter.

References

Anon. (eds) (1946) *Theory and Practice in Historical Study: A Report of the Committee on Historiography* (Bulletin 54), New York: Social Sciences Research Council.

Anon. (1954) *The Social Sciences in Historical Study: A Report of the Committee on Historiography* (Bulletin 64), New York: Social Sciences Research Council.

Benson, J. K. (1977) "Organizations: A dialectical view," *Administrative Science Quarterly*, 22(1): 1–21.

Berlin, I. (1960) "History and theory: The concept of scientific history," *History and Theory*, 1(1): 1–31.

Boddewyn, J. (1965) "The comparative approach to the study of business administration," *Academy of Management Journal*, 8(4): 261–267.

Boldizzoni, F. (2011) *The Poverty of Clio: Resurrecting Economic History*, Princeton, NJ: Princeton University Press.

Booth, C. and Rowlinson, M. (2006) "Management and organizational history: Prospects," *Management & Organizational History*, 1(1): 5–30.

Braverman, H. (1974) *Labor and Monopoly Capital: The Degradation of Work in the Twentieth Century*, New York: Monthly Review Press.

Breisach, E. (2007) *Historiography: Ancient, Medieval, and Modern*, 3rd edn, Chicago, IL: The University of Chicago Press.

Burnham, J. (1941) *The Managerial Revolution: What Is Happening in the World*, New York: John Day.

Carroll, C. E. (2002) "Introduction," *Journal of Organizational Change Management*, 15(6): 556–562.

Carter, C., McKinlay, A. and Rowlinson, M. (2002) "Introduction: Foucault, management and history," *Organization*, 9(4): 515–526.

Chandler, A. D. Jr. (1962) *Strategy and Structure: Chapters in the History of the Industrial Enterprise*, Cambridge, MA: MIT Press.

Clark, P. and Rowlinson, M. (2004) "The treatment of history in organization studies: Toward an 'historic turn'?" *Business History*, 46(3): 331–352.

Cochran, T. C. and Miller, W. (1942) *The Age of Enterprise: A Social History of Industrial America*, New York: Macmillan.

Coraiola, D. M., Foster, W. M. and Suddaby, R. (2015) "Varieties of history in organization studies," in P. Genoe McLaren, A. J. Mills and T. G. Weatherbee (eds), *The Routledge Companion to Management and Organizational History*, London: Routledge, pp. 206–221.

Curti, M. (1946) "Foreword," in Anon. (eds), *Theory and Practice in Historical Study*, New York: Social Sciences Research Council, pp. vii–ix.

Decker, S. (2015) "Mothership reconnection: Microhistory and institutional work compared," in P. Genoe McLaren, A. J. Mills and T. G. Weatherbee (eds), *The Routledge Companion to Management and Organizational History*, London: Routledge, pp. 222–237.

Decker, S. (2016) "Paradigms lost: Integrating history and organization studies," *Management & Organizational History*, 11(4): 364–379.

Delany, W. (1960) "Some field notes on the problem of access in organizational research," *Administrative Science Quarterly*, 5(4): 448–457.

Delany, W. (1963) "The development and decline of patrimonial and bureaucratic administrations," *Administrative Science Quarterly*, 7(4): 458–501.

Fombrun, C. J. (1989) "Convergent dynamics in the production of organizational configurations," *Journal of Management Studies*, 26(5): 439–458.

Frost, P. (1980) "Toward a radical framework for practicing organization science," *Academy of Management Review*, 5(4): 501–507.

Godelier, E. (2009) "History, a useful 'science' for management? From polemics to controversies," *Enterprise and Society*, 10(4): 791–807.

Godfrey, P. C., Hassard, J., O'Connor, E. S., Rowlinson, M. and Ruef, M. (2016) "Introduction to special topic forum: What is organizational history? Toward a creative synthesis of history and organization studies," *Academy of Management Review*, 41(4): 590–608.

Goldman, P. (1994) "Searching for history in organizational theory: Comment on Kieser," *Organization Science*, 5(4): 621–623.

Goodman, R. S. and Kruger, E. J. (1988) "Data dredging or legitimate research method: Historiography and its potential for management research," *Academy of Management Review*, 13(2): 315–325.

Gottschalk, L. (1963) *Generalization in the Writing of History*, Chicago, IL: The University of Chicago Press.

Green, A. and Troup, K. (eds) (2016) *The Houses of History: A Critical Reader in History and Theory*, 2nd edn, Manchester: Manchester University Press.

Hage, J. (1978) "Toward a synthesis of the dialectic between historical-specific and sociological-general models of the environment," in L. Karpik (ed), *Organization and Environment: Theory, Issues and Reality*, London: Sage, pp. 103–145.

Kantraw, A. M. (ed) (1986) "Why history matters to managers," *Harvard Business Review*, 64(1): 81–88.

Kieser, A. (1987) "From asceticism to administration of wealth: Medieval monasteries and the pitfalls of rationalization," *Organization Studies*, 8(2): 103–113.

Kieser, A. (1989) "Organizational, institutional, and societal evolution: Medieval craft guilds and the genesis of formal organizations," *Administrative Science Quarterly*, 34(4): 540–564.

Kieser, A. (1994) "Why organization theory needs historical analyses—And how this should be performed," *Organization Science*, 5(4): 608–620.

Kipping, M., Kurosawa, T. and Wadhwani, R. D. (2017) "A revisionist historiography of business history: A richer past for a richer future," in J. F. Wilson et al. (eds), *The Routledge Companion to Business History*, London: Routledge, pp. 19–35.

Kipping, M. and Üsdiken, B. (2008) "Business history and management studies," in G. Jones and J. Zeitlin (eds), *The Oxford Handbook of Business History*, Oxford: Oxford University Press, pp. 96–119.

Kipping, M. and Üsdiken, B. (2014) "History in organization and management theory: More than meets the eye," *Academy of Management Annals*, 8(1): 535–588.

Kipping, M. and Üsdiken, B. (2015) "Turning how and where? The potential for history in management and organizational studies," in P. Genoe McLaren, A. J. Mills and T. G. Weatherbee (eds), *The Routledge Companion to Management and Organizational History*, London: Routledge, pp. 372–379.

Kipping, M. and Westerhuis, G. (2012) "Strategy, ideology, and structure: The political processes of introducing the M-form in two Dutch banks," in S. J. Kahl, B. S. Silverman and M. A. Cusumano (eds), *History and Strategy* (Advances in Strategic Management, 29), Bingley, UK: Emerald, pp. 187–237.

Kobrak, C. (2009) "The use and abuse of history as a management tool: Comments on Eric Godelier's view of the French connection," *Enterprise and Society*, 10(4): 808–815.

Lawrence, B. S. (1984) "Historical perspective: Using the past to study the present," *Academy of Management Review*, 9(2): 307–312.

Leblebici, H. (2014) "History and organization theory: Potential for a transdisciplinary convergence," in M. Bucheli and R. D. Wadhwani (eds), *Organizations in Time: History, Theory, Methods*, Oxford: Oxford University Press, pp. 56–99.

Leblebici, H. and Shah, N. (2004) "The birth, transformation and regeneration of business incubators as new organisational forms: Understanding the interplay between organisational history and organisational theory," *Business History*, 46(3): 353–380.

Louzek, M. (2011) "The battle of methods in economics: The classical Methodenstreit—Menger vs. Schmoller," *American Journal of Economics and Sociology*, 70(2): 439–463.

Maclean, M., Harvey, C. and Clegg, S. (2016) "Conceptualizing historical organization studies," *Academy of Management Review*, 41(4): 609–632.

Maclean, M., Harvey, C. and Clegg, S. (2017) "Organization theory in business and management history: Present status and future prospects," *Business History Review*, 91(3): 457–481.

McNeil, K. (1978) "Understanding organizational power: Building on the Weberian legacy," *Administrative Science Quarterly*, 23(1): 65–90.

Meyer, M. W. and Brown, M. C. (1977) "The process of bureaucratization," *American Journal of Sociology*, 83(2): 364–385.

Mouzelis, N. P. (1967) *Organisation and Bureaucracy: An Analysis of Modern Theories*, Chicago, IL: Aldine Publishing.

O'Sullivan, M. and Graham, M. B. W. (2010) "Guest editors' introduction—Moving forward by looking backward: Business history and management studies," *Journal of Management Studies*, 47(5): 775–790.

Pettigrew, A. M. (1990) "Longitudinal field research on change: Theory and practice," *Organization Science*, 1(3): 267–292.

Popp, A. (2009) "History, a useful 'science' for management? A response," *Enterprise and Society*, 10(4): 831–836.

Ranson, S., Hinings, B. and Greenwood, R. (1980) "The structuring of organizational structures," *Administrative Science Quarterly*, 25(1): 1–17.

Richter, R. (1988) "Views and comments on Gustav Schmoller and the Method enstreit: Editorial preface," *Journal of Institutional and Theoretical Economics (JITE)/Zeitschrift für die gesamte Staatswissenschaft*, 144(3): 524–526.

Rowlinson, M. (1988) "The early application of scientific management by Cadbury," *Business History*, 30(4): 377–395.

Rowlinson, M. (1995) "Strategy, structure and culture: Cadbury, divisionalization and merger in the 1960s," *Journal of Management Studies*, 32(2): 121–140.

Rowlinson, M. (2004) "Historical perspectives in organization studies: Factual, narrative, and archeo-genealogical," in D. E. Hodgson and C. Carter (eds), *Management Knowledge and the New Employee*, Burlington, VT: Ashgate, pp. 8–20.

Rowlinson, M. and Carter, C. (2002) "Foucault and history in organization studies," *Organization*, 9(4): 527–547.

Rowlinson, M. and Delahaye, A. (2009) "The cultural turn in business history," *Entreprises et Histoire*, 55: 90–110.

Rowlinson, M. and Hassard, J. (1993) "The invention of corporate culture: A history of the histories of Cadbury," *Human Relations*, 46(3): 299–326.

Rowlinson, M. and Hassard, J. (2013) "Historical neo-institutionalism or neo-institutionalist history? Historical research in management and organization studies," *Management & Organizational History*, 8(2): 111–126.

Rowlinson, M. and Hassard, J. (2014) "History and the cultural turn in organization studies," in M. Bucheli and D. Wadhwani (eds), *Organizations in Time: History, Theory, Methods*, Oxford: Oxford University Press, pp. 147–165.

Rowlinson, M., Hassard, J. and Decker, S. (2014) "Research strategies for organizational history: A dialogue between historical theory and organization theory," *Academy of Management Review*, 39(3): 250–274.

Rowlinson, M., Jacques, R. S. and Booth, C. (2009) "Critical management and organizational history," in M. Alvesson, T. Bridgeman and H. Willmott (eds), *The Oxford Handbook of Critical Management Studies*, Oxford: Oxford University Press, pp. 286–303.

Rowlinson, M. and Procter, S. (1999) "Organization culture and business history," *Organization Studies*, 20(3): 369–396.

Stern, F. (ed) (1973) *The Varieties of History: From Voltaire to the Present*, 2nd edn, New York: Vintage.

Suddaby, R. (2016) "Toward a historical consciousness: Following the historic turn in management thought," *M@n@gement*, 19(1): 46–60.

Suddaby, R., Foster, W. M. and Mills, A. J. (2014) "Historical institutionalism," in M. Bucheli and D. Wadhwani (eds), *Organizations in Time: History, Theory, Methods*, Oxford: Oxford University Press, pp. 100–123.

Tiffany, P. (2009) "Does history matter in business?" *Enterprise and Society*, 10(4): 816–830.

Üsdiken, B. and Kieser, A. (2004) "Introduction: History in organization studies," *Business History*, 46(3): 321–330.

Üsdiken, B. and Kipping, M. (2014) "History and organization studies: A long-term view," in M. Bucheli and D. Wadhwani (eds), *Organizations in Time: History, Theory, Methods*, Oxford: Oxford University Press, pp. 33–55.

Vaara, E. and Lamberg, J.-A. (2016) "Taking historical embeddedness seriously: Three historical approaches to advance strategy process and practice research," *Academy of Management Review*, 41(4): 633–657.

Wadhwani, R. D. and Bucheli, M. (2014) "The future of the past in management and organization studies," in M. Bucheli and R. D. Wadhwani (eds), *Organizations in Time: History, Theory, Methods*, Oxford: Oxford University Press, pp. 3–30.

Weatherbee, T. G. (2012) "Caution! This historiography makes wide turns: Historic turns and breaks in management and organization studies," *Management & Organizational History*, 7(3): 203–218.

White, H. V. (1966) "The burden of history," *History and Theory*, 5(2): 111–134.

Whittington, R. and Mayer, M. (2000) *The European Corporation: Strategy, Structure, and Social Science*, Oxford: Oxford University Press.

Zald, M. N. (1990) "History, sociology, and theories of organization," in J. E. Jackson (ed), *Institutions in American Society: Essays in Market, Political and Social Organizations*, Ann Arbor, MI: University of Michigan, pp. 81–108.

Zald, M. N. (1991) "Sociology as a discipline: Quasi-science and quasi-humanities," *The American Sociologist*, 22(3): 165–187.

Zald, M. N. (1993) "Organization studies as a scientific and humanistic enterprise: Toward a reconceptualization of the foundations of the field," *Organization Science*, 4(4): 513–528.

Zald, M. N. (1996) "More fragmentation: Unfinished business in linking the social sciences and the humanities," *Administrative Science Quarterly*, 41(2): 251–261.

4 Evidence
Identifying History in Top Management Journals

Introduction

The growing calls for "more history" in management and organization studies were based on the implicit assumption that history—however defined—had a very negligible presence within the extant literature. While a cursory reading of that literature probably confirmed such an impression, a more systematic, quantitative examination would allow to obtain some indication of the degree to which history has actually found a place in management and organizational research and in what ways— as well as gaining some sense of whether or not these calls had any effect so far. Such an effort was made first by Rowlinson and Hassard (2013) and then by Leblebici (2014)—though both studies remained rather limited in terms of the periods covered, the journals surveyed and the articles included in the analysis.

The present chapter will report the results of a more recent and broader survey of changes in both the timing and the types of history that can be found in the empirical and conceptual literature on management and organizations. Like the previous studies, it will focus on journal articles, since, following the scientistic turn (Chapter 2, this volume), management and organization studies have increasingly been driven by publications in journals rather than books. Consequently, the number of journals has expanded over time—though, not unexpectedly, not all have been equally influential in the development of the discipline. A more stringent test of the extent to which history has featured in the management and organization studies literature therefore requires, as done by the surveys mentioned previously, to focus on what have come to be considered the leading journals—though with an extended temporal scope, a slightly larger number of journals and a somewhat broader definition of what to include in "history".

An important caveat should be noted up-front that was also recognized by the authors of the previous studies (Rowlinson and Hassard 2013; Leblebici 2014) and pointed out by others (e.g. Suddaby, Foster and Mills 2014; Maclean, Harvey and Clegg 2016): No such survey is likely to be exhaustive, namely because research incorporating history may not always be identifiable through database searches, not least because authors might not understand their work as such and therefore refrain from using the term history in the title or the abstract. Such a survey can still be useful, not only to obtain some indication of the degree to which history has found a place in management and organizational research but also to identify long-term trends—including a possible recent surge.

The chapter begins by providing a brief overview of the extant studies, as well as their limitations, followed by a discussion of how the journals and articles for the present survey were selected and why. The major part of the chapter first identifies two basic types of publications in management journals related to history: The first type of articles addresses the history of management as a practice and/or discipline; the second contributes to theorizing in studies of management and organizations. The latter will then be dissected further, distinguishing between those articles where history is a source of qualitative or quantitative data and those where it is a driver or moderator within the theoretical model itself. Building on these journal publications, the final part of the chapter develops a framework for delineating the different ways in which history has been linked with theory—the major concern in management and organization studies (see Chapters 1 and 2, this volume; see also, Maclean et al. 2016; and for a similar, more intuitively derived framework, Kipping and Üsdiken 2014). Publications in other formats, especially books, can then be inserted as additional exemplars into this framework—as will be the case in the subsequent chapters of this volume.

Needle in a Haystack? History in the Management and Organization Studies Literature

Previous Surveys and Their Limitations

As noted, so far there have only been two attempts to explore the extent to which history has featured in the management and organizational literature, and they only included a small number of journals and covered relatively brief periods of time. The first of these was done by Rowlinson and Hassard (2013) who examined three leading US-based journals, namely, the *Academy of Management Journal* (AMJ), *Administrative Science Quarterly* (ASQ) and *Organization Science* for the period 1991 to 2010. Confining their survey to empirical articles and excluding those that made only passing reference to history or were based on recent data, they located 55 studies that they considered "historical with some empirical content" (Rowlinson and Hassard 2013: 118). About two-thirds of these were quantitative, with around half of them involving event history analyses. Their analysis of these articles remained limited. They did not examine, for instance, whether there had been any changes in the frequency and types of historical studies over time.

Leblebici (2014) conducted a similar survey that covered the first decade of the 2000s. Included in this survey were both doctoral dissertations (100 altogether) and journals: again, AMJ, ASQ and *Organization Science*, as well as the European-based *Organization Studies* (OS). Based on a somewhat loosely specified criterion of "historical data, analyses or narrative", Leblebici (2014: 60) located a greater number of articles—102 altogether, 76 of which were in the three journals that Rowlinson and Hassard (2013) had examined—despite covering only half of the period. Importantly, Leblebici (2014: 90) observed an increase in journal articles during the period studied, particularly in ASQ and OS. He also identified an increasing trend in doctoral dissertations where "historical data or perspectives" were used (Leblebici 2014: 58). Notably, though, the doctorates he included were confined only to those completed in the US and a few Canadian business schools.

That dissimilar results have been reported in these two surveys probably has to do with divergent interpretations of what is to be considered "history" within management and organizational research. Moreover, while Leblebici (2014) did find an increase of both historical journal publications and dissertations, he only surveyed a brief period, which makes it difficult to ascertain long-term trends. The survey presented in this chapter aims to address both these limitations.

Objectives and Scope of the Present Survey

Building on the earlier studies, the present journal survey was guided by three main considerations. First, the search for history was to be in what can be considered the "mainstream" management literature represented by publications in "leading" outlets. Second, in line with the discussion in the introductory chapter on the domain of this book, the main focus was history within the context of management (including strategy) and organization studies (see also Leblebici 2014). Third, the survey needed to identify articles that had a significant historical dimension.

Given these considerations, the survey proceeded in three steps. The first step involved the selection of journals to be examined, which was driven by two main criteria. One of these had to do with confining the survey to journals that are widely deemed as the "top" ones in management and organization studies. The second related to including journals based not only in the US, which are typically treated as the most prominent, but also their major followers based in Europe (see Üsdiken 2014).

In operational terms the present *Financial Times* (FT) 50 list was used to determine the journals to be included in the survey. Using this list as the basis of journal selection satisfied both of the criteria mentioned earlier. For many, the FT list is seen as comprising journals with the highest status (see Üsdiken 2014). The list has become increasingly salient, particularly outside the US, as research published in these journals constitutes one of the dimensions used by the FT in ranking business schools. What started out as a selection of 38 journals a year after the FT began to publish its international rankings in 1999 became the FT40 in 2003 (Wedlin 2006: 89). This particular list included only US-based journals in management and organization studies (see Burgess and Shaw 2010: 632). Yet this changed when the list was revised and expanded once in 2010 (becoming FT45) and then again in 2016 (becoming FT50). Two journals in the aforementioned subject areas from outside the US were added in the 2010 revision and another one in 2016.

In all then, the FT50 list currently comprises nine academic journals in management (including strategy) and organization studies, six of which are US-based and three are located in Europe. These are, from the US, AMJ, *Academy of Management Review* (AMR), ASQ, *Journal of Management* (JoM), *Organization Science* and *Strategic Management Journal* (SMJ) and from Europe, *Human Relations*, *Journal of Management Studies* (JMS) and OS. It is these nine outlets that constituted the basis of the journal survey. Clearly, this is a selection based on present-day assessments of "quality", but as Üsdiken (2014) has discussed in some detail, all of these journals have been recognized as such, indeed historically, in various other lists and reviews. Admittedly, using these journals does incorporate a bias toward research that is published in the English language. Nevertheless, not only have these journals become somewhat more internationalized over time (Üsdiken 2014) but they also serve as apposite indicators of the extent to which history has been able to penetrate into the "mainstream", understood here as work that gets reported in these kinds of outlets.

Locating studies that could be in some way related to history involved a search for "histor*" in titles and abstracts, covering the entire lifetime of all nine journals until the end of 2017 (for the dates that each journal began publication, see Table 4.1). In cases where some of the older journals did not have any abstracts in their early years, only the titles were used. The search was based on full articles and research notes only (hereafter articles). Book reviews, editorials, special issue introductions and invited papers—such as the "*Vita Contemplativa*" and "Peripheral Vision" sections in OS and the "Crossroads" section in *Organization Science*—were excluded. So were comments, rejoinders and exchanges, as in the "Dialogue" section in AMR. Applying these rules, a total of 626 articles were identified that had the term "histor*" in their titles and/or abstracts.

The second step involved screening out articles that were not dealing with management, strategy or organizations. Specifically, the following

Table 4.1 Articles on management history and history of management and organization studies (MOS) in select management, strategy and organization journals[a]

	1961–1980		1981–2000		2001–2017		Totals	
	Management History	*History of MOS*	*Management History*	*History of MOS*	*Management History*	*History of MOS*	*Management History*	*History of MOS*
Academy of Management Journal (1958)	6	1					6	1
Academy of Management Review (1976)		2	2	5			2	7
Administrative Science Quarterly (1956)		1	1	1			1	2
Human Relations (1947)		1	1	5	4	9	5	14
Journal of Management (1975)		1	3	5	1	8	4	14
Journal of Management Studies (1964)		1		4	1	2	1	7
Organization Science (1990)				6		5	1	11
Organization Studies (1980)			1	3	5	9	5	12
Strategic Management Journal (1980)				2		1		3
Totals	6	6	8	31	11	34	25	71

a Years when journals began publication are shown in parentheses.

kinds of articles were removed from the set of 626 that were obtained with the initial search:

1. Articles that were at individual or group levels of analyses, where the reference would typically be to career, work, occupational or group histories.
2. Articles that were outside the domain of this volume, namely, industrial relations, psychology, social psychology or other business specialisms such as marketing, accounting, production management or information technology.

Eliminating these articles reduced the set to 508, now comprising only those related to management, strategy and organizations.

In the final step, the aim was to distinguish those articles that genuinely had a historical dimension. To this end, the following three kinds of articles were eliminated from the previous set:

1. Articles in which the only reference to history in the title and/or the abstract was to event history as the method used in the analyses.
2. Articles in which terms like history or historical were mentioned only *en passant* or in a cursory fashion—ensured by perusing the entire text when there was doubt from the title and/or the abstract that this could be the case.
3. Articles where variables or data pertained to a very brief recent history or process, expressed for instance in days, weeks, months or quarters.

As a result of this final screening, articles that were thought to have a significant historical dimension were reduced to a total of 287.

And Then There Were Two . . . Types of Studies With a Historical Dimension

The 287 articles that the survey eventually yielded as involving history in some significant manner could be classified into two broad categories. First, 96 articles were categorized as focusing on the *history of management* or *the history of management thought,* with a considerable portion of the latter actually being on the history of the academic literature on a management topic, concept, theory, model or method. Their overall number increased over time, which probably has to do with the development of management and organization studies as an academic discipline and, possibly even more so, with the monopolization of management writing by academics after the late 1960s and early 1970s (see Chapter 6, this volume).

Table 4.1 presents the distribution of the 96 articles on the history of management and management thought over time and across the nine journals. As the table shows, in the 1960s and the 1970s articles on management history were at par with those that dealt with the history of management and organization studies as an academic discipline. Notably, all of the management history articles in this period appeared in the US-based AMJ, while those on the history of the discipline were spread across a broader range of journals. The table also shows that after 1980 AMJ became practically closed to history articles of both kinds, as did other established US-based journals, namely, AMR and ASQ, after 2000 (see also Chapter 6, this volume).

What became the predominant pattern of focusing on the history of the discipline rather than management history per se is also apparent in Table 4.1. Since the early 1980s, this type of article outnumbered the ones on management history on the order of three to one. The meager appearance of studies on management history in leading journals is also indicated by the publication of only 19 articles over a period of almost four decades since 1980, amounting on average to about one paper every two years. Table 4.1 also points to a marginal increase in the number of management history articles in the post-2000 period. This finding appears to capture, as will be discussed in some detail in Chapter 7 of this volume, the emergence of approaches that have taken a critical position vis-à-vis the "classic" or "orthodox" view of management history (see, for the latter, Chapters 5 and 6, this volume). Notably, all but one of these articles have been published in non-US-based journals, namely, OS, *Human Relations* and JMS, as have the majority of the papers on the history of management and organization studies. The critical orientation in both of these two types of history appears to have been inspired by the increasing calls for greater engagement with history discussed in the preceding chapter of this volume.

The remaining 191 articles were classified as using history in one form or another in conjunction with *theorizing on management and organizational phenomena*. The articles constituting this category were distinct from those on the history of management and management thought in one or both of two ways: Either history featured in these articles as a source of data or evidence to test or develop theory; or history (or the past) itself was made an integral part of theoretical models covering organization- or field-level phenomena. Notably, the number of all these articles that linked history and theory is almost double those on the history of management and management thought, indicating a greater interest than is usually assumed in relating history to theorizing in management and organization studies.

The distribution over time and across journals of the articles that in some way linked history and theory is presented in Table 4.2. One result that stands out in this table is the increase in such articles over time for the entire journal set. The upward trend is particularly apparent during

Table 4.2 Articles linking history and theory in select management, strategy and organization journals[a]

	1951–1960	1961–1970	1971–1980	1981–1990	1991–2000	2001–2010	2011–2017	Total
Academy of Management Journal (1958)				3	2	9	11	25
Academy of Management Review (1976)				3	6	1	5	15
Administrative Science Quarterly (1956)	2	3	5	10	6	2	7	35
Human Relations (1947)					3	5	2	10
Journal of Management (1975)				1			1	2
Journal of Management Studies (1964)				1	9	10		20
Organization Science (1990)					5	10	9	24
Organization Studies (1980)				2	5	9	15	31
Strategic Management Journal (1980)				1	13	4	11	29
Totals	2	3	5	21	49	50	61	191

a Years when journals began publication are shown in parentheses.

the 2010s, despite the figures reported being for seven years rather than a full decade, as in the preceding periods. Also notable, though, is the considerable presence of historically oriented articles in the 1980s and the 1990s when scientization in management and organizational research was becoming solidified and when calls for greater engagement with history had only begun to emerge.

The same table also shows that there have been differences across journals. Frequencies are to some degree affected by special issues or forums, as in the case of JMS (O'Sullivan and Graham 2010) and AMR (Godfrey et al. 2016), though the publication of special issues is in itself an indication, as mentioned in Chapter 1 of this volume, of an expanding interest. In any case, there also appear to be some broad patterns. Until 1980 ASQ was the only journal among the ones that existed at the time in which articles based on a link between history and theory appeared. And during the 1980s ASQ remained the outlet, which published most of the history and theory papers (see also Ventresca and Mohr 2002). However, a number of newcomer journals appear to have shifted the panorama after 1990. It was two of the newer organization studies journals, one based in Europe (OS) and the other in the US (*Organization Science*), and a US-based strategy journal (SMJ) that have published the most history and theory articles in the last three decades. These journals are followed by two general management outlets, one from the US (AMJ) and the other from the UK (JMS), and then ASQ. The theory journal AMR and two others (*Human Relations* and JoM) have published the least number of history-related articles, the latter two probably due to a greater focus on individual and group behavior in organizations.

As already mentioned, articles categorized as linking history and theory varied in whether history was used mainly as a source of data or was made a part of theories on management and organizations. There was also variation within each of these two ways of relating to history. Methods of analysis varied in empirical studies, as did the nature of data that were used or generated from history. And when integrating history into theory, it could feature as a major driver in the theoretical model or as a moderator of relationships between its main constructs. The next section will discuss each of these two potential uses of history and their specific manifestations (namely in terms of methodology) in more detail.

Two Souls: History and Theory in Management and Organizational Research

Backing It All Up: History as Evidence and a Source of Data

From the perspective of social sciences at large, as well as management and organization studies, historical research has typically been regarded as a qualitative methodology (e.g. Swanson and Holton 2005; Suddaby and Greenwood 2009; Berg and Lune 2014; Bansal, Smith and Vaara 2018). Yet as mentioned in Chapter 3, Rowlinson, Hassard and Decker (2014), for example, have considered quantitatively based "serial history" a historical research strategy like corporate, analytically structured and ethnographic histories (see also Jacques 2006; Maclean et al. 2016). Somewhat differently, Ventresca and Mohr (2002: 805) identified historical research as one of the approaches among "archival research methods", which they defined broadly as involving the study of "documents and textual materials produced by and about organizations". These archival methods also included what the authors referred to as "ecological approaches" and "new archivalism". In the case of the former, evidence on the histories of individual organizations was used to create and quantitatively analyze large longitudinal data sets (see also Chapter 9, this volume). In contrast, what they labeled new archivalism treated historical or contemporaneous documents and texts themselves as data, which were then analyzed by formal methods such as content analysis, while retaining the interpretive possibilities of historical or qualitative research.

History did serve as a basis for developing both qualitative and quantitative data in the studies identified through the journal survey. This subsection will show that each of these types of data had their variants due to the specific nature of the data that was obtained and how they were subjected to analysis.

Its Natural Place? Historical Data in Qualitative Research

The journal survey suggests that the use of history in qualitative research has been increasing over time. The steady growth in articles which have engaged with the history of organizations or historical sources qualitatively appears to be a reflection of the increasing legitimacy that qualitative research has been garnering in management and organization studies at large (Üsdiken 2014). The turn to qualitative research more broadly started out in the 1980s and the 1990s, mainly in the UK, as a challenge to the dominance of US-led hypothetico-deductive research (Üsdiken 2010; see also Chapter 2, this volume). It was even viewed as a form of "resistance" to the latter kind of work that was conceived at the time as representing the "mainstream" (Symon et al. 2008). Times have changed, and qualitative research has found greater reception, albeit more so among European-based researchers and journals. Nevertheless, lately some penetration into US-based journals has also been taking place (see e.g. Bansal et al. 2018). Indeed, the increase in history-based qualitative work seems to be a part of, and benefited from, the expansion of qualitative research more broadly.

Articles in which history featured as a source of qualitative data were in the main case studies—though there was also a small group of work in which historical material or histories of particular organizations were used as case vignettes. A few of the studies were conceptual pieces, which did, however, use historical books or the authors' prior historical work for illustrative purposes (e.g. Yates and Orlikowski 1992; King 1995). Case studies would typically be on a single or a small number of organizations—though there were also instances when they were on an entire market, industry or organizational field (e.g. McKendrick and Carroll 2001). All of these studies were characterized not by resorting to history as a "qualitative" method per se (as pointed out earlier), but rather by using history as a source of "data" in conducting qualitative research. They would therefore often be referred to as a "case history" or a "historical case study". What distinguished them as a historically oriented qualitative mode of inquiry was the longitudinal nature of the data and the analyses, occasionally covering long time spans (e.g. Mintzberg and Waters 1982) or, less frequently, drawing upon data that came from some time in the distant past (e.g. Pajunen 2006; Murmann 2013; Kim, Croidieu and Lippmann 2016).

Historical case studies would follow the conventions of case research prevalent at the time they were conducted. Names of organizations would often be disguised, though there were instances where the identity of the organization was disclosed (e.g. Côté, Langley and Pasquero 1999). Documents of various kinds, some produced by the organizations themselves, were often a major source of data, although the latter might not necessarily be referred to as archives. Other forms of qualitative data collection would frequently be involved, such as retrospective or contemporaneous interviews, questionnaires, participant observation or site visits. Indeed, in some instances historical data could be used as a supplement to what was essentially an ethnographic study (e.g. Labatut, Aggeri and Girard 2012). Also, this latter study is one of the only two cases among all articles—both, not unexpectedly, published in a European journal, which were described as genealogical (see also Knights and Morgan 1995), posited as one of the forms for writing counter-histories (see Chapter 7, this volume).

Notably though, historical case studies also appear to have followed the pattern in which qualitative research at large has developed in management and organization studies and have therefore undergone change over the course of time. The early articles from the 1960s and the 1970s were case histories presented in narrative form, which was guided by theoretical concepts and ideas (see e.g. Warriner 1961; Stern 1979). Although there was mention of "data" or even "historical data", little information was provided on how they were obtained, and references to sources were made in a limited and somewhat cursory manner. A separate methods section did begin to appear in the 1980s (e.g. Mintzberg and Waters 1982) and became largely established by the end of the 1990s. While the typically narrative account developed from the authors' interpretations was maintained, some more information was being provided on how the data were analyzed. And by the late 1990s, more systematic procedures of analysis started to appear, developing toward the use of increasingly established procedures in qualitative research, such as thematic coding, in order to achieve greater rigor (see e.g. Gioia, Corley and Hamilton 2013; Kim et al. 2016).

This was to be accompanied by case studies that represented what Ventresca and Mohr (2002) had identified as the new archival approach. These would be studies that relied predominantly, if not entirely, on documentary material and used, at least in part, some method of formal analysis. The source of data could be organizational archives (e.g. Pajunen 2006) or various kinds of texts such as association proceedings, journals and books (e.g. Kahl, King and Liegel 2016). The types of methods employed included network analysis (e.g. Pajunen 2006), content analysis (Kahl et al. 2016) or cognitive mapping (Bingham and Kahl 2013). A particularly notable example among these is Murmann's (2013) study, where parallels are drawn between comparative-historical and comparative case study methods and an attempt made, as the author puts it, to combine "the traditional methods of historians with social science methods" (Murmann 2013: 62).

While it was mainly these kinds of case studies that were preponderant and expanded in the ways described earlier, the narrative form of historical analysis—confusingly at times also referred to by their authors as "cases" or "case studies"—persisted, though to a lesser and diminishing degree. What distinguished this type of research from the case studies described previously, however, was that historical material was not viewed as data to be analyzed by procedures of qualitative research, but rather as the basis for constructing narrative histories, "a sequence of logically and chronologically related events organized by a coherent plot" (Rowlinson et al. 2014: 254). Overall, these were studies that represented what Rowlinson et al. (2014: 251) have dubbed "analytically structured history" in which "conceptually defined structures and events are narrated"—pointing to Chandler's (1962) book as a prime example.

Some additional features separated these narrative histories from historical case studies. First, narratives were based invariably on "archival" sources in the broad sense that the term is used in management and organizational research (see Ventresca and Mohr 2002) with very rare and limited recourse to other forms of data collection, such as interviews. Not all of them relied on primary sources or archives, however. Indeed, few did (e.g. Rowlinson 1995; Mutch 2007), while the majority were, much like the quantitative work described later, based on various kinds of publicly available secondary sources, such as company reports, articles in newspapers and trade periodicals, government documents and biographies. Second, with respect to the level of analysis, these narrative histories tended to cover fields or industries relatively more than the historical case studies discussed earlier (e.g. Leblebici et al. 1991; Bryman 1997 and various articles in the O'Sullivan and Graham 2010 special issue in JMS). But when the narrative did concern a single organization or a small number of organizations, their identity would invariably be revealed. Third, these articles often followed established conventions of historical writing. A greater proportion, for example, did not have a separate methods section. Information about sources would be provided either briefly in the text or listed in an appendix. And when there was a specified part, it would either describe historical methods or use terms like "research design" rather than "methods"—with the latter being a rare occurrence (e.g. Farjoun 2002). Finally, although there were instances that were based on shorter and more recent histories, the more pronounced tendency was to draw upon historical material from well in the past, in one case, for example, going all the way back to the Roman Republic (Carmeli and Markman 2011).

On a final note, the low level of narrative histories and the parallel marked growth of historical studies that are framed as qualitative research may indicate a convergence of the former with the latter, possibly due to the increasing popularity of qualitative work and to expectations on the part of management journals and their editors and reviewers. An example is Farjoun's (2002) article, which is described, as mentioned earlier, as a "qualitative historical analysis" and includes a separate methods section.

Feeding the Beast? Historical Data in Quantitative Research

Studies in which quantitative data pertaining to history were employed would rely almost entirely on publicly available secondary sources, such as directories, catalogs, censuses, trade journals, legislative documents or historical books, though there were rare cases where unpublished material or archives were used (e.g. Ingram and Inman 1996; Tripsas 1997). The trademark of all these studies was quantitative analysis on large samples of organizations, which could be either of the exploratory or hypothesis-testing kind.

There was some variation among research based on quantification of historical data with respect to the time span covered by the data and the analysis, as well as the extent to which history was used to frame the study. In one type of studies, quantitative data would be generated for a large sample of companies based on individual company histories constructed from secondary sources. This data set would then be employed in a cross-sectional analysis without any reference to the historical context (e.g. Miller and Friesen 1980). In a second type, a historical background would be provided on the issue that was being addressed, but would again be followed by a cross-sectional analysis with recent data (e.g. Glynn and Abzug 2002). There was also a third type, which included studies that were in effect examples of what Ventresca and Mohr (2002) identified as the ecological approach to archival research (see also Chapter 9, this volume). In these studies, data would be compiled for entire populations of organizations or a particular industry for a long time span often extending to the present (e.g. Carroll and Delacroix 1982) or for a somewhat shorter period well in the past (e.g. Kuilman and Li 2009).

There were two versions, however, of this particular type of quantitative study. What differed between the two versions was the way in which history was incorporated. In one version, historical information was provided only to supplement the longitudinal quantitative analysis, which typically included the entire period for which data had been compiled. In the other version, the study would be framed by a historical analysis, which in some instances would even serve as the basis for hypothesis development (e.g. Ingram and Inman 1996). The latter type of studies too would often rely on data and analysis that pertained to the entire period covered by the historical account (e.g. Ingram and Inman 1996; Lounsbury 2002), though there were also cases where the quantitative analysis, though still longitudinal, would be limited to a recent part of the history (e.g. Sherer and Lee 2002).

In the Driving Seat: History as Part of Theoretical Models

As already mentioned, in addition to research where history served as a source of qualitative or quantitative data, there were articles that made history, or the "past", a part of their theoretical framework(s) (see also Chapters 10 and 11, this volume). These articles were united in assigning history (or the past) the role of a driver or a moderator in shaping management and organizational phenomena. Indeed, in this journal survey, there were almost as many articles of this kind as there were of the kind where history was used as a source of data. Articles within this group were also heterogeneous in various ways, such as the nature of the study and the types of data and methods of analysis used in empirical studies.

Quantitative studies far outnumbered the qualitative ones among this group of articles. Indeed, there were very few qualitative studies, mostly appearing within the last couple of decades, an interesting recent example being a study by Gao et al. (2017), which, based on oral histories of long-lived firms, developed a historically grounded concept ("reputation") as the main driver of survival and performance in emerging economies. Like in this case, most of the qualitative studies were at the organizational level, whereas the quantitative studies, despite a preponderance of organizational level research, more often extended to more macro levels, such as populations and communities (e.g. Marquis, Davis and Glynn 2013; see also Chapters 10 and 11, this volume).

While more limited in number, there were some studies which combined the identification and narrative presentation of different historical time periods with quantitative analyses. The typical format of these articles would involve providing a description for the time periods in question, followed by some form of quantitative analysis (e.g. Thornton 2002). These descriptions would generally be in the form of a narrative developed from secondary sources and possibly interviews. Likewise, the data employed in the quantitative analyses would be derived from a variety of secondary sources. Occasionally, there were articles where the conditions and the outcomes for each period were also presented in narrative form (e.g. Jones 2001). Rare were studies that would be based at least in part on organizational archives (e.g. Mutch 2016).

And, not surprisingly, there were a considerable number of conceptual or theory papers. A substantial portion of these articles were concerned with the question of integrating history with theorizing on management and organizations, almost all of which have been discussed in Chapter 3 of this volume. Among others, some would include illustrative historical vignettes or some historical analysis based on prior published histories (e.g. Calori et al. 1997). There was also some variation with respect to the level at which the effects of history were conceptualized. Some would attribute a deterministic role to history at the macro level, arguing, for example, that organizations as we know them today have been historically constructed (e.g. Clegg 1981). Others would postulate the effects of history at societal levels to account for present-day variations across countries in organizational forms and administrative practices (e.g. Whitley 1991; Calori et al. 1997). Still others would focus on how historical experiences may play out at the regional level (e.g. Lippmann and Aldrich 2016). And a final group of articles would posit how organizational histories may be conditioning later actions (e.g. Schrempf-Stirling, Palazzo and Phillips 2016).

Putting It All Together: A Framework for Combining History and Theory

The review of the results of the journal survey in the foregoing sections leads back to the question of the relationship between history, broadly understood, and theorizing on management and organizations. This issue was raised earlier in Chapter 3 (this volume), and two main approaches were identified, labeled, respectively, by their proponents as "historical organization studies" (Maclean et al. 2016) and "organizational history" (Rowlinson et al. 2014). As discussed in some depth in Chapter 3, although distinct in their proposals, these two approaches are at one in looking for a "synthesis" between history and organization and management theory.

The framework developed here takes a broader perspective in the sense that it does not involve a search for synthesis, but rather seeks to identify the different research programs and currents in which history has been used or has found a place in theory and theorizing. It is based on earlier work (Kipping and Üsdiken 2014) but has been revised by drawing upon the journal survey as well as a broader literature that includes articles that have not been detected by the survey, such as research published in other disciplines like sociology, as well as other outlets such as books and book chapters.

Given the preeminence of theory in management and organization studies, the first of the two dimensions on which the framework is based concerns the nature of the relationship between history and theory, with the latter viewed here in the social science sense of a coherent scheme for understanding or explaining social phenomena. This dimension distinguishes between two broad forms that the relationship between history and theory can take:

1. History may serve as a source of data or evidence to test, modify or develop theory. This is referred to as "history *to* theory". In terms of the classification developed based on the journal survey, the category that includes studies where history has been used as a source of data and evidence exemplifies this approach.
2. History (or the past) may itself be an integral part of a theoretical model, as a driver (or moderator) of the relationships among or influences upon organizational fields or populations, as well as the characteristics, actions and outcomes of individual organizations. This is referred to as "history *in* theory". In this case, it is the group of studies identified through the journal survey as incorporating history as a driver or moderator of management and organizational phenomena that exemplifies this approach.

The second dimension relates to the methodological orientation in empirical studies within research programs that involve linking history with theory and distinguishes between qualitative and quantitative approaches as follows:

1. As mentioned, from a social science perspective, historical research has been viewed as a qualitative methodology. Indeed, as the preceding review of journal publications has shown, there have been a number of empirical studies that have developed historical narratives, though based more on secondary rather than primary archival sources. There have also been historical case studies, typically adhering, however, to the conventions of case study research on management and organizations. As qualitative research gained greater legitimacy and expanded, historical material began to be increasingly used as a source of data for qualitative studies, also following the more recent tendencies within the latter toward more formal methods of analysis.

2. As the journal survey has also shown, links to history have not been confined to qualitatively oriented research. Indeed, historical sources of various kinds, often publicly available, have been frequently used to construct large-scale organizational data sets for quantitative analysis. This quantitative orientation has been paramount so far, particularly in empirical research that has drawn upon theoretical formulations where historical constructs have been a main ingredient.

Juxtaposing these two dimensions yields the two-by-two matrix presented in Figure 4.1. Chapters in Part III of the book will be elaborating on and extending this framework. The detailing of the framework in these chapters will be structured not on the basis of specific studies, but rather around broad theoretical perspectives or research programs. Individual articles will be used, though, to demonstrate how in actual terms history has been employed either for the purposes of developing, refining and testing theory or as an integral part of theoretical models.

History-Theory Relationship

		History *to* Theory	History *in* Theory
Methodology	Qualitative	Traditional historical studies or History as a source of qualitative evidence and data	Analytically structured history
	Quantitative	History as a source of quantitative evidence and data	History as a driver or moderator

Figure 4.1 Combining history, theory, and methodology: A framework

But before turning to the detailed overview of the various research programs, Part II of the book will summarize the other body of literature, which covered about one-third of the articles identified in the present survey—a literature where history is not part of theorizing on management and organizations, but where the latter is itself the object of historical research. And it will do so by drawing on a much broader set of publications concerned with the history of management and management thought.

References

Bansal, P., Smith, W. K. and Vaara, E. (2018) "From the editors: New ways of seeing through qualitative research," *Academy of Management Journal*, 61(4): 1189–1195.

Berg, B. L. and Lune, H. (2014) *Qualitative Research Methods for the Social Sciences*, 8th edn, Harlow: Pearson Education.

Bingham, C. B. and Kahl, S. J. (2013) "The process of schema emergence: Assimilation, deconstruction, unitization and the plurality of analogies," *Academy of Management Journal*, 56(1): 14–34.

Bryman, A. (1997) "Animating the pioneer versus late entrant debate: An historical case study," *Journal of Management Studies*, 34(3): 415–438.

Burgess, T. F. and Shaw, N. E. (2010) "Editorial board membership of management and business journals: A social network analysis study of the Financial Times 40," *British Journal of Management*, 21(3): 627–648.

Calori, R., Lubatkin, M., Very, P. and Veiga, J. (1997) "Modelling the origins of nationally-bound administrative heritages: A historical institutional analysis of French and British firms," *Organization Science*, 8(6): 681–696.

Carmeli, A. and Markman, G. D. (2011) "Capture, governance, and resilience: Strategy implications from the history of Rome," *Strategic Management Journal*, 32(3): 322–341.

Carroll, G. R. and Delacroix, J. (1982) "Organizational mortality in the newspaper industries of Argentina and Ireland: An ecological approach," *Administrative Science Quarterly*, 27(1): 169–198.

Chandler, A. D. Jr. (1962) *Strategy and Structure: Chapters in the History of the Industrial Enterprise*, Cambridge, MA: MIT Press.

Clegg, S. (1981) "Organization and control," *Administrative Science Quarterly*, 26(4): 545–562.

Côté, L., Langley, A. and Pasquero, J. (1999) "Acquisition strategy and dominant logic in an engineering firm," *Journal of Management Studies*, 36(7): 919–952.

Farjoun, M. (2002) "The dialectics of institutional development in emerging and turbulent fields: The history of pricing conventions in the on-line database industry," *Academy of Management Journal*, 45(5): 848–874.

Gao, C., Zuzul, T., Jones, G. and Khanna, T. (2017) "Overcoming institutional voids: A reputation-based view of long-run survival," *Strategic Management Journal*, 38(11): 2147–2167.

Gioia, D. A., Corley, K. G. and Hamilton, A. L. (2013) "Seeking qualitative rigor in inductive research: Notes on the Gioia methodology," *Organizational Research Methods*, 16(1): 15–31.

Glynn, M. A. and Abzug, R. (2002) "Institutionalizing identity: Symbolic isomorphism and organizational names," *Academy of Management Journal*, 45(1): 267–280.

Godfrey, P. C., Hassard, J., O'Connor, E. S., Rowlinson, M. and Ruef, M. (2016) "Introduction to special topic forum: What is organizational history? Toward a creative synthesis of history and organization studies," *Academy of Management Review*, 41(4): 590–608.

Ingram, P. and Inman, C. (1996) "Institutions, intergroup competition and the evolution of hotel populations around Niagara Falls," *Administrative Science Quarterly*, 41(4): 629–658.

Jacques, R. S. (2006) "History, historiography and organization studies: The challenge and the potential," *Management & Organizational History*, 1(1): 31–49.

Jones, C. (2001) "Co-evolution of entrepreneurial careers, institutional rules and competitive dynamics in American film, 1895–1920," *Organization Studies*, 22(6): 911–944.

Kahl, S. J., King, B. G. and Liegel, G. (2016) "Occupational survival through field-level task integration: Systems men, production planners, and the computer, 1940s–1990s," *Organization Science*, 27(5): 1084–1107.

Kim, P., Croidieu, G. and Lippmann, S. (2016) "Responding from that vantage point: Field position and discursive strategies of legitimation in the U.S. wireless telegraphy field," *Organization Studies*, 37(10): 1417–1450.

King, A. (1995) "Avoiding ecological surprise: Lessons from long-standing communities," *Academy of Management Review*, 20(4): 961–985.

Kipping, M. and Üsdiken, B. (2014) "History in organization and management theory: More than meets the eye," *Academy of Management Annals*, 8(1): 535–588.

Knights, D. and Morgan, G. (1995) "Strategy under the microscope: Strategic management and IT in financial services," *Journal of Management Studies*, 32(2): 191–214.

Kuilman, J. G. and Li, J. (2009) "Grades of membership and legitimacy spillovers: Foreign banks in Shanghai, 1847–1935," *Academy of Management Journal*, 52(2): 229–245.

Labatut, J., Aggeri, F. and Girard, N. (2012) "Discipline and change: How technologies and organizational routines interact in new practice creation," *Organization Studies*, 33(1): 39–69.

Leblebici, H. (2014) "History and organization theory: Potential for a transdisciplinary convergence," in M. Bucheli and R. D. Wadhwani (eds), *Organizations in Time: History, Theory, Methods*, Oxford: Oxford University Press, pp. 56–99.

Leblebici, H., Salancik, G. R., Copay, A. and King, T. (1991) "Institutional change and the transformation of interorganizational history of the U.S. radio broadcasting industry," *Administrative Science Quarterly*, 36(3): 333–363.

Lippmann, S. and Aldrich, H. (2016) "A rolling stone gathers momentum: Generational units, collective memory, and entrepreneurship," *Academy of Management Review*, 41(4): 658–675.

Lounsbury, M. (2002) "Institutional transformation and status mobility: The professionalization of the field of finance," *Academy of Management Journal*, 45(1): 255–266.

Maclean, M., Harvey, C. and Clegg, S. (2016) "Conceptualizing historical organization studies," *Academy of Management Review*, 41(4): 609–632.

Marquis, C., Davis, G. F. and Glynn, M. A. (2013) "Golfing alone? Corporations, elites and nonprofit growth in 100 American communities," *Organization Science*, 24(1): 39–57.

McKendrick, D. G. and Carroll, G. R. (2001) "On the genesis of organizational forms: Evidence from the market for disk arrays," *Organization Science*, 12(6): 661–682.

Miller, D. and Friesen, P. (1980) "Archetypes of organizational transition," *Administrative Science Quarterly*, 25(2): 268–299.

Mintzberg, H. and Waters, J. A. (1982) "Tracking strategy in an entrepreneurial firm," *Academy of Management Journal*, 25(3): 465–499.

Murmann, J. P. (2013) "The coevolution of industries and important features of their environments," *Organization Science*, 24(1): 58–78.

Mutch, A. (2007) "Reflexivity and the institutional entrepreneur: A historical exploration," *Organization Studies*, 28(7): 1123–1140.

Mutch, A. (2016) "Bringing history into the study of routines: Contextualizing performance," *Organization Studies*, 37(8): 1171–1188.

O'Sullivan, M. and Graham, M. B. W. (2010) "Guest editors' introduction—Moving forward by looking backward: Business history and management studies," *Journal of Management Studies*, 47(5): 775–790.

Pajunen, K. (2006) "Stakeholder influences in organizational survival," *Journal of Management Studies*, 43(6): 1261–1288.

Rowlinson, M. (1995) "Strategy, structure and culture: Cadbury, divisionalization and merger in the 1960s," *Journal of Management Studies*, 32(2): 121–140.

Rowlinson, M. and Hassard, J. (2013) "Historical neo-institutionalism or neo-institutionalist history? Historical research in management and organization studies," *Management & Organizational History*, 8(2): 111–126.

Rowlinson, M., Hassard, J. and Decker, S. (2014) "Research strategies for organizational history: A dialogue between historical theory and organization theory," *Academy of Management Review*, 39(3): 250–274.

Schrempf-Stirling, J., Palazzo, G. and Phillips, R. A. (2016) "Historic corporate social responsibility," *Academy of Management Review*, 41(4): 700–719.

Sherer, P. D. and Lee, K. (2002) "Institutional change in large law firms: A resource dependency and institutional perspective," *Academy of Management Journal*, 45(1): 102–119.

Stern, R. N. (1979) "The development of an interorganizational control network: The case of intercollegiate athletics," *Administrative Science Quarterly*, 24(2): 242–266.

Suddaby, R., Foster, W. M. and Mills, A. J. (2014) "Historical institutionalism," in M. Bucheli and D. Wadhwani (eds), *Organizations in Time: History, Theory, Methods*, Oxford: Oxford University Press, pp. 100–123.

Suddaby, R. and Greenwood, R. (2009) "Methodological issues in researching institutional change," in D. A. Buchanan and A. Bryman (eds), *The Sage Handbook of Organizational Research Methods*, London: Sage, pp. 176–195.

Swanson, R. A. and Holton, E. F. III (eds) (2005) *Research in Organizations: Foundations and Methods of Inquiry*, San Francisco, CA: Berrett-Koehler.

Symon, G., Buehring, A., Johnson, P. and Cassell, C. (2008) "Positioning qualitative research as resistance to the institutionalization of the academic labour process," *Organization Studies*, 29(10): 1315–1336.

Thornton, P. H. (2002) "The rise of the corporation in a craft industry: Conflict and conformity in institutional logics," *Academy of Management Journal*, 45(1): 81–101.

Tripsas, M. (1997) "Unraveling the process of creative destruction: Complementary assets and incumbent survival in the typesetter industry," *Strategic Management Journal*, 18(Summer SI): 119–142.

Üsdiken, B. (2010) "Between contending perspectives and logics: Organizational studies in Europe," *Organization Studies*, 31(6): 715–735.

Üsdiken, B. (2014) "Centres and peripheries: Research styles and publication patterns in 'top' US journals and their European alternatives, 1960–2010," *Journal of Management Studies*, 51(5): 764–789.

Ventresca, M. J. and Mohr, J. W. (2002) "Archival research methods," in J. A. C. Baum (ed), *The Blackwell Companion to Organizations*, Oxford: Blackwell, pp. 805–828.

Warriner, C. K. (1961) "Public opinion and collective action: Formation of a watershed district," *Administrative Science Quarterly*, 6(3): 333–359.

Wedlin, L. (2006) *Ranking Business Schools: Forming Fields, Identities and Boundaries in International Management Education*, Cheltenham: Edward Elgar.

Whitley, R. D. (1991) "The social construction of business systems in East Asia," *Organization Studies*, 12(1): 1–28.

Yates, J. and Orlikowski, W. J. (1992) "Genres of organizational communication: A structurational approach to studying communication and media," *Academy of Management Review*, 17(2): 299–326.

Part II

5 Beginnings

Early Writings on Management History

Introduction

The practice of management, as understood today, is widely seen to have originated with the first and, more importantly, the second industrial revolutions in the late eighteenth and nineteenth centuries, respectively (see, e.g. Engwall, Kipping and Üsdiken 2016: Ch. 2)—which has not prevented some of those studying its history to search for and locate the "idea" of management in much earlier times, as will be discussed in this and the following chapter. A sustained effort to trace and structure the history of management practice and to write a "history of management thought", as it came to be called, had to wait until after World War II—when (a) management practice had become more mature and accepted, as compared to, say, personal ownership, and (b) the study of management itself, as well as those individuals and organizations providing it, more systematically strived—and increasingly succeeded—to be perceived as "scientific", akin to other academic disciplines (see Chapter 2, this volume).

However, reflections on the origins and history of management and management thought did start earlier, at the beginning of the twentieth century, contemporaneous with—and partially driven by—efforts to systematize management itself, usually subsumed under the label scientific management or Taylorism (see Engwall et al. 2016: Chs. 2 and 5). This chapter will first summarize these early reflections, conducted in particular by some of those teaching "commerce", as it used to be referred to at the time. While these writings did not find much resonance during the interwar period, their themes would reappear as management history came into its own. The chapter then looks at the more numerous efforts in the immediate post–World War II period, marked by a highly influential series of books by Lyndall B. Urwick and Edward Brech and a growing number of histories of management written predominantly by consultants and practicing managers, while academics only took on this subject at a more sustained level since the 1960s, as will be discussed in the subsequent chapter.

When It All Began: Early Histories of Management

The first management publications to deal explicitly with "history" were a series of articles and books written by Edward D. Jones, a professor of commerce and industry at the University of Michigan (Jones 1912, 1913, 1914). Jones had a utilitarian take on history, believing that principles and policies of administration could be distilled from history. However, as very little was available on the history of administration in business, one had to turn to other realms. Thus, his first article, published in three parts in *The Engineering Magazine* in 1912 (reprinted separately in combined form in 1913), was based on military history from which he elaborated on the lessons that could be drawn for business executives. Jones's history went as far back as the Roman army and Julius Caesar, interspersed with examples from figures like Frederic the Great and Napoleon, as well as, with great admiration, the German military force after the mid-nineteenth century. From military history, the business executive could learn, for example, the importance of initiative and discipline.

In a lengthier book published a year later, Jones (1914) added histories of science and diplomacy, which he thought could also serve as "models" for the "business administrator". The history of science would provide examples of how open-mindedness, thoroughness and cooperation were important, while that of diplomacy could demonstrate the virtues of manners, tactfulness, esthetics and ethics. In addition to explicit reference to the "utility of the study of history" in developing principles of administration, Jones's article and books are notable in at least one other respect. The first sentence of his initial article (Jones 1912: 1, and the reprint, 1913: 1) read: "The art of administration is as old as the human race". This opening statement foreshadowed what was to become a standard claim in much of the later literature to justify the study of the history of management (e.g. Wren 1972) or of organizations (e.g. Starbuck 2003).

A doctoral dissertation by Horace B. Drury (1915), an instructor at Ohio State University, took history more seriously in that it attempted to unearth the origins and provide an assessment of the scientific management movement, which was still emerging at the time. Drury's (1915) history began by reviewing some of the early initiatives reported at the meetings of the American Society of Mechanical Engineers (ASME), especially after the attention of its membership began to turn toward "management of works", as formulated initially by the society's vice-president and later president Henry R. Towne (1886: 429) in a paper that has since been considered a landmark in turning attention to management (see e.g. Merrill 1960: 58; Mee 1963: 22). While acknowledging these origins, Drury (1915: 32) was quick to add that ASME members' principal concern was with the "wages problem" and that scientific management was different from anything that had been done before (p. 53). He then noted that although Taylor's first presentation at ASME was in 1895, he had been carrying out his work since the early 1880s (p. 54) and therefore suggested that the "genesis" of scientific management needed to be considered in two stages, the first up to 1895 and the second from then on until 1903. The latter date marks Taylor's (1903) "Shop Management" paper presented at an ASME meeting, which for Drury was when scientific management had become "complete" (Drury 1915: 66).

Drury (1915: 17–18) also provided a firsthand account of how the term scientific management was coined—ironically without Taylor himself being present. It happened at a meeting in late 1910, convened by the then attorney, later US Supreme Court associate judge Louis D. Brandeis (Wren 1972: 182), who was preparing for the hearings before the US Interstate Commerce Commission to argue against the appeal of various railroads for higher freight rates. Though not consequential with respect to the decision of the commission, these hearings, Drury (1915: 20) argued, were a turning point for increased public awareness of scientific management—with Taylor also using the term in the title of the book that he published the following year (Taylor 1911). In addition, Drury (1915: 88–119) had a chapter on what he called "lives of the leaders", which foreshadowed the focus on the so-called pioneers in much of the later literature in the form of biographies or biographical compilations. For him, the leaders of scientific management included, in addition to the "great leader" Frederick W. Taylor (p. 16), Henry L. Gantt, Carl G. Barth, Horace K. Hathaway, Morris L. Cooke, Sanford E. Thompson, Frank B. Gilbreth and Harrington Emerson—names that have subsequently been made familiar through numerous books and articles.

Not many followed these initial efforts by Jones and Drury during the interwar years. Management textbooks did proliferate, though with no or only limited attention to the past, as their major preoccupation was with expounding scientific management and/or offering principles and methods for administration, management, organization or other business functions (see, e.g. George 1968: 188–195). Neither did past thought or practices feature in the initial university-based journals dedicated to business in the US, namely the *Harvard Business Review* and *The University Journal of Business*, both of which began publication in 1922 as mentioned earlier (see Chapter 2, this volume). The latter was renamed *The Journal of Business of the University of Chicago* in 1928 and then the *Journal of Business* in 1954. And, somewhat surprisingly maybe, the *Bulletin of the Business Historical Society*, which began publication in 1926 and was renamed *Business History Review* in 1954, did not pay much attention to the history of management either.

When a few of the textbooks did make a link to the past, it was usually in the form of the first couple of chapters or so being devoted to a history of industry in the US and to what had begun to be referred to as the "management movement" (e.g. Lansburgh 1923; Anderson 1928). Industrial history in these accounts went back to the American colonies or even to the Middle Ages. Thus, the readers were told that the early 1880s ushered in a new era in the US, characterized by faster technical progress, the expansion of markets, increase in competition as well as growth in enterprise size and, as highlighted by some, tensions between capital and labor. The central claim was that these new conditions—or the "second industrial revolution", as it came to be called (Alford 1928: 3)—made administration and management more significant, leading to the emergence of the management movement and the search for science, the beginnings of which were attributed singularly—and different from Drury (1915)—to Taylor. That scientific management was not uncontested was acknowledged, though together with the claim that its "value" had become apparent over time. Reflecting the time of writing, these books also contained conjectures on how World War I and the depression of the early 1920s in the US positively affected management in the sense of a growing appreciation for the human factor and a more cooperative attitude toward labor, despite a continuing anti-union stance.

A more detailed account can be found in a series of conferences that Harlow S. Person delivered during an "evening course for executives" organized by the US Bureau of Personnel Administration in 1924–1925 (see Metcalf and Urwick 1940: 26). Previously a faculty member and then the head of the Amos Tuck School at Dartmouth College and later recognized as having given "scientific management a new academic respectability" (George 1968: 105), Person (1926), like Drury (1915), saw the origins of the so-called management movement in the initiatives of the engineers that preceded Taylor. He also went beyond Drury (1915) by suggesting that developments occurred in three phases in the period from 1880 to 1910: The first two phases involved attention to wage and cost issues. After 1900 the focus turned toward "organization" and "system". For Person (1926: 206), too, however, the movement was revolutionized in 1911 and took a distinct route toward becoming more "scientific" with Taylor, who he referred to as a "genius". This should not be surprising given that he was one of the founders of the Taylor Society in 1912, later served as its president and, at the time of writing, was the managing director (Bruce and Nyland 2001; see further on the Taylor Society Chapter 7, this volume). Person thought that a proper understanding of scientific management required a distinction between "administration" and "management" (see also Person 1924). The former was the "highest function" providing "general direction", whereas management referred to "technical processing". So, he argued, "administration could not be scientific in the same sense that management can be" (Person 1926: 217), which can possibly be read as a move to salvage the attribution of science at least to management, given the at times hostile approach of business people. Finally, Person (1926: 191) also thought that "management" was "not something new". Yet unlike Jones (1912) and many later writers of management history, he was less presumptuous about its origins, as he believed that it "has existed from the beginning of enterprise".

The 1920s and the 1930s also saw the publication of a number of biographies focusing on those individuals who would later be called the pioneers. Best-known among them is probably the first of numerous biographies of Taylor by Copley (1923), who was the one to label him the "father of scientific management", an expression often used since then, though Lansburgh (1923: 25) had also referred to Taylor as the "father of modern scientific industrial management". There was also a biography of Henry L. Gantt written by Leon P. Alford (1934), who himself came to be considered a pioneer by later authors (Urwick 1956: 192–195; see also later). Gantt was one of Taylor's closest associates, though they did part ways at some stage (Alford 1934: 79). He is known for his emphasis on the human factor and is also famous for the "Gantt Chart", developed initially for the US military during World War I and later used as a standard tool for project management (Wren and Bedeian 2018: 127–129). Metcalf and Urwick (1940) brought together a brief biography of Mary Parker Follett, who has been variously referred to as a "pioneer" (Urwick 1956: 132–137), a "philosopher" (George 1968: 130–132) or a "political philosopher" (Wren 1972: 300–310)—the latter partly because she had no industrial experience. Included in the volume were the papers she delivered between 1925 and 1928 and in 1932 at the conferences organized by the US Bureau of Personnel Administration mentioned earlier. For Metcalf and Urwick (1940: 9), too, Follett was a "political and business philosopher" whose ideas were ahead of her time not least because of her emphasis on the individual and the group, as well as the dynamic aspects of organization.

Ideas Matter: The Transition Toward Histories of Management Thought

Setting the Stage: Initial Exemplary Works

Following the growth of the literature on administration and management and the emergence of some novel approaches—including what came to be known as "human relations"—during the interwar years, two more comprehensive histories appeared immediately after World War II. One was a three-volume publication by two British authors, Lyndall F. Urwick and Edward F. L. Brech on *The Making of Scientific Management*. Urwick had a long pedigree as a "propagator of management" (Engwall et al. 2016: 112), which included directing the ultimately short-lived International Management Institute in Geneva and co-founding the Urwick, Orr & Partners consulting firm (Brech, Thomson and Wilson 2010). The first volume of the book was dedicated to *Thirteen Pioneers* (Urwick and Brech 1945) and the subsequent ones to, respectively,

Management in British Industry (1946) and *The Hawthorne Investigations* (1948). We learn from Harry A. Hopf's (1947: 3) review that the making of the book went back to the war years, as the first and the second volumes appeared between 1940 and 1946 as monthly articles in a British business journal called *Industry Illustrated*.

Apart from being the first of its kind—a "pioneering work" in Hopf's (1947: 14) words—Urwick and Brech's (1945, 1946, 1948) book was notable in various other ways. Volume I was an initial example of a focus on the "pioneers". Urwick and Brech's list included three of Drury's (1915) "leaders"—Taylor, Gantt and Gilbreth as well as the latter's wife, Lillian Gilbreth whom Drury had not acknowledged. In addition, there were Charles Babbage, Henri Fayol, Mary Parker Follett, B. Seebohm Rowntree, Walter Rathenau, Henry L. Chatelier, Charles de Fréminville, Henry S. Dennison and Edward T. Elbourne, as well as Robert Owen, who was mentioned as a pioneer in the second volume. So, for Urwick and Brech (1945: 20–27), the aspiration to make management "scientific" began around the 1830s with Babbage, an English mathematician and scientist credited with being the "father of the computer" (Witzel 2003: 20) and continued with Taylor and the other pioneers that they identified. Not surprisingly, other than Babbage and Follett, those in the list were either consultants or industrialists, mostly associated with scientific management. In any case, all of them continued to be acknowledged, albeit in varying degrees, in the histories that were to follow (see e.g. Wren 1972; Witzel 2012).

A notable feature of Urwick and Brech's list of pioneers is its internationality, as it includes six Americans, three British, three French and one German. This particular selection possibly had to do with Urwick and Brech being British and the book, as the original articles, being intended for a British audience. More importantly perhaps, it seems indicative of their view that the "scientific" approach to management had been developing internationally, particularly in what they referred to as the "great nations" (Urwick and Brech 1945: 155). The second volume was focused on Britain and thus differed from the earlier histories, which were only concerned with what had been happening in the US. A central premise in this volume was that Britain was the first country to industrialize and therefore had a long history of management thinking and practice that preceded Taylor.

However, Urwick and Brech (1948) returned toward the US in their third volume with the aim of informing the "British management movement" (p. x) about the investigations in Western Electric's Hawthorne factory carried out in the 1930s by Elton Mayo and his associates. In their opinion, these studies and the themes that were derived from them about human relations within work organizations were also contributing to the development of scientific management: "quite simply [. . .] Scientific Management means, thinking scientifically instead of traditionally or customarily about the processes involved in the control of the social groups who co-operate in production and distribution" (p. 9; capital letters in the original). It was this view though that opened their book to criticism, for one, by Hopf (1947), who was recognized later by none other than Urwick (1956: 232–237) himself as one of the pioneers (see later).

Thus, even before seeing the third volume Hopf (1947: 5) was critical of what he called the "broad approach" by Urwick and Brech. In his view, the term "scientific management" should only be used for the work of Taylor and his associates. Following Drury (1915) and Person (1926), Hopf considered Taylor as an inventor, while Urwick and Brech (1946: 7) saw him as someone who only synthesized what was done before. Incidentally, Taylor (1911: 139) himself had conceded that "scientific management does not involve any great invention", but it does "involve a certain *combination* of elements which have not existed in the past" (emphasis in original). Neither did Hopf agree with according similar status to all the pioneers identified by Urwick and Brech (1945), proposing instead a revised list (Hopf 1947: 14) that distinguished between those he thought were *the* pioneers (Taylor, Gantt and the Gilbreths—all Americans), the "disciples and practitioners" (Le Chatelier, Fréminville, Dennison, Elbourne and Rowntree) and the "independents" (Babbage, Fayol, Follett and Rathenau).

At about the same time, a history of management was published in the US by George Filipetti (1946), a professor at the University of Minnesota. His preface stated that the book was written "in the hope that it would prove useful for business and labor leadership", while he also thought that it could "serve in the training of students" (p. iii); apparently it was based on a course he was teaching. Indeed, Filipetti's book needs to be acknowledged as the first textbook in this transition period, especially in its revised version (1953), which added an appendix with questions for discussion. That the book took this form appears to indicate that a market was believed to exist—or emerging—in the US for a textbook on the history of management.

The book itself was essentially a compendium of book summaries presented in chronological order. For Filipetti the "modern" management movement had started with Taylor. A highly positive assessment of scientific management was provided in the first half of the book with half a chapter (1946: 117–128), for example, devoted to reviewing and rebutting the pro-labor observations in the Hoxie report (1915) prepared for the US Commission on Industrial Relations. Although writing clearly from an American perspective, Filipetti (1946) also turned to Europe, summarizing in detail Fayol's (1917) book and Devinat's (1927) survey on the dissemination of scientific management among European countries—the latter part populated with frequent references as to how this had come about because of Taylor's influence. The Hawthorne studies were covered in detail too, though differently from Urwick and Brech (1948), since Fili-petti (1946) surrounded them by summaries of books from union leaders. This allowed him to argue that there had been an increasing rapproche-ment between management and labor, since the former had come to accept unions as legitimate and the latter acknowledged the benefits of science in management.

In all, not only did Filipetti herald the academicization of management history but also the "classic" or "evolution" view that was to character-ize most of the later book-length treatises. Unlike evolutionary theory associated with variation and the mechanisms of selection and retention, the "evolution" of management in this sense was seen as a progression in response to objective needs (cf. Jacques 2006; Lippmann and Aldrich 2014). An accompanying implicit assumption in this view was that ideas were closely followed by practice. Thus, a major theme running through Filipetti's (1946) book is that management thinking and practice had been moving, albeit in a checkered manner, toward a greater appreciation of "scientific thinking" and the application of the "scientific method". While often using the term "scientific management" in a broad sense, he was at times more careful in his terminology than Urwick and Brech, referring, for example, to what he thought was an extension of Taylor to top management issues as "scientific industrial administration" (p. 242). The heyday for "science in management", he believed, had arrived in the aftermath of World War II, as there was an expansion and refinement in the use of techniques developed earlier, which were joined by newer ones as well as novel forms of attention to the human factor (Filipetti 1953: 309–312). At the same time, the Cold War environment crept into the revised edition, since Filipetti thought that "American techniques and philosophy have produced a result which is the strongest possible *refu-tation of the Marxian theory of increasing misery*" (p. xiv; emphasis in original).

These two histories published immediately after World War II pro-vided the initial examples of two separate streams of writing that were to continue until management history came into its own as a sub-discipline toward the later part of the 1960s (see Chapter 6, in this volume): one were the—sometimes commissioned—books by practitioners (at times together with academics) intended for a managerial audience; the other were the increasing number of publications by authors affiliated with universities, like Filipetti, which came to serve as initial steps toward an academic literature on management history.

Making It Count: Histories for Practitioners by Consultants and Managers

Within the practitioner-oriented stream a notable addition was Urwick's (1956) *Golden Book of Management* that he had compiled for the

International Committee of Scientific Management (*Comité international de l'organisation scientifique* or CIOS). The book included a much-extended list of "pioneers", 70 in total, with their biographies and major works. Probably because it was done for CIOS, this list was even more international than Urwick and Brech's (1945) earlier one. It included names from seven more countries in addition to the four that were represented in the first round (US, Britain, France and Germany). The earliest "pioneers" were again from Britain, though starting this time with James Watt Jr. (the son of the inventor James Watt, known for his development of the steam engine) and Matthew R. Boulton (the son of father Watt's partner, Matthew Boulton). Urwick and Brech (1946: 24) had already credited Boulton and Watt's Soho Foundry in Birmingham at the beginning of the nineteenth century as the "earliest example of scientific management in practice".

Next, the American Management Association (AMA), a practitioner organization founded in 1923 (see Chapter 2, this volume) and the largest at the time (Bridgman, Cummings and Ballard 2019: 84), entered into the picture under the leadership of its long-time president Lawrence A. Appley with two consecutive publications: the *Classics in Management* compiled by Harwood F. Merrill (1960), an officer of AMA, and *Gantt on Management* edited by Alex W. Rathe (1961a), who was linked to AMA but was also a professor at New York University. The second book was published in cooperation with ASME to commemorate the centennial of Gantt's birth. It followed the tradition of books on a single "pioneer", though in this occasion by reprinting sections of Gantt's writings. According to Appley (in Rathe 1961a: 9), Gantt's ideas were not widely known and the book was published as a "service to the management community" by offering "guidelines", as claimed in the subtitle.

Classics in Management was the first example of a different genre in the focus on pioneers. Rather than biographical sketches, it brought together papers or excerpts from books by a number of the early writers whom Merrill (1960: 11) referred to as the "old masters". For him, the compilation was "a history of management philosophy written by those who made this history" (p. 17). With the exception of Russell Robb, a manager of public utilities in the US who wanted to show what business could learn from military organization, all the writings were from individuals in the list of pioneers in Urwick and Brech (1945) and/or Urwick (1956), to whom Merrill (1960: 8) gave due credit. *Classics in Management* was yet another clear example of the evolution approach to management and management thought: It started with the early ideas, for instance, by crediting Captain Henry Metcalf, a military officer, with mentioning for the first time, in 1885, the possibility of a "science of administration" (Merrill 1960: 14, 47). Then there were Taylor and Fayol and, eventually, the greater attention to the human factor. Indeed, for Merrill (1960: 13) management history had been a "straight-line progression".

This approach aligns with what appears to be the book's main aim of contributing to the "professionalism project" of management. A *bona fide* profession, as management was claimed to be, should have a history, and its practitioners needed to know this history. As Appley wrote in his foreword (p. 5), "Since management is a profession, does there not then exist a 'classic' body of management literature? And since it exists, should not the professional manager be familiar with it?"

Management history as well as professionalism also featured in a handbook edited by Harold B. Maynard, whose consulting firm was one of the largest in the US at the time (see Engwall et al. 2016: 170–172). All of the chapters in the handbook were authored by American managers, including one on the history of management, written by Curtis H. Gager, a former senior executive at the Coca-Cola Company. He echoed Appley in stating that the US had "entered a period of professionalism" and that managers should know how management had historically developed (Gager 1960: 72). Differently from Merrill (1960), and somewhat akin to Jones (1912), mentioned earlier, Gager's search for the origins of management went back to ancient times, aiming to provide a sense of continuity since the old civilizations: "the story of the development of management is essentially the story of mankind" (Gager 1960: 69; see Thomas, Wilson and Leeds 2013 for similar observations in histories of strategic management). After some detailed references to Hammurabi's Code, the Old Testament, Greek philosophers and the Roman Empire, in what by then was becoming a somewhat standard narrative, Gager (1960) turned to the industrial revolution in Britain, mentioning Boulton and Watt Jr., Owen and Babbage as the "pioneering steps" (p. 62). Then came the industrial revolution in the US and, of course, Taylor, who deserved, according to Gager, most of the credit for the emergence of a "science of business management" (p. 69). Interestingly, after briefly referring to Fayol, the narrative ended without any reference to Mayo's human relations.

Yet another list of "Pioneers in Management" was featured in *The Encyclopedia of Management* by Carl Heyel (1963: xxiii). Intended for American executives, a large proportion of its contributors were also managers. The list was an abridged version of Urwick's (1956) pioneers, stripped of the non-Americans other than Boulton (placed at the top), Owen, Babbage, Fayol and Rowntree. The few more recent authors who were added included Urwick himself as well as his co-author Luther Gulick, Lawrence A. Appley and Peter Drucker. Interestingly, despite figuring as one of Urwick's pioneers, Mayo was not included in the general list but placed among the "pioneers" of personnel management (Heyel 1963: 669–672).

Staying in the Shadows: Limited Contributions by Academics

In this period, histories of management and management thought written by academics remained rudimentary, appearing mainly in the form of journal articles in the *Business History Review* (BHR), the *Journal of the Academy of Management*—the *Academy of Management Journal* (AMJ) after 1963—and the *Administrative Science Quarterly* (ASQ), with the latter two having started publication in the second half of the 1950s (see Chapter 2, this volume). A few papers also began to be presented at the expanding annual conferences of the Academy of Management (AoM).

The focus on pioneers also continued within academic circles. There were the occasional biographies, including a doctoral dissertation (Jaffe 1957) on Leon P. Alford, who had himself written about Gantt (see earlier). While some of the journal articles covered those who had previously been identified as pioneers, others brought in new names or gave known pioneers new relevance. Thus, Follett was highlighted again as someone who had moved beyond the preoccupation in her own time with management techniques, instead upholding business as an institution of great significance (Sethi 1962). Alford's co-author Alexander H. Church, despite being mentioned by Urwick (1956), was seen as neglected by Joseph A. Litterer (1961a), who portrayed him as akin to Fayol, since, unlike Taylor, he had focused on the whole enterprise and the function of management. Obituaries could also get published in the AoM's journal at the time, like the one by Rathe (1961b) for Hopf, whom Urwick, in his commentary, referred to as one of the "second flight of pioneers" (p. 241). Another commemorative piece in the same journal introduced Chester I. Barnard, who had not so far been included among the "pioneers"— though would be placed among the personnel management pioneers by Heyel (1963: 671). In that earlier piece Wolf (1961: 167, 172) characterized him as a "philosopher" with a "tremendous impact on the development of management theory".

The large US corporations became another object of study, namely in a series of articles by Ernest Dale, who highlighted the "systematic approach" to management these companies had developed in the early decades of the twentieth century. Thus, for him Alfred P. Sloan Jr. of General Motors, "rather than Taylor, was a pioneer of scientific management" (Dale 1956: 52). This was, because what Taylor and his followers did was "science *for* management", whereas "Sloan's administrative ideology and 'scientific' methodology [. . .] were applicable at the top level" (p. 52; emphasis in original)—a claim that echoed Litterer's (1961a) view on Church. Dale's second article was a study of the DuPont Company, this time based on primary sources (Dale 1957). The company as whole, he argued, had developed "systematic management" early on, though he also singled out some members of the DuPont family and its executives as "management pioneers" (p. 58). In an accompanying piece, Dale and Meloy (1962) focused on one of the latter, Hamilton MacFarland Barksdale, who, in their view, was not well-known but needed to be recognized as a "pioneer thinker and contributor" (p. 130) with respect to what he had achieved in systematizing management. While Barksdale was not on Urwick's (1956) list, for Dale and Meloy (1962: 152), he was a candidate "to enter the haven of the 'immortals of management' ". Already in 1960, Dale compiled his earlier articles into a book, together with his two additional studies on more recent reorganizations in large American corporations. The "pioneers" were now relabeled the *Great Organizers*, a title that also pointed to Dale's objective of proposing an experience-based approach to "theory" on organization, which, he believed, would serve practitioners best when confronting major organizational problems.

Accompanying this focus on the "pioneers" were publications that returned to examining particular "movements" or themes that had been taken up in some of the previous literature. Eilbirt (1959), for instance, in an article published in BHR examined the historical roots of personnel management. Drawing on practitioner writings in the first two decades of the twentieth century, he posited that the "employment management movement", which arose from the blending of scientific management and the older tradition of welfare work, resulted by the 1920s in the acceptance of personnel administration as a specialized staff function within large US businesses (see Chapter 6, this volume, for similar views). Welfare work and employment management also featured in Ling's (1965) history, as parts of the first (prior to 1890) and the second (1890–1920) stages in the development of the personnel function in the US. The third, post-1920, stage involved the influences of Hawthorne and similar studies, the Great Depression and World War II, altogether leading, according to Ling, to increased significance and elevated status of personnel in American business organizations.

Litterer, whose work on Church has already been mentioned, published two additional articles in BHR drawing on his PhD dissertation, focusing on the period between 1870 and 1900 (Litterer 1961b, 1963). Based on a study of the practitioner literature, he dubbed what he believed to be the predominant approach of the time as "systematic management" (Litterer 1961b: 474), reviving—though without referencing—a distinction made much earlier by the manager Henry P. Kendall (1914) between "unsystematized", "systematized" and "scientific" management. He showed in particular that "systematic management" had a history before DuPont and General Motors, identified as pioneers by Dale (see earlier). Litterer also was more detailed regarding the meaning of this notion, suggesting that it involved precise definitions of management duties and responsibilities, standardized ways to carry them out and specific systems of information gathering and dissemination (Litterer 1963: 389), the main concern being "directing and controlling" (Litterer 1961b: 476). Being even more precise in his timing, Leland H. Jenks (1960) identified the period of 1895–1904 as the "innovative decade" (p. 421) in the US, because it saw not only the origins of Taylor's scientific management but also, more broadly, of the industrial engineering "profession" and the institutionalization of a "management movement" mainly due to the emergence of specific associations. The theme that there was a history which preceded Taylor was also revived by John H. Hoagland (1955), who had written a doctoral dissertation on Babbage. In a paper at the AoM conference, he argued strongly against "the often told *tale* of management foundations being laid by Frederick W. Taylor" (p. 15; emphasis added), citing not only the work of Babbage but also of others going back to the eighteenth century and ultimately claimed that there was little originality in Taylor's work.

Scientific management remained nevertheless a major focus of research and debate at the time. While many writings provided a highly positive assessment of Taylorism (e.g. Boddewyn 1961), others diverged from the acclaim that scientific management had usually received in the literature. Milton J. Nadworny (1955), for example, drew on primary sources to provide a historical account on the development of the relations between Taylorism and labor in the US, suggesting that two stages could be distinguished: At the beginning, Taylorism was characterized by an authoritarian, anti-union philosophy that led to worker hostility. Yet after 1920, there was a rapprochement—as Filipetti (1946) had already suggested earlier. According to Nadworny (1955), not only had later proponents of Taylorism begun to accept unions but the unions themselves had become increasingly accommodating of scientific management because of wage improvements that could be obtained due to increases in productivity (see also Chapter 7, this volume). While agreeing with Nadworny (1955) overall, Aitken (1960) showed, in a detailed historical case study, how the introduction of Taylorism at the Watertown Arsenal of the US Ordnance Department eventually led to a strike. As a result, in 1915 the US Senate banned the use of time study and incentive payments in US government contracts. This case also demonstrated the less-than-truthful relations that Taylor had with other consulting engineers and the ways he was personally involved in the struggle to prevent a negative ruling by the Senate. Nadworny (1957), too, showed, again in a study based on primary sources, how competition and hostility had developed between Taylor and his "disciples", on the one hand, and the Gilbreths, on the other, around the use of time vs. motion study and how this conflict remained hidden until 1920.

These in-depth, focused studies were accompanied by publications that took longer-term perspectives, largely repeating in their own ways what had been said before, yet also serving as precursors of book-length treatises that were to come later. In these essays or book chapters, histories were narrated by identifying stages of development or by offering classifications of prior approaches. A case in point is John F. Mee's (1963) collection of lectures, again based on a doctoral dissertation (Bedeian 1976: 97). They were delivered with Ford Foundation funding, as a part of its post–World War II efforts to promote the professionalization of management and the scientization of its research (see Engwall et al. 2016: 149–152; also Chapter 2, this volume). Mee's (1963) account squarely belongs into the evolution view, where management "thought"—or "philosophy" or "theory", as variably referred to in the text—is seen to have developed in distinct stages in parallel with the change from owner-managers to professional managers. Although earlier ideas and practices are acknowledged—as demonstrated by the chronological bibliography at the end of the book, which starts in 1831, the first or "generative" stage is reserved for Taylor's scientific management. The second stage, extending to the 1930s, was one in which the concepts of "organization" and "system" prevailed—which is reminiscent of Dale's view (see earlier), followed by the so-called "management process" approach—with the original formulation attributed, as typically done, to Fayol (see later). The fourth stage was still in the making, shaped by the criticisms of the "process" view and the advent of behavioral, decision-making and quantitative approaches, which Mee hoped—as did many management writers at the time—would result in a new synthesis.

Another piece expressing similar hopes but offering a somewhat different classification was a chapter by Joseph L. Massie (1965), which appeared in the very first *Handbook of Organizations* (March 1965). He also posited that management as a separate discipline emerged with Taylor, while observing in passing that "individual ideas on management and administration date back for more than two thousand years" (Massie 1965: 387). Massie's specific focus, however, was on what he referred to as "classical management theory". For him, too, it began with Fayol's (1917) formulation of management functions as planning, organization, command, coordination and control, accompanied by a list of management principles. He then reviewed the additions that had been made to Fayol's framework and principles in the 1920s and the 1930s by American (as well as British) managers and consultants such as Henry S. Dennison, James D. Mooney, Alan C. Reiley, Oliver Sheldon and Urwick, as well as Follett and the rare academic, Luther H. Gulick. The period until the mid-1950s was described as one where the same themes were elaborated by management consultants and business school academics. Massie (1965) then claimed that over the following decade "classical" theory was becoming divided into "traditional" and "neoclassical" approaches. The latter included writings that took an empirical approach (e.g. Dale; see earlier) or viewed management less as a science and more as a practice (e.g. Drucker; see Engwall et al. 2016: 135).

Enter "Theory", Kind of: Going Beyond Management History

In parallel, some American academics began to identify their engagement with history not as pertaining to management or management thought, but rather to "organization theory" or "organization research". Reference to a "theory of organization" had already been made since the mid-1930s (see e.g. Gaus, White and Dimock 1936: 66–91; Gulick 1937: 1–45). However, this particular reorientation appears to have been fueled by the publication of books such as March and Simon's (1958) *Organizations* and Haire's (1959) collection *Modern Organization Theory*, as well as the broader post–World War II push in the US toward scientizing the study of business and administration (see Chapter 2, this volume). As William G. Scott (1961: 8), the author of the initial article in this stream, put it: "As a foundation [. . .] rests administrative science. A major element of this science is organization theory". Likewise, George B. Strother (1963: 4) referred to the "concern with the social science of organization" in a paper delivered in a seminar, which again benefited from a Ford Foundation grant. These authors were grappling with defining and garnering acceptance for this new "science" or "theory" of organization. A history was needed both for legitimation by reference to intellectual roots and to show how the current endeavors were different from and superior to prior formulations.

But what they covered with respect to the past was not all that different from what had been told before about the history of management or management thought. In a blatant example, Hoagland (1964) repeated what he had said in his 1955 paper (see earlier), but this time under the heading "organization research". Scott (1961: 8) did have something to add, though; he was the first to coin the labels "classical", "neoclassical" and "modern" in his three-stage "evolutionary" classification. However, what he included in the former two stages was not more than those new labels. His "classical doctrine" started with Taylor and continued with Mooney and Reiley (see earlier), while the "neoclassical theory" was associated with the "human relations" school that had developed from the Hawthorne studies. The "modern" was the last stage in this evolution and was characterized by the conception of organizations as a "system", as well as its integrative nature and an empirical research base. Similarly, Strother (1963) in his search for origins, much like the writers on management history, went back all the way to the Greek philosophers. But while his narrative on the twentieth century was similar to what had been written before, differently from others he referred to bureaucracy and the writings of Max Weber. Importantly, while suggesting that there were similarities between Weber's description of bureaucracy and the "classical organization theorists", he was careful to also point at their differences, not least with respect to central concerns and methodology.

There were other departures from the earlier trends in the writings on management history, not only with respect to the disciplinary focus but also in terms of the geographic scope which had centered on the US—with the early exception of Urwick and Brech's work and the more widespread recognition of some non-American pioneers such as Owen, Babbage and Fayol. An early book to take such a broader perspective was Reinhard Bendix's (1956) *Work and Authority in Industry*. Unlike almost all writers on the history of management, Bendix was a sociologist, who fled Germany in 1938, did his training at the University of Chicago and joined the University of California at Berkley in 1947. His book was a comparative-historical study of four "cases", namely England and Russia during early industrialization and the US and the German Democratic Republic (GDR) after the development of large-scale industry. It showed that early and late stages of industrialization involved a change from a dominant entrepreneurial class toward salaried management (or "industrial bureaucrats") together with the increasing size and complexity of enterprises. There were also differences among these countries as to the autonomy of industrial actors from the state, which was high in England and the US and low in Tsarist Russia and socialist East Germany.

What was also different in Bendix's (1956) analysis from what was written before and, for that matter, later, was his characterization of management thought as an "ideology", defined as the ways in which entrepreneurs and/or managers attempted to legitimize and retain their privileges and authority to elicit obedience and effort from labor. His main argument was that ideologies varied according to societal conditions, in particular, the stage of industrialization and autonomy from the state. Thus, whereas in England and the US ideologies were developed by enterprise owners and managers, in pre-revolutionary as well as Soviet Russia and in countries under its influence, i.e. East Germany, they were framed by centralized rulers, be it the tsar or the party. With respect to the histories of management summarized previously, Bendix argued that the significance of the approaches that had originated in the US did not lie in the techniques that were promoted, but rather in the impact they had on managerial ideologies. That these approaches could be flexibly interpreted and selectively appropriated facilitated their use as ideological tools. Thus, for example, while Taylor's specific methods did not spread easily and were not readily welcomed by employers, the notion of scientific management, in contrast, served to reorient managerial ideology by reframing the role and definitions of success for entrepreneurs and managers, as well as what could and should be expected from workers. Much the same could be said, according to Bendix, about Mayo and his human relations approach which, again, met with resistance from US managers and did not spread widely. But contrary to the limited actual use of human relations practices, its language was adopted much more readily.

Two books by British academics focusing on the UK case also provided a more critical assessment of extant views on the history of management and management thought. In his study, the economic historian Sidney Pollard (1965), based at the University of Sheffield, searched for the roots of "modern management" in the early industrial revolution—the period between 1750 and 1830. Pollard's principal concern was not to single out pioneers or innovative techniques, but rather to identify the challenges that emerged with industrialization, as well as the prevalent attitudes and actions among what were then often owner-entrepreneurs. Surely, mainstays of management history such as the Soho Foundry, Babbage and Owen got frequent mention in his book. Yet for Pollard, these were idiosyncratic practices and ideas that remained largely on paper or in the minority. His main conclusion therefore was that a generalized knowledge base—a "management theory" or "science", in Pollard's terms—had not emerged by the end of the period investigated. Neither was a managerial class in sight, other than in a few specific industries. Indeed, Pollard's (1965: 271) final verdict was that management in this period was not an "initiator of change", but rather an adaptive response to the novel conditions during the industrial revolution.

In the other book, John Child (1969), who was at the time affiliated with the London Business School, traced the history of British management thought from the early twentieth century until the 1960s. He defined management thought as "the body of writings and other recorded material which has been directed towards the assessment and improvement of managerial authority, performance and status" (p. 22). For him, like for Bendix, management thought, driven in Britain mainly by managers and consultants, served both a legitimating—or ideological—and a technical function (p. 23). Thus, in his view, the early stages before the 1920s were characterized by an emphasis on legitimation of managerial authority, not least due to a context of industrial strife. The interwar years then saw a move toward technical content in the form of human relations ideas and the "management principles" or "management process" approach, as well as a strengthening of the science claim. During World War II and the following decade, as British management came under criticism, it was Mayo's human relations that rose to prominence both with its promises of democratic relationships and worker contentment and, purportedly, its science-based techniques. Child also observed, however, that during the interwar years and after World War II the reach of human relations ideas to managers was limited and required "selling" on the part of management thinkers—though human relations did appear to capture the imagination of some labor leaders. What eventually followed, according to Child (1969), was a decline in British management thought which came about, in his view, because of the challenge from social science research to its universalistic claims and value-laden advocacy of management writers.

Conclusion

This chapter has summarized the early development of what became known as management history and history of management thought from its origins in the early twentieth century. It has shown that these studies became dominated since the interwar period and, even more so, during the first two decades after World War II by a concern with the "pioneers" and an effort to periodize the "evolution" of management and management thought, increasingly through the identification of successive stages. Authors came from various backgrounds. Practicing managers and consultants tended to target their writings at practitioners, while academics would address their peers—apparent through a growing number of journal articles—or, at times, a wider audience. With few exceptions, notably Urwick and his co-authors, most studies originated in the US and concentrated on the pioneers and the evolution in that country. The 1960s saw some dissenting voices, namely those looking—though often superficially—at history from a broader "organization theory" perspective, and others questioning the universalistic claims of the extant literature—both in terms of geography and ontology. But these critics had to wait their turn, since, as shown in the next chapter, "classic" management history retained the upper hand—at least temporarily—by obtaining recognition as a sub-discipline within the US academic context at the end of the 1960s.

References

Aitken, H. G. J. (1960) *Taylorism at Watertown Arsenal: Scientific Management in Action, 1908–1915*, Cambridge, MA: Harvard University Press.

Alford, L. P. (1928) *Laws of Management Applied to Manufacturing*, New York: Ronald Press.

Alford, L. P. (1934) *Henry Lawrence Gantt: Leader in Industry*, New York: Harper and Brothers.

Anderson, A. G. (1928) *Industrial Engineering and Factory Management*, New York: Ronald Press.

Bedeian, A. G. (1976) "Management history thought," *Academy of Management Review*, 1(1): 96–97.

Bendix, R. (1956) *Work and Authority in Industry: Ideologies of Management in the Course of Industrialization*, New York: John Wiley and Sons.

Boddewyn, J. (1961) "Frederick Winslow Taylor revisited," *Journal of the Academy of Management*, 4(2): 100–107.

Brech, E., Thomson, A. and Wilson, J. F. (2010) *Lyndall Urwick, Management Pioneer: A Biography*, Oxford: Oxford University Press.

Bridgman, T., Cummings, S. and Ballard, J. (2019) "Who built Maslow's pyramid? A history of the creation of management studies' most famous symbol and its implications for management education," *Academy of Management Learning & Education*, 18(1): 81–98.

Bruce, K. and Nyland, C. (2001) "Scientific management, institutionalism, and business stabilization: 1903–1923," *Journal of Economic Issues*, 35(4): 955–978.

Child, J. (1969) *British Management Thought: A Critical Analysis*, London: George, Allen & Unwin.

Copley, F. B. (1923) *Frederick W. Taylor: Father of Scientific Management*, vols I–II, New York: Harper and Brothers.

Dale, E. (1956) "Contributions to administration by Alfred P. Sloan, Jr., and GM," *Administrative Science Quarterly*, 1(1): 30–62.

Dale, E. (1957) "Du Pont: Pioneer in systematic management," *Administrative Science Quarterly*, 2(1): 25–59.

Dale, E. (1960) *The Great Organizers*, New York: McGraw-Hill.

Dale, E. and Meloy, C. (1962) "Hamilton MacFarland Barksdale and the DuPont contributions to systematic management," *Business History Review*, 36(2): 127–152.

Devinat, P. E. (1927) *Scientific Management in Europe*, Geneva: International Labour Office.

Drury, H. B. (1915) *Scientific Management: A History and Criticism*, PhD thesis, New York: Columbia University.

Eilbirt, H. (1959) "The development of personnel management in the United States," *Business History Review*, 33(3): 345–364.

Engwall, L., Kipping, M. and Üsdiken, B. (2016) *Defining Management: Business Schools, Consultants and Media*, New York: Routledge.

Fayol, H. (1917) *Administration Industrielle et Générale: Prévoyance, Organisation, Commandement, Coordination, Contrôle*, Paris: H. Dunod et E. Pinat.

Filipetti, G. (1946) *Industrial Management in Transition*, rev. edn, 1953, Chicago, IL: Richard D. Irwin.

Gager, C. H. (1960) "Management throughout history," in H. B. Maynard (ed), *Top Management Handbook*, New York: McGraw-Hill, pp. 35–73.

Gaus, J. M., White, L. D. and Dimock, M. E. (1936) *The Frontiers of Public Administration*, Chicago, IL: The University of Chicago Press.

George, C. S. (1968) *The History of Management Thought*, Englewood Cliffs, NJ: Prentice-Hall.

Gulick, L. (1937) "Notes on the theory of organization—With special reference to government in the United States," in L. Gulick and L. Urwick (eds), *Papers on the Science of Administration*, New York: Columbia University, pp. 1–45.

Haire, M. (ed) (1959) *Modern Organization Theory*, New York: Wiley.

Heyel, C. (ed) (1963) *Encyclopedia of Management*, New York: Reinhold Publishing.

Hoagland, J. H. (1955) "Management before Frederick Taylor," *Academy of Management Proceedings*, 15–24.

Hoagland, J. H. (1964) "Historical antecedents of organization research," in W. W. Cooper, H. J. Leavitt and M. W. Shelly II (eds), *New Perspectives in Organization Research*, New York: John Wiley and Sons, pp. 27–38.

Hopf, H. A. (1947) *Historical Perspectives in Management*, New York: Hinkhouse.

Hoxie, R. F. (1915) *Scientific Management and Labor*, New York: D. Appleton and Company.

Jacques, R. S. (2006) "History, historiography and organization studies: The challenge and the potential," *Management & Organizational History*, 1(1): 31–49.

Jaffe, W. J. (1957) *L. P. Alford and the Evolution of Modern Industrial Management*, New York: New York University Press.

Jenks, L. H. (1960) "Early phases of the management movement," *Administrative Science Quarterly*, 5(3): 421–447.

Jones, E. D. (1912) "Military history and the science of business administration," *The Engineering Magazine*, 44(1): 1–6; 44(2): 185–190; 44(3): 321–326.

Jones, E. D. (1913) *Business Administration: The Scientific Principles of a New Profession*, New York: The Engineering Magazine Co.

Jones, E. D. (1914) *The Business Administrator: His Models in War, Statecraft, and Science*, New York: The Engineering Magazine Co.

Kendall, H. P. (1914) "Unsystematized, systematized and scientific management," in C. B. Thompson (ed), *Scientific Management: A Collection of the More Significant Articles Describing the Taylor System of Management*, Cambridge, MA: Harvard University Press, pp. 103–131.

Lansburgh, R. H. (1923) *Industrial Management*, New York: John Wiley and Sons.

Ling, C. C. (1965) *The Management of Personnel Relations: History and Origins*, Homewood, IL: Richard D. Irwin.

Lippmann, S. and Aldrich, H. (2014) "History and evolutionary theory," in M. Bucheli and D. Wadhwani (eds), *Organizations in Time: History, Theory, Methods*, Oxford: Oxford University Press, pp. 124–146.

Litterer, J. A. (1961a) "Alexander Hamilton Church and the development of modern management," *Business History Review*, 35(2): 211–225.

Litterer, J. A. (1961b) "Systematic management: The search for order and integration," *Business History Review*, 35(4): 461–476.

Litterer, J. A. (1963) "Systematic management: Design for organizational recoupling in American manufacturing firms," *Business History Review*, 37(4): 369–391.

March, J. G. (ed) (1965) *Handbook of Organizations*, Chicago, IL: Rand McNally.

March, J. G. and Simon, H. A. (1958) *Organizations*, New York: Wiley.

Massie, J. L. (1965) "Management theory," in J. G. March (ed), *Handbook of Organizations*, Chicago, IL: Rand McNally, pp. 387–423.

Mee, J. F. (1963) *Management Thought in a Dynamic Economy*, New York: New York University Press.

Merrill, H. F. (ed) (1960) *Classics in Management*, New York: American Management Association.

Metcalf, H. C. and Urwick, L. (1940) *Dynamic Administration: The Collected Papers of Mary Parker Follett*, New York: Harper and Row.

Nadworny, M. J. (1955) *Scientific Management and the Unions, 1900–1932*, Cambridge, MA: Harvard University Press.

Nadworny, M. J. (1957) "Frederic Taylor and Frank Gilbreth: Competition in scientific management," *Business History Review*, 31(1): 23–34.

Person, H. S. (1924) "Scientific management: A brief statement on its nature and history," in E. E. Hunt (ed), *Scientific Management Since Taylor*, New York: McGraw-Hill, pp. 5–13.

Person, H. S. (1926) "Basic principles of administration and of management," in H. C. Metcalf (ed), *Scientific Foundations of Business Administration*, Baltimore, MD: Williams and Wilkins, pp. 191–254.

Pollard, S. (1965) *The Genesis of Modern Management: A Study of the Industrial Revolution in Great Britain*, Cambridge, MA: Harvard University Press.

Rathe, A. W. (ed) (1961a) *Gantt on Management: Guidelines for Today's Executive*, New York: American Management Association.

Rathe, A. W. (1961b) "Harry Arthur Hopf: Scholarly practitioner and pioneer in management," *Journal of the Academy of Management*, 4(3): 235–244.

Scott, W. G. (1961) "Organization theory: An overview and an appraisal," *Journal of the Academy of Management*, 4(1): 7–26.

Sethi, N. K. (1962) "Mary Parker Follett: Pioneer in management theory," *Journal of the Academy of Management*, 5(3): 214–221.

Starbuck, W. H. (2003) "The origins of organization theory," in H. Tsoukas and C. Knudsen (eds), *The Oxford Handbook of Organizations: Meta-theoretical Perspectives*, Oxford: Oxford University Press, pp. 143–182.

Strother, G. B. (1963) "Problems in the development of a social science of organization," in H. J. Leavitt (ed), *The Social Science of Organizations: Four Perspectives*, Englewood Cliffs, NJ: Prentice-Hall, pp. 3–37.

Taylor, F. W. (1903) "Shop management," *Transactions of the American Society of Mechanical Engineers*, 24: 1337–1480.

Taylor, F. W. (1911) *The Principles of Scientific Management*, New York: Harper & Brothers.

Thomas, P., Wilson, J. and Leeds, O. (2013) "Constructing 'the history of strategic management': A critical analysis of the academic discourse," *Business History*, 55(7): 1119–1142.

Towne, H. R. (1886) "The engineer as an economist," *Transactions of the American Society of Mechanical Engineers*, 7: 428–432.

Urwick, L. (1956) *The Golden Book of Management: An Historical Record of the Life and Work of Seventy Pioneers*, London: Newman Neame.

Urwick, L. and Brech, E. F. L. (1945, 1946, 1948) *The Making of Scientific Management*, vols I–III, London: Management Publications Trust.

Witzel, M. (2003) *Fifty Key Figures in Management*, London: Routledge.

Witzel, M. (2012) *A History of Management Thought*, London: Routledge.

Wolf, W. B. (1961) "Chester I. Barnard (1886–1961)," *Journal of the Academy of Management*, 4(3): 167–173.

Wren, D. A. (1972) *The Evolution of Management Thought*, New York: Ronald Press.

Wren, D. A. and Bedeian, A. G. (2018) *The Evolution of Management Thought*, 7th edn, Hoboken, NJ: Wiley.

6 Orthodoxy
Establishing and Defending Classic Management History

Introduction

While the number of publications on management history and the history of management thought, in particular those written by academics, increased quite significantly during the first two decades after World War II, their place within the expanding universe of management research still appeared rather tenuous. This was at least the opinion of some of the insiders, with Jenks (1960: 447), for instance, characterizing management history as a "neglected field". Writing five years later, Massie (1965: 387) started his chapter in James March's *Handbook of Organizations* by stating that "management thought, as an identifiable and separate field of study, is relatively immature".

Both authors appear to have been overly pessimistic. By the end of the same decade, the very first textbook entitled *The History of Management Thought* had been published (George 1968). Even more importantly, in 1969 "management history" was included among the seven "interest groups" that were set up for the first time within the US-based Academy of Management (AoM)—originally founded in 1936 and by then already the largest organization for management academics. And when these interest groups were turned into "professional divisions" in 1971, now ten altogether, so was management history, "designated as Division 1" (Greenwood 2015: 175). And probably most importantly, in a survey conducted in 1967 among mostly American AoM members, approximately 20 percent of the respondents identified the history of management thought as an area of their "current research interests". With this level of appeal, management history actually outranked about two-thirds of the subject areas that were listed in the survey (Young et al. 1967: 206–207).

This chapter first details the efforts that, by the early 1970s, allowed management history to claim its place among the mainstream of management research in the US, focusing on the publication of the first two textbooks, which signaled a certain maturity and institutionalization of the field, and a growing number of journal articles, which suggested an active community of scholars. However, as the chapter discusses subsequently, during the 1970s and 1980s management history became more and more marginalized, since management research in the US was increasingly driven by the "natural science" paradigm, which made publishing in mainstream journals increasingly difficult for management historians and eventually led to the establishment of the *Journal of Management History* (JMH) in the mid-1990s. Despite the growing marginalization, most scholars perpetuated what could be called the "classic" or "orthodox" view, changing, at most, terminology rather than substance, with both established and new textbooks being published along the same lines into the twenty-first century.

Claiming a Place in the Mainstream

Compared to the first post–World War II decades, publications on the history of management and of management thought came increasingly from academics. On the one hand, by the late 1960s and early 1970s the previous and ongoing research had developed a sufficiently large body of knowledge to be summarized in a textbook intended for broader audiences, in particular students. On the other hand, new research on the topic continued leading to additional conference papers and articles—though, as the subsequent section will show, the latter found access to the mainstream journals increasingly challenging.

Bringing It All Together: Publication of the First Textbooks

Strictly speaking, Mee's 1959 dissertation, *A History of Twentieth Century Management Thought*, should probably be considered the first attempt to bring the growing body of knowledge on management history together. However, it was never published as such—though it did influence his lectures on the topic, which were then put together into a book (Mee 1963; see Chapter 5, this volume). A first textbook, intended as such, was authored by Claude S. George (1968), at the time a professor at the University of North Carolina, with a second edition published in 1972. The other textbook was written by Daniel S. Wren (1972), a professor at Florida State University who moved to the University of Oklahoma the following year and is now emeritus professor there. The book was called *The Evolution of Management Thought* rather than *The History of Management Thought* and is still in print, with a seventh edition published in 2018; from the sixth edition in 2009 onward it was co-authored by Arthur G. Bedeian, now emeritus professor at Louisiana State University (Wren and Bedeian 2018).

George's (1968) book combined various features of the preceding literature. To start, it was yet another example of searching for the "beginnings" of management in ancient civilizations. The remainder of the book consisted of two parts, the first focusing on particular individuals and the second offering a classification of "schools of thought". To start the first part, the Soho Foundry was once again introduced as an "early" scientific management practice and Owen as the "father of personnel management" (George 1968: 56, 61). The attention then shifted to the US, ending with the interim conclusion that, as the nineteenth century drew to a close, "management as a separate field had finally come into being" (George 1968: 85). A full chapter was devoted to scientific management, followed by "major contributors" in the early twentieth century that included names like Gantt and Emerson as well as, from outside the US, Fayol, who was considered equal in stature to Taylor. Next, there was a list of "minor writers" and "critics", the latter only including Hoxie (see Chapter 5, this volume). The final chapter on individual contributors included those who George (1968: 123–135) called the "managerial philosophers", comprising not only Follett and Barnard who had previously been endowed with this label (see Chapter 5, this volume) but also, among others, Mayo, Mooney and Urwick.

In the second part of the book, George classified the "schools of thought" into "traditional" or "classical" (i.e. scientific management), "behavioral" (i.e. human relations), "management process" (represented, in his view, by Fayol and Mooney) and "quantitative" (i.e. management science and operations research). George had little qualms about the influence that the development of these schools of thought had on managerial practices. And neither did he see a tension in the increasing academicization and scientization of the study of management, quite unlike Child (1969), who published his book more or less at the same time (see Chapter 5, this volume). Thus, for George (1968: 178), the "new brand of management [. . .] was one incorporating all the findings of the sociologists and psychologists, yet still managing to be quantitatively oriented with [a] goodly portion of scientific methodology". Most astounding perhaps is the "general theory of management" that George (1968: 168–170) put forth toward the end. It was presented in the form of a mathematical model—an indication not only of the hopes prevalent at the time for developing such a theory but also for the rising influence of scientism.

For Wren (1972: 3), too, "management is as old as man [*sic*]". There was again the claim that there had been management, for example, in Egypt, the Bible, Greece, Rome and the Catholic Church. Wren then turned his attention to the industrial revolution in Britain, together with the usual mentions of Babbage and Owen, who were labeled "management pioneers in the factory system" (pp. 63–79). His history subsequently focused on the US only—as acknowledged at the very beginning of the book. Those from the outside, who were seen to have made major contributions, like Fayol, were occasionally brought in—though always with reference to when their writings reached the US. Differently from George, Wren structured his US history chronologically, identifying three evolving "eras": "scientific management", "social man [*sic*]", and "modern". With considerable similarity to some of the preceding stage models and periodizations (e.g. Scott 1961), this classification turned out to have an enduring effect on the coverage of history in introductory textbooks on management in the US. Wren's main thesis was a functionalist one with a focus on techniques and principles of managing (cf. Bendix 1956; Child 1969; Chapter 5, this volume). He believed that the evolution of management thought that he identified through these three eras was the result of responses to changes in what he called the "cultural milieu", which included, with specific reference to the US, the "economic", "social" and "political" facets influencing the job of management. According to Wren (1972), as conditions and "needs" changed, thinking changed, and so did the managers' understanding of their role as well as their practices.

With respect to the three eras, for Wren (1972), "scientific management" was a product of the conditions that led to the emergence of large-scale organizations in business. This era covered, of course, Taylor and his followers. Particularly new, however, was the inclusion of Max Weber into this stage of evolution. Wren made him, together with Fayol, into a progenitor of "administrative theory". While Weber was actually referring to his description of bureaucracy as an "ideal type", the way Wren portrayed it, he had taken "an administrative viewpoint in his *bureaucratic ideal*" (p. 234; emphasis added; see also Strother 1963; Chapter 5, this volume). Readers were told not only that Weber's "concept of the best administrative system is strikingly analogous to that of Taylor" but also that, like Fayol, Weber "attempted to present administrative schemes for coping with large-scale organizations" (Wren 1972: 231, 234). This interpretation remained very much the same in later editions of the book (see later) and, very importantly, it became a kind of basis for the way Weber was treated in much of the US literature (see also McNeil 1978 for a review of similar interpretations by early sociologists of organizations in the US and Chapter 7, this volume for critical assessments of these views).

The shaping of the "social man" [*sic*] era had to do with the post-Depression conditions and the New Deal environment, which, according to Wren (1972: 403), made "people, not production, [. . .] the main concern of the administrator". This stage, as one would expect, started with the Hawthorne studies, followed by Follett and Barnard, whom Wren (1972: 300) viewed as "integrators" linking this era with its predecessor, scientific management. The book moved on to discuss writers such as Mooney, Urwick and Gulick, whom some of the authors mentioned in the previous chapter (e.g. Massie 1965) had characterized as "classical". Also included was, for example, Ralph C. Davis, a practitioner and consultant turned professor, who had been an early promoter of the management process and principles approach (see also Mee 1965).

Wren's (1972) "modern" era was even more eclectic—inevitable in a sense for those writing management history in the US at that time, including, as mentioned, George (1968), due to the various and varied advances in the academic literature in business and management after World War II. Primacy was reserved for developments in the so-called management process and principles approach, with an emphasis on the "search for unity", which Wren (1972) thought was lacking at his time of writing. Nevertheless, he still seemed to be hopeful—in line with the prevailing aspirations at the time—regarding the ability to build a general theory of management (p. 492). Moreover, entire chapters were devoted, on the one hand, to what Wren called "organizational humanism", or the "search for harmony" and, on the other, to quantitative approaches. The former included both the post-Hawthorne extensions in human relations and developments in organization theory, as also mentioned in Chapter 5 (this volume), and the latter referred in particular to operations research and systems theory. According to Wren (1972: 491), these new developments were all "demanded" by the conditions of the modern era. That management thinking was now taken over entirely by "management scholars" did not constitute a notable change for Wren, based probably on the implicit assumption that armed with the tools of science they would continue to serve managers—like the practitioners and the consultants had done in the past.

Progressing . . . a Bit: Further, Albeit Limited Expansion of the Literature

In addition to the publication of these two textbooks, during the 1970s and the 1980s research continued, though only moderately, as can be gathered from the number of relevant publications in journals as well as the papers presented at the AoM conferences. While some of the latter were based on original sources, only a few of them were eventually published as journal articles. Notably, several of these writings came from authors based in countries other than the US, like Australia and Canada. Moreover, new book-length empirical studies were extremely rare. The journal articles that did appear were mainly of three kinds. One group followed earlier patterns by focusing on the so-called pioneers, in particular but not only those related to scientific management; the second traced the history of specific management concepts; while the third aimed at revising established views, often based on the examination of original sources.

Among the first group, Gullett and Duncan (1975), for example, wanted to show that there were pre-Hawthorne "industrial humanists", singling out Dennison (see Chapter 5, this volume) for the employee representation plan he had introduced in his company in 1919, which, they claimed, was somewhat unique in terms of the extent of worker participation. Muhs (1982) also referred to employee representation plans by uncovering files from the consulting company founded by Emerson, one of the leading figures in scientific management (Engwall, Kipping and Üsdiken 2016: 69–70; see also Chapter 5, this volume). The author argued that Emerson was in favor of worker participation as long as it did not take the form of a class struggle or mounted a challenge to the authority of managers. Turning to exemplary practices before Taylor, Reid (1986: 415) reported on the "card system of cost accounting and production control" that Captain Metcalf (see Chapter 5, this volume) introduced initially in the early 1880s at the Frankford Arsenal, which he headed at the time, followed by organizations where he was put in charge later on. Other studies made incremental additions to the previous literature, such as Jelinek's (1980) article on Church (see Chapter 5, this volume) or Parker's (1984) article on Follett's views about control in organizations.

With respect to the pioneers, the literature was also extended to those from outside the US. Breeze (1985), for instance, added some biographical information on Fayol as well as one of his fellow managers, Joseph Carlioz. Likewise, Marsh (1975) published a research note on Karol Adamiecki, the Polish engineer, who was recognized by Urwick (1956: 107–110) as one of the pioneers and had received a mention by Wren (1972: 181) because of the "harmonogram" that he had developed in 1896—a workflow chart similar to but preceding that of Gantt. Perhaps most notable was Wren's (1980) article that examined the diffusion of scientific management and the Gantt chart in what was then the Soviet Union. Based on secondary sources, he suggested that there was limited reception of scientific management in the period between 1917 and 1929, despite the support the idea had received from Lenin. The Gantt chart was a different matter, as it did make inroads through the consulting projects undertaken between 1929 and 1931 by Walter N. Polakov, a Russian emigrant to the US and an associate of Gantt (see also Petersen 1986). However, the use of the Gantt chart came to a halt during Stalin's "Great Purge" in the late 1930s.

In a series of later articles based on novel sources, Petersen (1986, 1989, 1990) shed some more light on the implementation of scientific management in the US with research on Gantt as well as Major General William Crozier, the chief of ordnance for the US Army (see, on the Watertown Arsenal, Chapter 5, this volume) and on the failure of Taylorist methods at the US Navy yards (see also Nelson 1980: 137–167). Nelson and Campbell (1972) used the Bancroft Company as a case to illustrate the competition in the early twentieth century between the Taylor system and "welfare work" to obtain the support of American businessmen. Welfare work could contain a range of activities but was broadly understood as involving "special consideration for physical comfort wherever labor is performed; opportunities for recreation; educational advantages and the providing of suitable sanitary homes [. . .], plans for saving and lending money, and provisions for insurance and pensions", as defined by the National Civic Federation in the US (quoted by Nelson and Campbell 1972: 3). Nelson and Campbell's study showed that in this particular company, welfare work eventually superseded Taylorist approaches. In any case, during World War I the two currents had converged to create "personnel management" (see Chapter 5, this volume; also earlier). In a subsequent article Nelson (1974) argued that despite Taylor's claim to offer a "partial solution to the labor problem", this was the weakest part of Taylorism. For him, the Taylor system was in that sense only an extension of what had come to be known as "systematic management" (see Chapter 5, this volume). Attempts to deal with worker problems originated instead from legal changes and from employers who tried to improve working conditions and introduced various forms of welfare work (see also Nelson 1980: 16–19 and, for an alternative view, Chapter 7, this volume).

As mentioned, the second group of articles focused on the history of particular management concepts and traced their evolution, ending with the "modern" ways in which they were or needed to be understood and implemented. Giglioni and Bedeian (1974), for example, wrote on what they referred to as "control theory". They started with the formulations by "pioneers" such as Taylor, Emerson and Church on control and then moved on to Fayol, Urwick and Davis. The latter, they believed, with their focus on "management process", after the 1950s laid the foundations for "the development of a science of management control theory" which executives could, even at that stage, use for guidance (Giglioni and Bedeian 1974: 301). Another example was Van Fleet and Bedeian (1977) who wrote a "history" of the concept of "span of management", claiming origins in antiquity but dating its formal recognition to the early 1800s mainly within the context of the military. Bracker (1980) did the same for the concept of "strategy", maintaining that its first mention was in the Old Testament and referring to its later use in political and military settings until it was brought into business after World War II.

Probably most interesting was a third group of articles that were based on original research. Some of these studies were aimed at revising established views about scientific management as well as the Hawthorne studies. Not unexpectedly, these articles also prompted some controversy. Wrege and colleagues, for example, questioned the authenticity of Taylor's famous pig-iron experiments (Wrege and Perroni 1974) and pointed to Taylor's use of a part of a draft book by one of his associates, Cooke (see Chapter 5, this volume), in the *Principles of Scientific Management* (1911), without due credit (Wrege and Stotka 1978; see also Wrege and Greenwood 1991: 97–117, 175–190). These articles, as well as the broader criticisms of scientific management coming from those adhering to the human relations view, led, among others, Fry (1976) to write in defense of Taylor. An even stronger rebuttal came from Locke (1982) who not only claimed that most of the more general criticisms of Taylorism were not valid but also argued that the evidence provided by Wrege and colleagues was questionable. In an interesting addition to this debate, Bluedorn and his colleagues (1985: 130) showed that Wrege and Perroni's (1974) critique had little impact on management textbooks. They checked 25 introductory texts referring to Taylor's pig-iron experiments. All but two of them followed Taylor's description and made no reference to the doubts about their authenticity raised by Wrege and Perroni (1974).

The Hawthorne experiments also became the subject of criticisms—in fact, even more so. The very first critique came from Gilson (1940) in her review of one of the major publications drawing on the Hawthorne studies, *Management and the Worker* (Roethlisberger and Dickson 1939). Gilson herself has been regarded as one of the "pioneers" aiming to combine scientific management with welfare measures (Wrege and Greenwood 1982). She was particularly critical of the Hawthorne book because of the lack of any reference to unions. Gilson (1940: 99) also thought that the study was "naïve", because what it presented as a "discovery" would have already been known to anyone who had any shop floor experience or was aware of the publications available at the time. Sociologists soon joined the critics, pointing to the pro-management bias in the project as well as Mayo's conservative political convictions and questioning the scientific credibility of the research (see Gillespie 1991: 257–260 for a review; cf. Muldoon 2017). These claims led to controversy which then spilled over to the management literature. Among those defending the Hawthorne studies and their researchers was Shepard (1971), for example. While admitting that some of the criticisms were justified, he dismissed suggestions that the resulting writings were misleading and insisted that the main contribution of these studies was to unravel the "economic man" assumption that had prevailed before. By contrast, based on interviews with three surviving participants in the Hawthorne experiments, Greenwood and his colleagues (1983) argued that the selections were not conducted the way the researchers had portrayed them in their writings and that some of the supposed results were simplified, if not misleading, i.e. money was actually considered important by the workers and supervisors were not necessarily friendly.

As mentioned, book-length studies based on original sources were rare. One such exceptional study was by Yates (1989). It examined in great depth the origins of one particular mainstay of the management history literature, the notion of "systematic management" introduced by Litterer (1961; see Chapter 5, this volume) with respect to US businesses in the late nineteenth century. Her research focused on the development of "formal internal communication" as part of a change in "philosophy" which "promoted rational and impersonal systems in preference to personal and idiosyncratic leadership for maintaining efficiency in a firm's operations" (Yates 1989: 1). Based on archival sources from a railroad company and two manufacturing firms, she found that internal communication based mainly on written documents turned into a managerial tool for control and coordination in the late nineteenth and early twentieth centuries. This came about through the change in management philosophy and methods toward "systems", together with the development of technology such as the typewriter and the emergence of new genres of internal communications like reports, memoranda and meetings.

While all of these publications, and in particular the empirically based ones, furthered the body of knowledge about management history, they could not prevent the field from becoming ever more marginal within the rapidly growing and scientizing universe of management research (see Chapter 2; this volume).

Drifting to the Margins: The Effect of "Scientization" on Management History

Closing Doors: Reduced Publication Opportunities in Mainstream Management Journals

As already mentioned in Chapter 4 (this volume; see especially Table 4.1) and as the preceding review shows, one strong indicator for the increasing marginalization of the history of management and management thought during the 1970s and 1980s can be found in the types of journals, where studies on these topics could be and were published, as well as the actual number of articles appearing in these journals. Thus, while such articles could and did get published in the *Academy of Management Journal* (AMJ) until the mid-1970s, the doors of the journal became practically shut, when, in 1976, as a response to expanding scientism in management research, AoM decided to reserve AMJ for empirical— meaning, at the time quantitative—studies and to launch its companion, the *Academy of Management Review* (AMR). The editorial announcing this decision (Miner 1974) stated that the new journal would be publishing "conceptual papers", which included "theoretical pieces, literature reviews, *historical analyses*, essays and commentary" (p. 405; emphasis added)—implying a treatment of history as "conceptual". And AMR did indeed serve as a home for historical writing until the mid-1980s. More receptive was the *Journal of Management*, launched in 1975 by the Southern Management Association in the US, a regional division of AoM. However, even there, articles on the history of management or management thought were becoming sparse after the late 1980s (van Fleet 2006)—with the focus shifting toward historical reviews of the academic literature (see Table 4.1 in Chapter 4, this volume).

A similar pattern can be gauged from the papers presented at AoM conferences. During the 1970s and 1980s, on average only about three papers on the history of management and management thought got published in full in the conference proceedings, constituting slightly above three percent of all the full papers that were included (*Academy of Management Proceedings*, 14 November 2017). But during the last few years of the 1980s history papers all but disappeared. In fact, concerns emerged as to whether the continuously small size of the Management History Division would threaten its survival, given the AoM's criteria during the 1980s that required a division to have at least four percent of the total membership in order to be viable. The threat was overcome when in 1990 the AoM president assured that the Management History Division would be exempt from this criterion—purportedly because of the "status" it had gained as "Division 1" when divisions were established in the early 1970s (Greenwood 2015: 182–183). That research and writing on these topics remained marginal was also apparent from Wren (1987) issuing yet another call for a greater interest in teaching and researching management history. Most indicative perhaps was the limited actual research that he could refer to, which consisted of a few rather dated doctoral dissertations and the articles that were reviewed earlier in this chapter.

The response to the increasing difficulties of publishing history articles in major management journals and an attempt to rekindle interest in research on the history of management and management thought was the creation of a dedicated journal in the mid-1990s. According to Regina Greenwood (2015), discussions to set up such a publication had started in the late 1980s among members of the Management History Division at the AoM. It took a while for these efforts to come to fruition. Eventually MCB University Press, renamed Emerald Publishing in 2001, accepted to launch what was to be called the *Journal of Management History* (JMH), with its first issue appearing in 1995 (Greenwood 2015). The new journal was greeted with enthusiasm and optimism, as it purportedly promised to provide a new avenue for championing the cause of management history (see, e.g. Carson and Carson 1998). Yet worries did not cease. Concerns continued to be voiced about the unwelcome reception by leading US journals (e.g. van Fleet 2008) and, perhaps even more strongly, the limited space that was allowed for teaching management history in US business schools (Bedeian 2004; Van Fleet and Wren 2005; Smith 2007).

Initially, it appeared that the initiative would be rather short-lived, as JMH ceased publication in 2000, becoming "incorporated" into *Management Decision*, another journal of the same publisher. However, JMH did regain a separate identity in 2006, again under the auspices of the Emerald Group and has since continued publication, officially recognized as being affiliated with the AoM's Management History Division (Jain and Sullivan 2015). A study on the initial five years of the journal (1995–1999) concluded that it provided a base for discussions on the "history of management concepts and practices" so that the development of particular research areas in management could be appreciated and used for further advancement of the field (Hardy, Gibson and Buckley 2015: 417). The "new" JMH from 2006 was envisioned as standing on the same footing, perpetuating the approaches and traditions that had developed mainly within the academic context in the US after World War II (see earlier). In his inaugural editorial of the resurrected journal, Lamond (2006: 6), for example, saw the task of JMH and its authors as responding to the "need to examine more closely the historical development of management concepts and practices, with a view to how they inform the present and 'shape what we are and what we do' ".

Like in the short-lived first period of publication, some of the articles that appeared in JMH after 2006 were geared toward tracing the historical development of management concepts or topics, especially more topical ones such as quality management, entrepreneurship, social responsibility and corporate governance. Yet the predominant focus continued to be on historical figures, particularly Taylor, Fayol, Follett and Barnard, and lately, similar to patterns identified later for edited collections, also on the more recent US contributors and "gurus" (e.g. Peter Drucker, W. Edwards Deming, Alfred D. Chandler Jr., Herbert Simon and Douglas McGregor). The reviews on JMH (Crocitto 2015; Hardy et al. 2015; Jain and Sullivan 2015) indicate that in the first five years of the journal around 50 percent and then up to 2009 about 40 percent of the articles were about individuals. Thus, what ultimately surprises most is that management historians, despite the obvious marginalization, and even existential threat they faced within the broader community of management academics in the US, did not revisit and revise their research priorities. Instead, they continued along the well-trodden "orthodox" lines of inquiry.

Doubling Down: The "Classic" View Persists

Wren's textbook was published in a fifth edition in 2005, though now under the title *The History of Management Thought*—maybe to signal defiance against all odds? The sixth edition in 2009, however, reverted to the original title and also, for the first time, included a co-author, Arthur G. Bedeian (see earlier). For the most recent seventh edition, both the title and the authorship remained unchanged (Wren and Bedeian 2018). A comparison of Wren's (1972) original book with Wren and Bedeian's 2018 version more than four decades later indicates only limited changes in the overall approach and narrative. The three-stage process of progression from "scientific management" to "social person" (instead of "man" in the original) and then to "modern" remained the same, though the latter term is no longer used and is replaced by "Moving Onward: The Near Present". The "cultural framework", changes in which were believed to influence developments in management practice and thought, is still there with the addition of a "technological facet" to the earlier economic, social and political aspects. And Weber again sits side by side with Fayol. Although the parallels with Taylor are no longer mentioned, Weber is still presented as attempting, like Fayol, "to develop methods for managing large-scale organizations" (Wren and Bedeian 2018: 187; see also Bedeian 2004: 96 and later).

What has changed most is the treatment of the last stage in the progression of management thought. Apart from some updated coverage, including, for instance, population ecology, transaction costs and agency theory, and the introduction of present-day popular topics such as ethics, corporate social responsibility and globalization, there are two particularly notable changes: First, taking the Fayolian management "functions" or "management process" approach as a unifying framework is no longer present. However, there is still reference to the somewhat elusive notion of "general management theory", apparently understood as the unfolding of Fayolian ideas into strategic management (Wren and Bedeian 2018: 338). Second, the somewhat hesitant hope in the original book that "general systems theory" and/or "comparative management" might offer a "potential for synthesis" is not upheld any more (cf. Wren 1972: 524). The authors appear to have come to terms with integration being out of sight among the different practical and theoretical pathways that they have identified in the post–World War II era.

Book-length treatises on the history of management or management thought in countries other than the US have remained relatively rare, confined, at least in the English language, to the UK. Brech's (2002) collection spanning the period from the mid-nineteenth to the later part of the twentieth century is one example. The five volumes cover the management models and the literature in Britain over this period, as well as the various organizational bodies that were established to advance the cause of professional management and management education. A more recent example is Wilson and Thomson's (2006) history of management in Britain, which begins with the late eighteenth century and then traces management development, thought and practice until the end of the twentieth century.

There is another author who has done much over the last two decades to propagate the classic perspective of management history—though with a somewhat more international focus than most others: Morgen Witzel, a Canadian who had studied history and worked as an independent writer before moving to the UK in 1995 to lecture at the London Business School until 1999. His debut in management history was with an edited collection of 600 biographies (Witzel 2001). And the first of his authored books traced the "evolution" of management (Witzel 2002).

It was of a popular kind with little referencing and with vignettes on some of the individuals included in his earlier biographical compilation. Nevertheless, the book did demonstrate Witzel's "classic" approach to writing management history. This was to become more apparent in a textbook that he published a while later purportedly with "cases", which were in fact brief histories of different organizations, mostly companies, collated from secondary sources (Witzel 2009). True to the spirit of the classic view, what Witzel appears to want to teach is that the past needs to be studied because it could inspire new ways of looking at management practice in the present and possibly in the future. There is also a strong conviction that management has a very long and proud history, that much of what now goes as management has roots in the past and that the kind of problems faced by managers and the core aspects of managing are essentially timeless. Witzel's (2009) book does differ however from Wren and Bedeian's (2018) in that management and business activity are treated somewhat synonymously; his history is actually structured according to business functions such as marketing, finance and human resource management, among others.

In his subsequent, more academic treatise Witzel (2012) turned to a chronological layout, starting with ancient times, moving to the Middle Ages and then to the industrial revolution and eventually to scientific management and human relations. He nevertheless explicitly stated that he does not fully subscribe to an "evolutionary"—read: progressive—approach because the "long path of management thought is littered with the wreckage of good ideas that failed" (p. 6). Still, a functionalist interpretation persisted, as he also said that "new ideas about management emerge because new ideas about management are needed" (p. 4). And he admitted to having "generally portrayed management thought in a positive light" (p. 234). Witzel's proclivity to equate management with a full range of business activities showed itself in this book too, though in this instance largely in a separate chapter where he also included topics such as the development of business education and management consulting. And, notably, Witzel diverged from Wren's (1972) legacy of treating the development of twentieth-century management thought as a singular trajectory by sidestepping from his chronological progression and including a chapter on Europe. While largely devoted to Britain, the chapter also considered France, highlighting Fayol, and Germany, mentioning academics of the early twentieth century, including Weber, as well as industrialists such as Rathenau (see Chapter 5, this volume). Most notable, of course, is that although Fayol and Weber appear in the same chapter, different from the view propagated by Wren (1972) and Wren and Bedeian (2018), Weber is not portrayed as a management theorist who had sought methods for increasing efficiency in large-scale organizations.

Still Focusing on Individuals: From "Pioneers" to "Innovators" and Back

Prominent management history writers also maintained the tradition of publishing compilations of early writings or biographical collections. Wren (1997), for instance, edited a book that contained articles or excerpts from books mostly from the last two decades of the nineteenth century. There were also a few earlier pieces from Adam Smith, Charles Babbage and, perhaps most interestingly, from a book that Charles Dickens (1842) wrote after his travels to the US. In the introduction, Wren (1997: xiv–xvi) highlighted that even the English observers tended to view American management and workers in a more positive light than their own. Dickens's impressions of the factories that he visited in Lowell, Massachusetts, added to this message, as he appeared to be impressed with the way that the female workers were dressed, their cleanliness and healthiness, as well as the conditions in the factory and the houses where they were boarded. He did mention though that they were quite young and that there were also a few children around. These young women, Dickens observed, worked on average 12 hours a day, though only for nine months due to the laws of this particular state, since they were expected to be educated during the remaining three months. Dickens's positive impressions notwithstanding, the editors of a more recent edition of his book, from which Wren took the piece, did make the point that "nowhere in America at this time were factory workers treated so paternally as here", i.e. where Dickens had visited (Wren 1997: 331).

More than a decade later, Bedeian (2011) followed with a more comprehensive collection. This four-volume compendium exemplified the tendency in the post-2000 literature of expanding the focus on notable individuals from the pioneers to those of more recent times, thus making such compilations more convergent with evolution histories. Indeed, Bedeian's (2011) collection was very much in line with his co-authored book with Wren (Wren and Bedeian 2018)—short of the management science part and the present-day popular topics that were mentioned earlier. The first volume of the compendium and a good part of the second are devoted to scientific management. The second volume also included a part that again put Fayol together with Weber. Volume III started with the Hawthorne studies, also covering Follett and Barnard, as well as some of the early so-called classical writers with a part on Urwick, for example. The last volume covered the early writings of post–World War II American academic authors such as Abraham Maslow and Frederick Herzberg who have been influential in the development of what is now referred to as organizational behavior.

The tendency to extend the time horizon forward to prominent individuals of the more recent period was heralded by an earlier compilation by Wren and Ronald Greenwood. Its title was already indicative in that it referred to "management innovators" rather than "pioneers" (Wren and Greenwood 1998). This book also extended the scope of the "classic" literature on pioneering individuals by moving beyond manufacturers and consultants to include progenitors of other business activities categorized under headings such as "sellers" and "financiers". The biographies in the first part of the book do go back to American business people of the nineteenth century, including the likes of Eli Whitney, Henry Ford, Richard W. Sears and J. P. Morgan. The second part includes household names such as Taylor, the Gilbreths, Follett, Barnard and Mayo. It then extends, like Bedeian's (2011) anthology, to Maslow, Herzberg, McGregor and to the major promulgators of the quality movement, i.e. W. Edwards Deming and Joseph Juran, and eventually to Peter Drucker—a category by himself according to Wren and Greenwood (1998) who refer to him as the "guru". In other ways, this collection too was a continuation of the patterns set by the classic view. The center of attention is again the US, with only two names from Japan included: Yoichi Ueno, the "father of Japanese administrative science", and Taiichi Ohno, who played a key role in devising the Toyota Production System. Notably though, they are both credited, among their other achievements, with successfully importing and adapting methods developed in the US. The professed aims of this collection were similar to some of the books in the early 1960s claiming that management is a profession and that managers should be aware of its history. We are told at the beginning, for example, that the volume is intended for "an audience of contemporary managers, aspiring managers, and students of management who wish to gain a historical perspective on their profession" (Wren and Greenwood 1998: ix).

The Wren (1997) and the Wren and Greenwood (1998) anthologies appear to have caught the imagination of publishers in conjunction with a new set of editors who were only partially involved in academia. Wood and Wood (2001, 2002a, 2002b, 2003, 2004), for example, in keeping with the classic view, started by editing compendia on Fayol, Taylor, Ford, the Gilbreths and Mayo for a new Routledge series. Yet taking the new tendency to extend the time horizon of what was considered "history" of management thought even closer to the present, their later collections included many more recent well-known academics and consultants.

For Witzel too, the study of individuals served as a way to trace the development of management ideas and practices. As mentioned earlier, his first book brought together 600 biographies of those viewed as having contributed to management thought and practice (Witzel 2001). True to the spirit of the classic view, the collection stretches to philosophers, clergymen, monarchs and businesspeople from ancient times, the oldest entry dating back to 2000 BC. The subsequent coverage is likewise eclectic and extends all the way to present-day business people such as

Bill Gates and Michael Dell, founders of Microsoft and Dell Computers, respectively. Similar to Urwick (1956) with his *Golden Book*, apparently Witzel's (2001) ambition was to make his collection international. Nevertheless, he did acknowledge overall American dominance, indicated, for instance, by the fact that contributors to his volume from the US by far outnumbered those from other countries. Moreover, a later abridged version included only the 260 or so US-based individuals (Witzel 2005). In between, Witzel (2003) published another abbreviated version containing the biographies of only 50 "key figures" that he authored himself. The intent of the book was otherwise the same, though the timeline of entries was cut on both ends, as the collection now went back only as far as the sixth century BC and stopped with Bill Gates.

Witzel's most recent book to focus on individuals, co-edited with Malcolm Warner, has been somewhat different, though the tendency to take management thinking to the present day was still there (Witzel and Warner 2013). The chapters were comprehensive reviews that described and assessed each individual's contributions and influence. In addition, the book was notably more focused in its conception of "management", since it did not include influential names from other business disciplines such as marketing or finance, which had been part of Witzel's earlier biographical compilations. This collection was also narrower in scope both with respect to the time frame and the range of individuals who were selected. The pro-management view was again there, as Witzel and Warner (2013: 3) added that one of the criteria they employed was to include those who "believed in the importance of management and emphasized its positive role in organizations, business and society". The history now began with Taylor and included other historically significant figures treated as the "pioneers" such as the Gilbreths, Fayol and Barnard. Consultants and academics who came to be known in the immediate aftermath of World War II were then covered, followed by academics from more recent times. Thus, no businesspeople were selected other than Fayol and Barnard. This choice appears to have been driven by the programmatic title of the book: *Management Theorists*. Interestingly, of course, now Taylor, Fayol and others in the "pioneers" part of the book were labeled as "theorists"—though not all the chapters on these individuals necessarily refer to them in this manner.

Conclusion

By the end of the 1960s and the early 1970s, it looked like management history and the history of management thought had come into their own, with two major textbooks bringing together the research efforts of the previous decades. But any elation that the academics pursuing these kinds of studies might have felt at becoming AoM's "Division 1" was short-lived. Within the next two decades the increasing scientization of management research made it more and more difficult, and at the end largely impossible, to publish their papers in the mainstream management journals. And while the creation of their own specialist journal, JMH, in 1995 and its re-establishment in 2006, after a six-year hiatus, provided a new outlet, it actually illustrated, even cemented, the marginal and precarious status of the discipline.

If any lessons were learned from these developments, they did not extend to the persistence of what has been referred to here as the "classic" or "orthodox" view of management history, which centered around the evolution of management thought over time through progressive stages—driven by some functional logic pointing to the "needs" of managers—and the more or less in-depth descriptions of the contribution by an ever-growing number of "pioneers"—gradually including a few more individuals from outside the US. Partially driven by an editorial logic, changes to this orthodoxy were minimal and usually little more than cosmetic, including, for instance, a renaming of the pioneers as "innovators"—though, more recently, Witzel returned to the earlier nomenclature—and a broadening of the temporal, geographic and functional scope of those included.

This lack of intellectual development not only left the traditional history of management and management thought in an almost vegetative state, with few new authors joining the fold—though mostly espousing the classic ways. It also created an opening for those with a more critical take on the history of management and even the idea of management thought. Like the scholars beholden to the classic view, they could draw on some, though way fewer, earlier publications (see Chapter 5, this volume). And while the classic view became increasingly marginalized after a brief moment in the sun, the critical scholars kept pushing from the—thematic and geographic—margins toward the mainstream. Their efforts eventually became intertwined—intellectually and institutionally—with initiatives aiming to "revive" the role of history in management studies—initiatives, which, in the most recent period, even included attempts to wrestle control over Division 1 from the remnants of the erstwhile orthodoxy.

References

Academy of Management Proceedings, http://proceedings.aom.org/site/misc/archive.xhtml (accessed 14 November 2017).

Bedeian, A. G. (2004) "The gift of professional maturity," *Academy of Management Learning & Education*, 3(1): 92–98.

Bedeian, A. G. (ed) (2011) *Evolution of Management Thought*, London: Routledge.

Bendix, R. (1956) *Work and Authority in Industry: Ideologies of Management in the Course of Industrialization*, New York: John Wiley and Sons.

Bluedorn, A. C., Keon, T. L. and Carter, N. M. (1985) "Management history research: Is anyone out there listening?" *Academy of Management Proceedings*, 130–133.

Bracker, J. (1980) "The historical development of the strategic management concept," *Academy of Management Review*, 5(2): 219–224.

Brech, E. F. L. (2002) *The Evolution of Modern Management: A History of the Development of Managerial Practice, Education, Training and Other Aspects in Britain from 1852 to 1979*, 5 vols, Bristol: Thoemmes Press.

Breeze, J. D. (1985) "Harvest from the archives: The search for Fayol and Carlioz," *Journal of Management*, 11(1): 43–54.

Carson, P. and Carson, K. D. (1998) "Theoretically grounding management history as a relevant and valuable form of knowledge," *Journal of Management History*, 4(1): 29–42.

Child, J. (1969) *British Management Thought: A Critical Analysis*, London: George, Allen & Unwin.

Crocitto, M. (2015) "Learning from the past to envision the future: A five-year review 2005–2009," *Journal of Management History*, 21(4): 453–493.

Dickens, C. (1842) *American Notes for General Circulation*, Paris: A. and W. Galignani.

Engwall, L., Kipping, M. and Üsdiken, B. (2016) *Defining Management: Business Schools, Consultants and Media*, New York: Routledge.

Fry, L. W. (1976) "The maligned F. W. Taylor: A reply to his many critics," *Academy of Management Review*, 1(3): 124–129.

George, C. S. (1968) *The History of Management Thought*, Englewood Cliffs, NJ: Prentice-Hall.

Giglioni, G. B. and Bedeian, A. G. (1974) "A conspectus of management control theory: 1900–1972," *Academy of Management Journal*, 17(2): 292–305.

Gillespie, R. (1991) *Manufacturing Knowledge: A History of the Hawthorne Experiments*, Cambridge: Cambridge University Press.

Gilson, M. B. (1940) "Review of *Management and the Worker* by F. J. Roethlisberger and William J. Dickson," *American Journal of Sociology*, 46(1): 98–101.

Greenwood, R. A. (2015) "A first look at the first 30 years of the first division: The management history division," in B. Bowden and D. Lamond (eds), *Management History: Its Global Past and Present*, Charlotte, NC: Information Age Publishing, pp. 173–189.

Greenwood, R. G., Bolton, A. A. and Greenwood, R. A. (1983) "Hawthorne half a century later: Relay assembly participants remember," *Journal of Management*, 9(2): 217–231.

Gullett, C. R. and Duncan, W. J. (1975) "Henry Dennison and employee representation: A counterpoint in management thought," *Journal of Management*, 1(1): 9–14.

Hardy, J. H. III, Gibson, C. and Buckley, M. R. (2015) "Looking back: A quantitative review of the *Journal of Management History*, 1995–1999," *Journal of Management History*, 21(4): 410–420.

Jain, A. K. and Sullivan, S. (2015) "Adjusting to the unexpected a review of the *Journal of Management History* from 2000 to 2004," *Journal of Management History*, 21(4): 421–438.

Jelinek, M. (1980) "Toward systematic management: Alexander Hamilton Church," *Business History Review*, 54(1): 63–79.

Jenks, L. H. (1960) "Early phases of the management movement," *Administrative Science Quarterly*, 5(3): 421–447.

Lamond, D. (2006) "Management and its history: The worthy endeavour of the scribe," *Journal of Management History*, 12(1): 5–11.

Litterer, J. A. (1961) "Systematic management: The search for order and integration," *Business History Review*, 35(4): 461–476.

Locke, E. A. (1982) "The ideas of Frederick W. Taylor: An evaluation," *Academy of Management Review*, 7(1): 14–24.

Marsh, E. R. (1975) "The harmonogram of Karol Adamiecki," *Academy of Management Journal*, 18(2): 358–364.

Massie, J. L. (1965) "Management theory," in J. G. March (ed), *Handbook of Organizations*, Chicago, IL: Rand McNally, pp. 387–423.

McNeil, K. (1978) "Understanding organizational power: Building on the Weberian legacy," *Administrative Science Quarterly*, 23(1): 65–90.

Mee, J. F. (1963) *Management Thought in a Dynamic Economy*, New York: New York University Press.

Mee, J. F. (1965) "Pater Familiae et Magister," *Academy of Management Journal*, 8(1): 14–25.

Miner, J. B. (1974) "Editorial comment," *Academy of Management Journal*, 17(3): 405.

Muhs, W. F. (1982) "Worker participation in the progressive era: An assessment by Harrington Emerson," *Academy of Management Review*, 7(1): 99–102.

Muldoon, J. (2017) "The Hawthorne studies: An analysis of critical perspectives, 1936–1958," *Journal of Management History*, 23(1): 74–94.

Nelson, D. (1974) "Scientific management, systematic management, and labor, 1880–1915," *Business History Review*, 48(4): 479–500.

Nelson, D. (1980) *Frederick W. Taylor and the Rise of Scientific Management*, Madison, WI: University of Wisconsin Press.

Nelson, D. and Campbell, S. (1972) "Taylorism versus welfare work in American industry: H. L. Gantt and the Bancrofts," *Business History Review*, 46(1): 1–16.

Parker, L. D. (1984) "Control in organizational life: The contribution of Mary Parker Follett," *Academy of Management Review*, 9(4): 736–745.

Petersen, P. B. (1986) "Correspondence from Henry L. Gantt to an old friend reveals new information about Gantt," *Journal of Management*, 12(3): 339–350.

Petersen, P. B. (1989) "The pioneering efforts of Major General William Crozier (1855–1942) in the field of management," *Journal of Management*, 15(3): 503–516.

Petersen, P. B. (1990) "Fighting for a better navy: An attempt at scientific management (1905–1912)," *Journal of Management*, 16(1): 151–166.

Reid, W. H. (1986) "The development of Henry Metcalf's card system of shop returns at Frankford Arsenal, 1880–1881," *Journal of Management*, 12(3): 415–423.

Roethlisberger, F. J. and Dickson, W. J. (1939) *Management and the Worker*, Cambridge, MA: Harvard University Press.

Scott, W. G. (1961) "Organization theory: An overview and an appraisal," *Journal of the Academy of Management*, 4(1): 7–26.

Shepard, J. M. (1971) "On Alex Carey's radical criticism of the Hawthorne studies," *Academy of Management Journal*, 14(1): 23–32.

Smith, G. (2007) "Management history and historical context: Potential benefits of its inclusion in the management curriculum," *Academy of Management Learning & Education*, 6(4): 522–533.

Strother, G. B. (1963) "Problems in the development of a social science of organization," in H. J. Leavitt (ed), *The Social Science of Organizations: Four Perspectives*, Englewood Cliffs, NJ: Prentice-Hall, pp. 3–37.

Taylor, F. W. (1911) *The Principles of Scientific Management*, New York: Harper & Brothers.

Urwick, L. (1956) *The Golden Book of Management: An Historical Record of the Life and Work of Seventy Pioneers*, London: Newman Neame.

Van Fleet, D. D. (2006) "The *Journal of Management*'s first 30 years," *Journal of Management*, 32(4): 477–506.

Van Fleet, D. D. (2008) "Doing management history: One editor's views," *Journal of Management History*, 14(3): 237–247.

Van Fleet, D. D. and Bedeian, A. G. (1977) "A history of the span of management," *Academy of Management Review*, 2(3): 356–372.

Van Fleet, D. D. and Wren, D. A. (2005) "Teaching history in business schools, 1982–2003," *Academy of Management Learning & Education*, 4(1): 44–56.

Wilson, J. F. and Thomson, A. (2006) *The Making of Modern Management: British Management in Historical Perspective*, Oxford: Oxford University Press.

Witzel, M. (ed) (2001) *Biographical Dictionary of Management*, 2 vols, Bristol: Thoemmes Press.

Witzel, M. (2002) *Builders and Dreamers: The Making and Meaning of Management*, London: Pearson Education.

Witzel, M. (2003) *Fifty Key Figures in Management*, London: Routledge.

Witzel, M. (ed) (2005) *The Encyclopedia of the History of American Management*, Bristol: Thoemmes Press.

Witzel, M. (2009) *Management History: Text and Cases*, London: Routledge.

Witzel, M. (2012) *A History of Management Thought*, London: Routledge.

Witzel, M. and Warner, M. (eds) (2013) *The Oxford Handbook of Management Theorists*, Oxford: Oxford University Press.

Wood, J. C. and Wood, M. C. (eds) (2001) *Henri Fayol*, 2 vols, London: Routledge.

Wood, J. C. and Wood, M. C. (eds) (2002a) *F. W. Taylor*, 4 vols, London: Routledge.

Wood, J. C. and Wood, M. C. (eds) (2002b) *Henry Ford*, 2 vols, London: Routledge.

Wood, J. C. and Wood, M. C. (eds) (2003) *Frank and Lillian Gilbreth*, 2 vols, London: Routledge.

Wood, J. C. and Wood, M. C. (eds) (2004) *George Elton Mayo*, 2 vols, London: Routledge.

Wrege, C. D. and Greenwood, R. G. (1982) "Mary B. Gilson—A historical study of the neglected accomplishments of a woman who pioneered in personnel management," *Business and Economic History*, 11: 35–42.

Wrege, C. D. and Greenwood, R. G. (1991) *Frederick W. Taylor: The Father of Scientific Management—Myth and Reality*, Homewood, IL: Business One Irwin.

Wrege, C. D. and Perroni, A. G. (1974) "Taylor's pig-tale: A historical analysis of Frederick W. Taylor's pig-iron experiments," *Academy of Management Journal*, 17(1): 6–27.

Wrege, C. D. and Stotka, A. M. (1978) "Cooke creates a classic: The story behind F. W. Taylor's principles of scientific management," *Academy of Management Review*, 3(4): 736–749.

Wren, D. A. (1972) *The Evolution of Management Thought*, New York: Ronald Press.

Wren, D. A. (1980) "Scientific management in the U.S.S.R., with particular reference to the contribution of Walter N. Polakov," *Academy of Management Review*, 5(1): 1–11.

Wren, D. A. (1987) "Management history: Issues and ideas for teaching and research," *Journal of Management*, 13(2): 339–350.

Wren, D. A. (ed) (1997) *Early Management Thought*, Aldershot: Dartmouth Publishing.

Wren, D. A. (2005) *The History of Management Thought*, 5th edn, Hoboken, NJ: Wiley.

Wren, D. A. and Bedeian, A. G. (2018) *The Evolution of Management Thought*, 7th edn, Hoboken, NJ: Wiley.

Wren, D. A. and Greenwood, R. G. (1998) *Management Innovators: The People and Ideas That Have Shaped Modern Business*, New York: Oxford University Press.

Yates, J. (1989) *Control Through Communication: The Rise of System in American Management*, Baltimore, MD: The John Hopkins University Press.

Young, S., George, C. S., Johnson, R. A., Pederson, C. A., Reed, K. A. and Shull, F. A. (1967) "Research activities and interests of the Academy membership—A summary," *Academy of Management Journal*, 10(2): 205–207.

7 Alternatives

Emergence and Expansion of Critical Views

Introduction

During the first two decades after World War II, there had already been some critical studies on the history of management thought, in particular by Bendix (1956) and Child (1969) (see Chapter 5, this volume). They questioned not only the—largely implicit—ontological assumptions of the extant literature and its functionalist assertions in terms of management ideas purportedly responding to managerial "needs". They also challenged the progressive aspirations underlying the evolution or stage models prevalent in most of the writings on management history. And they adopted a more comparative and international outlook by moving beyond the geographic scope of the "classic" or "orthodox" literature which had focused almost exclusively on the US—and related even ideas and actors from other countries to their reception and impact there. However, these critical approaches found little resonance in the discipline as it became institutionalized toward the late 1960s and early 1970s and did not find more of a following even as management history became ever more marginalized within the broader community of management scholars in the subsequent decades. On the contrary, as shown in the previous chapter, rather than changing or even questioning the established views, management historians dug in.

As this chapter will show, already since the 1970s there was an opportunity for revising classic accounts of management history with what subsequently came to be referred to as labor process theory, which radically challenged the extant interpretations of what much of "orthodoxy" considered the starting point for today's business practice: scientific management. But the original historical orientation in this highly critical literature soon vanished and history never took hold in a related, but broader and more mainstream version, Critical Management Studies (CMS). After these false starts, critical approaches in management history only took off at a larger and more sustained pace since the 1990s and in particular over the past two decades—a development partially supported by the establishment, in 2006, of a new journal, *Management & Organizational*

History (MOH), based in the UK. In the following we provide an overview of these efforts, dividing them into two different categories: First, we look at revisionist histories of management—revisionist in the sense that they aim to provide alternatives to the established narratives both regarding the supposed progressive "evolution" of management thought and specific management ideas. Secondly, the chapter discusses a variety of what could be called "counter-histories", which often draw on conceptualization from French scholars, in particular Michel Foucault and Bruno Latour. In addition, the final section draws attention to a growing body of work that transcends the almost single-minded focus of most management history, including some of the critical approaches, on the US.

'Twas All Rather Different: Revisionist Histories

As noted, there had already been some criticisms of both Taylor and the Hawthorne studies within the classic view—though they remained limited in scope, were dismissed by other authors and ignored within summary publications (see Chapter 6, this volume). A more radical critique of scientific management based on Marxism arose in the 1970s but relatively soon shed the original link with and interest in history. Revisionist accounts of the history of management and management thought, this time coming from more mainstream management scholars, only arose again since the 1990s as will be detailed next.

False Starts: Labor Process Theory and Critical Management Studies

An early opportunity to question and revise the extant orthodoxy arose in the mid-1970s with the publication of Harry Braverman's seminal book on *Labor and Monopoly Capital* (Braverman 1974). Written from a Marxist perspective, his work constituted a direct challenge to the core of the classic management history literature, which—without any real exception—put Taylor's scientific management at the origins of modern management and its progressive evolution, while searching for and acknowledging some earlier ideas and their manifestations. Braverman did not question the central role played by Taylor, but, rather than deifying him, saw scientific management as ultimately responsible for the de-skilling of workers, since it allowed transferring the control over the labor process in terms of both conception and execution to engineers and managers who ultimately acted on behalf of monopoly capital.

His "labor process theory", as it came to be called, was largely ignored by orthodox management historians, who did not seem to want to dignify the radical reinterpretation of their key actor's role with a response. It did have a considerable influence, however, on management scholarship, mainly in the UK, where sociologists dominated research. A Labor

Process Conference (LPC) was organized for the first time in Manchester in 1983. It attracted a growing number of international participants, was held outside the UK for the first time in 2004, in Amsterdam, and is still ongoing (Smith 2008; ILPC, 20 April 2020). Labor process theorizing also became one of the intellectual foundations for CMS, which emerged in the 1990s in the UK and Scandinavia—though it took a more encompassing view that also incorporated various other ideas, including from poststructuralism (Alvesson and Willmott 1992; Fournier and Grey 2000). Lacking an explicit link to Marxism, CMS was more palpable to a broader swath of academics and became an interest group and then, in 2008, a division in the Academy of Management (Özkazanç-Pan and Donnelly 2018, 29 July 2019) as the latter tried to increase its appeal to audiences outside the US.

Eminently historical in its origins, labor process theory initially prompted some scholarship that drew at least partially on original sources and was often comparatively oriented, while aiming to contribute to theoretical debates. One example is the work by Craig Littler, whose doctoral dissertation drew, among others, on the archives of the Bedaux Consultancy to examine in some depth the introduction and consequences of scientific management in Britain and then compared the British case with the US and Japan (see Littler 1982 for the revised published version). Later writings in this tradition, and even more so those associated with CMS, showed less and less interest in history and used data and methods more akin to mainstream management research (see, e.g. the annotated bibliography in Smith 2008). Yet this did not prevent the proponents of a "historic turn" in management studies from claiming its heritage (see Chapter 3, this volume).

Talk Matters: Theorizing the Evolution of Management Discourses and Models

The mainstream management scholars providing revisionist views on the history of management and management thought usually took the latter part of the nineteenth century as their starting point, unlike many of the classic "evolutionary" accounts that typically began by searching for early manifestations of management in ancient times. Yet not unlike the conventional histories, the focus of the revisionists was also on the US. The first of these articles that aimed at revising the established evolution narrative was by Barley and Kunda (1992). They suggested that management thinking in the US, rather than developing in a linear path of progress, oscillated between "normative" (people oriented) and "rational" (technology and technique oriented) forms of control. The normative forms and the periods they dominated were labeled "industrial betterment" (1870–1900), "human relations" (1923–1955) and "organizational culture and quality" (1980–early 1990s), while the rational versions were called "scientific management" (1900–1923) and "systems rationalism" (1955–1980). The emergence of these pendulum swings between the normative and the rational, these authors argued, were conditioned, respectively, by long waves or Kondratieff cycles of economic expansion and contraction. Barley and Kunda (1992: 389) reasoned that this was because in economic downturns profitability appeared to depend on the management and motivation of employees, whereas during periods of expansion profits rested on the investment in and efficient use of capital. At the same time, they also pointed out that the rational forms of control appeared to have been more influential all along the way, even in periods that seemed dominated by the normative ones.

In addition to questioning the stage-by-stage progression of American managerial thought, Barley and Kunda's (1992) "pendulum thesis" was distinct in at least three more ways. First, the language was different. Predating later critical work, management thought or theories were construed, akin to Bendix (1956; see Chapter 5, this volume), as managerial ideologies or rhetorics, defined as "a stream of discourse that promulgates, however unwittingly, a set of assumptions about the nature of the objects with which it deals". The "objects of rhetorical construction [were] typically [. . .] corporations, employees, managers, and the means by which the latter can direct the other two" (Barley and Kunda 1992: 363). They also pointed out that the rise of each managerial ideology had to do with backing by particular interest groups. Second, differently from conventional histories, where thinking and practice have been treated as intertwined, Barley and Kunda's (1992) history was confined to the ideational level, not addressing whether ideas were related to actual practices. Third, their work also involved an attempt to develop a general theory from history (see Kipping and Üsdiken 2014; Chapters 8 and 9, this volume). The central theoretical proposition they derived was that the oscillation between normative and rational forms of control rested on the dualism in Western—and thus, Anglo-American—culture about achieving social order through *Gemeinschaft* or *Gesellschaft*, i.e. "organic" or "mechanistic" solidarity (Barley and Kunda 1992: 385–386).

Barley and Kunda (1992) had conjectured that their theory would predict the surge of another rational rhetoric together with an economic upswing. Some empirical support to this prediction was provided by Abrahamson (1997: 524) whose findings suggested that, with management notions such as downsizing and reengineering on the rise in the 1990s, a new rational rhetoric that he called "flexible rationalism" could be emerging. Also challenging Barley and Kunda's (1992) theorizing, Abrahamson (1997) tested their pendulum thesis against what he called "performance-gap" theory, which posited that the prevalence of management rhetorics will be associated with the extent they promised to deal with issues of labor turnover and union activity across businesses. Abrahamson's (1997) empirical findings suggested that the pendulum and performance-gap theories were complementary. The pendulum thesis accounted for the emergence of new management rhetorics, whereas performance-gap theory was associated with their prevalence during and beyond the periods in which they emerged.

The last in this line of attempts to theorize US management history was a study by Bodrožić and Adler (2018). Contrary to similar earlier studies, these authors explicitly justified their focus on the US, stating that the country "was increasingly central in the world economy over the past two centuries and served as the main locus of innovation in management models for most of the period". As this quote shows, their preferred term was "management models", which they defined as "a distinct body of ideas that offers organizational managers precepts for how best to fulfill their technical and social tasks" (Bodrožić and Adler 2018: 86). Different from Barley and Kunda (1992), Bodrožić and Adler's (2018: 106) "neo-Schumpeterian theory" placed long waves of consecutive "technological revolutions" (railroads and steam power, steel and electrical power, automobile and oil, computers and telecommunication) at the core of their explanatory effort. The problems that these technological revolutions generated for management, they argued, led to organizational innovations or new "paradigms", namely, the professionally managed firm, the factory, the corporation and the network.

"Nested" within the changes brought about by the emergence of these different organizational paradigms were two cycles of model development, a primary one that arose from the new paradigm and a secondary "balancing cycle" that followed as a response to the problems generated by the implementation of the former. Human relations, for example, served as a balancing cycle for scientific management, which arose as the factory was ushered in by the steel and electrical power revolution. So was quality management for the strategy and structure model that developed with the advent of the corporation paradigm, which resulted from the automobile and oil revolution (Bodrožić and Adler 2018: 92–93). Thus, differently from the pendulum thesis which saw alternations in management ideologies as manifestations of Western cultural dualism, for Bodrožić and Adler (2018: 106–107), management models should be regarded as "poles of a dialectical contradiction": the "second pole in the pair opposes the first but also presupposes it, and the two do not simply oscillate as a pendulum but are eventually synthesized before a new technological revolution renders that synthesis obsolete".

While departing from the linear stage models of evolution in the classic view, Barley and Kunda (1992) as well as Bodrožić and Adler (2018) ultimately retained a functionalist and efficiency-oriented perspective by attributing changes in the identified management discourses and models to, respectively, Kondratieff cycles and technological revolutions. The latter did accord a role to agency in the creation and diffusion of management models, though with little detail regarding the part that competing—or colluding—interests play in these processes.

. . . And So Does Context: "Politicizing" the History of Management Thought in the US

A separate stream of revisionist literature, including contributions both from within and, increasingly, outside the US, adopted a critical orientation toward the historiography of management thought in the US. This literature was mainly concerned with how the social and political context and/or political motivations may have shaped the development of particular management ideas and practices, as well as the ways in which histories of management were constructed. These authors namely exposed and criticized the inherent functionalism in most of the classic histories—and their accompanying portrayal of management as a politically neutral activity. They made greater reference to ideology and how it served a legitimatizing function for management. Implicit universalism was a subject of critique too, given the typical neglect of contexts in the emergence and popularization of management ideas. A particular focus of attention were the omissions in management historiography and their implications for present-day understandings. Others framed the development of management ideas or, rather, ideologies as struggles between the "left" and the "right" of the political spectrum. This was accompanied in some cases by calls for forging links with the CMS literature (e.g. Bruce and Nyland 2011; see also Booth and Rowlinson 2006).

Based on an examination of articles published in three prominent American engineering magazines in 1879–1932 Shenhav (1995: 557), for example, suggested that the emergence and development of the "systematization" discourse (see Chapters 5 and 6, this volume) was a "product of professional, cultural and political forces" and "not necessarily of functional and economic needs". The ascendancy of this discourse rested on the professionalization struggles of mechanical engineers who also benefited from the political context of the Progressive Era in the US (1900–1917) and succeeded in promoting systematization as a solution to industrial strife. Shenhav (1995: 581) also made the important point that understanding the growth of management ideas required studying the "idiosyncratic factors that were at work in a particular society in the specific period".

Ruef and Harness (2009) also pointed to a lack of attention to context in classic histories due to the search for affinity between ancient practices and present-day management. Examining the period of rising polarization around slavery in the US (1831–1861) and the late stages of the Roman Republic (circa second century BC to first century AD), they argued that management ideologies arose together with practical aspects (cf. Bendix 1956) as responses to the legitimacy crises that elites were facing in each of these agrarian societies. What we learn from these cases is that, unlike what has been told in conventional historiography, even in these slavery-bound agrarian settings "management" needed to be legitimized in the face of opposition and resistance. Moreover, according to Ruef and Harness (2009: 604) the two examples indicated a need to "confront the conceptual historicism surrounding 'management' and the risk of interpreting it anachronistically". Slavery had already been taken up by Cooke (2003), though with the purpose of revealing its omission—or in his terms "denial"—in management historiography. He saw "management" in slave plantations in that the overseers were like "salaried managers" and their practices were not much different from what has been labeled scientific or classical management. The exclusion of antebellum slavery from US management history, Cooke (2003: 1896) argued, contributed to the social legitimation of management by avoiding "associations with oppression and exploitation".

Echoing Cooke (2003), Frenkel and Shenhav (2006) drew upon post-colonial theories, arguing that management had its roots in the administration of Western colonies—roots which were, however edited out of its historiography. As a case in point they referred to the omission of the bureaucratic model for colonial administration devised and later published by Lord Cromer—the British consul general who governed Egypt between 1883 and 1907. Likewise, Elton Mayo's racial and ethnocentric references never got mentioned in later writings on human relations. For Frenkel and Shenhav (2006: 859) such omissions served, on the one hand, to "purify" the Western management canon and, on the other, for the ideas that were included such as Mayo's human relations, to hide the distinctions that existed between the colonizers and the colonized. Already earlier, Cooke (1999) had pointed to similar omissions in the post–World War II management literature, which, he suggested, had edited out ideas about organizational change and development originating from the political "left". Similarly, Cooke, Mills and Kelley (2005) argued with respect to action research in the Cold War context that the establishment of its technicist managerial version had been facilitated rather than the alternative formulation oriented toward social issues and change (Cooke 2006).

A major issue in this revisionist literature concerned the way both scientific management and human relations had been portrayed by the classic view, but also by the proponents of labor process theory. Thus, with respect to scientific management, for Nyland and Heenan (2005: 1371) "that a liberal left tradition had been a significant influence in management thought and debate through the interwar years was all but eradicated from the discipline's history by the 1960s". That this happened, they argued, had to do with the earlier focus on the hostility between scientific management and labor that portrayed Taylorism as authoritarian. Hence, the later endeavors on the part of the Taylor Society, founded in 1912 by Taylor's followers, toward the democratization of management, which eventually failed however, had been ignored. For Nyland and Heenan (2005), not unlike Shenhav (1995), this neglect was associated with the broad tendency to view management activity and knowledge about management as devoid of the political context. More in general, Nyland and his colleagues challenged what they referred to as the "demonization" of Taylor and scientific management (Nyland 1996; Nyland and Bruce 2012). They portrayed Taylorism as a broad organizational reform program, which not only entailed replacing rule-of-thumb methods by science but also foresaw cooperation between management and labor—even more so in the later part of Taylor's life (see, e.g. Nyland 1996: 986). And they saw relations between scientific management and labor unions develop from outright hostility to softening and then mutual appreciation after 1919 (e.g. Nyland 1996: 989). From then until the 1950s, the Taylor Society played a prominent role in this rapprochement, as it "moved to the left of the political spectrum" (Nyland 1996: 1013) and aimed to advance "a program of progressive reform within and beyond the workplace" (Nyland, Bruce and Burns 2014: 1150), which brought it to advocate workplace and societal-level codetermination similar to the International Labor Organization (ILO).

Regarding the Hawthorne studies and the resulting human relations ideas, O'Connor (1999a) took an explicitly political view, showing how ideologies and interests were at play (see Gillespie 1991 for an earlier study along similar lines). More specifically, she demonstrated how a network of actors coalesced around the promotion of this approach and its techniques as a panacea to problems of industrial strife. These actors included the Harvard Business School (HBS); business leaders, with John D. Rockefeller Jr. as the most prominent member; and Elton Mayo, the researcher and spokesperson for the Hawthorne studies. Thus, Rockefeller generously funded Mayo and his research, which in turn helped HBS to develop its legitimacy not only as a training ground for the managerial elite but also as the "savior of capitalism". And human relations legitimized management's authority over labor and appealed to business executives concerned by the expansion of what were seen as radical, socialist orientations among workers. As O'Connor (1999a: 129) put it, "Mayo convinced business leaders that his agenda would solve their worries, if not despair, about labor strife and about the viability of the U.S. economic and political order amid the shocks of economic depression, industrial conflict, and alternative political ideologies". According to O'Connor (1999a), Mayo succeeded because he was offering an apolitical solution to what were essentially political problems. He provided managers with a philosophy and tools that were detached from material conditions and could help deal with the vagaries of worker psychology and behavior by changing their attitudes, making them happy and cultivating a better fit with the workplace—ideas that served as the building blocks for present-day organizational behavior and human resource management (O'Connor 1999b).

Hassard (2012) added to the revisionist literature on human relations by examining the effects of the political and the social context of the Hawthorne studies, focusing in particular on the struggles against unionization, the Hawthorne plant and its owner, Western Electric—influences not sufficiently taken into account so far (cf. Gillespie 1991). Following others (e.g. Bruce 2006), Hassard (2012) also questioned the popular attributions of the emergence of the concern with the human factor to the Hawthorne studies and Elton Mayo, pointing to practices geared toward guarding worker well-being at Western Electric before the start of the research at Hawthorne—practices that exemplified welfare capitalism and paternalism as earlier responses to escalating industrial conflict and as ways to prevent unionization.

Building on their earlier work and O'Connor (1999a, 1999b), Bruce and Nyland entered this debate by arguing that the reasons why Taylor and his followers were "demonized", while Elton Mayo was "deified", were inherently political (Bruce and Nyland 2011; Nyland and Bruce 2012; Bruce and Nyland 2017). While criticizing O'Connor (1999b) for not recognizing the "democratic" element in scientific management, they agreed with her view that the human relations approach was posed as a humane remedy for the authoritarianism and economic basis of scientific management (Nyland and Bruce 2012). And like O'Connor (1999a) they contended that what human relations actually proposed was control through governing the minds and emotions of workers, disregarding issues such as pay and working conditions (Bruce and Nyland 2011: 386). Workers were presented as irrational and facing problems of psychological and social adjustment. So, what Mayo offered to the conservative business community was a set of ideas and practices that suited their interests, as it "enabled them to deny that workers should become active participants in workplace decision-making and in wider society" (p. 384). That human relations gained popularity and became established in its purportedly humanistic form had to do with the allegiances and support that Mayo was able to muster. In addition, as O'Connor (1999a) also argued, it had to do with the political context involving both fears of communist threats and of worker radicalism as well as attempts on the part of business to regain their prerogative to manage following the New Deal era. The eventual outcome was that by the 1960s the industrial democracy stance of the liberal wing of the Taylor Society was overcome by Mayo's human relations.

These revisionist histories were largely ignored by the recent classic literature. O'Connor (1999a, 1999b), for example, is not referenced either in Witzel's (2012) or Wren and Bedeian's (2018) books. Responses to the revisionist critique were also few and far between and tended to focus on details. For example, regarding claims that Mayo was not a central figure in the development of the Hawthorne studies, Smith (1998) argued that he was both pivotal and not predominantly oriented toward management interests.

'Twas the Total Opposite, Actually: Counter-Histories

There is another, more radical though ultimately marginal, challenge to both the classical and the critical views on management history, outlined in the previous chapters and earlier, which are characterized by document-based empirical research and the ambition to reveal the past in an objective manner. In contrast, these "counter-historical" approaches, as they are referred to here, view history as socially constructed and inherently subjective. While united in their opposition to what they call "realist" or "factual" history, the literature that can be classified as counter-history has developed in two different directions, respectively, under the influence of Foucault's postmodernism and Latour's actor–network theory (ANT)—though at times with some overlaps.

Cue in Foucault: Archaeologies and Genealogies

Critics have characterized Foucault as being "anti-historical" or "anti-historian" and questioned whether his "historical" writing can be considered history (see Rowlinson and Carter 2002: 531–535 for a detailed critique). Neither has history featured much in the Foucauldian literature in organization studies (Carter, McKinlay and Rowlinson 2002). Indeed, even his followers have observed that the importance of history for Foucault originates "not from an interest in the past, but from a deep commitment to understand the present" (Burrell 1988: 225) or that "his analyses were histories of the present" (Jacques 1996: 14). Nevertheless, for his proponents, Foucault was a "critical historian" taking a "counter-historical" position (Cummings and Bridgman 2011: 78). His view of history was that it was not "objective" and that it served to legitimize the "current establishment" (Cummings, Bridgman and Brown 2016: 38–41). This anti- or counter-historical stance was the basis of Foucault's "archeological" and "genealogical" (or archeo-genealogy) methods. Cummings and Bridgman (2011: 80) contended that Foucault's archeology "encourages us to identify reasons why different views emerge as truthful in different ages". For Foucault, the emergence of such truths had to do with the modes of thought or episteme and discourses prevalent in particular historical periods over a broad range of domains, imposing rules from which there was no possibility of breaking away (Burrell 1988). In genealogy, identified as a later stage in Foucault's work (Burrell 1988), history was deemed a "series of interpretations" that became received as truths not due to an overriding episteme, but rather due to interests and power relations at play, which at once shut down other possibilities of learning (Cummings and Bridgman 2011: 80).

The first claim to a Foucauldian archeo-genealogical—or rather archeological—approach to the history of management and management thought was by Jacques (1996). His book is posited as one on the history of the employee, though it is also about management. Like most of what has been reviewed previously, Jacques's focus is on the US, though he does explicitly acknowledge that US-specific history has often been told as if it were universally valid. Indeed, one of the main claims in the book is that what is currently put forth as management knowledge or research has been framed in ways that are based on American values. That Jacques (1996) sees this as a problem has much to do with his view that these American values are of an industrial society. They would not fit into the postindustrial period and thus are not likely to be of use to anyone in the upcoming era. Jacques (1996: 9, 19) positioned his work as an alternative to both "managerialist", i.e. classic, and "critical" histories. The "discursive perspective" adopted in the book follows from Foucault's archaeo-genealogical approach and aims to unravel the development of knowledge about organizations. Like Foucault, Jacques (1996: ix) stated at the outset that his interest was not really in the past, but rather "to better understand the post-industrial future into which most-industrialized countries are now heading". So, the history of the employee can serve as "a prologue to developing knowledge about the post-industrial worker" (Jacques 1996: 11).

Jacques (1996) started his history with "excavations" that go back to the period from the late eighteenth to the latter part of the nineteenth century. This period, which he labeled "Federalist reality", marked the "pre-history" of management—and the employee—in the US and was structured around a "frontier vision" and "personal community relationships" (pp. 22–26). Like Foucault's episteme, the "common sense" or the discourse of the period was epitomized by progress, action orientation, belief in the capacities of the average person and in the lack of conflict between individual interests and the social good (pp. 39–40). The Federalist social order was disrupted by the rise of big business and heightened levels of industrial strife in the last decades of the nineteenth century. A new industrial reality and "common sense" emerged, as did the construction of the employee and, as a nonlabor form of the latter, the manager, buttressed by the discourse of objectivity and professionalism associated with science and university education. In Jacques's view, this new era in the US corresponded to Foucault's description of the arrival of industrial modernity in Europe or, again in Foucault's terms, the "disciplinary society" (pp. 97–99). The new "common sense" entailed "classification", "quantification" and "rationalization" (pp. 99–110). Jacques then went on to develop his main argument that this "common sense", tainted by Federalist cultural values, has persisted to the present day.

Thus, in his view, management knowledge has not been evolving over time, and much of what has been presented as new more recently already existed in similar ways at the turn or the initial decades of the twentieth century (pp. 156–157). The contribution of a Foucauldian historical perspective then, Jacques claimed, was to provide an awareness of the historical context and the roots of a pervading common sense, so that new possibilities could be considered in the move to a postindustrial era.

Shenhav (1999: 19), whose book was discussed earlier, also posited that he was taking a genealogical approach. For Shenhav, too, his history of management stood in opposition to both evolutionary and neo-Marxist views. His claim to a genealogical approach was based on the aim to take "ideas and practices back in time to their original breeding ground, to isolate their meanings and to search for existing alternatives and objecting views" (Shenhav 1999: 7). In line with this aim he took issue with some of the earlier historical observations on American management, such as when the so-called "managerial revolution" had taken place, as well as arguing that what passes as management thought or theory has been socially constructed and reflected the ideologies of its proponents. For him, the managerial revolution dated back to the late nineteenth and early twentieth centuries (1879–1932). It emerged as a professional project of mechanical engineers capitalizing on the political ideologies prevalent in the US within this period. Drawing also upon actor-network theory (see later), he proposed that this could be achieved because mechanical engineers were able to "translate" the ideas of science, systematization and standardization from the technical to the organizational world. What came out of this "translation" was the "social construction of organizations and labor as 'engineerable'" (p. 72). These endeavors were not uncontested, however, since what the engineers were proposing meant a shift of power from manufacturers to engineers, and the contribution of systematization to greater profits was not always clear. This was also when the idea of management rationality or efficiency—today seen as natural—was formulated. Its construction was "conflictual, debated and circular", creating opposition by manufacturers as well as unions and generating controversy among groups of engineers (p. 58). While offered as an objective and neutral concept and posited as serving the public interest, rationality reflected the ideologies of its advocates in their struggles against owners and in controlling labor unrest. Despite contestation, endeavors on the part of engineers did culminate in a distinction between ownership and management, with the latter and its systems cast as apolitical and both a "profession" and a "science".

Cummings and his colleagues (e.g. Cummings and Bridgman 2011; Cummings et al. 2016) followed in the footsteps of Foucault in a more purist fashion. They drew upon the last phase in Foucault's work, dubbed "interpretive analytics", which sought to combine archeology and genealogy. A major theme in this approach has been that emergent scientific fields tend to establish themselves on a history that rests on some great figure. In revisiting the manner in which Weber has been typically included in management textbooks, for example, Cummings and Bridgman (2011) began by pointing to how his contribution has been dated to 1947—the year Talcott Parsons's translation was published—and how he has been placed among the so-called classical organization "theorists" (see also Chapters 5 and 6, this volume). They then proceed to Foucault's archeology, suggesting that this can explain why Weber has been presented as an advocate of bureaucracy "with reference to the specific set of views and values, or episteme, that emerged in the United States in the middle of the 20th century" (Cummings and Bridgman 2011: 83). In an effort to demonstrate Foucault's approach in full, the genealogical part in the article traced the changes that have been made in descriptions of Weber's views over the nine editions (between 1993 and 2008) of a particular management textbook. Cummings and Bridgman's (2011) proclaimed purpose was to show how particular interpretations, such as that of Parsons in this case, may persist. Yet this does not necessarily mean, according to Cummings and his colleagues, that interpretations are fixed. They can change with alterations in the context and political concerns. What the particular exercise by the authors demonstrated however, was continuity. The differences that could be identified were, as the authors also admit, "subtle". Nevertheless, they were convinced that despite being subtle there was a "significant development of the historical narrative to reflect contemporary concerns" (Cummings and Bridgman 2011: 88).

Likewise, Cummings et al. (2016) wanted to show that the "unfreeze-change-refreeze" model widely attributed to Lewin in the change management literature was a posthumous construction. Their claim was that this model was not an important part of Lewin's writings, but was rather made to be foundational mainly after 1980 by "others' repackaging and marketing" (Cummings et al. 2016: 35). The genealogical part of the study traced the ways in which Lewin was referenced initially in the 1950s and the 1960s and later from the 1980s onwards. Archeology involved the identification of the conditions in the 1980s, which influenced the framing of the "unfreeze-change-refreeze" model as the basis of change management, such as the search for competitive differentiation by both US industry and management consulting firms, as well as relevance concerns by academics. The demise of the organizational development approach also helped. The eventual outcome, according to Cummings et al. (2016), was a questionable foundation for change management.

For Cummings and his colleagues, resorting to Foucault and offering these counter-histories was to serve a more prominent aim, namely, to include this kind of history in management education, which, in their opinion, would help develop a critical attitude toward history and historiography. Such an approach, they believed, should help history play another important role by encouraging prospective practitioners to be more creative and envision other possibilities for the future of management. The same view is repeated in what Cummings and colleagues (2017) presented as *A New History of Management*—a book drawing upon their former writings as well as publications by others (e.g. Hassard 2012). Their message for academic studies of management history is that following Foucault's paths to counter-history should open up the possibilities to be freed from the ways that history has been conventionally told and received and, thus, to be able to "think differently" (Cummings et al. 2017: 38).

Cue in Latour: ANTi-History

Latour's actor-network theory (ANT) has been invoked to develop another form of counter-history that has been dubbed "ANTi-History" (Durepos and Mills 2012). The foremost concern of this approach is to take issue with the ways that historical work is carried out and to lay claim to an alternative way of doing history. Its proponents accept that the past has existed. Yet, the argument goes, it cannot be captured as it has actually been lived. So, what we have as history are only subjective representations, which are "highly contingent, fragile, political and fluid" (Durepos, Mills and Weatherbee 2012: 270). Critique is mounted against the truth and accuracy claims of "modernist" or "realist" history, as well as the "relativist" or "plural" histories of the postmodernists. Proposed instead is a third alternative of doing history, called "relationalism". Talking about the past in relational terms means looking at the "politics" in the construction of the "representations of the past", as actors form networks by bringing in and altering other actors. It is from these relations that distinct and shared accounts of the past are produced (p. 271). Relationalism also enables revealing the "multiplicity"—understood as versions of one representation—in the way the past has been told and the relations between them by tracing the dispersion of "localized" accounts and "translations" through time and space without privileging any of these accounts over the others (p. 269).

The proponents of ANTi-History have a broad agenda, as they aim primarily to engage with the broader call for a "historic turn" in management and organization studies (see earlier and Chapter 3, this volume) and to link this form of history with the CMS literature (Durepos and Mills 2012). The past of management thought and practice constitutes only one facet of their interests. What they have offered empirically in this respect has been confined to demonstrative examples to illustrate what their relationist approach involves. One such example has been based on the translation and later treatment of Weber's work—like in some of the writings mentioned previously. Differently from those, however, their conclusion has been that "a 'Parsonian' Weber cannot be any less, nor any more, 'truly' Weberian than a 'Bendixian' [. . .], 'Cleggian' [. . .] or

'Shenhavian' [. . .] version" (Mills, Weatherbee and Durepos 2014: 237). The search for an accurate representation is, according to these authors, a futile exercise.

Other Worlds: Expanding the Critical Perspective Geographically

As noted throughout the previous chapters, much of the literature in management history and the history of management thought focused almost exclusively on the US case. And even if the origins of some of the ideas outside the US were acknowledged, it was their influence on the US that was studied. This remains largely true for the critical views presented in this chapter so far—even if the counter-histories sought their inspiration from French scholars. However, within the critical perspective there are studies that took a more international and comparative approach—though almost always anchored to the US. Moreover, and possibly more consequentially, there is now a new journal, based in the UK, which might help institutionalize and internationalize a more critical research agenda.

Moving Beyond the US: Comparative and Diffusion Studies

A pioneer of comparative studies going beyond—and even excluding— the US was Robert R. Locke, starting in the 1980s. His first book offered an examination of the academic business literature and higher education in business and engineering from the late nineteenth century until World War II with a focus mainly on Germany, together with some comparison to France and Great Britain (Locke 1984). Particularly notable about this book was its coverage of "business economics" (*Betriebswirtschafts-lehre*—BWL) that had developed in Germany as an academic and educational specialty after the turn of the century (see also Chapter 2, this volume). The BWL tradition had been entirely ignored in US-based histories of management thought, other than a brief mention in Witzel's (2012) recent book. Following Locke (1984), there have been additional studies on the pre–World War II diffusion of BWL to other countries, such as the one by Üsdiken, Kieser and Kjaer (2004), who examined the influence of the German BWL in Denmark and Turkey. In his second book, Locke (1989) did study the US and the scientization of management studies there after World War II—what he called the "new paradigm"—but focused primarily on the diffusion of the US business school model to Germany, France and Great Britain. Subsequently, a considerable literature has examined the American influence on the development of management education elsewhere (e.g. as an early example, Amdam 1996), though some of these studies have also considered the impact of Germany as a role model during the first half of the twentieth-century years (see, e.g. the various country cases in Engwall and Zamagni 1998).

A comparative study more germane to the history of management was Mauro F. Guillén's (1994) book on the development of three management "models" in the US (scientific management, human relations and the "structural approach" associated mainly with forms of organizing the enterprise) and their reception in Germany, Spain and Great Britain. Like Bendix (1956) and others, Guillén (1994: 3) regarded management "models" or "paradigms" as including both ideological and technical elements, the former referring to "rationalizations of the system of hierarchical authority in the firm". The study considered the reception and the spread of ideologies and techniques separately, distinguishing also between the roles played by management "intellectuals", an elite national group of individuals who generated and received the models, and the large body of management "practitioners" who used the techniques.

Guillén's (1994) book was an early exemplar of challenges to classic histories. First, like other critical authors, he questioned the economistic and technological basis of evolution in the classic accounts, which attributed the development of management thinking to the search for more efficient ways of responding to changing conditions. The second, and not unrelated, challenge was to the universalism of these approaches, which assumed this pattern to be similar in different societal contexts. Thus, Guillén's (1994: xi) main argument was that the adoption of management models could not be accounted for only by the "scientific value of the theories supporting them" or "purely economic and technological factors". Institutional conditions, which differed across countries, were at play too. They included the mentalities of the business elite, the influence of professional groups, the role and actions of the state and the attitudes of labor (p. 21). As these institutional conditions differed across countries, their relative influence on the timing, sequencing and extent of adoption of the three models varied. In the US, for example, where early industrialization made the country conducive to the emergence of new management models, their development was primarily driven by the activities of professional groups, starting with engineers and efficiency experts, followed by psychologists and sociologists promoting human relations and then academics as well as management consultants championing ideas about how large businesses should be organized.

For Guillén (1994), the manner in which the models were patterned and the extent of their adoption in the three importer countries depended mainly on institutional factors such as the involvement of the state and the dominant mentalities of the business elite. In Germany, for instance, the reception that scientific management, or rather its adaptation as "rationalization", enjoyed during the interwar years had to do with the role model that the state provided as well as the Protestantism and modernist orientations of the business elite. In Spain, by contrast, the reception of scientific management was meager until World War II, while human relations became widely endorsed, though largely in ideological terms and only after the early 1950s. This pattern was due to sanctioning by the state and the influence of the Catholic social doctrine on business mentality. Great Britain had an early trajectory somewhat similar to Spain, but diverged with the adoption of the structural approach after the 1960s, where it resembled the US and Germany. Overall, while recognizing the leading role of the US, Guillén (1994) did not make much of the US influence in shaping the post–World War II patterns in the three countries. By contrast, a significant subsequent literature examining the diffusion of US productivity, corporate, industrial relations and technological models to Europe and Japan after World War II identified broad processes of "Americanization", while also recognizing adaptation and even resistance by the multiple actors involved (e.g. Djelic 1998; Kipping and Bjarnar 1998; Zeitlin and Herrigel 2000; see also Chapter 12, this volume).

Additional studies within the critical perspective have examined the diffusion of specific management ideas to other countries, considering in particular the role of varying institutional factors as well as "carriers" in facilitating or hindering such transfer processes. Thus, with respect to scientific management Kipping (1997) examined the adoption of Taylorist methods in Britain, Germany and France during the interwar years and the immediate aftermath of World War II. He showed that the more pronounced reception of scientific management in Germany relative to the other two countries had to do with the channels provided by national-level institutional frameworks, which were developed with government backing. And for the entry of Taylorism into the management discourse in China and Japan during the interwar years, Morgan (2006) and Vaszkun and Tsutsui (2012), respectively, pointed to the role of students sent for education to the US, apparently with encouragement by Taylor himself, and of various business associations. For the Israeli case, Kalev, Shenhav and De Vries (2008) singled out the recently founded State of Israel as having a major role in the establishment of scientific management–based "joint productivity councils" during the 1950s, showing how state actors drove the spread of this management model by framing it in nationalistic terms. Their study is also an example for using a historical case to compare and extend theory (see Chapters 8 and 9, this volume).

There has also been some work on the spread of the US human relations model. For Israel, Frenkel (2005) showed that scientific management and human relations were brought to the country co-terminously in the 1950s. Within a context of large-scale US aid, the state, the national labor union and private employers were identified as the major actors partaking in the transfer of these models. Drawing upon ANT, her central argument was that the politics of the interrelations among these actors resulted in a "translation" of these models both in the meanings attributed to them and in the ways that they were implemented (see also Chapter 12, this volume).

Better to Be Different? Institutionalizing a Critical and International Perspective

Publishing articles with a critical view on the history of management and management thought received a boost with the establishment of a new journal, *Management & Organizational History* (MOH), in 2006. MOH was conceived and based in Britain (Cummings et al. 2017: 13). Its co-promoters and two of its first editors, Charles Booth and Michael Rowlinson, aimed to link the journal with what they viewed as an emergent "historic turn" (see Chapter 3, this volume). The range of topics to be published in this journal was meant to be broad, since the historic turn called for a reorientation that would primarily involve engagement with the predominantly ahistorical nature of theorizing on management and organizations (Booth and Rowlinson 2006; see also Clark and Rowlinson 2004; Üsdiken and Kieser 2004). In addition, it was meant to entail addressing questions of historical methods and the philosophy and theory of history. As indicated by the name of the journal, "organizational history" was proposed as a new sub-discipline distinct from business history (see also Chapter 3, this volume). Other topics that could benefit from a historical turn and presumably find space in the pages of the journal were corporate culture, business ethics and corporate social responsibility (Booth and Rowlinson 2006).

Thus, unlike the *Journal of Management History*, which was relaunched that same year after having originally been founded in 1995 (see Chapter 6, this volume), MOH was not meant to address the inability of management historians to publish in the mainstream management journals, but to exploit opportunities arising from what appeared like a growing interest in historical perspectives and approaches among many management scholars, enticing them both as readers and authors. To what extent these ambitions have been and continue to be fulfilled remains an open question. Recent developments permit some doubt. Thus, in 2013, the original publisher SAGE, whose interests are predominantly in management, sold the journal to Taylor & Francis, which also publishes the journal *Business History*. And the current MOH editor is affiliated with the business history community rather than with management or even management history—though the ambition seems to be to maintain an openness for a variety of authors and topics as well as a broad appeal.

Whatever their respective futures, the coexistence of JMH and MOH since 2006 reflects the divergence that unfolded over the past few decades in studying the history of management and management thought. On one side, the classic view of management history—variously referred to by the critics as "mainstream" or "orthodox"—that had taken shape since the late 1960s largely within the American academic environment continued very much in the same way, incorporating only limited changes (see Chapter 6, this volume). On the opposite side, the revisionist literature began to expand since the 1990s and took a distinctly critical position vis-à-vis the established historiography. Adding further to this divergence was the emergence of "counter-histories" that were radically opposed to the view of history as objective knowledge. These alternative approaches originated mainly from outside the US and, as such, they were also a part of a growing internationalization of the literature on management history both with respect to contributors and the settings that were studied. The increasing contribution by authors based outside the US in both journals is shown in Table 7.1, though in JMH US-based authors still account for about half of all articles since 2006—nevertheless down from three-quarters or more before. In MOH American authorship has always been rather low. And even when combining authors from the US and UK, they make up only about half the contributions.

Table 7.1 Authorship by country of affiliation in the *Journal of Management History* (JMH) and *Management & Organizational History* (MOH)[a,b]

	JMH 1995– 2005	Share in total	JMH 2006– 2017	Share in total	MOH 2006– 2017	Share in total
United States	145.00	74.7%	154.18	53.0%	34.33	14.0%
United Kingdom	16.00	8.3%	28.58	9.9%	88.92	36.1%
Canada	10.83	5.6%	19.08	6.6%	23.58	9.6%
Australia	10.00	5.2%	26.42	9.1%	7.00	2.9%
Israel	3.00		1.00		1.00	
New Zealand	2.00		6.50		2.00	
Netherlands	2.00		5.00		11.17	
Finland	1.00		3.50		15.75	
Sweden	1.00		2.75		7.42	
Japan	1.00		1.00			
Germany	0.50		2.33		5.00	
South Korea	0.33		0.67			
Brazil	0.33				3.00	
France			6.50		7.08	
Lebanon			3.75			
Italy			3.50		6.08	
Switzerland			3.00		1.00	
India			2.50			
Singapore			2.50			
Denmark			2.00		12.83	
Ireland			2.00		3.33	
Spain			2.00		1.00	
Portugal			1.00		2.67	
Estonia			1.00			
Greece			1.00			
Mexico			1.00			
Saudi Arabia			1.00			

(*Continued*)

Table 7.1 (Continued)

	JMH 1995–2005	Share in total	JMH 2006–2017	Share in total	MOH 2006–2017	Share in total
UAE			1.00			
China			0.73			
Kuwait			0.67			
Norway			0.50		3.00	
Hong Kong			0.50			
Hungary			0.50			
Russia			0.50			
Malaysia			0.33			
South Africa			0.25		2.00	
Sri Lanka			0.25			
Belgium					2.00	
Turkey					1.33	
Argentina					1.00	
Austria					1.00	
Cyprus					1.00	
Nigeria					1.00	
Morocco					0.50	

a Only articles were considered. Countries were assigned a score of 1 in the case of single-authored articles or when multiple authors were all from the same country. If multiple authors of an article were from different countries, the score of 1 was partitioned according to the share of authors from each country. In the case of double appointments, the affiliation listed first was considered.

b For the period 2001–2005 when JMH was incorporated into *Management Decision* (see Chapter 5, this volume) articles that were included were those that had been designated as (a) "Focus on Management History" (in 2001), (b) "Journal of Management History" (2002–2005) and (c) in one case as part of a special issue on "Management History". As the journal did not appear to be always consistent in these designations, articles that had among their keywords "management history" or "management and history" were also included.

Conclusion

Over the past three decades, there has been a considerable growth of publications that adopt a more or less critical view when researching the history of management and management thought. Taking the coexistence of two journals, JMH and MOH, as a simple indicator, both the classic and the critical perspective are now equally well-established. Again, drawing on the journals as proxies, the authors for the latter tend to be more international. Also, a number of the different approaches within the critical perspective had their origins outside the US, though still in Anglo-Saxon countries, i.e. the UK and Canada. Moreover, in their intellectual foundations, the counter-histories summarized previously draw on two well-known French scholars, Foucault and Latour. Nevertheless, in their thematic focus, the vast majority of the critical literature remains anchored to the US—though it has added more comparative research and an extensive literature examining the diffusion of US management ideas in different national and institutional contexts, as well as the associated difficulties.

Compared to the survival mode of the management historians tethered to the classic view (Chapter 6, this volume), there has clearly been an ambition among many of those laboring in the critical perspective to have their historical approaches taken more seriously within mainstream management research or, even more ambitiously, to contribute to a "historic turn" within that mainstream (see also Chapter 3, this volume). On the whole, that ambition has not been realized, some exceptions notwithstanding, most of which seem to have come from mainstream scholars taking a detour into history. This, one could contend in line with the overall argument in this book, has to do with the difficulties inherent in combining the different underlying conceptions of "science" and "theory" in history and management. The overview in this chapter has pointed to some opportunities, which did not really come to fruition. One was cut short prematurely: labor process theory; it quickly veered away from its origins in management history and never even got close in its CMS incarnation—despite repeated calls addressed specifically at that audience. The other drew on theorists that have by and large remained outside the mainstream of both history and management research, Foucault and Latour, and—for those drawing on the latter—have yet to demonstrate their empirical validity. In this respect, it might be worthwhile comparing the success that Latourian approaches have had in accounting research as well as science and technology studies (STS), which is, however, beyond the scope of this book.

Overall, therefore, the history of management and management thought has remained on the margins of management and organization studies—decidedly so for its classic variety and only a bit less for its critical perspective. But this does not mean that "history", in the broad conceptualization introduced earlier, has not played a role in management research. As the following Part III of the book will show, it actually has been an important and integral—though not always immediately and easily visible—component in many different research programs.

References

Abrahamson, E. (1997) "The emergence and prevalence of employee management rhetoric's: The effects of long waves, labor unions, and turnover, 1875 to 1992," *Academy of Management Journal*, 40(3): 491–533.

Alvesson, M. and Willmott, H. (eds) (1992) *Critical Management Studies*, London: Sage.

Amdam, R. P. (1996) *Management, Education and Competitiveness: Europe, Japan and the United States*, London: Routledge.

Barley, S. R. and Kunda, G. (1992) "Design and devotion: Surges of rational and normative ideologies of control in managerial discourse," *Administrative Science Quarterly*, 37(3): 363–399.

Bendix, R. (1956) *Work and Authority in Industry: Ideologies of Management in the Course of Industrialization*, New York: John Wiley and Sons.

Bodrožić, Z. and Adler, P. S. (2018) "The evolution of management models: A neo-Schumpeterian theory," *Administrative Science Quarterly*, 63(1): 85–129.

Booth, C. and Rowlinson, M. (2006) "Management and organizational history: Prospects," *Management and Organizational History*, 1(1): 5–30.

Braverman, H. (1974) *Labor and Monopoly Capital: The Degradation of Work in the Twentieth Century*, New York: Monthly Review Press.

Bruce, K. (2006) "Henry S. Dennison, Elton Mayo, and human relations historiography," *Management & Organizational History*, 1(2): 177–199.

Bruce, K. and Nyland, C. (2011) "Elton Mayo and the deification of human relations," *Organization Studies*, 32(3): 383–405.

Bruce, K. and Nyland, C. (2017) "Human relations," in A. Wilkinson, S. J. Armstrong and M. Lounsbury (eds), *The Oxford Handbook of Management*, Oxford: Oxford University Press, pp. 39–56.

Burrell, G. (1988) "Modernism, post modernism and organizational analysis 2: The contribution of Michel Foucault," *Organization Studies*, 9(2): 221–235.

Carter, C., McKinlay, A. and Rowlinson, M. (2002) "Introduction: Foucault, management and history," *Organization*, 9(4): 515–526.

Child, J. (1969) *British Management Thought: A Critical Analysis*, London: George, Allen & Unwin.

Clark, P. and Rowlinson, M. (2004) "The treatment of history in organization studies: Toward an 'historic turn'?" *Business History*, 46(3): 331–352.

Cooke, B. (1999) "Writing the left out of management theory: The historiography of the management of change," *Organization*, 6(1): 81–105.

Cooke, B. (2003) "The denial of slavery in management studies," *Journal of Management Studies*, 40(8): 1895–1918.

Cooke, B. (2006) "The Cold War origin of action research as managerialist cooptation," *Human Relations*, 59(5): 665–693.

Cooke, B., Mills, A. J. and Kelley, E. S. (2005) "Situating Maslow in Cold War America: A recontextualization of management theory," *Group & Organization Management*, 30(2): 129–152.

Cummings, S. and Bridgman, T. (2011) "The relevant past: Why the history of management should be critical for our future," *Academy of Management Learning & Education*, 10(1): 77–93.

Cummings, S., Bridgman, T. and Brown, K. G. (2016) "Unfreezing change as three steps: Rethinking Kurt Lewin's legacy for change management," *Human Relations*, 69(1): 33–60.

Cummings, S., Bridgman, T., Hassard, J. and Rowlinson, M. (2017) *A New History of Management*, Cambridge: Cambridge University Press.

Djelic, M.-L. (1998) *Exporting the American Model: The Post-War Transformation of European Business*, Oxford: Oxford University Press.

Durepos, G. and Mills, A. J. (2012) "Actor-network theory, ANTi-History and critical organizational historiography," *Organization*, 19(6): 703–721.

Durepos, G., Mills, A. J. and Weatherbee, T. G. (2012) "Theorizing the past: Realism, relativism, relationalism and the reassembly of Weber," *Management & Organizational History*, 7(3): 267–281.

Engwall, L. and Zamagni, V. (eds) (1998) *Management Education in a Historical Perspective*, Manchester: Manchester University Press.

Fournier, V. and Grey, C. (2000) "At the critical moment: Conditions and prospects for critical management studies," *Human Relations*, 53(1): 7–32.

Frenkel, M. (2005) "The politics of translation: How state-level political relations affect the cross-national travel of management ideas," *Organization*, 12(2): 275–301.

Frenkel, M. and Shenhav, Y. (2006) "From binarism back to hybridity: A postcolonial reading of management and organization studies," *Organization Studies*, 27(6): 855–876.

Gillespie, R. (1991) *Manufacturing Knowledge: A History of the Hawthorne Experiments*, Cambridge: Cambridge University Press.

Guillén, M. (1994) *Models of Management: Work, Authority and Organization in a Comparative Perspective*, Chicago, IL: The University of Chicago Press.

Hassard, J. (2012) "Rethinking the Hawthorne studies: The Western Electric research in its social, political and historical context," *Human Relations*, 65(11): 1431–1461.

ILPC, www.ilpc.org.uk/PreviousConferences.aspx (accessed 20 April 2020).

Jacques, R. (1996) *Manufacturing the Employee: Management Knowledge from the 19th to 21st Centuries*, London: Sage.

Kalev, A., Shenhav, Y. and De Vries, D. (2008) "The state, the labor process, and the diffusion of managerial models," *Administrative Science Quarterly*, 53(1): 1–28.

Kipping, M. (1997) "Consultancies, institutions and the diffusion of Taylorism in Britain, Germany and France, 1920s to 1950s," *Business History*, 39(4): 67–83.

Kipping, M. and Bjarnar, O. (eds) (1998) *Americanization of European Business: The Marshall Plan and the Transfer of US Management Models*, London: Routledge.

Kipping, M. and Üsdiken, B. (2014) "History in organization and management theory: More than meets the eye," *Academy of Management Annals*, 8(1): 535–588.

Littler, C. R. (1982) *The Development of the Labour Process in Capitalist Societies*, London: Heinemann.

Locke, R. R. (1984) *The End of the Practical Man: Entrepreneurship and Higher Education in Germany, France and Great Britain, 1880–1940*, Greenwich, CT: JAI Press.

Locke, R. R. (1989) *Management and Higher Education Since 1940: The Influence of America and Japan on West Germany, Great Britain and France*, Cambridge: Cambridge University Press.

Mills, A. J., Weatherbee, T. G. and Durepos, G. (2014) "Reassembling Weber to reveal the-past-as-history in management and organization studies," *Organization*, 21(2): 225–243.

Morgan, S. L. (2006) "Transfer of Taylorist ideas to China, 1910–1930s," *Journal of Management History*, 12(4): 408–424.

Nyland, C. (1996) "Taylorism, John R. Commons, and the Hoxie report," *Journal of Economic Issues*, 30(4): 985–1016.

Nyland, C. and Bruce, K. (2012) "Democracy or seduction? The demonization of scientific management and the deification of human relations," in

N. Lichtenstein and E. Tandy Shermer (eds), *The American Right and Labor: Politics, Ideology, and Imagination*, Philadelphia, PA: University of Pennsylvania Press, pp. 42–76.

Nyland, C., Bruce, K. and Burns, P. (2014) "Taylorism, the International Labour Organization, and the genesis and diffusion of codetermination," *Organization Studies*, 35(8): 1149–1169.

Nyland, C. and Heenan, T. (2005) "Mary van Kleeck, Taylorism and the control of management knowledge," *Management Decision*, 43(10): 1358–1374.

O'Connor, E. S. (1999a) "The politics of management thought: A case study of the Harvard Business School and the Human Relations School," *Academy of Management Review*, 24(1): 117–131.

O'Connor, E. S. (1999b) "Minding the workers: The meaning of 'human' and 'human relations' in Elton Mayo," *Organization*, 6(2): 223–246.

Özkazanç-Pan, B. and Donnelly, P. (2018) "5-year review," https://cms.aom.org/about-us/new-item5 (accessed 29 July 2019).

Rowlinson, M. and Carter, C. (2002) "Foucault and history in organization studies," *Organization*, 9(4): 527–547.

Ruef, M. and Harness, A. (2009) "Agrarian origins of management ideology: The Roman and antebellum cases," *Organization Studies*, 30(6): 589–607.

Shenhav, Y. (1995) "From chaos to systems: The engineering foundations of organization theory, 1879–1932," *Administrative Science Quarterly*, 40(4): 557–585.

Shenhav, Y. (1999) *Manufacturing Rationality: The Engineering Foundations of the Managerial Revolution*, Oxford: Oxford University Press.

Smith, C. (2008) www.ilpc.org.uk/Portals/56/ilpc-docs/ILPC-Background.pdf (accessed 27 July 2019).

Smith, J. H. (1998) "The enduring legacy of Elton Mayo," *Human Relations*, 51(3): 221–249.

Üsdiken, B. and Kieser, A. (2004) "Introduction: History in organization studies," *Business History*, 46(3): 321–330.

Üsdiken, B., Kieser, A. and Kjaer, P. (2004) "Academy, economy and polity: Betriebswirtschaftslehre in Germany, Denmark and Turkey," *Business History*, 46(3): 381–406.

Vaszkun, B. and Tsutsui, W. M. (2012) "A modern history of Japanese management thought," *Journal of Management History*, 18(4): 368–385.

Witzel, M. (2012) *A History of Management Thought*, London: Routledge.

Wren, D. A. and Bedeian, A. G. (2018) *The Evolution of Management Thought*, 7th edn, Hoboken, NJ: Wiley.

Zeitlin, J. and Herrigel, G. (eds) (2000) *Americanization and Its Limits: Reworking US Technology and Management in Post-War Europe and Japan*, Oxford: Oxford University Press.

Part III

8 History to Theory
Institutional Theories and Process Studies

Introduction

Examining a single or a few organizations was largely abandoned as research on management and organizations moved increasingly toward scientization, accompanied by a quest for—or some might say, obsession with—theorizing. While in initial stages of this scientistic trajectory the turn was toward cross-sectional comparative studies, later there was increasingly a move toward longitudinal research (see Chapter 2, this volume). Within this broad pattern there has been some early recognition of the importance of studying specific cases (Eisenhardt 1989)—with an ensuing debate about how many cases there should be and how they need to be analyzed (Dyer and Wilkins 1991; Eisenhardt 1991). There have also been repeated calls by some of the discipline's great for taking on "samples of one" (e.g. March, Sproull and Tamuz 1991) or "theory building from cases" (e.g. Eisenhardt and Graebner 2007)—combined with suggestions of how to do it. And "case study research" is generally included in methodology handbooks for management (see, e.g. Berg and Lune 2014, possibly as the most prominent) and has its own widely cited manual now in its sixth edition (Yin 2017). Indeed, indicative of a somewhat revived interest in and increasing legitimation of qualitative research more broadly, calls for case studies, including historical ones, have recently been appearing in the core journals of the discipline (e.g. Bansal, Smith and Vaara 2018).

Historical cases, however, have not figured prominently among those used to generate, elaborate, modify or question theories in management and organizational research—though Chandler's (1962) book on the emergence of the multidivisional form of organization in DuPont, General Motors, Standard Oil and Sears Roebuck during the interwar period has been included among the exemplary early studies in organization theory (Eisenhardt 1991; see also Chapter 2, this volume). This seems understandable, given the nature of historical data, which often tend to be spotty and definitely less consistent and coherent than those generated by interviews and observations for instance (see, e.g. Lipartito

2014)—making theorizing more challenging. To wit, those who have recently tried to publish work based on such sources in management journals—animated by that call for "more history"—will remember their frustration when receiving the following—or similar—comment from a reviewer: "great story, but what's your contribution to theory".

Nevertheless, upon closer inspection, there have actually been a considerable number of examples in mainstream management and organizational research where historical cases of one or several organizations, as well as those of organizational collectivities, have been used for theorizing. As shown in Chapter 4 (this volume), given the broad thrust toward scientization, history has also served as a source of data for large-scale quantitative studies in a diverse range of research programs, which will be covered in this chapter and Chapter 9. The remainder of the present chapter discusses select examples mainly from two research programs, which have used historical cases or quantitative research in building, modifying and extending theories—institutional theory, both in its "old" and "new" varieties, and process studies. Within these two broad approaches, what later came to be known as old institutionalism within institutional theory and process studies have been based more on case studies of individual organizations. New institutionalism, on the other hand, with somewhat of an increasing turn toward the use of history, has relied on both case-based and quantitative research, typically, though, at the level of organizational fields.

Which Way? Two Institutionalisms on Different Paths From History to Theory

Institutionalism in organizational analysis is a broad research program that extends into many areas of research (see e.g. Greenwood et al. 2017). What eventually came to be labeled "neo-institutional theory" (Greenwood and Hinings 1996) has now become the most influential theoretical current within management and organization studies. Following early work in the late 1970s, DiMaggio and Powell (1991) introduced the term "new institutionalism" to demarcate an approach that was distinct from what they referred to as "old institutionalism". As DiMaggio and Powell (1991: 12) remarked, the new version "traces its roots to 'old institutionalism' [. . .], yet diverges from that tradition substantially". These authors did also point out that the "old" and the "new" were united in questioning rational-actor models and acknowledging environmental and cultural influences upon organizations. New institutionalism differed from the old one, however, in its conception of institutionalization as occurring at the level of fields or society rather than at the organizational level. Moreover, the emphasis was on stability and persistence rather than change. The new institutional approach also stressed the quest for legitimacy and the ensuing isomorphism among organizations in a given field. Unlike old institutionalism, a limited role was accorded to agency, interests and power in organizational action (for a more detailed comparison, see DiMaggio and Powell 1991: 11–15).

Another difference, not highlighted by DiMaggio and Powell (1991), concerned the relation of the two institutionalisms to history. While the "old" institutionalism actually built its theoretical framework on organizational history, the room for this type of historical research seemed nonexistent, or at least severely limited, for new institutional theory because of its preoccupation with the field level of analysis and a primary concern with convergence among organizations toward similar structures and practices, or "isomorphism", within the same organizational field (Hirsch and Lounsbury 1997). Early empirical work relied on quantitative studies, even when historical data happened to be used. It was only in response to criticisms of how new institutional theory was initially formulated and following calls for integration with old institutionalism (Greenwood and Hinings 1996; Selznick 1996; Hirsch and Lounsbury 1997), that a turn began toward studying change, which led to greater recourse to history and case studies—though together with quantitative research and more so at the field level. In what follows, the chapter first examines how the "old" institutionalism derived theory from (historical) cases and then discusses the uses of history for building or extending theories in a number of research programs within the neo-institutional paradigm.

How It All Started: Institutionalism From the TVA to a Theory of "Organizational Character"

As mentioned earlier, the now so-called "old" institutionalism has been characterized, among the various ways in which it differed from new institutional theory, by a focus on institutionalization at the organizational level and an accompanying attention to the history of organizations. Those associated with this program had conducted their early research on specific, often iconic, organizations and their historical development. Selznick's (1949) study of the Tennessee Valley Authority (TVA), a US government agency established as part of the New Deal during the 1930s, is probably the best-known among these cases. But there were various other studies of organizations by early institutionalists, such as Charles K. Warriner's (1961) account on the creation of a watershed treatment agency in Kansas and Burton R. Clark's (1972) research on three famous American liberal arts colleges—Antioch, Reed and Swarthmore (see also Perrow 1986: 157–177 for a critical review). All of these were characterized by a developmental approach.

But it was Selznick in particular who has been viewed as the progenitor of old institutionalism, as set forth in his book *Leadership in Administration* (Selznick 1957), which drew mainly upon his research on the TVA (see earlier) as well as on the Bolshevik Party in Soviet Russia (Selznick

1952)—with the latter carried out when he was associated with the RAND Corporation, a global policy think tank. The book's main aim was to advance the idea of "institutional leadership" in large organizations, which, according to Selznick (1957: 5), was "marked by a concern for the evolution of the organization as a whole, including its changing aims and capabilities" and meant "viewing the organization as an institution". Thus, he made a distinction between "organization" and "institution", with the former signifying an "expendable tool, a rational instrument engineered to do a job", and the latter "more nearly a product of social needs and pressures—a responsive, adaptive organism" (p. 5). The turning of organizations into institutions—or the process of "institutionalization"—involved the development of a distinctive "character", embodying values and commitments, as well as an accompanying "competence", i.e. capabilities to carry out policies. Yet at the same time, institutionalization reduced flexibility and served as a source of resistance to change, since it made the organization captive to its own history (Selznick 1996).

Selznick (1957: 103) believed that organizations had a "natural history" and that the "interpretation of organizational behavior required a historical perspective". This was because character, capabilities and limitations were products of the organization's history and therefore called for historical sensitivity on the part of analysts of organizations as well as institutional leaders—the latter because their "critical decisions" at least in part shaped these developmental processes (Selznick 1957: 102–107). Thus, using the terms of this volume, Selznick's analysis involved a "history *to* theory" approach. Also, foreshadowing studies examining the influence by founders (see Chapter 10, this volume), he thought that one set of critical decisions by "institutional leaders" entailed selecting the "social bases" of the organization in the early stages of its lifetime, or the "segments of the environment to which operations will be oriented" (Selznick 1957: 104). The commitments generated thereby, he argued, would shape the future evolution of the organization. At the same time, Selznick acknowledged that these "decisions" often did not reflect the free will of organizational leaders, but were imposed on them by the particular circumstances. He nevertheless concluded that the "study of institutions" required "a genetic and developmental approach, an emphasis on historical origins and growth stages" (p. 141). In sum, according to Selznick (1996: 271), institutional theory was about tracing "the emergence of distinctive forms, processes, strategies, outlooks, and competences as they emerge from patterns of organizational interaction and adaptation".

However, as Fombrun (1989) observed in the late 1980s, little additional work of the kind had been forthcoming since the early studies mentioned previously. One of the rare, more recent examples of this tradition, though with an explicit emphasis on founder influence—and therefore also as an example of a "history *in* theory" approach—was Kimberly and Bouchikhi's (1995) case study on the early history of a highly successful French retailer of computer hardware and software (see for further detail on this study Chapter 10, this volume). Quantitative studies that have drawn upon old institutionalist ideas have also been rare (see for an exception Kraatz, Ventresca and Deng 2010).

Bring in the New: Developing Neo-Institutional Theory

As mentioned previously, at the outset there seemed to be little room for history in new institutionalism because of the primary concern with convergence to a similar form or isomorphism within organizational fields (Hirsch and Lounsbury 1997). Nevertheless, given an inherent time element in isomorphic and legitimation processes, even in some of the very early empirical studies aiming to develop and establish new institutionalism, some use was made of historical data. More historical cases could also be seen as this approach moved toward the study of change.

Original empirical studies were geared toward demonstrating the salience of institutional effects on organizations with a view to providing empirical support to and substantiating the theory. Rowan (1982), for example, in one of the earliest empirical neo-institutional studies, aimed to show the utility of an institutional approach to account for changes in administrative structures in the public school system in California. The research relied on organizational-level historical data from 1930 to 1970 on public schools in 33 cities. Based on this evidence, the author constructed historical narratives encompassing alterations in the "institutional environments" and the additions of specialist positions in health, psychological and curriculum services within these school districts. The interpretations derived from these historical accounts pointed to significant institutional influences on administrative expansion. Using the same data, Rowan (1982) also carried out a quantitative comparison between the new institutional and the predominant "structural" or "contingency" theory of the time to show that the former needed to be taken into account in studying organization structures as it complemented the latter.

In another early and much quoted study, Tolbert and Zucker (1983) used data on 167 cities in the US to examine the adoption of civil service reforms by municipal governments during the period 1880–1935. Findings showed that in states where adoption was not mandated by law, variables pertaining to city conditions predicted adoption in early, but not later, stages. The outcome of the study was the well-known two-stage model of diffusion, which posited that early adopters of innovations are driven by efficiency considerations, whereas late adoption occurs under institutional influences as the particular innovation gains a taken-for-granted character. While not drawing on organizational-level data, the findings of a subsequent study by Baron, Dobbin and Jennings (1986) on the origins and diffusion of "modern" employment practices in the US during the second quarter of the twentieth century provided support for the two-stage model, highlighting namely the significant role played by state intervention in the process, in particular during World War II.

As mentioned earlier, in response to the critique pertaining to the limits of neo-institutional theory to account for change, a turn began toward studying the creation of institutions, processes of institution-alization and institutional change, which led to greater recourse to history. Indeed, historical case studies aiming to develop theorizing about field-level change had already begun to appear in the early 1990s, moti-vated by the lack of attention in the new institutionalism of the time to issues of change and contestation within organizational fields. To extend neo-institutional theory to these concerns, institutional theorists moved beyond attributing institutional change to external forces and turned to endogenous sources of change. Thus, using primary historical evidence, DiMaggio (1991) showed how a new model of the art museum emerged in the US as an alternative to the one that had been established by the 1920s. He also demonstrated how this "reform" was promulgated through a professionalization project and the struggles that it generated at the field level. Brint and Karabel (1991) examined the transforma-tion of community colleges in the US toward a vocational orientation in the 1960s and 1970s. Theoretically, these authors were drawing upon "old" institutionalism, which, as a whole, had exhibited more interest in and use of history than the new institutional version did at the outset (see earlier). What primarily distinguished Brint and Karabel's (1991: 355) historical analysis was the view they took of organizational fields as "arenas of power relations". Thus, not only did they make an early call for greater attention to studying the development of organizational forms and the processes of institutional change within the new institu-tionalism research program, they also highlighted the value of taking an historical approach in doing so.

Another frequently cited early study which focused on endogenous sources of institutional change and explicitly drew upon publicly avail-able archival sources has been the work by Leblebici and his colleagues (1991) on the US radio broadcasting industry during the period 1920–1965. As the authors themselves put it, "our objective is to present his-torically grounded descriptive material and develop a set of conjectures for understanding institutional change" (p. 333). Their historical narra-tive showed that in each of the three periods they identified in the evolu-tion of radio broadcasting in the US as a privately operated activity, new practices came from the marginal organizations in the field, which were looking for practical solutions to their problems of generating value. These practices turned into conventions at the field level as they came to be endorsed by the dominant actors, when the latter began to face increased competition. Yet another cycle of change started as the new order prompted marginal actors to search for new solutions, leading the researchers to conclude that "institutional change is the product of endogenous forces that are associated with the historical evolution of the field itself" (Leblebici et al. 1991: 360).

Holm (1995), in another highly cited early study, traced the creation, establishment and decline of an organizational form, the "mandated sales organization" (MSO) within the Norwegian fishery sector through the period 1930–1994. Although not making any direct reference to history, the narrative that he constructed was intended to demonstrate how a "nested-systems" view of institutions could illuminate the rise and demise of the MSO. Based on the idea that institutions are multilayered and are at once "frameworks" and "products" of action, this perspective and the MSO story, according to Holm (1995: 418), showed that there was "much room for endogenous change" and that, "while institutional change might be triggered by external events, the outcome will be shaped through internal processes structured by the institutions themselves". More explicitly historical in its design and the sources used is the study by Hargadon and Douglas (2001), which examined the institutional change instigated by Edison's electric lighting system from the announcement of his discovery in 1878 until 1892, when electric lighting eventually displaced gas lighting in New York. These authors proposed the notion of "robust design" to account for why Edison's innovation was able to replace established institutions. Robust design refers to actions or strategies that contain elements of preexisting meanings and rationales, as well as those that are not exposed and are flexible enough to accommodate new conditions as they arise. The former increase chances of effectiveness in the short run, while the latter do so over the longer run.

In another historical study, Schneiberg (2005) considered perspectives from economic and sociological institutionalism to ask the question why a long period of stability in the American property insurance field from the 1860s to the 1940s was followed in the 1950–1970 period by radical institutional change. The change involved a shift from "association and state rate regulation" to "price-competitive markets" and "vertically integrated hierarchies" (Schneiberg 2005: 97, 98). As Schneiberg (2005: 95) put it, he was "using historical analysis [. . .] to construct, rather than test, theory, using the strength of a case study approach". Based on historical narratives developed for each period, Schneiberg argued that institutional change could be endogenously driven and that radical change could occur when both material and institutional factors, including challenges from those in the periphery, were conjoined. In reaching this conclusion, he also pointed to the utility of combining economic and sociological approaches in accounting for institutional change. A more recent example of deeply historical work, this time regarding field formation, is a study by Maclean et al. (2018). These authors used the archives of the Hilton Hotels Corporation from its establishment in 1949 until its founder, Conrad Hilton, stepped down in 1967 to show how political ideology—anti-communism in this case—can be instrumental in the formation of a field, the multinational hotel industry. Notably though, Maclean and her colleagues combined the archival material with the coding of speeches by Conrad Hilton over the same period. Together, these data were used in a qualitative analysis based on thematic coding to identify the forms of political processes that were involved.

In the meantime, various studies using historical data have pursued more standard agendas in neo-institutional theory, such as institutional effects on organizations and how the latter deal with such pressures. Earlier examples of such studies have typically been quantitatively based. Glynn and Abzug's (2002) two-part investigation of isomorphism in company names and its impact on legitimacy, for example, was grounded on a review of naming patterns among US firms from 1800 to the 2000s. Also using quantitative methods and data that stretched beyond a century (1874–1995), Washington and Ventresca (2004) developed and tested the argument that institutional structures need not necessarily only generate conformity but could also serve as sources of organizational change and diversity. Their study showed that the inclusion of one of the three sport programs (basketball, ice hockey or lacrosse) in US colleges and universities was based in part on coherence with prior strategy as well as on field-level influences—in this case, membership in a national association and peer emulation, which served to support these organizational-level changes.

There appears to have been a more recent turn toward adopting qualitative approaches in these kinds of studies when employing historical data. Kim, Croidieu and Lippmann (2016: 1418), for instance, turned to the early stages (1913–1927) of the wireless telegraphy field in the US in order to "craft theory" on how field positions of organizations shape their discursive strategies for gaining legitimacy during the emergence of a field. Thematic coding of selected articles in trade journals published, respectively, by a central and a peripheral organization showed that discursive strategies varied with field location. And in a clear-cut case of history to theory, Hampel and Tracey (2017) studied publicly available historical documents and the archives of Thomas Cook's travel agency to develop a model of how organizations can shift from a state of stigma to gaining legitimacy. Stigmatization was defined to occur when an organization's "salient audiences mark it out, publicly shame its conduct as highly inappropriate, and express strong moral disapproval of it" (p. 2175). The period used for the study was from 1861 when the agency was founded until 1877 when its acceptance by "elite" audiences was affirmed. Also subjecting the historical material to thematic coding, the authors derived what they called a "dialogical model of organizational destigmatization" (p. 2187).

Here Come the Dynamos: Institutional Entrepreneurship and Institutional Work

Greenwood and Suddaby (2006: 29) defined institutional entrepreneurs as "organized actors who envision new institutions as a means of advancing interests they value highly". Among the early studies mentioned previously, Leblebici et al. (1991) and Holm (1995) had already made reference to the notion of "institutional entrepreneurship", originally introduced by DiMaggio (1988, 1991). Some of the later work building on this idea was historically based too—though the particular approaches and the methodologies adopted varied. In general, studies that were "process-centric" rather than "actor-centric" (Hardy and Maguire 2008: 199) tended to be more historically oriented.

As one of the early examples, Rao's (1998: 916) "case study" on the creation of nonprofit consumer watchdog organizations (CWOs), such as Consumers Research (CR) and Consumers Union (CU) in the US during the 1930s, aimed to show how the formation of "new organizational forms requires an institutionalization project wherein the theory and values underpinning the form are legitimated by institutional entrepreneurs" (p. 914). In his view, "historical research on the origins of an organizational form provides greater breadth than conventional ethnography and enables us to derive a historically informed understanding of organizations" (p. 921). A fascinating story in itself, Rao's (1998) narrative began with the precursors of CWOs from the turn of the century, followed by a description of how institutional entrepreneurs, capitalizing on the social context of the time, created first the CR and then, due to an internal scission, its rival CU—with both framed by different values and norms. The narrative extended to the late 1950s showing how the shaping of organizational forms is a political process. The eventual convergence between the two organizations was achieved only when the CU gradually tempered its pro-labor stance as it came under coercive pressures, including being investigated as a "Communist-front organization" (Rao 1998: 941).

The study by Munir and Phillips (2005) on institutional change, which attributed the transformation of photography, from being a "professional" field to becoming a "popular" activity, to institutional entrepreneurship on the part of Kodak, was also historical. It covered the period from 1882, when Kodak introduced its roll-film camera, until the late 1930s, when this new technology had become well-established (p. 1670). Although based on historical evidence, this study is distinct in that it relied on discourse analysis both as a theoretical frame and methodology. Thus, the variety of primary and secondary sources consulted for this period served as "texts" to be analyzed to identify the various forms of discourse employed by Kodak to shape the meaning of the new technology in line with its interests. The outcome, as the authors put it, was a "discursive theory of institutional entrepreneurship" (p. 1682).

Mutch (2007: 1132) brought in Margaret Archer's notion of "autonomous reflexive", i.e. the personal attributes of "individualism, prioritization of work and contextual discontinuity", to examine institutional entrepreneurship and institutional change using an historical example. As he pointed out, the "advantage of historical forms of inquiry is that we can take documents and other forms of evidence formulated for an entirely different purpose and interrogate them" (p. 1130). The case chosen was that of Sir Andrew Barclay Walker, who introduced a novel way of running public houses in mid-nineteenth-century Liverpool. His innovation included using salaried managers rather than tenants, coupled with building a managerial hierarchy and a comprehensive accounting system—practices that then spread locally and nationally. Mutch (2007: 1124) provided an actor-centric account, though he was careful to note that Walker's "aim was to be an entrepreneur rather than an 'institutional entrepreneur', but the consequence of the former project was innovation in organizational practice".

Greenwood and Suddaby (2006) also interpreted the creation of a new organizational form—called multidisciplinary practice—within the professional business services field in Canada as a case of institutional entrepreneurship. Theirs was a study which combined historical analysis with other qualitative methods such as interviews and content analysis. Nevertheless, it is a good example of history to theory, as it was motived by "elaborating" existing theory and led to the development of what the authors called a "process model of elite institutional entrepreneurship" (Greenwood and Suddaby 2006: 31, 42). It was referred to as "elite" because differently from Leblebici et al.'s (1991) work (see earlier), these authors found that it was not the marginal, but the "central actors that became the institutional entrepreneurs" (Greenwood and Suddaby 2006: 27). Wright and Zammuto (2013) added a new perspective to this literature, again with an historical study. They examined the county cricket field in England during the period 1919–1967. Based on the archives of a London-based cricket club that "governed English cricket" as well as on published primary and secondary sources, they constructed a "process model" of institutional change in a mature field. Their model demonstrated the intermediary role that "middle-status" actors in between those at the center and the periphery play in top-down and bottom-up institutional change processes (Wright and Zammuto 2013: 322).

David, Sine and Haveman's (2013) study on the development of "professional management consulting" as an organizational form, as well as a field in the US, provides another case of studying institutional entrepreneurship by using an historical approach. The authors explicitly stated that they "draw on the early history of the management consulting field to build theory about how institutional entrepreneurs legitimate new kinds of organizations in emerging fields" (p. 356). Their historical investigation focused in particular on the activities of the founders of three firms, who pioneered the professional management consulting firm during the interwar years, which resulted in this organizational form becoming widely accepted prior to World War II. Based on the historical narrative, the authors developed a series of general propositions concerning how the legitimacy of a new organizational form may be enhanced in an emerging field and how these processes may differ from institutional entrepreneurship in mature fields.

Historical events or accounts of organizational histories have also appeared among a few organizational-level studies of "institutional work"—a notion introduced, like institutional entrepreneurship, to bring agency into neo-institutional theory. Lawrence and Suddaby (2006: 215) have defined institutional work as "purposive action of individuals and organizations aimed at creating, maintaining and disrupting institutions". As Decker (2015) has pointed out, studies on institutional work have tended to cover short periods of time due to the type of qualitative methodologies that are typically employed. Nevertheless, Rojas (2010), for example, used a historical case, the episode of student protests known as the "Third World Strike" at San Francisco State College between November 1968 and March 1969, portraying the ways the then college president acquired greater powers and altered the institutional frames guiding the organization as institutional work. Based on archives and secondary sources, his narrative account illustrated a "process model of power and institutional change" (Rojas 2010: 1264) in that the acquisition of managerial power was enabled and yet also constrained by changes in the institutional context.

In a study with similar theoretical motivations but different methodologies, Bisel, Kramer and Banas (2017) started by observing that the institutional work literature had paid limited attention to the role of organizational history. Theirs, by contrast, was a "historical case study" involving an anonymized gymnastics organization in the US for training athletes to compete at the highest international level, such as the Olympics. The study relied on life history or in-depth retrospective interviews with the founder, her daughter, coaches, staff, athletes and parents, since for the authors such interviews enabled tapping into typically unreported aspects of past organizational lives. The historical narrative was structured according to the research questions guiding the study and helped them propose a new concept, "institutional resistance leadership" (IRL), which was defined as "activities that influence others to recognize and resist the flow of institutional influences on local team and organizational practices" (Bisel et al. 2017: 412). IRL at the organizational level spearheaded attempts toward institutional entrepreneurship to challenge dominant norms of training highly promising athletes to win Olympic medals, which was thwarted, however, since these norms were an entrenched institution.

Holding It All Together—In a Dynamic Way: Institutional Logics

Evolving from neo-institutionalism in organization studies, the institutional logics approach has also been linked to history both theoretically and empirically. Based on Friedland and Alford's (1991) conception of society as an interinstitutional system whereby central institutions embody different logics, organizational fields have come to be "viewed as having their own logics nested within societal level institutional orders" (Goodrick and Reay 2011: 375). And, as Ocasio, Mauskapf and Steele (2016: 679) have proposed, "societal logics provide foundational principles that can be used in the creation, maintenance, and disruption of more situated field-level logics".

Within this framework institutional logics has been defined as "socially constructed, historical patterns of cultural symbols and material practices, including assumptions, values, and beliefs, by which individuals and organizations provide meaning to their daily activity, organize time and space, and reproduce their lives and experiences" (Thornton, Ocasio and Lounsbury 2012: 2; see also Haveman and Gualtieri 2017). Moreover, based on Friedland and Alford's (1991: 249) view that societal logics have "specific historical limits", "historical contingency" has been deemed as "a key meta-theoretical assumption of the institutional logics approach" (Thornton and Ocasio 2008: 108). In support of this core aspect, early studies as well as various others have shown that relationships among variables differed across historical periods when distinct institutional logics were prevalent within organizational fields. Historicizing the organizational effects of institutional logics serves as an example of what is considered within the framework of this book as "historically cognizant" research and will therefore be discussed in some detail in Chapter 12.

In addition, however, there have been a range of studies, which have taken a historical perspective to examine institutional change within the framework of the institutional logics approach and/or to show and theorize how field-level institutional logics emerge and develop and may shift or coexist over time. An example is Sine and David's (2003) study, which returned to the idea of the impact of exogenous shocks to examine change in institutional logics. Their historical analysis of the electric power industry in the US over the period 1935–1978 showed how the 1973 oil crisis led to the deinstitutionalization of a homogeneous industry structure dominated by large public utilities. The ensuing change in institutional logics of power generation coupled with new legislation resulted in opening up a vast range of new entrepreneurial opportunities. Rao, Monin and Durand (2003), in contrast, examined sources of change internal to a field in their research on the replacement of institutional logics and role identities of classical French cuisine by those of nouvelle cuisine. Their study combined a historical account based on secondary sources and interviews with quantitative analyses. The narrative traced the development and institutionalization of classical cuisine from the first half of the nineteenth century to the 1960s and the emergence of the nouvelle cuisine era after 1970. Nouvelle cuisine was described as an identity movement that spurred institutional change. The quantitative part of the study for the latter period involved testing hypotheses on factors thought to account for why actors would shift from a traditional to a new logic.

Dunn and Jones (2010) studied American medical education to argue that in professional fields institutional change need not necessarily involve a shift from a dominant logic to another, but that multiple logics could coexist over long periods. Their analytically structured historical narrative showed how two distinct logics (science and care) became institutionalized in this field during 1910–1959, followed by increased tension and contestation between the two. Based on hypotheses derived from this narrative, Dunn and Jones (2010) quantitatively examined through content-analytic methods the factors that led to a relative emphasis on one or the other of the science or care logics during the period of rivalry between the two (1967–2005). Another example of how organizations respond to institutional pressures—more specifically to multiple logics—is Dalpiaz, Rindova and Ravasi's (2016: 349) "in-depth, longitudinal case study of the Italian household goods manufacturer Alessi". While the history of Alessi goes back to 1921, the authors focused on the period from 1970 to 2000, after the company had established itself as the leader in tableware. The narrative that they constructed was based on the coding of various publications as well as documents from the company archives and two rounds of interviews, which demonstrated that over the course of this period Alessi had combined the logics of "industry" and "art" in different ways. Dalpiaz et al. (2016) identified the organizational practices associated with these different "recombinant strategies" to then propose a process model of how combining logics enhances organizational agency to create new products and markets.

The institutional logics approach has also been extended to the study of professions. So has been the idea of coexisting, often contending, multiple logics. In an exemplary study, Goodrick and Reay (2011) focused on the history of pharmacy in the US to examine how multiple institutional logics impinged upon the work of pharmacists. As these authors have put it, very much along the lines of the history to theory approach, their research goal was "to develop theory about how different logics can collectively be reflected in professional work by examining a historical case study of US pharmacists" (Goodrick and Reay 2011: 373–374). Their historical narrative spanned the period from 1852, when a national association was founded, up to the present day—temporally bracketed into five eras as identified by the literature on US pharmacy history. The narrative analysis examining the strength of four institutional logics (professional, corporate, market and state) on pharmacy practice enabled the authors to develop the notion of "constellation of logics", as well as identifying the different types of such multiple logic combinations and to propose that relationships among multiple logics need not necessarily be competitive but could also be cooperative.

Although not stemming from the institutional logics framework, other research and theorizing on occupations and professions that drew upon neo-institutional theory has also relied on historical data. Kahl, King and Liegel (2016: 1087), for instance, aimed to "develop middle-range theory about integrative approaches and the survival of occupations" through studying strategies employed by the professional associations of "systems men" [*sic*] and "production planners" following the entry of computers into US business in the mid-1950s up to the 1990s. And Croidieu and Kim (2018: 3) sought "an alternative theoretical model to address the inadequacies of professionalization theory to account for [. . .] cases of legitimate but non-professionalized forms of expertise" by analyzing texts on amateur radio operators in the US between 1899 and 1927. They described their study as an "in-depth historical investigation" (Croidieu and Kim 2018: 4), while Kahl et al. (2016: 1085) called theirs a "theoretically informed, comparative historical analysis". Notably, though, in both cases the historical material was considered qualitative data and analyzed through methods such as content analysis or thematic coding.

What's Going On? Unrealized Potential in Process Studies of Organizations and Strategy

Early research on processes focused largely on organizational change (for an overview, see Üsdiken, Kipping and Engwall 2011). But while its leading proponents explicitly endorsed the use of historical cases and approaches, little empirical work followed their example and suggestions. This, as the following overview will show, has not changed much in the most recent period, despite calls for more history in what have overall been successfully expanding research programs, namely in process organization studies and strategy-as-practice.

Looking Inside: Process Organization Studies

An almost iconic early example of advancing theory based on historical research has been the history of the British company Imperial Chemical Industries (ICI) by Andrew Pettigrew (1985), which was based on the corporate historical archives as well as retrospective interviews. Importantly in the context of this chapter, he used the historical data to advance theorizing. Thus, in a subsequent article, Pettigrew (1987) provided an extensive critique of the leadership and organizational change literatures at the time and instead, drawing on the ICI case, developed a new process model of organizational change that took into account not only its content, the "what" of the change, but also the outer and inner context in which it took place. But while taking history seriously, Pettigrew was wary of not focusing on history per se. Rather than being content with "case histories", he advocated turning them into "case studies" by going "beyond chronology to develop analytic themes" (Pettigrew 1990: 277). A similar position regarding the need to go from history to theory was taken by Van de Ven and Huber (1990: 213) as they spoke of "longitudinal" rather than "historical" research. Their main concern was to complement the—at the time—dominant input and output model of organizational change with "a 'process theory' explanation of the temporal order and sequence, in which a discrete set of events occurred based on a story or historical narrative". Like Pettigrew, though, they stressed that historical data should not be used to examine a specific change process focusing on its peculiarities but identifying its "underlying generative mechanisms or laws" (Van de Ven and Huber 1990: 213).

However, empirical studies based on these ideas remained sparse, if not entirely absent. Thus, while in their introduction to a "Special Research Forum on Change and Development Journeys into a Pluralistic World" for the *Academy of Management Journal* (AMJ) Pettigrew, Woodman and Cameron (2001: 700) again stressed the benefits of developing more "historical studies of industrial, institutional, and organizational change", none of the ten studies in the Special Research Forum actually undertook historical research—though the editors classified eight of them as focusing on "Time, History, Process, and Action" (p. 706). And even for those described as "longitudinal", the time periods covered were generally short and the research was usually conducted using observations, interviews and some surveys—with several studies investigating the individual and team rather than organizational levels, hence falling beyond the scope of this book. The one that seems closest to the concerns in this chapter is Siggelkow's (2001) work on the turnaround at Liz Claiborne covering the period between the late 1970s and the 1990s, which the author characterized as a "longitudinal case study" (p. 839). In terms of evidence, he relied on trade journals and magazines as well as retrospective interviews rather than the company archives. Importantly, Siggelkow (2001: 839) used the case solely "to illustrate the framework", i.e. not to generate his theoretical insights. While this is, therefore, strictly speaking, not a case of history to theory, it clearly shows the inherent dangers of examining unfinished processes rather than letting history play itself out: A few years after the completion of the study the company's performance deteriorated again, invalidating claims of its "renaissance"—and casting doubt on the theoretical framework the case was meant to illustrate (Kipping and Lamberg 2017: 311).

Over the past two decades, process organization studies became increasingly institutionalized as a research program, starting in particular with a foundational article by Ann Langley (1999), which proposed various strategies to establish that all-important link between process data and theory. Another important milestone was the publication of a "Special Research Forum on Process Studies of Change in Organization and Management" in AMJ in 2013 (Langley et al. 2013). There has also been an annual Process Organization Studies Symposium (PROS) since 2009 with an associated book series (*Perspectives on Process Organization Studies*) published by Oxford University Press. And a first handbook came out in 2017 published by SAGE (Langley and Tsoukas 2017). Through the symposium and the handbook, there has been an effort to connect process studies with some other major research programs, including obvious ones, like strategy-as-practice (see later) or organizational routines, and some less obvious ones, such as dynamic capabilities (see also Chapter 11, this volume).

And there has been some interest in historical research within the process organization studies community. One of the handbook chapters looked at "History in Process Organization Studies" (Kipping and Lamberg 2017), and there was also a panel at the 2018 symposium entitled "History Matters: The Value and Challenges of Historical Approaches to Organizational and Management Research". These might have been a reaction to the generic calls for "more history" in management studies, since, in terms of actual research, history continues to play a rather subdued role within this program—despite the previously mentioned auspicious antecedents and what appears to be a strong overlap/affinity between the "questions about how and why things emerge, develop, grow, or terminate over time" asked by process studies (Langley et al. 2013: 1) and what historical research has to offer. In their handbook chapter Kipping and Lamberg (2017: 309–312) also highlight the potential, pointing in particular at "focusing on past processes", "learning from complete processes with known outcomes" and "identifying alternative process outcomes", while lamenting that "process management scholars [. . .] have only rarely used history", which they attribute to greater familiarity with other methodologies (p. 303).

This is borne out by the 13 articles included in the AMJ Special Research Forum mentioned earlier (Langley et al. 2013: 2–3, Table 1). While almost all of the authors describe their approach as "longitudinal", only in three cases does the time period covered exceed five years. And two of these are quantitative analyses of published documents— articles and books in one case and corporate reports in another. The only study drawing on confidential internal records, which is what historians would call "archives", as well as publicly available documents from past periods (in this case 1919–1967), is the one on English county cricket by Wright and Zammuto (2013) discussed earlier. All the other contributions rely on "real-time data", i.e. they follow processes as they unfold, based mainly on participant observation and interviews as well as, occasionally, "archival data" which, in management research, tends to refer to contemporaneous printed documents rather than records from historical archives (see also Chapter 4, this volume). Not much else has been published that would suggest cause for optimism in terms of fulfilling the promising potential for historical studies advancing theorizing on organizational processes (for some additional examples and a more extensive discussion, see Kipping and Lamberg 2017; see also Chapter 12, this volume). The situation is not much better when it comes to historical cases in the strategy literature.

Inside Looking Out: Strategy-Making

For process research within strategy, a historical, longitudinal approach also seemed promising at the outset, but ultimately remained marginal again. Thus, the pioneering work by Henry Mintzberg and his colleagues since the late 1970s (now summarized in Mintzberg 2007) drew on long-term, in-depth case studies to examine strategic change and continuity, as well as strategy-making within the now well-known dichotomy of "deliberate" vs. "emergent" processes. The organizations studied were often from Canada—not surprising, given that Mintzberg was based in Montreal; generally covered long time periods, with some going back to the nineteenth century, namely his own institution McGill University between 1829 and 1880; and included private as well as public organizations, such as the retailer Steinberg (1917–1974), the National Film Board (1939–1975) and Air Canada (1937–1976). Mintzberg also tracked his own strategy as a researcher between 1967 and 1991. Among the few non-Canadian organizations were Germany's Volkswagen (1937–1972) and the US strategy in Vietnam from 1950 to 1973. The sources used for all of these case studies were predominantly of the written kind, both published and unpublished, with a rather sparse recourse to interviews.

Another researcher consistently advocating the use of longitudinal approaches in studying strategy-making and strategic change is Robert A. Burgelman. Over the decades, his approach became increasingly geared toward history to generate, or at least modify, theory. His initial work—which in hindsight he himself called "quasilongitudinal" (Burgelman 2011: 594)—had looked at the internal corporate venturing (ICV) process in a diversified organization (Burgelman 1983). For this particular study, he observed ongoing projects over a 15-month period but also retraced their history—though not with the objective of deriving theory from this particular part of the research (p. 224). In a later study that aimed at "a fruitful integration" "of ecological and strategic perspectives", he conducted a "field study" of the evolution of corporate strategy at Intel and used it "to refine and deepen the conceptual framework" in an iterative process (Burgelman 1991: 239; see, for the ecological perspective, Chapters 9 and 10, this volume). This time, in addition to interviews, he used internal documents covering Intel's history as well as other written sources (p. 240). And in a more recent programmatic article Burgelman (2011: 591) fully embraced the contribution of historical methods, which, he believed, in combination with grounded theorizing, could "generate novel conceptual frameworks that establish theoretical bridges between historical narratives and reductionist quantitative models" (see, for this kind of more contingent theorizing also Chapter 12, this volume)—an approach he tried to apply in writing the history of Hewlett-Packard between 1939 and 2016 (Burgelman, McKinney and Meza 2017).

Last but not least, over the years there were a number of studies on strategic change with an empirical focus on healthcare organizations from a group of researchers around Jean-Louis Denis and Ann Langley—with the latter, as seen earlier, also instrumental in developing process organization studies. Following in the footsteps of both Pettigrew and Mintzberg, in a first of these studies Denis, Langley and Cazale (1996) use a descriptive case history, based on internal documents and retrospective interviews, to "trace" the evolving relationship between the leadership group and strategic change in a general hospital, leading to a series of propositions regarding this relationship. A subsequent study was more ambitious in that it aimed "to develop a process theory of strategic change in pluralistic settings characterized by diffuse power and divergent objectives" based on the cases of five hospitals (Denis, Lamothe and Langley 2001: 809). It drew on real-time as well as retroactive research with data, including interviews, observations and documents, going back—though only for one of their cases—to 1980 (p. 814). Theoretical insights were developed by iterating deductive and inductive reasoning and pointed at the crucial importance of " 'coupling' between leaders, organization, and environment" to permit strategic change. Interestingly, and quite tellingly, in a more recent study, where they refer to the empirical data as a "case history", their aim was to illustrate a "phenomenon" they call "escalating indecision"—in this instance among a group of teaching hospitals—rather than to develop theory (Denis et al. 2011). Taken together, these studies highlight once again the difficulties inherent in creating a strong link between historical data and theory. Thus, the study with the lowest historical depth—though a comparative dimension—went furthest in its theoretical claims.

Strategy-making has also been an integral part of a new practice-oriented perspective within the broader strategy discipline, aiming to break the stranglehold of cross-sectional studies and the focus on performance. Instead, "Strategy as Practice research focuses on the micro-level social activities, processes and practices that characterize organizational strategy and strategizing" (Golsorkhi et al. 2015: 1; see, among the many other overview publications, also Vaara and Whittington 2012). Claiming a Mintzbergian heritage, strategy-as-practice originated in the UK and Scandinavia and has now become popular and institutionalized, organizing sessions and streams both at strategy-focused and the main management research conferences, such as the European Group for Organizational Studies (EGOS) and the Academy of Management (AoM). At the latter, it has an interest group called "Strategizing Activities and Practices", which, in 2019, counted over 700 members—almost the same as Critical Management Studies (CMS) and nearly twice as many as the Management History Division. A handbook was first published in 2010 and is now in its extended second edition (Golsorkhi et al. 2015). The handbook does contain a chapter on historical methods, with a historian added as a co-author for the second edition (Ericson, Melin and Popp 2015). It takes a predominantly social constructionist position with mainly generic references and very few empirical examples. This should not come as a surprise, since the number of studies within strategy-as-practice that use history to develop or modify theory is minimal. Like in process organization studies, the vast majority of the research relies on real-time ethnographic methods.

An early example among the rare exceptions is a study by Robert M. Grant (2003) that challenged existing theorizing regarding the limits of strategic planning in turbulent environments by examining "fundamental changes in the nature and role of strategic planning since the end of the 1970s" at eight large global oil companies (p. 492). While the topic sounds very historical, the eight case studies drew mainly on interviews with current corporate planners, though "some former planning managers were contacted". These interviews were "supplemented with information from case studies, research papers, and company reports and documents" (p. 497). A special issue of *Long Range Planning* commemorating Mintzberg's (1987) article on "Crafting Strategy" contained six additional case studies investigating strategic planning processes (Whittington and Cailluet 2008)—though only one of them, on General Electric, was historical (Ocasio and Joseph 2008). Unlike Grant (2003), it did use "historical documents from the GE corporate archives", in addition to published sources and interviews (Ocasio and Joseph 2008: 252), but its theoretical contribution, like in the case of Grant (2003), was mainly to "challenge conventional accounts of the rise and fall of strategic planning" (Ocasio and Joseph 2008: 248). Another empirical study relying on corporate archives, in addition to publicly available documents, is an article by Kipping and Cailluet (2010) that tracked the strategies of the Canadian aluminum producer Alcan in Europe from 1928 until its acquisition by Britain's Rio Tinto in 2007. While mainly providing a detailed historical narrative, the authors nevertheless contribute to theory, namely Mintzberg's distinction between emergent and deliberate strategies. Based on their study, they question Mintzberg's view regarding "imposed strategies" as extreme and rare instances of external control over strategy-making by suggesting that "in the case of Alcan, and probably of resource-based businesses *more generally*, different kinds of imposition seem to play an important role *most of the time*, be they in the form of cartels, highly interventionist governments, or pressures from commodity or stock markets" (Kipping and Cailluet 2010: 104; emphasis added).

Conclusion

Thus, when it comes to studies of organizations and organizational fields that draw on historical evidence to develop, extend or modify theory, the so-called "old" institutionalism is among the earliest examples, with Selznick using mainly his own case studies to develop a theory of "organizational character". In its newer version, institutionalism was fairly ahistorical at the outset, focused as it was on convergence and stability—akin to the end of history, so to speak. But as neo-institutional theory turned more expansive and started to encompass questions of change, historical case studies at organizational and field levels have become more commonplace and, for certain topics, such as institutional emergence almost taken for granted. Consequently, Suddaby and Greenwood (2009: 178), for instance, consider historical methods as one of the major "epistemological categories" for studying processes of institutional change, particularly apt when change is conceived as "a complex phenomenon in which multiple political and economic pressures coincide". Seen from a perspective of "taking history seriously", these are encouraging statements and developments.

In contrast, when it comes to other research programs examining organizational change processes, history was present almost from the outset, namely in the form of case studies, such as the one on the British company ICI by Pettigrew or the multiple cases used by Mintzberg and his colleagues to research strategy formation. But what looked like a promising combination during the 1980s never lived up to this promise when the corresponding research programs, respectively, "process organization studies" and "strategy-as-practice", grew and became institutionalized since the early twenty-first century. Despite a professed openness to history, researchers continued to rely on largely ahistorical data and the corresponding methods, namely observations and interviews. The potential that seemed obvious at the beginning has yet to be realized even to a relatively limited extent.

References

Bansal, P., Smith, W. K. and Vaara, E. (2018) "From the editors: New ways of seeing through qualitative research," *Academy of Management Journal*, 61(4): 1189–1195.

Baron, J. N., Dobbin, F. R. and Jennings, P. D. (1986) "War and peace: The evolution of modern personnel administration in U.S. industry," *American Journal of Sociology*, 92(2): 350–383.

Berg, B. L. and Lune, H. (2014) *Qualitative Research Methods for the Social Sciences*, 8th edn, Harlow: Pearson Education.

Bisel, R. S., Kramer, M. W. and Banas, J. A. (2017) "Scaling up to institutional entrepreneurship: A life history of an elite training gymnastics organization," *Human Relations*, 70(4): 410–435.

Brint, S. and Karabel, J. (1991) "Institutional origins and transformations: The case of American community colleges," in W. W. Powell and P. J. DiMaggio (eds), *The New Institutionalism in Organizational Analysis*, Chicago, IL: The University of Chicago Press, pp. 311–360.

Burgelman, R. A. (1983) "A process model of internal corporate venturing in the diversified major firm," *Administrative Science Quarterly*, 28(2): 223–244.

Burgelman, R. A. (1991) "Intraorganizational ecology of strategy making and organizational adaptation: Theory and field research," *Organization Science*, 2(3): 239–262.

Burgelman, R. A. (2011) "Bridging history and reductionism: A key role for longitudinal qualitative research," *Journal of International Business Studies*, 42(5): 591–601.

Burgelman, R. A., McKinney, W. and Meza, P. E. (2017) *Becoming Hewlett Packard: Why Strategic Leadership Matters*, New York: Oxford University Press.

Chandler, A. D. Jr. (1962) *Strategy and Structure: Chapters in the History of the Industrial Enterprise*, Cambridge, MA: MIT Press.

Clark, B. R. (1972) "The organizational saga in higher education," *Administrative Science Quarterly*, 17(2): 178–184.

Croidieu, G. and Kim, P. H. (2018) "Labor of love: Amateurs and lay-expertise legitimation in the early U.S. radio field," *Administrative Science Quarterly*, 63(1): 1–42.

Dalpiaz, E., Rindova, V. and Ravasi, D. (2016) "Combining logics to transform organizational agency: Blending industry and art at Alessi," *Administrative Science Quarterly*, 61(3): 347–392.

David, R. J., Sine, W. D. and Haveman, H. A. (2013) "Seizing opportunity in emerging fields: How institutional entrepreneurs legitimated the professional form of management consulting," *Organization Science*, 24(2): 356–377.

Decker, S. (2015) "Mothership reconnection: Microhistory and institutional work compared," in P. G. McLaren, A. J. Mills and T. G. Weatherbee (eds), *The Routledge Companion to Management and Organizational History*, London: Routledge, pp. 22–237.

Denis, J.-L., Dompierre, G., Langley, A. and Rouleau, L. (2011) "Escalating indecision: Between reification and strategic ambiguity," *Organization Science*, 22(1): 225–244.

Denis, J.-L., Lamothe, L. and Langley, A. (2001) "The dynamics of collective leadership and strategic change in pluralistic organizations," *Academy of Management Journal*, 44(4): 809–837.

Denis, J.-L., Langley, A. and Cazale, L. (1996) "Leadership and strategic change under ambiguity," *Organization Studies*, 17(4): 673–699.

DiMaggio, P. J. (1988) "Interest and agency in institutional theory," in L. Zucker (ed), *Institutional Patterns and Organizations*, Cambridge, MA: Ballinger, pp. 3–32.

DiMaggio, P. J. (1991) "Constructing an organizational field as a professional project: U.S. art museums, 1920–1940," in W. W. Powell and P. J. DiMaggio (eds), *The New Institutionalism in Organizational Analysis*, Chicago, IL: The University of Chicago Press, pp. 267–292.

DiMaggio, P. J. and Powell, W. W. (1991) "Introduction," in W. W. Powell and P. J. DiMaggio (eds), *The New Institutionalism in Organizational Analysis*, Chicago, IL: The University of Chicago Press, pp. 1–38.

Dunn, M. B. and Jones, C. (2010) "Institutional logics and institutional pluralism: The contestation of care and science logics in medical education, 1967–2005," *Administrative Science Quarterly*, 55(1): 114–149.

Dyer, W. G. Jr. and Wilkins, A. L. (1991) "Better stories, not better constructs to generate better theory: A rejoinder to Eisenhardt," *Academy of Management Review*, 16(3): 613–619.

Eisenhardt, K. M. (1989) "Building theories from case study research," *Academy of Management Review*, 14(4): 532–550.

Eisenhardt, K. M. (1991) "Better stories and better constructs: The case for rigor and comparative logic," *Academy of Management Review*, 16(3): 620–627.

Eisenhardt, K. M. and Graebner, M. E. (2007) "Theory building from cases: Opportunities and challenges," *Academy of Management Journal*, 50(1): 25–32.

Ericson, M., Melin, L. and Popp, A. (2015) "Studying strategy as practice through historical methods," in D. Golsorkhi et al. (eds), *The Cambridge Handbook of Strategy as Practice*, 2nd edn, Cambridge: Cambridge University Press, pp. 506–519.

Fombrun, C. J. (1989) "Convergent dynamics in the production of organizational configurations," *Journal of Management Studies*, 26(5): 439–458.

Friedland, R. and Alford, R. R. (1991) "Bringing society back in: Symbols, practices and institutional contradictions," in W. W. Powell and P. J. DiMaggio (eds), *The New Institutionalism in Organizational Analysis*, Chicago, IL: The University of Chicago Press, pp. 232–263.

Glynn, M. A. and Abzug, R. (2002) "Institutionalizing identity: Symbolic isomorphism and organizational names," *Academy of Management Journal*, 45(1): 267–280.

Golsorkhi, D., Rouleau, L., Seidl, D. and Vaara, E. (2015) "Introduction: What is strategy as practice?" in D. Golsorkhi, L. Rouleau, D. Seidl and E. Vaara (eds), *The Cambridge Handbook of Strategy as Practice*, 2nd edn, Cambridge: Cambridge University Press, pp. 1–30.

Goodrick, E. and Reay, T. (2011) "Constellations of institutional logics: Changes in the professional work of pharmacists," *Work and Occupations*, 38(3): 372–416.

Grant, R. M. (2003) "Strategic planning in a turbulent environment: Evidence from the oil majors," *Strategic Management Journal*, 24(6): 491–517.

Greenwood, R. and Hinings, C. R. (1996) "Understanding radical organizational change: Bringing together the old and the new institutionalism," *Academy of Management Review*, 21(4): 1022–1054.

Greenwood, R., Oliver, C., Lawrence, T. B. and Meyer, R. E. (eds) (2017) *The Sage Handbook of Organizational Institutionalism*, 2nd edn, London: Sage.

Greenwood, R. and Suddaby, R. (2006) "Institutional entrepreneurship in mature fields: The big five accounting firms," *Academy of Management Journal*, 49(1): 27–48.

Hampel, C. E. and Tracey, P. (2017) "How organizations move from stigma to legitimacy: The case of Cook's travel agency in Victorian Britain," *Academy of Management Journal*, 60(6): 2175–2207.

Hardy, C. and Maguire, S. (2008) "Institutional entrepreneurship," in R. Greenwood, C. Oliver, K. Sahlin and R. Suddaby (eds), *The Sage Handbook of Organizational Institutionalism*, London: Sage, pp. 198–217.

Hargadon, A. B. and Douglas, Y. (2001) "When innovations meet institutions: Edison and the design of the electric light," *Administrative Science Quarterly*, 46(3): 476–501.

Haveman, H. A. and Gualtieri, G. (2017) "Institutional logics," in *Oxford Research Encyclopedia, Business and Management*, doi:10.1093/acrefore/9780190224851.013.137.

Hirsch, P. M. and Lounsbury, M. (1997) "Ending the family quarrel: Toward a reconciliation of 'old' and 'new' institutionalisms," *The American Behavioral Scientist*, 40(4): 406–418.

Holm, P. (1995) "The dynamics of institutionalization: Transformation processes in Norwegian fisheries," *Administrative Science Quarterly*, 40(3): 398–422.

Kahl, S. J., King, B. G. and Liegel, G. (2016) "Occupational survival through field-level task integration: Systems men, production planners, and the computer, 1940s–1990s," *Organization Science*, 27(5): 1084–1107.

Kim, P., Croidieu, G. and Lippmann, S. (2016) "Responding from that vantage point: Field position and discursive strategies of legitimation in the U.S. wireless telegraphy field," *Organization Studies*, 37(10): 1417–1450.

Kimberly, J. R. and Bouchikhi, H. (1995) "The dynamics of organizational development and change: How the past shapes the present and constrains the future," *Organization Science*, 6(1): 9–18.

Kipping, M. and Cailluet, L. (2010) "Mintzberg's emergent and deliberate strategies: Tracking Alcan's activities in Europe, 1928–2007," *Business History Review*, 84(1): 79–104.

Kipping, M. and Lamberg, J.-A. (2017) "History in process organization studies: What, why, and how," in A. Langley and H. Tsoukas (eds), *The Sage Handbook of Process Organization Studies*, London: Sage, pp. 303–320.

Kraatz, M. S., Ventresca, M. J. and Deng, L. (2010) "Precarious values and mundane innovations: Enrollment management in American liberal arts colleges," *Academy of Management Journal*, 53(6): 1521–1545.

Langley, A. (1999) "Strategies for theorizing from process data," *Academy of Management Review*, 24(4): 691–710.

Langley, A., Smallman, C., Tsoukas, H. and Van de Ven, A. H. (2013) "Process studies of change in organization and management: Unveiling temporality, activity, and flow," *Academy of Management Journal*, 56(1): 1–13.

Langley, A. and Tsoukas, H. (eds) (2017) *The Sage Handbook of Process Organization Studies*, London: Sage.

Lawrence, T. B. and Suddaby, R. (2006) "Institutions and institutional work," in S. R. Clegg, C. Hardy, T. B. Lawrence and W. R. Nord (eds), *Handbook of Organization Studies*, 2nd edn, London: Sage, pp. 215–254.

Leblebici, H., Salancik, G. R., Copay, A. and King, T. (1991) "Institutional change and the transformation of interorganizational history of the U.S. radio broadcasting industry," *Administrative Science Quarterly*, 36(3): 333–363.

Lipartito, K. (2014) "Historical sources and data," in M. Bucheli and R. D. Wadhwani (eds), *Organizations in Time: History, Theory, Methods*, Oxford: Oxford University Press, pp. 284–304.

Maclean, M., Harvey, C., Suddaby, R. and O'Gorman, K. (2018) "Political ideology and the discursive construction of the multinational hotel industry," *Human Relations*, 71(6): 766–795.

March, J. G., Sproull, L. S. and Tamuz, M. (1991) "Learning from samples of one or fewer," *Organization Science*, 2(1): 1–13.

Mintzberg, H. (1987) "Crafting strategy," *Harvard Business Review*, 65(4): 66–75.

Mintzberg, H. (2007) *Tracking Strategies: Toward a General Theory*, Oxford: Oxford University Press.

Munir, K. A. and Phillips, N. (2005) "The birth of the 'Kodak moment': Institutional entrepreneurship and the adoption of new technologies," *Organization Studies*, 26(11): 1665–1687.

Mutch, A. (2007) "Reflexivity and the institutional entrepreneur: A historical exploration," *Organization Studies*, 28(7): 1123–1140.

Ocasio, W. and Joseph, J. (2008) "Rise and fall—Or transformation? The evolution of strategic planning at the General Electric Company, 1940–2006," *Long Range Planning*, 41(3): 248–272.

Ocasio, W., Mauskapf, M. and Steele, C. W. J. (2016) "History, society, and institutions: The role of collective memory in the emergence and evolution of societal logics," *Academy of Management Review*, 41(4): 676–699.

Perrow, C. (1986) *Complex Organizations: A Critical Essay*, 3rd edn, New York: Random House.

Pettigrew, A. M. (1985) *The Awakening Giant: Continuity and Change in ICI*, Oxford: Blackwell.

Pettigrew, A. M. (1987) "Context and action in the transformation of the firm," *Journal of Management Studies*, 24(6): 649–670.

Pettigrew, A. M. (1990) "Longitudinal field research on change: Theory and practice," *Organization Science*, 1(3): 267–292.

Pettigrew, A. M., Woodman, R. W. and Cameron, K. S. (2001) "Studying organizational change and development: Challenges for future research," *Academy of Management Journal*, 44(4): 697–713.

Rao, H. (1998) "Caveat emptor: The construction of nonprofit consumer watchdog organizations," *American Journal of Sociology*, 103(4): 912–961.

Rao, H., Monin, P. and Durand, R. (2003) "Institutional change in Toque Ville: Nouvelle cuisine as an identity movement in French gastronomy," *American Journal of Sociology*, 108(4): 795–843.

Rojas, F. (2010) "Power through institutional work: Acquiring academic authority in the 1968 Third World Strike," *Academy of Management Journal*, 53(6): 1263–1280.

Rowan, B. (1982) "Organizational structure and the institutional environment: The case of public schools," *Administrative Science Quarterly*, 27(2): 259–279.

Schneiberg, M. (2005) "Combining new institutionalisms: Explaining institutional change in American property insurance," *Sociological Forum*, 20(1): 93–137.

Selznick, P. (1949) *TVA and the Grass Roots: A Study in the Sociology of Formal Organization*, Berkeley and Los Angeles, CA: University of California Press.

Selznick, P. (1952) *The Organizational Weapon: A Study of Bolshevik Strategy and Tactics*, New York: Rand Corporation.

Selznick, P. (1957) *Leadership in Administration: A Sociological Interpretation*, Evanston, IL: Row, Peterson and Company.

Selznick, P. (1996) "Institutionalism 'old' and 'new'," *Administrative Science Quarterly*, 41(2): 270–277.

Siggelkow, N. (2001) "Change in the presence of fit: The rise, the fall, and the renaissance of Liz Claiborne," *Academy of Management Journal*, 44(4): 838–857.

Sine, W. D. and David, R. J. (2003) "Environmental jolts, institutional change, and the creation of entrepreneurial opportunity in the US electric power industry," *Research Policy*, 32(2): 185–207.

Suddaby, R. and Greenwood, R. (2009) "Methodological issues in researching institutional change," in D. A. Buchanan and A. Bryman (eds), *The Sage Handbook of Organizational Research Methods*, London: Sage, pp. 176–195.

Thornton, P. H. and Ocasio, W. (2008) "Institutional logics," in R. Greenwood, C. Oliver, K. Sahlin and R. Suddaby (eds), *The Sage Handbook of Organizational Institutionalism*, London: Sage, pp. 99–129.

Thornton, P. H., Ocasio, W. and Lounsbury, M. (2012) *The Institutional Logics Perspective: A New Approach to Culture, Structure and Process*, Oxford: Oxford University Press.

Tolbert, P. S. and Zucker, L. G. (1983) "Institutional sources of change in the formal structure of organizations: The diffusion of civil service reform, 1880–1935," *Administrative Science Quarterly*, 28(1): 22–39.

Üsdiken, B., Kipping, M. and Engwall, L. (2011) "Historical perspectives on organizational stability and change: Introduction to the special issue," *Management & Organizational History*, 6(1): 3–12.

Vaara, E. and Whittington, R. (2012) "Strategy-as-practice: Taking social practices seriously," *Academy of Management Annals*, 6(1): 285–336.

Van de Ven, A. and Huber, G. P. (1990) "Longitudinal field research methods for studying processes of organizational change," *Organization Science*, 1(3): 293–312.

Warriner, C. K. (1961) "Public opinion and collective action: Formation of a watershed district," *Administrative Science Quarterly*, 6(3): 333–359.

Washington, M. and Ventresca, M. J. (2004) "How organizations change: The role of institutional support mechanisms in the incorporation of higher education visibility strategies, 1874–1995," *Organization Science*, 15(1): 82–97.

Whittington, R. and Cailluet, R. (2008) "The crafts of strategy: Special issue introduction by the guest editors," *Long Range Planning*, 41(3): 241–247.

Wright, A. L. and Zammuto, R. F. (2013) "Wielding the willow: Processes of institutional change in English county cricket," *Academy of Management Journal*, 56(1): 308–330.

Yin, R. K. (2017) *Case Study Research and Applications: Design and Methods*, 6th edn, Los Angeles, CA: Sage.

9 History to Theory

Organizational Ecology, Economics, Resource Dependence

Introduction

Differently from the research reported in the previous chapter, where theoretical insights were often gained from the analysis of case studies examining one or more specific organizations or organizational fields, the studies reviewed next have almost exclusively resorted to history as a source of quantitative data. But while the empirical material, the level of analysis and the methodology used are different, these research programs still belong to what this book calls "history *to* theory" where the past is employed as a source of data or evidence with the purpose of developing, testing, refining or elaborating theory. If anything, because most of these programs focus on change over time—rather than convergence and stability—history by definition has been more central from the outset.

This was in particular the case for organizational ecology, a research program that began to develop in the 1980s—in large part as a reaction to the predominant adaptationist views of organizations at the time. Focusing on the emergence and survival—or decline and disappearance—of populations of organizations, it spearheaded the turn from cross-sectional to longitudinal quantitative analyses. Naturally, therefore, this research program had to rely on historical data spanning long periods—and did so not only in the original formulations of the main ecological theories but also their subsequent empirical extensions and conceptual revisions. And so have later attempts to integrate organizational ecology with neo-institutional theory, as well as the more recent stream of research on categories and categorization.

The bulk of this chapter will provide an overview of these kinds of studies that are in many ways emblematic for turning historical data into "strong", i.e. highly general and testable, theories. It should be noted here that some of the theories within the ecological approach also include history as an integral part of their explanatory models and therefore constitute cases of "history *in* theory", which will be discussed in Chapter 11. The remainder of the chapter will present additional—though much rarer—studies drawing on quantified historical evidence outside the ecological research program, associated instead with organizational economics and resource dependence theories.

Who Wants to Live Forever: Organizational Ecology

Initially known as "population ecology", organizational ecology is not a theory itself, but rather an umbrella term for a collection of theories. A central concern in this broad research program has been to account for the diversity of organizational forms and long-term organizational change. These issues have been addressed mainly through studies at the level of organizational populations—aggregates of organizations of the same type or with a common form. As two of the leading contributors to the development of organizational ecology have put it, "(r)esearch at the population level leads naturally to a concern with history because the study of population dynamics frequently requires analysis over long periods of time" (Hannan and Freeman 1989: 10). Ecological research has therefore relied on data obtained on entire or, in some cases, particular segments within organizational populations over long periods, based on the life histories of all organizations that have existed within a population. These historical data were then used in empirical tests for extending, developing and revising general theories—the ultimate aim of the ecological research program. From the outset, this focus on timeless theorizing has been made very explicit by the leading proponents of the ecological approach: "We are interested in developing and testing general arguments, ones that *apply to all kinds of populations in all kinds of contexts*" (Carroll and Hannan 1989: 546; emphasis added). Similarly, according to Hannan and Freeman (1989: 19), "organizational change has a timeless, ahistorical quality". It is this aim of creating (and testing) universal theory by using historical data that makes organizational ecology a prime example of what is considered here as history to theory.

Apart from relying extensively on historical data, ecological studies would also typically provide some historical account on the context as a background, as well as specific instances from the history of the population to demonstrate theoretical claims or to support the interpretation of the results. In considering the relationship between organizational ecology and history, Hannan and Freeman (1989: 10) suggested that "ecological research requires an understanding of the institutional contexts of organizational populations". Thus, changes in the political and/or the legal environment or in technology and the economic context would typically be included in the empirical analyses (Carroll et al. 2009). However, when such contextual variations, say the world wars, were identified in the histories of organizational populations, they would be incorporated only as additional influences or control variables for a more robust specification of generalizable models (see Isaac and Griffin 1989). For example, as Hannan and Freeman (1987: 940) wrote in their labor union study, "from our perspective one of the most important findings is that the estimated effects of density and the number of prior findings appear to be quite insensitive to the specification of environmental effects on founding rates".

A voluminous literature exists on organizational ecology and its collection of theories. Some of these studies have used data from the more recent past, but as the following overview of its major models will show, ecological research has typically covered long periods. Indeed, the relevant literature is replete with work that has made recourse to data extending back to the nineteenth and in a few cases even to the eighteenth century (see, e.g. Baum and Shipilov 2006; Bogaert et al. 2016).

The More, the Merrier—Up to a Point: Density Dependence

The mainstay of organizational ecology is the so-called density dependence model of legitimation and competition—to be found, according to the recent meta-analysis by Lander and Heugens (2017), in 131 studies which for the most part rely on long-term historical data. Thus, in developing and testing the original formulation of the density dependence model, Hannan and Freeman (1987, 1988) drew upon data on the full history of the labor union population in the US, spanning a period of 150 years from 1836, when the first labor union appeared, until 1985. As is typically the case in ecological research, the data were collated from a range of publicly available sources. In this "classic" version (Bogaert et al. 2016), the density dependence model proposed that increases in density, i.e. the number of organizations, in the early stages of a population—and the accompanying postulated increase in the legitimacy of the organizational form—leads to a growth of founding and a reduction of failure rates. But as the population grows further, higher levels of density result in greater competition for resources, which in turn lowers rates of founding and increases rates of failure.

Both the founding (Hannan and Freeman 1987) and the mortality (Hannan and Freeman 1988) study supported the density dependence model. A curvilinear relationship was obtained between density and rates of founding. In other words, greater intrapopulation competition—due to increases in density beyond a certain level—curbed founding rates. Likewise, the mortality study showed that failure rates were strongly affected by greater competition among unions. The impact of legitimation was also as predicted by the model in that higher density lowered rates of disbanding of a union until density reached a high level. In order to counter criticisms at the time that the density dependence model was likely applicable only to nonbusiness or small organizations that were free of external regulation, Ranger-Moore, Banaszak-Holl and Hannan

(1991) tested the model based on the founding of Manhattan banks and American insurance companies. They extended the time span even further back in history—1791–1980 in the case of the former and 1759–1937 for the latter—and found that the theory also held in the context of these business organizations.

The density dependence model was also tested internationally, again with historical data. Hannan and his colleagues (1995) did so based on the entire histories of the automobile industry in five European countries, namely, Belgium, Great Britain, France, Germany and Italy. In addition, Carroll et al. (1993) tested the model on German and American breweries. The automobile industry study spanned the period 1886–1981 with data obtained from two encyclopedias and other historical sources, which were used to construct life histories of automobile producers that existed within this period in these respective markets. The brewery study was based on company data between 1861 and 1988. Of the two studies, the one on automakers focused only on founding, i.e. entry rates, whereas the one on brewing examined both founding and disbanding rates. Both studies supported the predictions of the theory in all the included countries. In the automobile industry study, a reformulation of the density dependence model was also tested by hypothesizing that legitimation processes would operate cross-nationally at the "European-level" (i.e. the five countries together), whereas the effects of competition would be confined to the country level. Findings supported this hypothesis too for all countries but Britain. In other words, except in Britain, total density for the five countries positively contributed to the legitimation of automobile manufacturers in each country.

Dobrev (2001) offered another test of the density dependence model outside the US in a study on the founding rates of Bulgarian newspapers between 1846 and 1992. Three distinct historical periods were identified in this study: pre-socialist (1846–1948), socialist (1949–1989) and post-socialist (after 1990). Such a periodization, Dobrev argued (2001: 423), helped to deal with the oft-levied criticism of "ahistoricism and contextual imprecision" in ecological research. However, rather than addressing the finding that the density dependence model did not hold in the socialist period, his main argument—very much true to the spirit of ecological research—was that specifying historical changes was appropriate for "cases where tumultuous environments have interfered with the *natural organizational processes*" (emphasis added). Nevertheless, the separation between the pre- and post-socialist eras helped to show that while the density dependence model held in these two periods, the time frame of legitimation, i.e. the pace of increases in density, and the onset of competitive processes were faster in the latter period. This was because, Dobrev argued, newspapers emerging in the pre-socialist era as a novel organizational form had the typical difficulties of gaining legitimacy whereas those founded in the post-socialist period could gain legitimacy from newspapers that had existed in this distant past. These findings led Dobrev (2001: 441) to conclude somewhat differently from the broad pattern in organizational ecology that "it was imperative to investigate [. . .] legitimation with a great deal of historical precision and contextual accuracy".

A later major revision in the conceptualization of "organizational form" in the ecology literature led to yet another modification of the density dependence model (for earlier modifications in the model see Chapter 11, this volume). In initial formulations of ecological ideas organizational forms were defined as "blueprints for organizational action" and distinguished on the basis of a set of hierarchically ordered core properties, namely, "stated goals, forms of authority, core technology and marketing strategy" (Hannan and Freeman 1984: 156). The revised approach took an identity-based view of organizational forms and proposed "that identity gets conferred by outsiders (often called audiences), that audiences decide what features are relevant and that identity persists so long as the relevant audiences continue to hold the same default expectations for the organization" (Hannan 2005: 60). The ensuing revision of the density dependence model (Hannan, Pólos and Carroll 2007: 98) recognized that membership in a population need not be a binary—yes or no—question, but that individual organizations may have "partial" or different "grades" of membership in a population and may well be a member of more than one population. Following from this idea, two new concepts were offered which pertained to the legitimation of organizational populations: "fuzzy density" which referred to the sum total of the grades of memberships of organizations in a population and "contrast" which was related to the distinctiveness of the population from others, i.e. its average grade of membership (see also Hannan 2010).

The central idea in this revision was that the contribution of density to legitimation will be greater when population fuzziness is low. Bogaert, Boone and Carroll (2010) provided an early test of this revised version by examining the formation of the Dutch accounting industry in the period 1884–1939. The aim was to demonstrate the utility of the revised density dependence model for the emergence and legitimation of new organizational forms in accounting and to derive "general conceptual insights from [. . .] historical renderings" in earlier studies on specific instances of new form emergence (Bogaert et al. 2010: 116). Using the same concepts and again based on historical data, Kuilman and Li (2009) aimed at developing and empirically examining a theory on legitimacy transfers between an organizational population and its subpopulations. The study investigated the entry of foreign banks to Shanghai between 1847 and 1935 and showed that the legitimation of foreign banks overall had positive effects on entry rates in subpopulations of banks from different countries. Kuilman and Li (2009) also found, in line with Hannan et al.'s (2007) revised formulation, that subpopulations with higher grades of membership, i.e. constituting a greater proportion of the total population, contributed more to the legitimacy of the overall foreign bank population. Yet at the same time it was the subpopulations with low grades of membership which benefited most from the legitimacy of the overall population.

Scale or Scope? Resource Partitioning and Community Ecology

Another major theory in organizational ecology, resource partitioning, was also formulated and tested with historical data. Resource partitioning theory rests on a distinction between specialist and generalist organizational populations. Specialist organizations are characterized by a narrow and focused range of activities, while the generalists are geared toward broader and more diversified resource spaces or markets. Resource partitioning theory proposes that when economies of scale prevail, generalists have an advantage in the competition for the center of the market where demand is most dense. Yet when some generalists are eliminated due to competition and the market becomes concentrated, resources are released, which enables specialists to thrive in the periphery of the market. When originally developing this theory, Carroll (1985) collated data spanning 175 years—from 1800 to 1975—on local newspapers in seven metropolitan areas in the US. Based on this historical data, he showed that greater concentration at the center increased the failure rate of generalist newspapers while reducing it for the specialist newspapers at the periphery—thus generating a dual resource space for these two types of populations.

Various later tests and extensions of resource partitioning theory have also relied on historical data. To give a few examples, Mezias and Mezias (2000) examined resource partitioning in the initial stages of the American film industry from its inception in 1912 to 1929. Their findings not only supported the theory for specialist producers and distributors but also showed that specialists were more innovative—doing better in the creation of new film genres. Dobrev, Kim and Carroll (2002) studied the American automobile industry over the period 1885–1981. They found, in line with the resource partitioning model, that while overall niche width—i.e. being generalists—and location in the center of the market increased survival chances, these relationships were reversed under high industry concentration, meaning that mortality rates were lowered for specialists. Boone, Bröcheler and Carroll's (2000) study of the Dutch audit industry over the period 1896–1992, however, showed that resource partitioning predictions in this case held only during the unregulated period before 1971 but not afterwards. Swaminathan (2001) brought in the new formulation of identity-based organizational form (see earlier) in studying the post-Prohibition US wine industry from 1940 to 1990 to show that specialists (farm wineries) suffered if they deviated from their key identity elements of small size and high quality and were negatively affected if generalists (mass producers) were able to develop "robust identities" through the expansion of brands and high levels of advertising.

An additional type of research drawing on historical data are the so-called community ecology studies, which examine mutualistic or competitive relations among distinct yet resource interdependent organizational populations. Ruef (2000), for example, studied the US health-care sector during the period 1965–1994 to show that the emergence of novel organizational forms depended on the density and size of existing organizational populations. And in two additional studies—again based on historical data—he demonstrated how interpopulation competitive dynamics influenced the decline, revival and demise of organizational forms. A study on medical schools in the US over the period from 1765 to 1999 showed that competition from alternative forms (sectarian colleges and nursing schools), together with population inertia (delays in founding of new organizations), best accounted for the observed historical trajectory of the medical schools (Ruef 2004a). And another study covering the period 1860 to 1880 demonstrated the significant impact of competition by mid-sized and small farms on the disappearance of large-scale plantations in southern regions of the US after the Civil War (Ruef 2004b).

That Rare Beast: Qualitative Studies

Given their strong preference for quantitative research and, more recently, formalization (e.g. Hannan et al. 2007), ecologists have rarely turned to historical cases to develop theory. An early exception is Langton (1984), who employed ecological ideas in an attempt to account for bureaucratization in Josiah Wedgwood's British pottery firm in the late eighteenth century and to examine its spread to the whole pottery industry during the industrial revolution. More recently and more germane to the central concerns of the organizational ecology research program, McKendrick and Carroll (2001) studied disk array producers in the US as a historical case to extend theorizing on the emergence of organizational forms. Their research followed the previously mentioned turn in the ecology literature toward defining an organizational form as an identity "conferred by outsiders" (Hannan 2005: 60). The evidence in their case study supported neither the argument that formal associations will help legitimize a new form nor the classic density dependence account of legitimation increasing with the number of organizations. The explanation they provided for the failure of a distinct organizational form to emerge was the unfocused nature of the firms in the market. Not unexpectedly, a quantitative study followed—though one on the more recent past, the period from 1986, when a firm for the first time offered a software for disk arrays, until 1998. It showed that new firms with similar identities which are locally clustered tend to aid in the emergence of a distinct organizational form (McKendrick et al. 2003).

And the Twain Did Meet: Organizational Ecology and Institutions

The idea of bringing organizational ecology and neo-institutional theory together originated from the debate around the way in which the legitimation of organizational forms was construed in the density dependence model. As pointed out earlier, the classic version of this model focused on "cognitive" or "constitutive" legitimacy, which was postulated as arising from increasing numbers of organizations embodying a particular organizational form. This cognitive view, it was argued, ignored the sociopolitical bases of legitimation. Based on this critique, Baum and Powell (1995: 536) called for building an "institutional ecology" of organizations, which would involve "a more sophisticated theoretical understanding of the co-evolving nature of cultural understandings, organizational forms and resource constraints".

A range of studies followed this lead by seeking to combine ecological analyses with institutional ideas—though without necessarily referring to the label institutional ecology (see however, Baum and Oliver 1996; Marquis and Lounsbury 2007). These attempts were buttressed by views that the two perspectives were complementary and that they could be brought together in fruitful ways (e.g. Haveman and David 2008; Lander and Heugens 2017). As Dacin (1997: 46) put it, "[i]n this framework, the institutional environment is conceived of as the arena for ecological dynamics in that institutional forces prescribe institutionally driven selection criteria via which organizations are created or dissolved". Some of the research along these lines has also employed historical data to empirically assess and theorize the effects of institutional contexts on organizational evolution. In keeping with the ecological tradition, these studies have relied on quantitative analyses, either of an exploratory or hypothesis-testing nature. Nevertheless, as the exemplars reviewed next will demonstrate, not only have they used historical data but they also included varying degrees of historical analysis to provide either a background for or context-specific considerations in the development of research questions or hypotheses.

In one of the early studies, Dacin (1997: 47) aimed to "extend organizational ecology" by examining the effects of institutional norms on key characteristics of newly founded organizations. The setting was the Finnish press from 1771, when the first-ever newspaper was published, until 1963. The data included all the newspapers that were founded in this time frame, and the hypotheses were embedded in a historical account that covered the entire period. The specific issue that Dacin (1997) addressed was the impact of nationalistic norms on whether newspapers in Finland were founded in Finnish or Swedish, taking also into account economic and competitive factors. Her findings showed that both at the population and the local city levels nationalism had a positive effect on the founding of Finnish-language newspapers. Indeed, nationalism overrode economic demand conditions, as even in cities where Swedish was the predominant language nationalistic norms positively influenced Finnish newspapers and were negatively associated with the creation of papers in Swedish. Another example was a study by Dobbin and Dowd (1997) that drew upon the history of railroads in Massachusetts in the nineteenth and the early twentieth centuries to theorize on the effects of public policy on competition and business strategies. These authors showed that of the three policy regimes they identified, public capitalization (1826–1871) encouraged railroad foundings by expanding resource availability, whereas pro-cartel policies (1872–1896) did the same by dampening competition. By contrast, anti-trust policies (1897–1922) reduced foundings by increasing competition within the industry. Similar to what Dobrev (2001) found (see earlier), the predictions of the classic density dependence model only held when alterations in policy regimes were taken into account.

In another study Barron (1998) directly addressed the debate around legitimacy by using historical data and some historical analyses in research on the early stages in the development of two kinds of consumer loan providers, namely, credit unions and the so-called Morris Plan Banks. These two novel organizational forms had emerged in the US in the first decade of the twentieth century in a cultural environment adverse to borrowing money. The study examined the founding rates of credit unions and the growth rate of the single Morris Plan Bank in New York—as there could be only one in any city—over the initial 20 years (1914–1934) after these two types of loan providers first appeared in the city. He found that in this early period founding rates of credit unions were positively associated with increases in the density of the population, thus supporting the ecologists' view of cognitive legitimacy. The results also showed that his measures for "pragmatic" and "moral" legitimacy (see Suchman 1995) were positively related to founding rates. Since there was just one Morris Plan Bank in the city, only its growth rate could be examined. Barron (1998) therefore supplemented his quantitative analyses by resorting to historical evidence obtained from documents and newspapers of the time. Foreshadowing future studies on institutional entrepreneurship (see Chapter 8, this volume), this historical analysis suggested that both the credit unions and the Morris Plan Bank took an active role in promoting their moral legitimacy by joining what had turned into a kind of social movement at the time against the so-called "loan sharks".

Haveman and Rao (1997) studied the thrift industry in California during the period 1865–1928 to show how institutions co-evolved with organizational forms. These authors were primarily concerned with integrating institutional and ecological theories by focusing on the interaction between technical and institutional pressures and examining whether selection or adaptation drove population evolution. Yet they also brought in a historical perspective not only by studying organizations well in the past but also by demonstrating how the Progressive movement in American history influenced the rise and demise of different organizational forms. Haveman and Rao (2006) used the same data to address the question of whether change in institutional logics occurs in an incremental or a discontinuous fashion. Their analyses showed that thrifts were more likely to convert into similar or hybrid forms than into completely different ones, leading to incremental institutional change. They argued that this was because blending processes within this population were stronger than segregating processes—leading them to the broad theoretical statement that whether institutional change is incremental or discontinuous depends on the relative strength of blending or segregating processes among organizational forms.

In an extension of these studies, Haveman, Rao and Paruchuri (2007) showed, based on data for the 1906–1920 period, that new foundings and conversions to the bureaucratic form, distinct from the original logics of the thrift industry, were mediated by intermediate institutions, namely the Progressive media and the city-manager form of government. Along similar lines, Lounsbury (2002) traced the history of the field of finance in the US to show how a regulatory logic in place in the early 1930s gave way to a market logic by the 1980s. A complementary quantitative analysis, using historical data from 1945 to 1993, demonstrated that this shift, together with the emergence of finance as a specialized academic field, led to increased foundings of professional finance associations.

There was also a turn to examining interdependencies between organizational populations, which constituted, as discussed previously, one of the major preoccupations in ecological research. In this case, however, research issues that were taken up were not related to interdependencies that arose from technological differences or competition, but rather from institutions or sociopolitical conditions. Ingram and Simons, for instance, used historical data in two consecutive studies (Ingram and Simons 2000; Simons and Ingram 2003), which mainly focused on the effects of the state as well as population interdependencies on the evolution of a focal population. Both studies were set in the context of Israeli political history involving the British Mandate for Palestine, which began in 1923, followed by the founding of the State of Israel in 1948. This history afforded the authors a rare opportunity to assess the influence of the formation of a strong state in lieu of the weaker rule by the British.

Based on data ranging from 1920 to 1992, the first study examined the impact of this strong state and a powerful workers' federation—Histadrut, which existed since 1920 and was also viewed as a provider of an institutional framework—on the failure rates of workers' cooperatives. The study also considered the effects of organizational populations with rival or similar political ideologies on failure rates. Findings showed that the establishment of the Israeli state reduced the failure rate, as did membership in Histadrut. Notably, though, benefits associated with Histadrut membership were moderated by the founding of Israel, suggesting that the state was more influential as a provider of institutional order relative to an organizational federation. In considering political interdependencies among organizational populations, Ingram and Simons (2000: 26) characterized workers' cooperatives as "utopian-socialist". The growth of ideologically similar organizations, i.e. credit cooperatives and the kibbutz, had mutualistic effects on the survival chances of workers' cooperatives, while the expansion of the bank population, as bearers of an opposing capitalist ideology, increased failure rates—though only for those affiliated with Histadrut.

Their second study examined the effects of a similar set of antecedent conditions on the fate of the kibbutz population (Simons and Ingram 2003). The historical data stretched from 1910, when the first kibbutz was founded, up to 1997. A central concern was again the influence of the state, in this instance on the founding rates of the kibbutz. The authors showed that the formation of the State of Israel lowered founding rates, as the kibbutz arguably came to be viewed as a threat and thus were subjected to delegitimizing attacks on the part of the state. With respect to interdependencies among organizational populations, findings again confirmed that the expansion of capitalism, i.e. the number of corporations as well as alternative forms of settlements, such as the moshav—another type of a cooperative settlement—or the so-called development towns, also dampened the founding rates of the kibbutz.

Wade, Swaminathan and Saxon (1998) studied interdependencies among populations of similar organizations under varying regulatory regimes in different geographical locations by examining the prohibition of alcohol in the US from the mid-nineteenth through the early twentieth century. During this period laws banning the production and sale of alcohol were passed in quite a few US states, though they were not always long-lived and were often reversed. The study examined the effects of Prohibition laws in certain states on the population dynamics of breweries located in adjacent states where no such laws were introduced. Drawing upon both ecological and institutional theories, the authors proposed that anti-alcohol regulations in one state created resources, such as capital or customers, for brewery populations in adjacent states with no Prohibition laws, but at the same time generated normative pressures on these breweries through the spread of anti-alcoholism as a cultural norm. Findings, based on data from 1845 to 1918, showed that the resources created for adjacent no-Prohibition states did increase the founding rates of breweries there but had limited effects on the rates of failure. Normative pressures and the increase in the number of adjacent states with Prohibitions laws, in contrast, both dampened the rates of founding and increased failure rates in a no-Prohibition state.

Hiatt, Sine and Tolbert (2009) used a similar period and issue to theorize and empirically assess the effects of social movements on organizations. Thus, they examined the consequences of the activism of the Woman's Christian Temperance Union (WCTU) on two separate organizational populations, namely breweries and soft-drink manufacturers in the US during the period 1870–1920. Their quantitative analyses tested hypotheses derived from a historical investigation of the WCTU, based on published sources. What they showed was that the activities of the WCTU led to changes in the institutional environment, which then resulted in increasing failures of breweries, while generating at the same time opportunities for the founding of producers of nonalcoholic beverages.

Where You Belong: Categories and Categorization

Lately, there has been an expansion of interest in the notion of "categories" and processes of "categorization". Categories have been defined as "socially constructed partitions that divide the social space and the distinct meanings associated with them" (Negro, Koçak and Hsu 2010: 4) and categorization as a "process that involves lumping things into distinct clusters, rendering them cognizable, and creating shared understandings" (Lounsbury and Rao 2004: 969). The interest in categories and categorization systems has been evident in both ecological and institutional literatures. Common to both approaches has been the premise that organizations, markets and fields are subject to categorization. These category systems serve as schemes for social evaluation. The idea of "categorical imperative" follows from this in that actors are expected to conform to requirements of established categories in social life—as infringement of expectations is prone to adverse evaluation (Negro et al. 2010).

In ecological research, the turn toward the concept of categories has been associated mainly with the major revision, discussed earlier, in the conceptualization of organizational form as "form identity" conferred by external and internal audiences (Hannan 2005). Based on this view, a new population emerges when a number of organizations are regarded by audiences as similar enough to constitute a separate cognitive category different from those pertaining to other organizations. When the dimensions of this category—or collective identity—become codified with organizational proliferation and gain a taken-for-granted character, a form identity takes shape and an organizational form is born (Hannan et al. 2007). Thus, as Pólos, Hannan and Carroll (2002: 89) have put it, organizational forms are "recognizable patterns that take on rule-like standing and get enforced by social agents".

Some of the more recent work following this new orientation has also continued with the ecological tradition of making use of historical data. To provide a few examples, there is the study by Dobrev, Ozdemir and Teo (2006: 579), which aimed at adding to theory in community ecology by "extend[ing] the form concept as reflecting a social identity with both a constitutive and punitive standing". It was based on the history of Singaporean financial cooperatives, from the first cooperative in 1925 up to 1994. As the authors point out, they "employed historical evidence to make judgments about the boundaries between forms and populations with reference to established and emergent social identities". Despite being a hypothesis-testing quantitative study, the historical perspective enabled the authors to show that the identity overlap between emergent financial cooperatives and extant commercial banks both helped and hindered the evolution of cooperatives. Some degree of legitimacy transfer from banks to cooperatives notwithstanding, the growth of the cooperative population was impeded because their identity overlap with banks held back the establishment of cooperatives as a distinct category. And when financial cooperatives eventually became recognized as a separate category, they invited greater competition from commercial banks, ultimately preventing them from becoming dominant actors within the Singaporean financial industry.

The outcomes of crossing category boundaries or creating hybrid forms were addressed by Ruef and Patterson (2009) in the context of an early industry classification scheme introduced in the US—initially for purposes of credit rating. Their study was based on data for the post–Civil War period (1870–1900) obtained from the system developed by R. G. Dun and Company. Going back to the origins of the scheme enabled the authors to add to theory by examining the effects of a category system in the making. As Ruef and Patterson (2009: 516) acknowledged, "[t]he implementation of Dun's schema during the postbellum period offers a unique historical window onto a system of social classification in the process of emergence". Combining a historical narrative on the development of Dun and Company's system with quantitative analysis, they were able to show that in the early stages of the classification system's development, boundary crossings were likely to be less penalized by those assessing the credit worthiness of businesses. When the system became institutionalized, however, category violation led to lower credit ratings. Again, pointing to the value of a historical perspective, Ruef and

Patterson (2009: 517) concluded that "[i]n lieu of ahistorical accounts, our understanding of how society evaluates different forms of organizations becomes enriched by attention to cultural change in the evaluative schema themselves".

In another example very much along similar lines, Hsu, Negro and Perretti (2012) turned to the early stages of the US feature film industry. They also aimed "to develop theory", in this instance on the antecedents and consequences of crossing category boundaries by producing hybrid "products" (Hsu et al. 2012: 1429). Differently from Ruef and Patterson (2009), however, no history was provided in the empirical part, and the study rested entirely on quantitative analyses drawing upon data for the period 1912–1948. Findings, as expected, showed that mixing film genres was more likely for categories, i.e. genres, with fuzzier boundaries.

The idea of categories has gained considerable traction in the institutional literature, too, as the latter started paying greater attention to diversity and change (see Chapter 8, this volume). Various studies along institutionalist lines have resorted to history in addressing questions about category emergence, category change and the impact of categorization on organizations, linking these processes with key concerns in the institutional literature such as institutional change and institutional logics. In one of the early studies, Lounsbury and Rao (2004) examined the creation of new product categories within the US mutual fund industry, focusing on how new categories developed from existing classification systems. Core theoretical arguments were that stability and change in category systems are not only technical matters but also political processes and that whether reconfiguration in categories did or did not occur depended on the interaction between producers and field-level media such as trade magazines and industry directories. This was again a quantitative, hypothesis-testing study. But it did draw on longer-term data, namely, from 1944 to 1985, and the quantitative analyses were supplemented with interviews as well as "extensive historical research and analysis" (Lounsbury and Rao 2004: 973)—though the latter were used only in the presentation and interpretation of the results.

The creation of a new market category, in this instance satellite radio, was examined by Navis and Glynn (2010). Their study encompassed a relatively recent past (1990–2005)—inevitably, since satellite radio emerged in the US as a new market category only in the mid-1990s. While this was essentially a quantitative, hypothesis-testing study, the authors also provided a lengthy historical narrative bracketed into periods of "emergence" (1997–2001), "commercialization" (2002) and "early growth" (2003–2005). The historical narrative, according to Navis and Glynn (2010: 447), "sensitized us to processes of meaning construction, legitimation, and identity formation" and "revealed key inflections, tipping points, or threshold effects [. . .] that demarcated discrete periods in the market category's emergence and the achievement of legitimacy". The end product, based on bringing the narrative and quantitative findings together, was a theoretical model of new category emergence and legitimation. In contrast, Jones et al. (2012) presented a narrative history of how "modern architecture" emerged as a "de novo category" and evolved over the period 1870–1975 as it became established, then dominant and eventually taken for granted. This process was shaped, the authors argued, by two contending logics: the commercial and the professional. Taking a historical perspective enabled them not only to trace the evolution but also to address the question of how a de novo category originates. Their study was based on texts written by 17 well-known architects from the US and Europe, exemplary buildings that they constructed and reviews of their work by "professional" audiences. This material was then subjected to a content-analytic method ("network text analysis") to delineate the dual institutional logics at play and their impact on category formation and evolution.

In a recent qualitative study, Delmestri and Greenwood (2016) used the Italian spirit grappa for developing a theoretical model on how status recategorization takes place within mature status systems, through processes of what they refer to as "theorization" by the actors. As the authors put it, very much in line with the broad theme in this chapter, "[b]ecause our purpose is theory elaboration, we used an inductive historical approach [. . .] by analyzing a case study of the successful redefinition of a mature category" (Delmestri and Greenwood 2016: 514). Their story of grappa began in the 1960s when the spirit was considered a low-status product and initial attempts toward upgrading had failed. The historical account then showed how toward the late 1980s "premium grappa" had become a high-status product, also altering, by the late 1990s and 2000s, the perception of the overall grappa category. The data used to construct the narrative came from historical archives supplemented with interviews—though, like in many other cases, this material was subjected to thematic coding. Based on their analysis the authors argued that redefinition of the category was possible because of the particular form of theorization of the change by the actors involved, "meaning the way that proponents of change invoke 'culturally resonant claims' [. . .] to render ideas 'into understandable and compelling formats'" (Delmestri and Greenwood 2016: 514). They called this "theorization by allusion", which involved category "detachment", "emulation and "sublimation" (pp. 531–535). The authors generalized their findings for the case by suggesting that this form of theorization was likely to enable status shifts in mature settings, as it was a way of avoiding resistance and confrontation.

Not Much There: History and Organizational Economics

In contrast to the ecological research program, studies developed within organizational economics, such as transaction cost or agency theories (e.g. Gibbons and Roberts 2013), have largely been oblivious to the use of historical data. This has been the case both at the organizational and the macro levels. And the few exceptions at the macro level discussed here either took a critical view of organizational economics approaches or combined them with other organizational theory perspectives. In an early example, Lazerson (1995) compared the putting-out system prior to the second industrial revolution with the one that had emerged, among others, in the knitwear industry in Modena, Italy, after World War II. To analyze the past, Lazerson did not actually use historical sources, but instead relied on prior studies on the history of the putting-out system, while the examination of the system in Modena was based on interviews and some statistical material. The author began by pointing to the similarities, in terms of ownership, family involvement and specialization, as well as the differences between the two systems, such as a greater division of labor, more hired labor and greater state involvement in the modern form. While rejecting neo-institutional economics and neo-Marxian accounts, Lazerson (1995) did not see transaction costs playing a role in the organization of the knitwear industry in Modena either. Instead, he pointed to institutional aspects in the sociological sense, such as family ties, trust, commitment to the community and supportive regulatory frameworks.

Ingram and Inman (1996) combined ideas from neo-institutional economics with an organizational ecology approach in research on the history of the tourism industry in Niagara Falls on both sides of the border between Canada and the US. Covering almost two centuries, their historical narrative was based on both published and unpublished sources. It recounted the attempts by private actors throughout the nineteenth century—and the struggles among them—to deal with hucksters and reckless entrepreneurs who abused the tourists and the site, which, according to the authors, constituted a case of the "tragedy of the commons" (p. 632). According to their study, these attempts failed—contrary to what economic theories of the firm would have predicted. However, the rivalry between the two communities in Canada and the US facilitated the establishment of government reservation parks on both sides of the border toward the end of the nineteenth century. A second, quantitative part of the study was based on data spanning the period from the establishment of the parks to the 1990s. It examined the impact of these "government institutions" on the founding and failure rates of hotels on the Canadian and US sides. Extending the density dependence model, the results showed that there were competitive but no legitimation effects across the border—a finding that contradicted what had been found by ecologists in the five-country automobile industry study (see earlier). Moreover, the institutional structures, i.e. the parks, on the two sides were indiscriminate in their positive effects on hotel populations on the other side. For Ingram and Inman (1996) the historical analysis supported both institutional economists and organizational institutionalists in demonstrating the active role that organizations may play in the creation of institutions. Yet the findings also indicated that outcomes tended to differ from the expectations the actors had when striving for the creation of these institutions. Notably in the context of history to theory, Ingram and Inman (1996: 655) were explicit in crediting the historical empirical study for their ability to make this general claim.

Covering a similar long-term period, Toms and Filatotchev (2004) used the history of the Lancashire cotton textile industry in the UK between 1830 and 1980 to demonstrate the usefulness of a theoretical model which introduced a typology of network relationships among firms in an industry and aimed to account for how these relationships or network structures changed over time. Relying on prior business history research and some publicly available documents rather than original sources, the authors constructed a historical narrative, drawing selectively on the resource-based view of the firm, transaction cost theory and the resource dependence approach (see later). This narrative identified periods of "expansion" (1830–1914) and of "decline" (1920–1980) (p. 631) and showed that the predominant industrial district type network structures, which had formed during expansion and gave power to interlocked directors, served as an impediment to restructuring in the face of the industry's decline. By contrast, those firms that had previously tended to diversify toward capital providers from outside the industry were able to engage in strategic change. In addition to developing theory from history, Toms and Filatotchev (2004) situated history within their theoretical model (see Chapter 11, this volume) by suggesting that forms of network relationships inherited from the past inhibited or facilitated strategic change in organizations.

Another example, covering a more recent period, is a study by Jacobides (2005), which addressed the question of market emergence within the context of mortgage banking in the US between 1970 and 1990. During these decades, the mortgage banking industry disintegrated and three new markets emerged: "securitization and the secondary market for loans", "brokers and the market for closed loans", and "the market for mortgage servicing rights" (Jacobides 2005: 474). Again, no original historical sources were used; the study drew mainly on interviews with a wide range of industry participants as well as secondary historical data. Categorized by the author as "process research" (p. 468; see also Chapter 8, this volume), it presented not only a range of challenges to transaction cost theorizing but also an inductive model that went beyond the latter in accounting for the process of new market creation and the drivers behind it.

Studies using history as a source of data were even rarer when it comes to economic approaches addressing organizational-level phenomena. One example is the work by Bigelow and Argyres (2008) who tested quantitatively whether transaction cost theory (TCT) predictions also held for small firms. Using historical data on the entire population of automobile manufacturers in the US during its early stages of development in 1917–1933, they found support for the asset specificity argument in TCT, showing that unique engines and component systems with greater interdependencies were more likely to be produced internally. By contrast, their data did not support the small numbers argument, which suggests that a more limited number of suppliers would lead to making rather than buying. Moreover, like Toms and Filatotchev (2004), Bigelow and Argyres (2008) went toward a theoretical model incorporating the past, since they found that the extent of firms' prior experience in the automobile industry was positively associated with the internalization of production (see Chapter 11, this volume).

More recently Silverman and Ingram (2017) used eighteenth-century data on transatlantic shipping from Liverpool—which also involved slave trading—to test predictions derived from the so-called "incentive systems theory". This theory is based on a principal–agent view of "managing agents performing multiple tasks" and considers the principals' concern about balancing agents' efforts with respect to caring for the asset and/or for performance outcomes (p. 856). To this end the study examined the antecedents and performance outcomes of the part-ownership of vessels by captains—with performance defined as captains avoiding capture by the enemy during war times and obtaining profits from the voyage. The historical data provided a unique opportunity to test the theory's predictions in that the captains were often only minority owners of the vessels. According to incentive systems theory, relative to nonowner captains they would therefore be expected to care more about preserving the value of the asset, i.e. the vessel, and less about maximizing the surplus from the voyage. Corroborating the theory, Silverman and Ingram (2017) were able to show that (a) vessels were more likely to have part-owner captains during wartime voyages, (b) vessels of part-owner captains were less likely to be captured compared to nonowner captains, but (c) the former appeared to exert less effort with respect to profits from the voyage than the latter.

Nor Here: Resource Dependence

Initially, the resource dependence perspective, which theorized how the behavior of organizations was determined by its broadly defined external resources (Pfeffer and Salancik 1978), relied on cross-sectional analyses. However, in line with the broader move toward longitudinal analyses (see earlier), a few studies associated with this research program began to examine hypothesized relations based on historical and/or longitudinal data. For instance, to address the question of corporate control, Mizruchi and Bunting (1981) relied on data from 1904 to study board interlocks among 166 large American corporations. The historical evidence enabled them to assess the validity of alternative measures for gauging influence among corporations, since they compared the results from their analyses with the consensus that existed in the popular and academic literatures at the time with regard to the power of financial institutions. Mizruchi and Stearns's (1988) study is an example for the use of longitudinal data. Based on an examination of board ties of 22 large US industrial firms with financial institutions over the period 1956–1983, they contributed to resource dependency theory by showing that not only the decline in solvency and profitability of firms but also variations in the economic environment affected the extent of new appointments of financial directors to the boards of these industrial firms.

There has also been the occasional study with some form of a historical basis where resource dependence theory has been considered together with other theoretical perspectives to explain organizational actions. Halliday, Powell and Granfors (1993: 529), for example, used historical data to elaborate and test what they called a "theory of organizational transformations". Examining whether or not bar associations in the US during the period 1918–1950 moved from a voluntary, i.e. market-based, to a state-based form, they included variables derived from resource dependence, organizational ecology and neo-institutional theories. Their historical review and quantitative analyses showed that resource dependence and neo-institutional theories were complementary in that the shift to the state-based form was associated with difficulties in the acquisition of resources and legitimacy. Sherer and Lee (2002) obtained a similar result in a study on the shift of law offices in the US away from the almost a century-old standard for managing the careers of lawyers—an "up-or-out" system referred to as the Cravath model. Combining a historical account with a quantitative analysis, they showed that the movement away from the Cravath model was a joint outcome of human resource scarcities and the prestige of law offices that could pioneer or readily adopt alternative career models. Notably, both of these studies also pointed to institutional change—though in a way where the emergence and institutionalization of a new organizational form or practice does not eradicate a prior order but leads to the coexistence of both the old and the new. Equally notably, Halliday et al. (1993) have called for research on the post-1990 era, as they have recognized that their theory and findings might be limited to the historical context that they had studied. They surmised that findings for the more recent period might differ, given the signs of a reverse movement within an unfolding ideological shift toward privatization and reductions in state involvement.

An example for a "historical case study" based entirely on confidential internal archives is the work by Pajunen (2006: 1263), who combined resource dependence and network perspectives to develop a power-based model for "stakeholder influence identification". He then used this model to examine the processes of decline (1904–1907) and turnaround (1908–1912) in the early stages of the history of the Finnish pulp and paper firm Kymi, justifying his research strategy by suggesting that "historical analysis may offer opportunities to examine social dynamics and prevailing organizational structures in ways that cross-sectional research cannot" (p. 1265). The resulting historical narrative—structured according to the theoretical bases of the model identified—categorized and compared the stakeholders and their influence during these periods of decline and turnaround. Very much in the spirit of history to theory, Pajunen then used the historical analysis to develop a range of general propositions on how, in a crisis situation, actively managing "governing" stakeholders, i.e. those that have a direct bearing on the success of an organization, may increase the likelihood of organizational survival.

Conclusion

As this chapter has shown, already during the 1980s research on organizational ecology has been instrumental in breaking the stranglehold of cross-sectional research in management and organization studies—and it has done so largely and consciously by drawing on historical data. Importantly, researchers working within this broad perspective not only "collated" variables from historical sources but many of them also looked at the historical context of the populations of organizations they studied over time to generate and test their various theories. And they continued to rely on historical data as they subsequently refined and modified these theories—in part by combining them with insights from neo-institutional approaches. In contrast to the extensive use of historical data and, at times, historical cases in these two broad perspectives, other management research programs, namely those drawing on economic theories but also those looking at resource dependence, have made little use of history in their work.

Thus, both neo-institutional and ecological research programs have provided multiple examples of what this book refers to as history to theory. While the former with their initial focus on the stability of organizations and organizational fields came to history late, historical evidence was central to the latter from the outset because of the concern with the long-term survival of organizational forms. And while the data sources and the methods used to analyze this evidence differ, there is no doubt that both of these broad research programs are taking history seriously—though possibly not always in the way that most historians would like them to, nor in the way that those calling for more history or a "historic turn" might envisage. But while the overviews presented in these chapters show the often hidden and, at times, ignored role of historical evidence in mainstream management research, they also reaffirm the primordial preoccupation of management scholarship with theorizing—whatever the data.

The subsequent chapters in this part of the book present the second way in which this relationship between history and theory has been constructed, namely by incorporating the past within the theoretical models themselves, or as the book calls it, "history *in* theory".

References

Barron, D. N. (1998) "Pathways to legitimacy among consumer loan providers in New York City, 1914–1934," *Organization Studies*, 19(2): 207–233.

Baum, J. A. C. and Oliver, C. (1996) "Toward an institutional ecology of organizational founding," *Academy of Management Journal*, 39(5): 1378–1427.

Baum, J. A. C. and Powell, W. W. (1995) "Cultivating an institutional ecology of organizations: Comment on Hannan, Carroll, Dundon and Torres," *American Sociological Review*, 60(4): 529–538.

Baum, J. A. C. and Shipilov, A. V. (2006) "Ecological approaches to organizations," in S. R. Clegg, C. Hardy, T. Lawrence and W. R. Nord (eds), *The Sage Handbook of Organization Studies*, 2nd edn, London: Sage, pp. 55–110.

Bigelow, L. S. and Argyres, N. (2008) "Transaction costs, industry experience and make-or-buy decisions in the population of early U.S. auto firms," *Journal of Economic Behavior & Organization*, 66(3–4): 791–807.

Bogaert, S., Boone, C. and Carroll, G. R. (2010) "Organizational form emergence and competing professional schemata of Dutch accounting, 1884–1939," *Research in the Sociology of Organizations*, 31: 115–150.

Bogaert, S., Boone, C., Negro, G. and van Witteloostuijn, A. (2016) "Organizational form emergence: A meta-analysis of the ecological theory of legitimation," *Journal of Management*, 42(5): 1344–1373.

Boone, C., Bröcheler, V. and Carroll, G. R. (2000) "Custom service: Application and tests of resource-partitioning theory among Dutch auditing firms from 1896 to 1992," *Organization Studies*, 21(2): 355–381.

Carroll, G. R. (1985) "Concentration and specialization: Dynamics of niche width in populations of organizations," *American Journal of Sociology*, 90(6): 1262–1283.

Carroll, G. R., Feng, M., Le Mens, G. and McKendrick, D. G. (2009) "Studying organizational populations over time," in D. A. Buchanan and A. Bryman (eds), *The Sage Handbook of Organizational Research Methods*, London: Sage, pp. 213–229.

Carroll, G. R. and Hannan, M. T. (1989) "On using institutional theory in studying organizational populations," *American Sociological Review*, 54(4): 545–548.

Carroll, G. R., Preisendoerfer, P., Swaminathan, A. and Wiedenmayer, G. (1993) "Brewery and Brauerei: The organizational ecology of brewing," *Organization Studies*, 14(2): 155–188.

Dacin, T. (1997) "Isomorphism in context: The power and prescription of institutional norms," *Academy of Management Journal*, 40(1): 46–81.

Delmestri, G. and Greenwood, R. (2016) "How Cinderella became a queen: Theorizing radical status change," *Administrative Science Quarterly*, 61(4): 507–550.

Dobbin, F. and Dowd, T. J. (1997) "How policy shapes competition: Early railroad foundings in Massachusetts," *Administrative Science Quarterly*, 42(3): 501–529.

Dobrev, S. D. (2001) "Revisiting organizational legitimation: Cognitive diffusion and sociopolitical factors in the evolution of Bulgarian newspaper enterprises, 1846–1992," *Organization Studies*, 22(3): 419–444.

Dobrev, S. D., Kim, T.-Y. and Carroll, G. R. (2002) "The evolution of organizational niches: U.S. automobile manufacturers, 1885–1981," *Administrative Science Quarterly*, 47(2): 233–264.

Dobrev, S. D., Ozdemir, S. Z. and Teo, A. C. (2006) "The ecological interdependence of emergent and established organizational populations: Legitimacy transfer, violation by comparison, and unstable identities," *Organization Science*, 17(5): 577–597.

Gibbons, R. and Roberts, J. (eds) (2013) *The Handbook of Organizational Economics*, Princeton, NJ: Princeton University Press.

Halliday, T. C., Powell, M. J. and Granfors, M. W. (1993) "After minimalism: Transformation of state bar associations from market dependence to state reliance, 1918 to 1950," *American Sociological Review*, 58(4): 515–535.

Hannan, M. T. (2005) "Ecologies of organizations: Diversity and identity," *Journal of Economic Perspectives*, 19(1): 51–70.

Hannan, M. T. (2010) "Partiality of memberships in categories and audiences," *Annual Review of Sociology*, 36: 159–181.

Hannan, M. T., Carroll, G. R., Dundon, E. A. and Torres, J. C. (1995) "Organizational evolution in a multinational context: Entries of automobile manufacturers in Belgium, Britain, France, Germany, and Italy," *American Sociological Review*, 60(4): 509–528.

Hannan, M. T. and Freeman, J. (1984) "Structural inertia and organizational change," *American Sociological Review*, 49(2): 149–164.

Hannan, M. T. and Freeman, J. (1987) "The ecology of organizational founding: American labor unions, 1836–1985," *American Journal of Sociology*, 92(4): 910–943.

Hannan, M. T. and Freeman, J. (1988) "The ecology of organizational mortality: American labor unions, 1836–1985," *American Journal of Sociology*, 94(1): 25–52.

Hannan, M. T. and Freeman, J. (1989) *Organizational Ecology*, Cambridge, MA: Harvard University Press.

Hannan, M. T., Pólos, L. and Carroll, G. R. (2007) *Logics of Organization Theory: Audiences, Codes, and Ecologies*, Princeton, NJ: Princeton University Press.

Haveman, H. A. and David, R. J. (2008) "Ecologists and institutionalists: Friends or foes?" in R. Greenwood, C. Oliver, K. Sahlin and R. Suddaby (eds), *The Sage Handbook of Organizational Institutionalism*, London: Sage, pp. 573–595.

Haveman, H. A. and Rao, H. (1997) "Structuring a theory of moral sentiments: Institutional and organizational coevolution in the early thrift industry," *American Journal of Sociology*, 102(6): 1606–1651.

Haveman, H. A. and Rao, H. (2006) "Hybrid forms and the evolution of thrifts," *American Behavioral Scientist*, 49(7): 974–986.

Haveman, H. A., Rao, H. and Paruchuri, S. (2007) "The winds of change: The progressive movement and the bureaucratization of thrift," *American Sociological Review*, 72(1): 117–142.

Hiatt, S. R., Sine, W. D. and Tolbert, P. S. (2009) "From Pabst to Pepsi: The deinstitutionalization of social practices and the creation of entrepreneurial opportunities," *Administrative Science Quarterly*, 54(4): 635–667.

Hsu, G., Negro, G. and Perretti, F. (2012) "Hybrids in Hollywood: A study of the production and performance of genre-spanning films," *Industrial and Corporate Change*, 21(6): 1427–1450.

Ingram, P. and Inman, C. (1996) "Institutions, intergroup competition and the evolution of hotel populations around Niagara Falls," *Administrative Science Quarterly*, 41(4): 629–658.

Ingram, P. and Simons, T. (2000) "State formation, ideological competition, and the ecology of Israeli workers' cooperatives, 1920–1992," *Administrative Science Quarterly*, 45(1): 25–53.

Isaac, L. W. and Griffin, L. J. (1989) "Ahistoricism in time-series analyses of historical process: Critique, redirection, and illustrations from U.S. labor history," *American Sociological Review*, 54(6): 873–890.

Jacobides, M. G. (2005) "Industry change through vertical disintegration: How and why markets emerged in mortgage banking," *Academy of Management Journal*, 48(3): 465–498.

Jones, C., Maoret, M., Massa, F. G. and Svejenova, S. (2012) "Rebels with a cause: Formation, contestation, and expansion of the de novo category 'modern architecture,' 1870–1975," *Organization Science*, 23(6): 1523–1545.

Kuilman, J. G. and Li, J. (2009) "Grades of membership and legitimacy spillovers: Foreign banks in Shanghai, 1847–1935," *Academy of Management Journal*, 52(2): 229–245.

Lander, M. W. and Heugens, P. P. M. A. R. (2017) "Better together: Using meta-analysis to explore complementarities between ecological and institutional theories of organization," *Organization Studies*, 38(11): 1573–1601.

Langton, J. (1984) "The ecological theory of bureaucracy: The case of Josiah Wedgwood and the British pottery industry," *Administrative Science Quarterly*, 29(3): 330–354.

Lazerson, M. (1995) "A new phoenix? Modern putting-out in the Modena knitwear industry," *Administrative Science Quarterly*, 40(1): 34–59.

Lounsbury, M. (2002) "Institutional transformation and status mobility: The professionalization of the field of finance," *Academy of Management Journal*, 45(1): 255–266.

Lounsbury, M. and Rao, H. (2004) "Sources of durability and change in market classifications: A study of the reconstitution of product categories in the American mutual fund industry, 1944–1985," *Social Forces*, 82(3): 969–999.

Marquis, C. and Lounsbury, M. (2007) "Vive la résistance: Competing logics and the consolidation of U.S. community banking," *Academy of Management Journal*, 50(4): 799–820.

McKendrick, D. G. and Carroll, G. R. (2001) "On the genesis of organizational forms: Evidence from the market for disk arrays," *Organization Science*, 12(6): 661–682.

McKendrick, D. G., Jaffee, J., Carroll, G. R. and Khessina, O. M. (2003) "In the bud? Analysis of disk array producers as a (possibly) emergent organizational form," *Administrative Science Quarterly*, 48(1): 60–94.

Mezias, J. M. and Mezias, S. J. (2000) "Resource partitioning, the founding of specialist firms, and innovation: The American feature film industry, 1912–1929," *Organization Science*, 11(3): 306–322.

Mizruchi, M. S. and Bunting, D. (1981) "Influence in corporate networks: An examination of four measures," *Administrative Science Quarterly*, 26(3): 475–489.

Mizruchi, M. S. and Stearns, L. B. (1988) "A longitudinal study of the formation of interlocking directorates," *Administrative Science Quarterly*, 33(2): 194–210.

Navis, C. and Glynn, M. A. (2010) "How new market categories emerge: Temporal dynamics of legitimacy, identity, and entrepreneurship in satellite radio, 1990-2005," *Administrative Science Quarterly*, 55(3): 439–471.

Negro, G., Koçak, Ö. and Hsu, G. (2010) "Research on categories in the sociology of organizations," *Research in the Sociology of Organizations*, 31: 3–35.

Pajunen, K. (2006) "Stakeholder influences in organizational survival," *Journal of Management Studies*, 43(6): 1261–1288.

Pfeffer, J. and Salancik, G. R. (1978) *The External Control of Organizations: A Resource Dependence Perspective*, New York: Harper and Row.

Pólos, L., Hannan, M. T. and Carroll, G. R. (2002) "Foundations of a theory of social forms," *Industrial and Corporate Change*, 11(1): 85–115.

Ranger-Moore, J., Banaszak-Holl, J. and Hannan, M. T. (1991) "Density-dependent dynamics in regulated industries: Founding rates of banks and life insurance companies," *Administrative Science Quarterly*, 36(1): 36–65.

Ruef, M. (2000) "The emergence of organizational forms: A community ecology approach," *American Journal of Sociology*, 106(3): 658–714.

Ruef, M. (2004a) "For whom the bell tolls: Ecological perspectives on industrial decline and resurgence," *Industrial and Corporate Change*, 13(1): 61–89.

Ruef, M. (2004b) "The demise of an organizational form: Emancipation and plantation agriculture in the American South, 1860–1880," *American Journal of Sociology*, 109(6): 1365–1410.

Ruef, M. and Patterson, K. (2009) "Credit and classification: The impact of industry boundaries in nineteenth-century America," *Administrative Science Quarterly*, 54(3): 486–520.

Sherer, P. D. and Lee, K. (2002) "Institutional change in large law firms: A resource dependency and institutional perspective," *Academy of Management Journal*, 45(1): 102–119.

Silverman, B. S. and Ingram, P. (2017) "Asset ownership and incentives in early shareholder capitalism: Liverpool shipping in the eighteenth century," *Strategic Management Journal*, 38(4): 854–875.

Simons, T. and Ingram, P. (2003) "Enemies of the state: The interdependence of institutional forms and the ecology of the kibbutz, 1910–1997," *Administrative Science Quarterly*, 48(4): 592–621.

Suchman, M. C. (1995) "Managing legitimacy: Strategic and institutional approaches," *Academy of Management Review*, 20(3): 571–610.

Swaminathan, A. (2001) "Resource partitioning and the evolution of specialist organizations: The role of location and identity in the U.S. wine industry," *Academy of Management Journal*, 44(6): 1169–1185.

Toms, S. and Filatotchev, I. (2004) "Corporate governance, business strategy, and the dynamics of networks: A theoretical model and application to the British cotton industry, 1830–1980," *Organization Studies*, 25(4): 629–651.

Wade, J. B., Swaminathan, A. and Saxon, M. S. (1998) "Normative and resource flow consequences of local regulations in the American brewing industry, 1845–1918," *Administrative Science Quarterly*, 43(4): 905–935.

10 History in Theory
Imprinting and Path Dependence

Introduction

In addition to resorting to history as a source of data or evidence to test, develop or modify theory, some of the same research programs discussed in Chapters 8 and 9, as well as others, have integrated history into their theoretical models as a driver or moderator of organizational phenomena. The main premise in this diverse set of theoretical perspectives is that the past influences in some way the present and the futures of specific organizations and/or organizational aggregates. "History *in* theory" was the umbrella term introduced in Chapters 1 and 4 to characterize and distinguish the broad range of research programs where history has been incorporated as an element of theory (see also, Kipping and Üsdiken 2014). In this approach, history is not considered a source of "data" like in the literature reviewed in the preceding two chapters. Rather, it is incorporated into theory to capture the effects of past conditions or processes, either at the micro level of individual organizations or at the macro level of organizational aggregates. Incidentally, many of the studies along these lines have also tended to use historical data—though this has not always been the case.

The present chapter reviews two main theoretical ideas, namely, imprinting and path dependence, that feature prominently in the incorporation of history into management and organization theory. Imprinting and path dependence have, on the one hand, developed into research programs unto themselves, generating literatures and debates of their own. On the other hand, they have been included, singularly or jointly, as theoretical building blocks into existing major research programs. Thus, in addition to becoming a theoretical perspective in its own right, the notion of "imprinting" has been used in various research programs such as neo-institutionalism and organizational ecology. As for the notion of path dependence, when employed within theorizing in other research programs, it has often been interpreted rather flexibly, used either in a metaphorical sense or to mean past or history dependence more broadly. Indeed, with or without reference to "path dependence", it is in this sense of "past dependence" that history has also been frequently integrated into theoretical frameworks.

History Leaving a Lasting Presence: Imprinting

Its Own Past: Origins and Early Studies

The so-called "imprinting hypothesis" goes back to the seminal insight by Stinchcombe (1965) that the initial structural properties of new types of organizations were influenced by the social environment, in which they were first created, and that these initial features persisted over time despite environmental changes. In Stinchcombe's (1965: 153) own words, "organizational inventions that can be made at a particular time in history depend on the social technology available at the time" and, thus, "organizational forms and types have a history, and that history determines some aspects of the present structure of organizations of that type". The initial features of emergent organizational types are shaped by the "environing social structure", that is, "any variables which are stable characteristics of the society outside the organization" (Stinchcombe 1965: 142). Due to the persistence of these features, a "correlation" could be observed "between the time in history that a particular type of organization was invented" and the "structure of organizations of that type at the present time" (Stinchcombe 1965: 143). That initial structural characteristics persisted could be due, according to Stinchcombe (1965: 169), to the relative efficiency of the particular form for the purpose at hand, limited competition from alternative forms or the "traditionalizing forces, the vesting of interests, and the working out of ideologies" that serve to preserve them.

In a nutshell, Stinchcombe's (1965) original formulation included two propositions: First, the rate at which new organizations were founded and their initial structural properties were influenced by the environmental conditions in which they were created. Second, these initial features persisted over time despite changes in the environment. As will be seen later, some of the research building upon the notion of imprinting have considered and empirically examined Stinchcombe's theses *in toto*. Others have been inspired mainly by the first part of Stinchcombe's formulation and have studied the influence of founding conditions, environmental and/or internal, on a range of organizational, industry or population outcomes.

However, it took some time for Stinchcombe's ideas to be picked up in organizational research (Lounsbury and Ventresca 2002). While organizations had come to be seen as "open systems" at the time, the initial focus of research was not on examining the influence of external environments at their foundation, but on conceptualizing and measuring these environments and showing that they mattered for current organizational structures, processes and actions. In their overview of the literature, Marquis and Tilcsik (2013: 197) identify a first mention of "imprinting" in 1974—almost ten years after the publication of Stinchcombe's handbook chapter. But the first to explicitly draw on Stinchombe's propositions in terms of organization structures being influenced at their foundation by the external environment was Kimberly (1975) in a study that examined organizations for the handicapped in the US. He suggested distinguishing these organizations with respect to the "production" or "rehabilitation" orientation of their activities, together with attendant—though not so well specified—differences in their organization structures. Importantly, he argued that his present-day survey results regarding production or rehabilitation orientation depended on whether they were founded before or after the end of World War II. Kimberly (1975) also considered an alternative explanation, pointing out that the more recent interventions by the US government may have also led post–World War II organizations for the handicapped to be rehabilitation oriented.

In another early study, again framed with a view to showing the influence of the external environment—in this case, on bureaucratization, Meyer and Brown (1977: 370) addressed both parts of Stinchcombe's proposition, i.e. the influence of the founding environment and the persistence of the resulting structural properties. For these authors, the "fundamental sociological question [was] whether origins or environments dominate organizations". Taking a somewhat critical position, they also considered what would nowadays be referred to as the possibility of "imprint decay". Empirically, they looked at the formalization of personnel procedures within state, county and city finance agencies in the US. They did reason that origins were important because this was when organizations were most open to environmental influences. And to account for contemporaneous and later environmental influences, they considered the history of the civil service movement in the US and legislative changes made over time. In a nutshell, their findings led them to conclude that environmental conditions at the origins continued to influence the extent of formalization, though their influence diminished over time due to subsequent changes in that environment. Notably, their empirical analyses did not yield similar results for administrative structures such as the number of divisions, which, for Meyer and Brown (1977), indicated that the search for origin effects needed to take into account a rationale for why environments would be expected to influence structural components of organizations.

In subsequent decades research on imprinting grew significantly, partially through its association with neo-institutionalism as well as other research programs, partially on its own. This has resulted in the accumulation of a considerable amount of literature (see, for detailed reviews, Marquis and Tilcsik 2013; Simsek, Fox and Heavey 2015). Moreover, the theory has been extended, on the one hand, to even higher levels of analysis such as communities and, lately, the notion of categories (Rhee et al. 2017; see Chapter 9, this volume) and, on the other, to the level of the organization as well as even more micro levels, such as organizational components and even individuals (see e.g. Marquis and Tilcsik 2013). Recently, Simsek et al. (2015: 290) proposed the umbrella term "imprinters" which refers to the "sources of imprints" that, in their view, range from industries and communities to individuals. Similarly, the "imprinted entities" could be at different levels too, ranging from an individual to a network. Plus, as suggested by Marquis and Tilcsik (2013: 195), imprinting does not need to be confined to the founding stage but might also occur at other "brief sensitive periods of transition" such as mergers, when "the focal entity exhibits high susceptibility to external influences". Consequently, organizations, say, could experience several such "sensitive periods" in the course of their lifetime and become subject to several rounds of imprints, leading to various forms of sedimentation.

The expanding universe of imprinting research can be subdivided into four different directions—all of which, naturally, incorporated "history" into their theoretical models. The first of these, and possibly the most managerially relevant, investigated and theorized the influence of founders on immediate and later organizational actions and characteristics. The other three streams of research developed in line with and, to varying degrees, drew on the increasingly dominant neo-institutional theory in organizational research by looking at imprinting and, respectively, institutional environments, institutional logics and geographic communities.

People Matter: Founder Characteristics and Organizations

As discussed earlier, Kimberly (1975) was the first to explicitly use Stinchcombe's notion of imprinting. In a subsequent article, based on a study of the creation of a new medical school, he was also the first to point to the significant influence that founders could have in the early stages of the development of an organization (Kimberly 1979). As mentioned in Chapter 8, Kimberly also had a later article with Bouchikhi (1995), which reported a case study on the history of a French retailer of computer hardware and software from its founding in 1977 to 1990. They argued that it was the founder who had a strong influence on the creation of an organic structure and a communitarian culture that they observed after some 14 years when the firm had grown considerably. The authors also noted, however, that, with growth, internal and external pressures were making the founder's approach increasingly problematic. Indeed, one of their concluding statements foreshadowed the more recent interest in path dependency in organizations (Kimberly and Bouchikhi 1995: 16; emphasis in original):

What is perhaps of greatest interest theoretically is how the definition of core values early on, along with choice of domain, insistence by the CEO in maintaining a majority ownership position, and the nature of the early hires has set this organization on a particular trajectory which has become self-reinforcing and from which it is increasingly difficult to *choose* to deviate.

But it was Boeker who examined founder influences on early stage characteristics of organizations in a large sample study. Here, he considered for the first time the separate effects of the founding environment and founder characteristics on the initial strategies of firms (Boeker 1988) and on the initial importance of different business functions within the firm (Boeker 1989a). Founding environments over the period 1958–1984 were distinguished by identifying four distinct periods based on varying market conditions. Founder characteristics included functional and educational background and prior work experience. Retrospective interview and questionnaire data on a sample of US semiconductor firms provided partial support for both hypothesized environmental and founder effects. Boeker's (1989a, 1989b) studies on the relative significance of functional departments and on strategy (Boeker 1989b) also examined the effects of organizational characteristics, such as performance, age and ownership, on the persistence of—or change in—founding influences. Empirical support was again mixed. It should be noted that much like Meyer and Brown's (1977) research discussed previously, Boeker (1989a, 1989b) problematized imprint persistence by considering the effects of later conditions upon organizations. However, differently from the former, who had examined the impact of changes in the environment on imprint persistence, Boeker focused on the influences of organizational factors.

Organizational ecologists made an early contribution to this literature through a series of studies in the 1990s and the 2000s derived from a research project known as SPEC (Stanford Project on Emergent Companies) on a sample of young high-technology Silicon Valley firms. Differently from typical ecological research (see Chapter 9, this volume) data employed in this project was based not on archival sources, but collected through surveys, retrospective interviews and some documentary material. Altogether, SPEC-based research focused on one or more of three main themes: (a) the influence that founders' prior experiences had at the start-up phase; (b) the effects that these initial templates had on a range of other organizational practices and structures, as well as organizational outcomes; and, finally, (c) the persistence of imprints shaped by founders' initial choices and models. Exemplifying the first of these foci, Burton, Sørensen and Beckman (2002) showed that firms with founders previously employed by prominent firms were more likely to adopt more innovative strategies at the outset. Looking at the effects of initial founder choices on subsequent organizational arrangements, Baron, Burton and

Hannan (1996) showed that employment models of companies at the outset shaped later human resource policies and practices. With respect to imprinting effects, Beckman and Burton (2008) found that the way in which founding teams were initially structured and their prior experiences influenced subsequent top team structures as well as the prior experiences of top executives later recruited by the firm. According to these authors, the effects of founding structures on subsequent evolution was due to imprinting, whereas persistence in top team backgrounds could be attributed to homophily.

Overall, the SPEC studies provided considerable support for the enduring influences of early stages in the life of organizations and for imprinting, gauged in this case by founders' initial visions and models. As Baron, Hannan and Burton (2001: 1009) summarized in their article: "a broad conclusion of this analysis, and of others using the SPEC data, is that *origins matter*" (emphasis in original). It should be noted, however, that in all of these studies none of the firms in the sample had a lifespan longer than ten years at the time of data collection. Arguably, though, as researchers involved in the project have pointed out (see e.g. Hannan, Burton and Baron 1996), the firms that have been studied were operating in a highly dynamic environment, which would lead to the expectation of frequent change rather than the stability that was observed to a large degree.

Another example for founder influence and imprinting was the study by Johnson (2007) on the founding of the Paris Opera in the seventeenth century. This study differs from those reviewed in this section not only because it dealt with a case in the distant past and, arguably, imprinting effects over the long term but, more notably perhaps, because the author took an "agency-based" approach to imprinting. The narrative account aimed to show that the hybrid form of the Paris Opera combined elements from preexisting organizational models provided by the French "royal academy" and the "commercial theater". That a hybrid outcome emerged, Johnson suggested, was because the proposal made to Louis XIV by a poet, Pierre Perrin, to form the opera as a royal academy was altered by the former, since his preference was to have public performances. Johnson added that the fundamental features of this hybrid organizational form shaped at the very beginning persisted since then, though not much evidence is provided to that effect, as the main concern of the study was to develop general theory on the founding stage of the imprinting process. Given this primary aim of theory refinement—similar to many studies covered in Chapter 9 (this volume), Johnson used present-day concepts and considered Perrin's initiative as a case of "cultural entrepreneurship" molded by Louis XIV as a powerful "stakeholder". Her main argument then was that "imprinting is an agency-driven process of cultural entrepreneurship rather than a mechanical and discrete event" (Johnson 2007: 117).

Some recent studies have added the idea that imprints on founders through their prior educational experiences and employment are transferred to the firms that they set up and in turn influence strategies and performance outcomes of those firms. Hahn, Minolaa and Eddleston (2019), for example, showed that in Italian technology start-ups scientist founders—i.e. those with prior employment in universities or other research organizations—positively contributed to performance, which was operationalized as the volume of sales one year after founding. The authors attributed this positive effect to the openness of scientist founders to external knowledge—an orientation imprinted by their formative career experiences. The study also indicated that this relationship and its effects on performance were attenuated if scientist founders were reluctant to adopt practices from the business world, such as strategic planning, and maintained their noncommercial science orientation. In a somewhat similar study, Ding (2011) examined the effects of the educational backgrounds of founders on the early stage strategies of US biotechnology firms. She obtained empirical support for the hypothesis that firms with a higher proportion of founders holding PhDs were more likely to pursue in the first five years after founding an "open-science" strategy, indicated by the number of publications in academic journals. Ding (2011) controlled for prior employment with a measure similar to the one used in Hahn et al.'s (2019) study and found that employment effects became insignificant when the PhD variable was included in the analysis.

Marquis and Qiao (forthcoming) added to this literature by studying the relationship between the socialization of private enterprise founders in China into communist ideology and the internationalization of their firms. Their research showed that founders' ideological imprint—indicated by prior party membership—was negatively associated with both the cooperation of their firms with foreign capital in China and their investment in other countries. Differently from most of the studies reviewed earlier, Marquis and Qiao (forthcoming) also examined the effects of decay in ideological imprints instigated by changes in the "imprinter" (Simsek et al. 2015), in this case, the Chinese government. The indicators that the authors used to capture the degree to which founders were directly exposed to shifts in discourses and policies of the government pertaining to marketization—such as participation in political councils or industry social networks—indeed weakened the negative relationship between ideological imprinting and firm internationalization.

Context Matters: Initial Institutional and Economic Environments of Organizations

Besides the few studies mentioned previously that considered both environmental conditions and founders as possible sources of initial influences, a rare early study focusing on environmental effects at the industry level came from authors taking a neo-institutional approach. Baron, Jennings and Dobbin's (1988) historical research considered only the first part of Stinchcombe's thesis, i.e. that industries were influenced by the environmental conditions in place when they emerged. These authors examined how forms of worker control varied across industries and over time in the US during the period 1935–1946. Their aim was to develop an institutional perspective as an alternative to efficiency-based and labor process views on the formation of bureaucratic systems of control. And their study indeed showed that the adoption and the evolution of forms of control depended—in addition to factors such as unionization, technology and labor market conditions—on the institutional environment, in particular, the role of the state, and on the historical period when industries were founded.

Thereafter, it again took quite a while for another round of research to emerge with a focus on the effects of the founding environments. Given the expansion of the organization theory literature in the meantime, these more recent studies represent an eclectic mix of theoretical inspirations and substantive concerns—though generally with at least some reference to neo-institutional notions and ideas. Phillips and Kim (2009), for example, studied the relationship between organizational concerns with the preservation of their historical identity, rooted in the period of founding, and deceptive action by them as a form of decoupling. Data for the study came from record companies and recordings in the early stages of jazz music (1920–1929) in the US Midwest. The authors distinguished between what they referred to as "Victorian Era" and "Jazz Era" firms—depending on whether they were founded before or after 1917, when jazz began to be commercialized with the emergence of new firms geared toward meeting the "mass" demand for this African-American "lowbrow" music. Drawing on Stinchcombe (1965), they suggested that the earlier Victorian Era firms had been imprinted with a high-class identity given their association with the cultural elite of the time. They then showed that the Victorian Era firms tended to preserve their historical high-class identities even at the cost of not fully benefiting from emergent business opportunities, engaging with the latter only through deception, i.e. reproducing recordings under pseudonyms and without any advertising.

A series of studies examined the firm-level effects of what came to be referred to as "socialist imprinting" in the aftermath of the transition to a more market-oriented economy in Central and Eastern Europe. Kriauciunas and Kale (2006), for example, made a distinction between "socialist institutional imprinting" and "socialist market imprinting" and examined the degree to which Lithuanian firms remained under the influence of these imprints within the post-transition environment and how they could alter them. According to these authors, socialist institutional imprinting related to adherence to rules and output goals set by the state, while socialist market imprinting referred to a lack of competition and limited concern with efficiency and product quality. As expected, they found that socialist market imprinting had stronger negative effects than socialist institutional imprinting and that obtaining knowledge from free-market economies helped improve know-how. Notably, though, the data used in the study were based purely on a current survey and perceptual measures rather than historical evidence. In a follow-up study using the same methods, Shinkle and Kriauciunas (2012) covered four post-socialist transition countries. Here, they compared four dimensions of "competitive aspirations"—related to quality improvement, for example—of firms founded before and after the shift to a more market-oriented economy. They found that firms from the socialist era had lower aspirations in three of the dimensions. Interestingly, aspirations of socialist-era firms seemed to be even lower in countries that had moved further toward marketization.

Oertel, Thommes and Walgenbach (2016) followed the same direction in the context of the former German Democratic Republic (GDR) and the reunification of Germany. Their study examined the post-reunification failure rates of firms in the state of Thuringia, founded during the socialist era and, arguably, imprinted by the institutional environment then. Delineating three phases in the history of the GDR and distinguishing among them in terms of the centralization of decision-making with respect to firms, Oertel and his colleagues hypothesized that the failure rates of firms founded in the least centralized phase were lower in the immediate aftermath of reunification—finding support for this hypothesis. Failure rates for these firms increased, however, in later stages of reunification. The authors conjectured that the variation in the impact of the founding environment on later life chances was due to the different ways in which firms founded under more or less centralized conditions perceived and acted within the radically altered institutional context. Those that were founded in less centralized institutional conditions fell into a "competency trap" (Levitt and March 1988) as they tended to perceive that the routines that they had developed in the socialist era were serving them well after reunification and they were therefore less inclined to change. In contrast, those that were founded in the more centralized phases felt greater pressures to adapt, which in turn led to lower failure rates over a longer time frame.

Adding to this strand of research, Zhang, Tan and Tan (2016) compared the kind of networks developed by Chinese entrepreneurs in earlier and later stages of the transition toward a more market-oriented economy. Based on both qualitative and quantitative data, they showed that private entrepreneurs entering business in the regulatory and normative context of the early stage—the period from 1992 to 2001—developed networks based on strong political links and only a narrow range of market ties. In contrast, networks of entrepreneurs that founded their businesses in the later stage—from 2002 onward, when marketization had advanced further—were based less on political ties and instead on more extensive, though weaker, market links. So, not only did this study demonstrate yet again the influence of initial conditions on organizing but, importantly from an imprinting view, it also showed that the entrepreneurs of the early period did not alter the form that their networks had taken despite the change in regulatory and normative conditions.

Differently from the predominant view of imprint persistence as a constraint making organizations maladaptive when environmental conditions change, a few studies examined whether and in what ways characteristics ingrained at founding might actually serve as a source of adaptive behavior later on. One such example is a study by Marquis and Huang (2010) where the authors advanced the idea of what they called "exaptation", meaning that organizational capabilities developed as a response to institutional conditions at founding could be put to different use following institutional changes. Based on this theoretical reasoning, they showed that the involvement of US banks in acquisitions after the deregulation in 1978 was associated with variations in state-level restrictions on branch banking at the time these banks were founded. Thus, banks founded in states where statewide branching was not legally restricted were observed to have a greater tendency to engage in acquisitions following deregulation. This effect was strengthened by the extent of modernization, i.e. transportation infrastructure and urbanization, and weakened by the political culture, i.e. agrarian influence and Progressive support, in US states at the time when the banks were founded.

In a similar manner, Sullivan, Tang and Marquis (2014) reasoned that the nature of the network structures in which organizations were founded could influence their later learning behavior. Their research on US venture capital firms showed that firms that were founded in "small-world networks", i.e. "clusters where actors are closely linked to each other" and where "a few actors serve as bridges connecting different clusters" (Sullivan et al. 2014: 184), were more likely to engage in exploratory learning, indicated by investing in industries that they had not invested in before. The authors argued that this was because the routines developed at founding in small-world networks through direct and fast access to information led to continuous learning. The study also showed that this learning effect was positively moderated when firms subsequently had higher closeness centrality, i.e. were closely linked to the other actors, and brokerage positions, i.e. linked two other actors which were not connected.

The Past Really Matters: History, Institutional Logics and Organizations

Another group of studies have considered how history may serve as a source of multiple institutional logics that organizations may encounter. A main theme in these studies has been that not only is there a need to recognize that institutional logics are historically contingent (see Chapter 8, this volume) but also to consider the enduring effects of previously dominant logics—or how coexisting alternative logics may be historically rooted. Imprinting research along these lines has drawn on the increasing interest within neo-institutional theory in the concept of "community" as an institutional order and as a source of institutional pressures on organizations (e.g. Marquis, Glynn and Davis 2007; Thornton, Ocasio and Lounsbury 2012). The notion of community has been conceptualized in the institutional literature as "the populations, organizations, and markets located in a geographic territory and sharing, as a result of their common location, elements of local culture, norms, identity, and laws" (Marquis and Battilana 2009: 286).

In a study along these lines, Lounsbury (2007) showed that contending logics may be historically rooted in different communities and have long-term effects on the actions of firms. To this end, he investigated the diffusion of the practice of contracting to external money management firms within the US mutual funds industry between 1944 and 1985. Of the two competing logics during this period, the "trusteeship" one, oriented toward wealth preservation, originated in Boston in the 1920s, whereas the "performance" one, focusing on short-term returns, emerged in New York in the 1950s. His findings demonstrated that the adoption of external contracting by mutual funds in these two cities was motivated by different concerns—relative product costs vs. relative performance, suggesting the persistence of early imprints in each locality.

Another attempt to address the question of institutional complexity came from Greenwood et al. (2010). Based on a study of downsizing in Spanish manufacturing firms during the 1990s—a practice enabled by new legislation at the time—they showed how historically rooted state logics at the geographical community level and family logics moderated organizational responses to market logics. With respect to community-level influences, the authors distinguished between two versions of the state logic in Spain's history, namely a centralist one represented by the Franco regime and a decentralized approach ascribing primacy to regions. They found that downsizing tendencies were tempered in regions where the decentralized state logic as well as family ownership prevailed. Greenwood and his colleagues (2010: 535) interpreted their results as pointing to the "importance of an appropriate historical and cultural lens" and showing that "the intensity of community pressures, the form that they take, and the receptivity of particular organizations are contingent on history".

Another example of this line of work is a study by Raynard, Lounsbury and Greenwood (2013) on the present-day implementation of corporate social responsibility (CSR) practices by listed Chinese firms. For these authors, "contemporary institutional arrangements are the product of different temporal processes and different historical configurations of socio-political and cultural institutions" (Raynard et al. 2013: 247). In line with this view and drawing on imprinting theory, they examined whether the extent and types of CSR practices in Chinese firms varied according to the historical period when they were founded, namely, the eras of Mao Zedong (1943–1976), Deng Xiao Ping (1977–1992), post-Deng (1992–1999) and post-2000 governmentally prescribed CSR. The particular focus in the study was on the enduring effects of the previously dominant state logic of the Mao era—with an accent on state-owned enterprises and self-sufficiency, as opposed to that of Deng—with greater emphasis on efficiency and capitalist markets. The authors also considered whether the responses of Chinese firms to national-level institutional prescriptions, i.e. the introduction of CSR, varied across the historically imprinted local institutional contexts of different geographical communities. Supporting the view that prior logics are likely to continue to influence firm action under a new prevalent logic, the empirical analysis did show that firms founded during the Mao era scored higher in CSR "performance"—though there was large variability. Firms founded in the Mao era, the authors suggested, were imprinted with an "implicit" CSR concern, which then led them to respond more positively to present-day government prescriptions. Moreover, according to Raynard and colleagues, regional differences in the types of CSR practices also indicated, perhaps even more strongly, the legacies of the Mao and Deng era in each region.

Local Matters: Community-Level Imprinting and Institutional Legacies

The growing interest in communities within neo-institutional theory also led to studies that considered imprinting at the community level. This rudimentary stream of research developed two lines of inquiry. The first, following Stinchcombe (1965), focused on historical conditions in the local community as a source of imprints both on the community itself and on the organizations within it. The second reversed, in a sense, Stinchcombe's imprinting hypothesis by suggesting that organizations founded at some past period in a community endow or imprint that particular locality with an institutional infrastructure, which then provides an institutional legacy for the—possibly much—later founding of the same or different types of organizations. While some of the work in this genre has drawn upon institutional processes in accounting for long-standing effects, others have incorporated a path dependence perspective, suggesting that early historical events have been perpetuated through reinforcing effects of successive organizational foundings (see Greve and Rao 2014, for a review; also later).

Exemplifying the first line of inquiry, Marquis (2003) examined the community- and organizational-level imprinting effects of community histories on the extent to which directorship networks among firms were later locally based. The empirical analyses showed that in US cities that were established prior to the advent of air and automobile transportation, intercorporate networks at the time of research, i.e. 1986 and 2000, were still likely to be more locally based than in cities established later. The organizational-level hypothesis that firms in cities that emerged before air and automobile travel would be more likely to form their intercorporate ties locally was also supported. The main social mechanism that appeared to sustain early imprints, Marquis argued, was mimetism, since findings for the postulated influence of the presence of community-level institutional structures such as upper-class clubs, banks, and arts and culture organizations were mixed and not entirely consistent.

An example for the second direction of research is a study aimed at advancing a conceptualization of "local geographic communities" as "institutional fields" by Marquis, Davis and Glynn (2013: 42–43), defining community as "a significant population center within a relatively compact geographic area—in essence, a commutable distance" (p. 46). Their research examined the influence of "local cultural history and traditions" or the "institutional infrastructure" on the subsequent development of the nonprofit sector in that locality by empirically studying the relationships between the historical density of corporations and the later growth of elite and social welfare–oriented nonprofit organizations in the same community. In addition to considering a range of possible contemporaneous effects, they proposed that "patterns established early in a community's history tend to be enduring and to exert a contemporary influence", in this instance on the growth of nonprofits (Marquis et al. 2013: 45). Founding period effects for communities were conceptualized as the "early establishment of the business community" and measured, following Marquis (2003), as the number of corporations in each US city in the year 1905 (Marquis et al. 2013: 47). Findings did show that cities which had more corporations in 1905 were likely to experience greater growth in nonprofits over the period 1987 and 2002. Moreover, in cities where the corporate community was established early, the positive association between contemporaneous corporate density and the growth of elite-oriented nonprofit organizations—though not those of the social welfare kind—turned out to be stronger, suggesting, according to the authors, that the corporate elite were more likely to establish nonprofits that were mainly oriented toward serving themselves. In all, Marquis and his colleagues (2013: 54) viewed the contribution of their study to institutional theory as "showing how *historical forces* and the legacy of elite interactions continue to shape not only social outcomes but also interorganizational interactions within community fields. To a surprising extent, the *historical circumstances* of a city's growth had lingering effects on its present-day community dynamics" (emphases added).

Along similar lines, Greve and Rao (2012) proposed that the early founding of particular types of nonprofit organizations in a community generated a positive imprint for establishing nonprofits of another kind in the future. This was based on the authors' premise that history played a central role in the creation of an "institutional infrastructure" for collective action. The extent of early foundings of nonprofits generated variations in the institutional infrastructure, i.e. the "civic capacity" that communities possessed in developing different nonprofit organizations later. For Greve and Rao (2012: 641), these differences across communities were not only due to the initial conditions that they encountered but also to the path they embarked on subsequently, since "each organizational founding builds up capabilities that make another founding easier". Supporting these views, the study showed that municipalities in Norway were more likely to establish consumer cooperatives in the first half of the twentieth century the earlier they had created village fire associations and savings banks in the previous century. Rao and Greve (2018) extended this line of work to a study on the long-lasting influences of disasters in history. They examined the effects of the Spanish flu epidemic in Norway in 1918–1919 on the creation of retail cooperatives over the period 1920–1949. Their central premise was that the scale of disasters of this kind and its variation across localities was likely to weaken collective action and negatively influence the later creation of cooperative organizations—though in a gradually decaying manner over time. Findings did support this hypothesis. Yet results also showed that the "civic capacity" that the locality had before the outbreak of the epidemic—measured by the diversity of types of voluntary organizations in 1917—mitigated the negative effects of the disaster over the entire period. Again, history mattered.

In a recent study of how early ideological imprinting of mayors in China influenced state–business relationships, Wang, Du and Marquis (2019) included the communist legacy of the "province"—similar to the idea of community in earlier studies—as one of the moderators—the other being the economic development of the city—for the persistence of the effects of historical imprints on these mayors. The central premise of the study was that mayors' ideologies differed according to the historical period when they were first inculcated with communist ideology. These ideological imprints were then likely to endure with respect to the stance the mayors took regarding the participation of private firms in politics. The study's empirical analyses showed that city mayors that had been imprinted more strongly by communist ideology—as indicated by Communist Party membership prior to the 1978 market-oriented economic reforms—were less likely to grant deputy seats to privately held firms in one of the two main political councils at the city level or above (Wang et al. 2019). The authors also found that the negative effect of this historical imprint was stronger if the mayors had experienced the Cultural Revolution in China (1966–1976) at a younger age. Furthermore, the negative relationship toward political representation of private firms was strengthened in provinces that had come under communist rule earlier. In contrast, the economic development of the city led to imprint decay, since it apparently weakened the effects of the stronger socialization of mayors into communist ideology.

Staying on Track: Path Dependence

How It All Started: Origins and Definitions

The notion of path dependence originated in economics and economic history to account for how a technologically inferior standard can become prevalent, with the keyboard layout known as QWERTY used as a frequent example (e.g. David 1985). The core idea in this original formulation has been that temporally distant—possibly chance—events may, through a combination of reinforcing conditions, result in the dominance of and eventually a lock-in to a technological outcome that may not be the "optimal" one. Thus, as David (1985: 332) put it, in contrast to standard economic analysis, in path dependence, "the dynamic process itself takes on an *essentially historical* character" (emphasis in original). While David's work became subject to theoretical and empirically based criticisms from other economists and historians (see, for a critical summary of the debates, Lewin 2001), the notion of "path dependence"—and even more so the term—found widespread use in various management research programs to account for historical influences on organizations. Yet not infrequently, the use of the term has in various ways gone beyond the previously noted formulation (Sydow, Schreyögg and Koch 2009; Vergne and Durand 2010). Some authors, for example, have tended to associate path dependence with historical and institutional legacies (e.g. Djelic and Ainamo 1999) or with past or history dependence (e.g. Teece, Pisano and Shuen 1997; Suddaby and Greenwood 2009; Shipilov, Greve and Rowley 2010). Others (e.g. Marquis 2003; Greve and Rao 2012; Klüppel, Pierce and Snyder 2018) have tended to equate the term with persistence or with long-lasting effects of initial conditions. In a recent update Sydow and his colleagues (forthcoming) have documented many of the ways in which the subsequent literature has used their original theory—often rather loosely and, at times, misrepresenting it at least partially.

Initial formulations based on technological paths (e.g. David 1985) have more recently served as a source of inspiration for extensions to the study of organizations with a view to further specify the conditions and dynamics that path dependence entails and to demonstrate the role of history in how organizations or industries can become locked in. As defined by Sydow et al. (2009: 696), for example, "organizational path dependence" refers to "a rigidified, potentially inefficient action pattern built up by the unintended consequences of former decisions and positive feedback processes". Although different versions vary in some respects, they share the view that path dependence needs to be seen as an "historical process" made up of distinct phases. The phases in Sydow et al.'s (2009) "three-stage" model, for example, consist of a triggering event (i.e. initial decisions or actions), self-reinforcing dynamics and, finally, lock-in. Vergne and Durand (2011) are somewhat less specific with the characterization of their phases, referring to path origin, path development and path outcome.

Sydow and his colleagues acknowledged that, differently from market phenomena, triggering events in organizational contexts are not likely to be random but will be based on prior choices, that is to say, history, and can be intentionally driven. They also viewed the final stage of lock-in as leaving some room for interpretation and allowing some degree of choice, despite what has become a predominant form of action. And they did consider ways in which paths could be dissolved or intentionally broken (see also Sydow et al. forthcoming). Nevertheless, in their framework, whether a path will emerge is unpredictable in early stages, with the formation of paths often depending on "*hidden* dynamics" (Sydow et al. 2009: 702; emphasis added). Plus, the possibility of reversal is seen as bound by prior history leading to the particular path. Or, as Schreyögg and Sydow (2011: 322) have put it in an editorial introduction, "self-reinforcing mechanisms often unfold behind the backs of the actors and bring about an escalating situation with unexpected results". Understood in this manner, path dependence still stands in contrast to the alternative path creation perspective that it has instigated, which accords greater room to human agency—and less weight to history—in influencing all three of the phases referred to earlier (see, Garud and Karnøe 2001; Garud, Kumaraswamy and Karnøe 2010; Gruber 2010; Sydow et al. 2012; Bothello and Salles-Djelic 2018).

Although Sydow et al. (2009: 690) have explicitly stated that the framework they propose is a "theory of *organizational* path dependence" (emphasis in original), they have also suggested that the path dependence perspective may inform research at individual, network and industry or field levels. Still, more of the actual path dependence research has been at the organizational level—though there have also been studies at higher levels of analysis, combined typically with neo-institutional views. Overall, however, as the following overview will show, the traction gained by path dependence has been much lower compared to imprinting—partially due perhaps to the relative recency of extending the former to studies of organizations. In terms of the data and methods used, while imprinting research has often consisted of quantitative analyses, studies on path dependence have so far almost entirely been based on "historical" case studies, relying either on a combination of documentary evidence with interviews or entirely on interview-based data, though Vergne and Durand (2010) recently suggested moving away from case studies and embracing methods such as simulation and experimentation, a view also endorsed by Sydow and colleagues (forthcoming).

How It Works in Practice: Organizational Path Dependence

As noted, empirical research on path dependence—even at the organizational level—has remained rather limited so far (see Sydow et al. forthcoming for a review). One example is the case study by Schreyögg, Sydow and Holtmann (2011) on the "book club" division of Bertelsmann, a German media company. The main aim of the study was to demonstrate how Sydow et al.'s (2009) three-stage model of organizational path dependence (see earlier) could be applied to account for the strategic lock-in that Bertelsmann's book club began to experience in the 1990s and early 2000s. Particularly notable features of this study were that it spanned a long period of time (1945–2007) and was based on company archives supplemented with a few interviews. The study also showed what lock-in actually meant: While the company did engage in various strategic initiatives, all were abandoned after a few years and there was a return to the old strategy that had made it successful in the past. Neither did frequent changes of top management help in reversing the path that led the book club division to become locked in.

A few other studies have aimed at expanding the three-stage model by "contextualizing" path dependence. Koch (2011), for example, in a comparative case study of two German national newspapers over a relatively brief period (1999–2006), focused on the effects of the organizational context on the development of a "strategic path". To this end, Koch introduced the notion of "path inscription", which referred to the "repetitive dynamic" recursively shaping and adjusting "specific organizational resources and routines"—both in the form of a "strategically relevant self-reinforcing mechanism" and a "strategic pattern" (Koch 2011: 342–343). With respect to the relations between the organizational context and strategic path inscription, the two newspapers were similar in terms of inscribed mechanisms but differed in pattern inscription, which had to do with two aspects of the organizational context, namely, coherence, i.e. the absence of power contests, and pattern confirmation, i.e. the endorsement of the strategic path. The difference between the two newspapers in how coherent and confirmatory the respective organizational contexts were led to differences in the extent to which they could deviate from the enduring strategic pattern. According to Koch's interpretation, the better performance of one of the newspapers, measured in terms of circulation over time, could thus be accounted for by a relatively weaker organizational context in both of these aspects.

Maielli (2015) also conducted a study contextualizing path dependence—though inspired by evolutionary approaches to path dependence (e.g. Vergne and Durand 2011). It employed a conception of organizational contexts based on Marxian and Gramscian views, while at the same time considering the external environment as a source of influence. In addition, the study aimed to address the agency vs. structure debate in the path creation and path dependence literatures mentioned previously. For Maielli, organizational path dependence in the development of "meta-routines" needed to be couched in macro-level capital–labor relations, which were transposed to the organization level in the form of "structural hegemony", instigated, together with a consideration of "hegemonic projects", by competing groups within organizations. The author also distinguished between self-reinforcing "mechanisms" and processes, shaped, respectively, by market pressures and internal social relations. In those terms, lock-in therefore involved "a sustained 'imbalance' between externally generated self-reinforcing *mechanisms* and internally generated self-reinforcing *processes*" (Maielli 2015: 492; emphasis in original). Based on primary and secondary sources, the study examined these ideas by tracing the path-dependent development of the product mix of the Italian car manufacturer Fiat from the 1920s through the 1980s, which came to be characterized historically by a focus on the low-price end of the market—culminating in the fall of its market share from 1990 to 2009 both in Italy and Europe overall. In his analytical narrative, Maielli attributed the constitution of a Fordist path as a meta-routine geared toward less costly production to the pursuit of labor control, i.e. structural hegemony, at a critical juncture in the mid-1920s, which favored the hegemonic projects of process designers vis-à-vis those of the product designers. This selection was then reinforced by increasing returns as self-reinforcing processes, ultimately leading to a lock-in that limited the capability to cater to medium and upper segments of the market.

Finally, in a multiple-case study set in post-1978 market-oriented economic reforms in China, Jing and Benner (2016) also aimed at contextualizing path dependence by distinguishing favorable and unfavorable "institutional regimes". These varied regionally across firms that had historically produced for the military and, after the introduction of the reforms, were ordered to turn toward civilian markets. With an accompanying objective of reconciling path dependence and path creation views, the authors suggested that new path constitution was also likely to be path-dependent (Schneiberg 2007; also Vergne and Durand 2010). Drawing on qualitative, survey and some quantitative data covering the 30 years of the post-reform era, the authors argued that the perceived "opportunity spaces" provided by a more favorable institutional regime enabled firms operating in these different regions to more easily break away from the narrowed path. According to the authors, this path had been shaped through exploitative learning based on dealing with the military as the sole customer and under no competition. There was one firm though that was also able to break away from this path even in the unfavorable post-1978 institutional environment. Moreover, Jing and Benner (2016) suggested that the development of the paths created by these firms within the context of civilian markets also turned out to be path-dependent.

Parallels and Crossings: Path Dependence in Institutional Persistence and Change

Neo-institutional scholars concerned with how institutional arrangements are reproduced and become difficult to alter saw some parallels with the early formulations of path dependence in economic history (see earlier). Thus, Powell (1991: 193), for example, pointed to the link that could be made with institutional persistence, noting that the concept of path dependence describes the "surprising manner in which historical small events can become magnified by positive feedback", causing "the economy, under conditions of increasing returns, [to] dynamically lock itself in as a result of chance decisions that is neither guaranteed to be efficient, nor easily altered, nor predictable in advance" (see also Scott 2014: 144–145). Despite this interest and apparent intellectual affinity, the penetration of path dependence ideas into organizational institutionalism has been rather limited.

An early example that drew in part upon path dependence ideas is Farjoun's (2002) field-level study on the institutionalization, deinstitutionalization and re-institutionalization of pricing structures in online database services during its early stages of development from 1971 to 1994. Substantiated by qualitative documentary data over this period, the author proposed a "dialectical process model" where institutional development was posited as being "contested" and "path dependent". While the latter notion was introduced in a general sense—signifying that "present and future choices and trends depend on prior history" or that "past developments constrain and enable present ones" (Farjoun 2002: 848, 850), there were also references to path dependence concepts such as initial choices, self-reinforcing processes and historical inefficiency. Indeed, as Farjoun (2002: 869) put it in his conclusion, the "study shows that rather than reflecting a fit with contemporaneous technological and market conditions, institutional persistence is to a large extent a product of historical and at times arbitrary choices made a long time before and under different conditions". In addition to demonstrating how the pricing structure known as "connect-time" emerged and became institutionalized in a path-dependent manner, his narrative pointed to the dialectical nature of the process in that connect-time sowed the seeds of its demise due to the contradictions it embodied and the opposition it generated. Hence, the emergence of "flat-rate" pricing as the potential replacement was also path-dependent due to this prior history of contestation. Moreover, the flat-rate structure had been one of the alternatives available at the very beginning that could have become dominant initially.

An example for path dependence in institutional persistence and change—though not at the organizational field level but rather at the level of national economies—is a study by Schneiberg (2007). It took issue with the well-established view that US business had been characterized since the late nineteenth century by a singular institutional path comprising markets and large, for-profit corporations. Using data on six infrastructure industries, including agriculture and electrical utilities, Schneiberg demonstrated that at least in some regions of the country an alternative path consisting of publicly owned enterprises and cooperatives also emerged and persisted over time. Like Farjoun, he argued that histories of dominant institutional paths contained competing elements that could enable endogenous institutional change and the creation of new paths. The origins of these elements could be found at the critical junctures when the dominant path emerged—in the US case, the late nineteenth and early twentieth centuries. These elements were remnants of alternative institutional projects that—during the political struggles and conflicts at these junctures—had lost out to what came to be the dominant path. Such organizational legacies could later on serve as sources for institutional change and the creation of new paths. The alternatives residing in these legacies were reproduced by cross-sector borrowing or by capitalizing on forms and practices developed in prior historical periods. So, differently from the path creation approach mentioned earlier, for Schneiberg (2007: 72), path creation is path-dependent too, as "the evolution of alternatives was clearly determined by history, by prior organization and by the distribution of existing forms of enterprise".

A more recent exception to the broad tendency in path dependence research to rely on case studies is research on the diffusion of competitive new production technologies by Greve and Seidel (2015). They examined the competition between the technically similar DC-10 and L-1011 aircraft and its eventual outcome in terms of relative sales using hypothesis-based quantitative testing. The "puzzle" for the authors was that, despite initially having major design problems and a worse safety record, sales of the DC-10 came to exceed those of the L-1011 throughout the observation period 1972–1990. That the DC-10 turned out to be more successful was also indicated by the termination of the production of the L-1011 and the withdrawal of its producer Lockheed from the market for civilian aircraft. Empirical findings showed that the diffusion processes were similar for both the successful DC-10 and failed L-1011 production technologies, shaped as they were by the same social information antecedents—public knowledge of prior purchases and abandonments by airlines. Ultimately, according to Greve and Seidel, the success of the DC-10—despite design issues and ensuing fatalities—resulted from a chance event: The engine manufacturer for the L-1011 went into receivership, causing delivery problems and giving the DC-10 a one-year head start. It was this event that led to the divergent paths and different outcomes for the two types of aircraft.

Conclusion

Imprinting and path dependence are two prime examples of what this book is referring to as "history *in* theory". Given their temporal focus, the past, by definition, has to be an integral element in their theorizing. Part of their overall appeal lies in the ease with which they suggest that "the past matters"—an implication inherent in the terms themselves, which, in particular for path dependence, has resulted in some rather generic use of the expression(s). What needs to be stressed here is that, unlike historians, scholars in these research programs are usually not trying to examine the past per se but focus on gauging the influence it had on the present—or at least subsequent periods. They nevertheless have to study that past, so, depending on how far they go back, also rely on historical evidence in their work—though generally preferring those data sources and methods they are more familiar with, not unlike many of the "history *to* theory" research programs discussed in Chapters 8 and 9.

Despite their inherent similarities, the research programs on imprinting and path dependence also exhibit marked differences. In terms of the sheer volume of output, imprinting has been much more successful—despite the fact that for the first two decades after the initial formulation of the idea by Stinchcombe (1965) empirical studies remained few and far between. The eventual success seems tied to an association with neo-institutional theorizing, as the latter became more interested in change and the elements facilitating or hampering it. Moreover, some of the theories in organizational ecology also referred to imprinting—though to a lesser extent (see Chapter 11). This success came at a cost, however, since the imprinting notion was extended dramatically in terms of the levels of analysis and the conditions as well as the organizational or individual actors providing the imprinting or being imprinted and even the process itself now being seen as more continuous or at least intermittent. As a result, "imprinting theory"—if there ever was one—has become rather unspecific, and most of the research aims to contribute to other theoretical concerns, notably within the still expanding neo-institutional universe.

In contrast, path dependence is a relative newcomer within management and organization studies, with the first programmatic articles only appearing in the early twenty-first century—though the underlying ideas go back to the 1980s. This might be one of the reasons for the much less extensive research exploring and developing the concept. Moreover, it has only made limited inroads into research motivated by theoretical concerns emanating from neo-institutionalism. Another reason might be the need to conduct in-depth case studies over sufficiently long periods so as to fully reflect the process leading to an eventual lock-in. This has prompted some to focus on "path creation" instead, which requires less of a historical perspective and the commensurate historical sources—though some have suggested that path creation is in itself a path-dependent process.

References

Baron, J. N., Burton, M. D. and Hannan, M. T. (1996) "The road taken: Origins and evolution of employment systems in emerging companies," *Industrial and Corporate Change*, 5(2): 239–275.

Baron, J. N., Hannan, M. T. and Burton, M. D. (2001) "Labor pains: Change in organizational models and employee turnover in young, high-tech firms," *American Journal of Sociology*, 106(4): 960–1012.

Baron, J. N., Jennings, P. D. and Dobbin, F. R. (1988) "Mission control? The development of personnel systems in U.S. industry," *American Sociological Review*, 53(4): 497–514.

Beckman, C. M. and Burton, M. D. (2008) "Founding the future: Path dependence in the evolution of top management teams from founding to IPO," *Organization Science*, 19(1): 3–24.

Boeker, W. (1988) "Organizational origins: Entrepreneurial and environmental imprinting at the time of founding," in G. R. Carroll (ed), *Ecological Models of Organizations*, Cambridge, MA: Ballinger, pp. 33–51.

Boeker, W. (1989a) "Strategic change: The effects of founding and history," *Academy of Management Journal*, 32(3): 489–515.

Boeker, W. (1989b) "The development and institutionalization of subunit power in organizations," *Administrative Science Quarterly*, 34(3): 388–410.

Bothello, J. and Salles-Djelic, M.-L. (2018) "Evolving conceptualizations of organizational environmentalism: A path generation account," *Organization Studies*, 39(1): 93–119.

Burton, M. D., Sørensen, J. B. and Beckman, C. M. (2002) "Coming from good stock: Career histories and new venture formation," *Research in the Sociology of Organizations*, 19: 229–262.

David, P. A. (1985) "Clio and the economics of QWERTY," *American Economic Review*, 75(2): 332–337.

Ding, W. W. (2011) "The impact of founders' professional-education background on the adoption of open science by for-profit biotechnology firms," *Management Science*, 57(2): 257–273.

Djelic, M.-L. and Ainamo, A. (1999) "The coevolution of new organizational forms in the fashion industry: A historical and comparative study of France, Italy, and the United States," *Organization Science*, 10(5): 622–637.

Farjoun, M. (2002) "The dialectics of institutional development in emerging and turbulent fields: The history of pricing conventions in the on-line database industry," *Academy of Management Journal*, 45(5): 848–874.

Garud, R. and Karnøe, P. (2001) "Path creation as a process of mindful deviation," in R. Garud and P. Karnøe (eds), *Path Dependence and Path Creation*, Mahwah, NJ: Lawrence Earlbaum, pp. 1–38.

Garud, R., Kumaraswamy, A. and Karnøe, P. (2010) "Path dependence or path creation," *Journal of Management Studies*, 47(4): 760–774.

Greenwood, R., Díaz, A. M., Li, S. X. and Lorente, J. C. (2010) "The multiplicity of institutional logics and the heterogeneity of organizational responses," *Organization Science*, 21(2): 521–539.

Greve, H. R. and Rao, H. (2012) "Echoes of the past: Organizational foundings as sources of an institutional legacy of mutualism," *American Journal of Sociology*, 118(3): 635–675.

Greve, H. R. and Rao, H. (2014) "History and the present: Institutional legacies in communities of organizations," *Research in Organizational Behavior*, 34: 27–41.

Greve, H. R. and Seidel, M.-D. L. (2015) "The thin red line between success and failure: Path dependence in the diffusion of innovative production technologies," *Strategic Management Journal*, 36(4): 475–496.

Gruber, M. (2010) "Exploring the origins of organizational paths: Empirical evidence from newly founded firms," *Journal of Management*, 36(5): 1143–1167.

Hahn, D., Minolaa, T. and Eddleston, K. A. (2019) "How do scientists contribute to the performance of innovative start-ups? An imprinting perspective on open innovation," *Journal of Management Studies*, 56(5): 895–928.

Hannan, M. T., Burton, M. D. and Baron, J. N. (1996) "Inertia and change in the early years: Employment relations in young, high technology firms," *Industrial and Corporate Change*, 5(2): 503–536.

Jing, R. and Benner, M. (2016) "Institutional regime, opportunity space and organizational path constitution: Case studies of the conversion of military firms in China," *Journal of Management Studies*, 53(4): 552–579.

Johnson, V. (2007) "What is organizational imprinting? Cultural entrepreneurship in the founding of the Paris opera," *American Journal of Sociology*, 113(1): 97–127.

Kimberly, J. R. (1975) "Environmental constraints and organizational structure: A comparative analysis of rehabilitation organizations," *Administrative Science Quarterly*, 20(1): 1–9.

Kimberly, J. R. (1979) "Issues in the creation of organizations: Initiation, innovation, and institutionalization," *Academy of Management Journal*, 22(3): 437–457.

Kimberly, J. R. and Bouchikhi, H. (1995) "The dynamics of organizational development and change: How the past shapes the present and constrains the future," *Organization Science*, 6(1): 9–18.

Kipping, M. and Üsdiken, B. (2014) "History in organization and management theory: More than meets the eye," *Academy of Management Annals*, 8(1): 535–588.

Klüppel, L. M., Pierce, L. and Snyder, J. A. (2018) "The deep historical roots of organization and strategy: Traumatic shocks, culture, and institutions," *Organization Science*, 29(4): 702–721.

Koch, J. (2011) "Inscribed strategies: Exploring the organizational nature of strategic lock-in," *Organization Studies*, 32(3): 337–363.

Kriauciunas, A. and Kale, P. (2006) "The impact of socialist imprinting and search on resource change: A study of firms in Lithuania," *Strategic Management Journal*, 27(7): 659–679.

Levitt, B. and March, J. G. (1988) "Organizational learning," *Annual Review of Sociology*, 14: 319–340.

Lewin, P. (2001) "The market process and the economics of QWERTY: Two views," *The Review of Austrian Economics*, 14(1): 65–96.

Lounsbury, M. (2007) "A tale of two cities: Competing logics and practice variation in the professionalizing of mutual funds," *Academy of Management Journal*, 50(2): 289–307.

Lounsbury, M. and Ventresca, M. J. (2002) "Social structure and organizations revisited," *Research in the Sociology of Organizations*, 19: 1–36.

Maielli, G. (2015) "Explaining organizational paths through the concept of hegemony: Evidence from the Italian car industry," *Organization Studies*, 36(4): 491–511.

Marquis, C. (2003) "The pressure of the past: Network imprinting in intercorporate communities," *Administrative Science Quarterly*, 48(4): 655–689.

Marquis, C. and Battilana, J. (2009) "Acting globally but thinking locally? The enduring influence of local communities on organizations," *Research in Organizational Behavior*, 29: 283–302.

Marquis, C., Davis, G. F. and Glynn, M. A. (2013) "Golfing alone? Corporations, elites and nonprofit growth in 100 American communities," *Organization Science*, 24(1): 39–57.

Marquis, C., Glynn, M. A. and Davis, G. F. (2007) "Community isomorphism and corporate social action," *Academy of Management Review*, 32(3): 925–945.

Marquis, C. and Huang, Z. (2010) "Acquisitions as exaptation: The legacy of founding institutions in the U.S. commercial banking industry," *Academy of Management Journal*, 53(6): 1441–1473.

Marquis, C. and Qiao, K. (forthcoming) "Waking from Mao's dream: Communist ideological imprinting and the internationalization of entrepreneurial ventures in China," *Administrative Science Quarterly*.

Marquis, C. and Tilcsik, A. (2013) "Imprinting: Toward a multilevel theory," *Academy of Management Annals*, 7(1): 193–243.

Meyer, M. W. and Brown, M. C. (1977) "The process of bureaucratization," *American Journal of Sociology*, 83(2): 364–385.

Oertel, S., Thommes, K. and Walgenbach, P. (2016) "Organizational failure in the aftermath of radical institutional change," *Organization Studies*, 37(8): 1067–1087.

Phillips, D. J. and Kim, Y.-K. (2009) "Why pseudonyms? Deception as identity preservation among jazz record companies, 1920–1929," *Organization Science*, 20(3): 481–499.

Powell, W. W. (1991) "Expanding the scope of institutional analysis," in W. W. Powell and P. J. DiMaggio (eds), *The New Institutionalism in Organizational Analysis*, Chicago, IL: The University of Chicago Press, pp. 183–203.

Rao, H. and Greve, H. R. (2018) "Disasters and community resilience: Spanish flu and the formation of retail cooperatives in Norway," *Academy of Management Journal*, 61(1): 5–25.

Raynard, M., Lounsbury, M. and Greenwood, R. (2013) "Legacies of logics: Sources of community variation in CSR implementation in China," *Research in the Sociology of Organizations*, 39(Part A): 243–276.

Rhee, E. Y., Lo, J. Y., Kennedy, M. T. and Fiss, P. C. (2017) "Things that last? Category creation, imprinting, and durability," *Research in the Sociology of Organizations*, 51: 297–325.

Schneiberg, M. (2007) "What's on the path? Path dependence, organizational diversity and the problem of institutional change in the US economy, 1900–1950," *Socio-Economic Review*, 5(1): 47–80.

Schreyögg, G. and Sydow, J. (2011) "Organizational path dependence: A process view," *Organization Studies*, 32(3): 321–335.

Schreyögg, G., Sydow, J. and Holtmann, P. (2011) "How history matters in organisations: The case of path dependence," *Management & Organizational History*, 6(1): 81–100.

Scott, W. R. (2014) *Institutions and Organizations: Ideas, Interests and Identities*, 4th edn, Thousand Oaks, CA: Sage.

Shinkle, G. A. and Kriauciunas, A. P. (2012) "The impact of current and founding institutions on strength of competitive aspirations in transition economies," *Strategic Management Journal*, 33(4): 448–458.

Shipilov, A. V., Greve, H. R. and Rowley, T. J. (2010) "When do interlocks matter? Institutional logics and the diffusion of multiple corporate governance practices," *Academy of Management Journal*, 53(4): 846–864.

Simsek, Z., Fox, B. C. and Heavey, C. (2015) " 'What's past is prologue': A framework, review, and future directions for organizational research on imprinting," *Journal of Management*, 41(1): 288–317.

Stinchcombe, A. L. (1965) "Social structure and organizations," in J. G. March (ed), *Handbook of Organizations*, Chicago, IL: Rand McNally, pp. 142–193.

Suddaby, R. and Greenwood, R. (2009) "Methodological issues in researching institutional change," in D. A. Buchanan and A. Bryman (eds), *The Sage Handbook of Organizational Research Methods*, London: Sage, pp. 176–195.

Sullivan, B. N., Tang, Y. and Marquis, C. (2014) "Persistently learning: How small-world network imprints affect subsequent firm learning," *Strategic Organization*, 12(3): 180–199.

Sydow, J., Schreyögg, G. and Koch, J. (2009) "Organizational path dependence: Opening the black box," *Academy of Management Review*, 34(4): 689–709.

Sydow, J., Schreyögg, G. and Koch, J. (forthcoming) "On the theory of organizational path dependence: Clarifications, replies to objections, and extensions," *Academy of Management Review*.

Sydow, J., Windeler, A., Schubert, C. and Möllering, G. (2012) "Organizing R&D consortia for path creation and extension: The case of semiconductor manufacturing technologies," *Organization Studies*, 33(7): 907–936.

Teece, D. J., Pisano, G. and Shuen, A. (1997) "Dynamic capabilities and strategic management," *Strategic Management Journal*, 18(7): 509–533.

Thornton, P. H., Ocasio, W. and Lounsbury, M. (2012) *The Institutional Logics Perspective: A New Approach to Culture, Structure and Process*, Oxford: Oxford University Press.

Vergne, J.-P. and Durand, R. (2010) "The missing link between the theory and empirics of path dependence: Conceptual clarification, testability issue, and methodological implications," *Journal of Management Studies*, 47(4): 736–759.

Vergne, J.-P. and Durand, R. (2011) "The path of most persistence: An evolutionary perspective on path dependence and dynamic capabilities," *Organization Studies*, 32(3): 365–382.

Wang, D., Du, F. and Marquis, C. (2019) "Defending Mao's dream: How politicians' ideological imprinting affects firms' political appointments in China," *Academy of Management Journal*, 62(4): 1111–1136.

Zhang, C., Tan, J. and Tan, D. (2016) "Fit by adaptation or fit by founding? A comparative study of existing and new entrepreneurial cohorts in China," *Strategic Management Journal*, 37(5): 911–931.

11 History in Theory
Ecology, Strategy, Co-evolution

Introduction

As seen in the previous chapter, imprinting and path dependence are prime examples of what this book refers to as "history *in* theory", since the past occupies a central position within their theoretical models. But they are not the only ones. History also plays a major role in the theories of several other research programs, which will be discussed in some detail in this chapter. Among them, first and foremost, is organizational ecology which, as seen in Chapter 9, already drew extensively on historical data for its research. History is also an integral part of some of its main theoretical building blocks, in particular the notion of structural inertia.

While taking a somewhat different stance to the ecological research program in terms of a focus on the possibility of organizational adaptation, part of the strategy research attributed a similar role to history. Theorized as a source of competitiveness in stable environments, historically grounded routines and resources became an impediment to change in turbulent ones—with the increasingly popular notion of "dynamic" capabilities an attempt to combine an element of stability with the ability to change. Finally, located kind of in between the previous two is co-evolution—a somewhat more marginal research program that attempts to combine the selection and adaptation, as well as organization and environment perspectives, and, by definition, accords prominence to history.

In what follows, the chapter provides overviews of these three research programs based on select exemplary contributions. What should be noted here is that in all these theoretical approaches occasional reference has been made to imprinting or path dependence—though in ways formulated within the frameworks of the respective theories. Thus, references to path dependence in particular have typically been more in the general sense of past or history dependence rather than in the form of the specific formulations discussed in the previous chapter.

Origins Matter Here, Too: Organizational Ecology

Organizational ecologists were early in drawing upon Stinchcombe's (1965) theoretically rich essay. However, both in foundational statements (Hannan and Freeman 1977, 1984) and in early empirical research, references to Stinchcombe were related more to his propositions regarding (a) the impact of the social environment on rates of founding of new types of organizations and (b) the "liability of newness", i.e. the idea that younger organizations are likely to have higher mortality rates. The notion of imprinting received only passing mention, and when it did, it was in conjunction with these themes (see, for a similar observation, Singh and Lumsden 1990). Nevertheless, as will be seen later, the notion of imprinting did feature in some of the later work of organizational ecologists—mostly in research geared toward organizational-level phenomena. Though to a lesser extent, ideas inspired in part by the imprinting hypothesis have also featured in population-level analyses—initially with a primary focus on the effects of founding ecological conditions on survival chances of organizations. At the same time, some ecological theories, like the so-called Red Queen theory for example, have been based on predictions that go against the idea of imprinting. Still, history without reference to imprinting theory has featured in a number of other ways in accounting for population-level outcomes, interactions between populations, and, more recently, parent–progeny relationships and their effects on populations.

What Starts Well. . . : Founding Conditions and the Density Delay Model

Recognition of the importance of founding conditions, and hence history, came early within theorizing on organizational ecology (see also Singh and Lumsden 1990). Thus, one of the pioneering empirical studies in the ecological tradition (Carroll and Delacroix 1982) made a passing reference to imprinting—though specifically with regard to Stinchcombe's (1965) liability of newness thesis. The study examined newspapers in Argentina and Ireland over the periods 1800–1900 and 1800–1975, respectively, and showed that failure rates were age dependent (Carroll and Delacroix 1982). It also demonstrated that conditions at the time of birth had a role to play, since newspapers founded during periods of economic expansion and political stability as opposed to turmoil had higher chances of survival.

In another early study, Tucker, Singh and Meinhard (1990) examined the effects of founding conditions and imprinting as they related to organizational change rather than the population level. Their study looked at voluntary social service organizations in Toronto, Canada, over a relatively short time span of 13 years. The researchers considered (a) the founding environment from an "institutional" perspective, distinguishing two historical periods demarcated as favorable and unfavorable, as well as an "ecological" perspective in terms of density and resource concentration, and (b) the initial organizational characteristics, namely specialist vs. generalist strategies and board size. Rates of change were gauged, in organization ecology terms, both with respect to core features (e.g. goals and structure) and peripheral ones (e.g. sponsor or chief executive) (see later; also Chapter 9, this volume). The study yielded mixed results, some contrary to what the authors expected. It did indicate that, at least within the short time frame, environmental conditions at founding were more influential than the organizational ones, since the two historical institutional conditions and density had the strongest effects. Thus, organizations founded under favorable institutional conditions were more likely to make core changes, whereas those founded in adverse institutional environments tended toward peripheral changes. Density at founding also had positive effects on quite a few of the change dimensions, while the effects of resource concentration were more limited. The impact of organizational founding characteristics was only marginal and indeed, in the case of specialist vs. generalist strategies contrary to predictions, as generalists made core changes almost as often as the specialists did.

Greater attention to the influence of the time of founding of organizations on the evolution of organizational populations emerged with an attempt to theoretically account for a gap in the original density dependence model as to why density declined after populations reached peak density (see Chapter 9, this volume). This led to another revision and broadening of the density dependence model, based on Stinchcombe's (1965) idea that organizations were influenced by the conditions surrounding them at the time of founding.

The "density delay model", as it was called, included the density at the time of founding of cohorts of organizations in the population (Carroll and Hannan 1989). The argument was that in addition to the effects of contemporaneous density, high population density at founding would be associated with higher failure rates for organizations created under such conditions. The basis for this argument was that cohorts of organizations founded during periods of high density confronted greater competition, which in turn led to problems of resource accessibility. Even if these organizations were able to survive initial stages after founding, resource scarcity would hamper the movement to routine activities and the development of stable, formal structures. Moreover, because the market was crowded at times of high density, new organizations would find it difficult to compete with the established ones and would therefore need to settle for inferior resources (Carroll and Hannan 1989). And in line with what Stinchcombe (1965) had suggested, these conditions were expected to leave their mark and make organizations founded in high-density environments weaker competitors over their entire lifetime, leading to persistently higher rates of failure. Enduring higher mortality of organizations founded in such adverse conditions, it was argued, also accounted, albeit in part, for the decline in density after population peaks were reached. This was because a greater proportion of organizations were founded under high-density conditions as population density increased, which led to an increase in average failure rates (see also Hannan 1997). Carroll and Hannan (1989) obtained consistent support in empirical tests of these conjectures using historical data they had collected previously on five organizational populations: US labor unions and breweries, Irish and Argentinian newspapers, and newspaper publishers in San Francisco (see Chapter 9, this volume on prior studies based on these data; Carroll and Hannan 2000 for further evidence on density delay effects). It should be noted though that while the density delay model rests on Stinchcombe's (1965) idea that founding environments have long-lasting effects, relative to his broader notion of social structure, this model only considers resource scarcity and competitive conditions.

A more encompassing view of the imprinting idea was explicitly incorporated into the original density dependence model by Dobrev and Gotsopoulos (2010). In line with that model they argued that initial cohorts of organizations in a new population or industry suffered from a "legitimacy vacuum" due to an absence of familiarity with the new organizational form. Structures and routines created by the early entrants would thus be shaped by the uncertainty in the environment arising from the lack of constitutive legitimation at the population level and the resource acquisition problems that this condition generated. The renewal of these initial structures would in turn be difficult and, consequently, the hazard of mortality high throughout the lifetime of these early entrants. The authors went further by proposing a revision of the density delay model with respect to the scale of population increases at low levels of density. They suggested that small increases reduced mortality rates as they overrode competitive influences by contributing to increased legitimation, while, as the original version of the density delay model predicted, higher-level increases would elevate the hazard of mortality. Overall, the authors contended, their "arguments [were] essentially about the role of history for organizational evolution" (Dobrev and Gotsopoulos 2010: 1171). Empirical analyses of the available data on US, French and German automobile manufacturers (see Chapters 9, this volume) confirmed these ideas. However, results also showed that the hypothesized effects only held up for foundings in the formative stages of the population and were weakened for cohorts entering the population after it had matured.

When Things Get Sticky: Structural Inertia and History Dependence

The notion of structural inertia, understood as "limitations on the ability of organizations to adapt" (Hannan and Freeman 1977: 930), has been a cornerstone in the organizational ecology research program. Indeed, structural inertia theory has served as the basis of the selection—as opposed to adaptation—approach that has characterized organizational ecology. Because existing organizations are likely to find it difficult to alter their strategy and structure at the pace environments change, organizational change comes about through the creation of new kinds of organizations and the replacement of old ones. Inertia is viewed as both an outcome of population-level processes of selection and a characteristic of individual organizations. Regarding the former, Hannan and Freeman (1984: 154) argue that in "modern societies" selection processes favor "reliability" and "accountability". Regarding organizations, they gain these capacities through the "reproduction" of their structures and routines, which at the same time, however, serve as the basis of inertia. Thus, in organizational ecology terms, organizations that have high inertia, i.e. are resistant to change, have better survival chances. The term "structure" in structural inertia theory relates to the core—as opposed to peripheral—features of organizations (Baum and Shipilov 2006; see also Hannan and Freeman 1984; Hannan et al. 2006; Chapter 9, this volume). Core features such as goals or forms of authority are likely to be more inert, whereas peripheral aspects, e.g. incumbents of top management positions in organizations, may be more amenable to change. Moreover, radical structural change, i.e. alterations in core features, is likely to reduce reliability and hence increase chances of failure (Hannan and Freeman 1984).

Structural inertia theory becomes linked to history in that organizational age has been identified as one of the main sources of inertia—together with size and complexity. Aging leads to the stabilization and reproduction of structures and practices as well as external relations, making organizations more inert and thus lowering rates of failure (Hannan and Freeman 1984). This is another way of stating the "liability of newness" hypothesis proposed by Stinchcombe (1965), which suggests that organizations have a higher risk of failure in their early years (see earlier). These original ideas have spurred a range of studies on the age dependence of failure rates, as well as alternative theoretical formulations referring to liabilities of "adolescence", "obsolescence" and "senescence". The liability of adolescence argument revised the liability of newness hypothesis only by suggesting that the risk of failure may rise not during the very early years, but after initial endowments of newly founded organizations are depleted—again diminishing with increasing organizational age though. By contrast, the notions of obsolescence and senescence refer to a "liability of aging", suggesting that older organizations run higher risks of failure—due, in the former case, to increasing misfit with the external environment and, in the latter, to problems in reproduction that aging may bring as a result of bureaucratization or internal politics (Baum and Shipilov 2006: 63–64). Notably though, empirical tests of these alternative formulations have produced mixed results (see, for reviews, Baum and Shipilov 2006; Carroll and Hannan 2000), leading Hannan, Pólos and Carroll (2007: 291) to admit that the question of age dependence remains a "recalcitrant problem".

In response to these alternative theoretical formulations and equivocal empirical results, ecologists have more recently begun to revisit the question of age dependence at both the population and organizational levels by drawing upon the identity- and audience-based shift in ecological thinking (see Chapter 9, this volume) and with a view to theoretical integration. With respect to organizational failure, the main idea now is that the "dynamics of the risk of failure depends crucially on early performance and on the *historical* pattern of resource accumulation" (Le Mens, Hannan and Pólos 2011: 116–117; emphasis added). Organizations are presumed to be subject to all three forms of liability identified in the previous literature, i.e. newness, adolescence and aging—albeit variably, due to the internal and external conditions that they encounter. Starting with the initial endowment at founding, organizations possess a stock of resources or "organizational capital", consisting of an amalgam of "financial resources" and "non-financial assets", which serves as a buffer against failure (Le Mens et al. 2011: 99). Depending on the appeal of what organizations have to offer in the category constructed by relevant audiences (see Chapter 9, this volume), they may—or may not—obtain resources from these audiences. Over time, a good performance increases the flow of resources and contributes to the growth of organizational capital, while low levels of performance lead to reductions.

These ideas are then brought together to suggest that (a) if an organization's initial "fitness" is above a threshold—determined by the amount of resources that the audience controls and the organization's cost structure, then organizational capital grows with age and the hazard of failure drops (liability of newness); (b) if initial fitness is lower than the threshold but rises above the threshold over time, the hazard of failure is initially high but then drops (liability of adolescence); and (c) if both initial and longer-term fitness remain below the threshold then the hazard increases with age (liability of aging). Later extensions along these lines have focused on age-related inertia, reiterating—albeit in different ways—the idea that inertia constrains organizational change. In these additional steps the same group of authors have attempted to demonstrate, again through mathematical formalism and empirical illustration, that aging reduces the speed at which organizations can change (Le Mens, Hannan and Pólos 2015a), especially when audience "tastes" drift, which leads to a deterioration of performance and, consequently, reductions in organizational capital and a heightened threat of failure (Le Mens, Hannan and Pólos 2015b).

In addition to this long-lasting interest in age dependence, structural inertia theory has prompted a turn among ecologists toward studying organizational-level change. Several among these studies have proposed that the research on change may benefit from considering the totality of organizations' past change experiences—a view that has enjoyed strong empirical support (see Baum and Shipilov 2006 for a review). Kelly and Amburgey (1991: 609), for example, suggested that "studies of organizational change require a historical perspective" which would consider organizations' prior history of changes. Based on this view, they advanced the idea of "momentum in change processes", which referred to organizational tendencies to repeat the types of changes that have been made in the past. In examining this idea, Kelly and Amburgey (1991) studied changes in a core organizational attribute, namely, product-market strategies, within the context of the US airline industry during the years 1962–1985. The study showed, in support of structural inertia theory, that older organizations were less likely to make changes in their product-market strategies. Even stronger empirical support was obtained for the idea of change momentum. Organizations that had greater prior experience with any of four types of product-market changes were more likely to make further changes of the same type.

Amburgey, Kelly and Barnett (1993) further developed the idea of history dependence with respect to organizational change and failure rates by considering structural inertia theory together with the idea of "change momentum". As mentioned earlier, the notion of change momentum refers to the tendency in organizations to repeat previous change actions—possibly irrespective of beneficial or dysfunctional consequences of prior change experiences. This is because of both the learning opportunities provided by past experiences and the propensity to act according to previously established routines. Thus, as Amburgey et al. (1993: 70) put it, "inertia also implies momentum—an organization in motion tends to stay in motion". In examining these ideas empirically, Amburgey and his colleagues studied changes in the content (general vs. specialized) and the publication frequency of Finnish newspapers over the period 1771–1963. Empirical results provided strong support to structural inertia theory. Changes in both content and frequency led to higher failure rates—an effect that was stronger for older organizations. The adverse effects of change were weakened, however, for all organizations with the time that passed after a change, since those that survived could gradually rebuild their "internal processes and external relationships" (Amburgey et al. 1993: 53). But at the same time the likelihood of making changes diminished with age. Moreover, results showed that changes in content or frequency depended on the number of previous changes of each type—thus supporting the idea of change momentum or history dependence of organizational change. However, there was also a historical decay effect in that recent changes were more likely to be repeated. In addition, results indicated that change momentum varied with what was being changed. Referring to Hannan and Freeman's (1984) hierarchy of core elements (see Chapter 9, this volume), the authors interpreted these findings as suggesting that while altering properties closer to the core—goals, for example, as indicated by content in this study—was more difficult, if a change was made in early years, the momentum generated persisted over the longer term. In contrast, properties more distant from the core—technology or strategy, indicated in this instance by frequency of publication—were easier to change, but despite an early change, momentum decayed more readily. Overall, there appeared to be "strong history dependence" both in rates of failure and in change rates (Amburgey et al. 1993: 70–71).

Similarly, studying niche shifts, i.e. changes in market position based on technologies used, by US automobile firms over the period 1885–1981 (see Chapter 9, this volume, for the source of this data), Dobrev, Kim and Carroll (2003) found that—in support of the change momentum argument—prior experience mattered and that organizational tendencies to change increased with the frequency of previous changes. They also showed that the positive effects of the number of prior changes were attenuated for larger firms and those pursuing a more generalist strategy, i.e. covering a broader niche. Most notably perhaps, the authors found that relative to firms with little previous change experience, those that had a higher number of prior changes were more likely to undertake change even when markets remained stable—thus demonstrating the inertial nature of this repetitive momentum. As Dobrev and his colleagues pointed out, this finding suggested that greater change momentum may lead to misinterpretations of the market environment. Results also indicated that while changes replicating accumulated change experience could be a source of survival advantage in appropriate external conditions, they might be hazardous when environmental demands shift. Notably, though, in a study on the Norwegian general insurance industry throughout almost the entire twentieth century, Greve and Rao (2006) did find an overall negative relationship between the number of prior niche changes and organizational failure, i.e. organizations changing niches more often were more likely to survive.

The Ever-Present Past: Population History and History of Competition

History, in the form of population age, has also featured in yet another revision of the original density dependence model (see Chapter 9, this volume; also earlier). In this formulation, history of organizational populations became a moderator of relationships between key theoretical constructs in organizational ecology (Hannan 1997). Motivated again by the theoretical question of why a decline was observed after populations reached a peak density—as well as why there were subsequent density increases in some populations, the core premise in this reformulation was that the effects of density are not "timeless" and that hence the "dependence of legitimation and competition on organizational density varies systematically over the history of a population" (Hannan 1997: 194). Population-level inertia was likely to be at play, it was thought, since both legitimation and competition became more "sticky" as a population grew older (p. 202). With respect to legitimation, stickiness would be due to greater institutionalization of the organizational form. And as the population was likely to become more structured with increasing age, diffuse competition among population members would take the form of rivalry among organizations with similar positions or strategies. The argument was that density would have strong effects on legitimation and competition during the early stages in the development of a population, which would diminish, however, as the population became older. Data on automobile industries in five countries, referred to earlier (see also Chapter 9, this volume) did support these predictions. Another study that shows the moderating effects of stages in the history of a population is the one by Agarwal, Sarkar and Echambadi (2002) on major product innovations that led to the creation of new industries over the period 1908–1991.

Furthermore, some organizational ecologists have viewed interorganizational competition as a history-dependent process—a view that rests on a population perspective but has both population- and organization-level implications. As Barnett and Pontikes (2005: 352) have put it, "research typically describes competition in terms of the organizational context at a given point in time, without explicit regard for the historical process that led to the current state". The so-called "Red Queen" theory addresses this gap by combining organizational ecology and organizational learning theories. As Barnett and Hansen (1996: 140) have explicated, the term Red Queen was appropriated from biology and refers to Lewis Carroll's book *Through the Looking Glass and What Alice Found There* (1896: 33), where the "Red Queen" explains to Alice that, despite all the running, they have not advanced because all the others have also been running: "*here*, you see, it takes all the running *you* can do, to keep in the same place" (emphases in the original). The core idea behind the theory is that competition deselects unfit organizations and triggers organizational learning as it leads to a search for ways to advance, such as refining existing practices or trying out new ones. Competition intensifies, since competitors embark on doing the same. Consequently, these processes continue in a self-reinforcing manner (see Barnett and Pontikes 2005). In other words, as surviving organizations become stronger competitors, so do their rivals—a dynamic that has been referred to as "Red Queen" evolution. Hence, an organization's viability and performance depend on both its own competitive history and that of its rivals. Survival chances of organizations improve by longer experiences with competition because of the learning effects but are at the same time negatively influenced by long competitive histories of competitors.

This ecological view of competition equally suggests, however, that history can also constitute a constraint, since past experience may be maladaptive in that organizations may fall into a "competency trap". This means that even when environmental circumstances change, organizations may adhere to structures and routines that have worked in the past (see also Levitt and March 1988) but are no longer valid in the present. Hence, the positive effects of a long competitive history may be confined to experiences in the recent past, whereas experiences in the distant past may in fact be harmful for survival. The same effects would also moderate the impact of the competitors. While extensive recent competitive experiences of rivals would generate adverse effects for the focal organization, the former's competitive histories in the distant past would reverse these effects. Furthermore, the impact of an organization's own competitive experiences will also depend on the variety of organizational cohorts that it has competed with in the past. Viability and performance will be negatively affected if an organization has had to compete with a greater number of cohorts because it will face greater difficulties in developing adaptive solutions to the varying and perhaps conflicting demands of competitors from these different cohorts (Barnett and Hansen 1996).

Empirical support for these predictions were obtained in studies on the failure rates of retail banks in the state of Illinois in the US during the period 1900–1993 (Barnett and Hansen 1996) and disk array manufacturers worldwide (Barnett and McKendrick 2004). Using the same data on Illinois banks, Barnett and Sorenson (2002) confirmed that Red Queen hypotheses were supported for foundings and organizational growth. However, in the Norwegian insurance industry study mentioned earlier, Greve and Rao (2006) found that past experiences of intense competition—operationalized as historical density, i.e. average density faced by organizations during the course of their history—did not reduce, but rather increased failure rates. What should be noted here is that—despite an emphasis on history—the Red Queen theory undermines the imprinting hypothesis and the density delay model, since it argues that competitive histories, rather than the founding conditions, shape outcomes such as failure rates (see also Swaminathan 1996). Notably, Barnett and Hansen (1996) did find separate density delay effects on failure when density at founding was included as a control variable. So did Greve and Rao (2006) in their Norwegian insurance industry study. In contrast, this was not the case in Barnett and Sorenson's (2002) research on bank growth rates using the same data on Illinois banks, which also considered density delay effects. Their findings showed that density delay had no significant effects on bank growth.

It Stays in the Family: Parents and Progenies

Some of the more recent research in the organizational ecology tradition has been examining the effects of the "genealogy of organizational populations" (Phillips 2002: 474)—not to be confused with Foucault's genealogy (see Chapter 7, this volume). The main idea behind this approach is that organizations founded with a past lineage are likely to borrow or inherit structures or routines from the "parents" that they are linked to or originate from. History or the past embodied in such links would in turn differentially affect survival chances of these organizations relative to those with no such lineage. The influence of history in this manner could be through the transfer of experiences gained by founders of new organizations in the parent organization or, more broadly, through resources or constraints passed on by the parents to their progenies.

In one of the early studies along these lines, Phillips (2002) examined the survival effects of the parent–progeny relationship among law firms in Silicon Valley over a period of 50 years. He found that "parenting", i.e. a member of the organization leaving to establish a new organization of the same kind, lowered the chances of survival for parent organizations. With respect to genealogical effects, more germane to the discussion here, findings showed that firms founded as progenies had higher survival chances relative to firms established de novo, particularly in their early years. This, according to Phillips (2002: 479), pointed to the value of being "imprinted" by the "fitness or viability" of the parent. However, the result that progenies whose founders had departed from a failing parent were more likely to fail indicated that it was not always the useful structures and routines that got transferred.

In addressing a somewhat similar issue in the context of the US personal computer industry from its birth in 1975 to 1994 Lange, Boivie and Henderson (2009) compared the impact that "corporate children", i.e. firms established by existing diversified businesses, and de novo firms with no such links had on failure rates within the population. Their findings showed that the density of parented firms reduced overall rates of failure, while de novo density led to more failures. Hence, the authors argued, corporate children contributed to the legitimacy of this new technology-based industry. Yet the de novo start-ups turned out to be stronger competitors because they were "imprinted at their birth with that technology and the demands that it creates" and were "unconstrained by parental inertia, giving them the freedom to move quickly and aggressively" (Lange et al. 2009: 187). In line with this inertia argument, results also demonstrated that firms created by older parents had higher failure rates, though this relationship was attenuated by the size of the corporate children.

Ellis et al. (2017) extended this approach to multiple generations of organizations, together with advocating an "agency-based transmission" view of the way founding environments influence organizations (see Chapter 10, this volume)—particularly when imprints involved tacit knowledge. Set in the context of the Israeli information technology industry, the study distinguished between two eras in the history of the State of Israel—labeled cooperative and competitive, which differed in both ideological and economic terms. In line with their agency-based view of imprinting, the authors argued that socioeconomic environments influence organizations through their founders and that it is the founders who serve as carriers of external influence not only on the organizations that they establish but also on other members in these organizations. Indeed, results showed that the first-generation "ancestral" founders who established their firms in the more market-based competitive era portrayed greater entrepreneurial knowledge or "proclivity", i.e. were likely to establish a larger number of start-ups (Ellis et al. 2017: 500). However, the founding environment had no direct effects on the entrepreneurial proclivity of the founders of the second-generation start-ups. Instead, the effect of founding conditions on second-generation founders was mediated by the founders of the first-generation firms.

Moreover and importantly from the authors' point of view, the transmission of entrepreneurial proclivity from first-generation founders was confined to second-generation start-ups by founders employed in first-generation firms. Likewise, the entrepreneurial tendencies of the founders of third-generation firms depended on the entrepreneurial proclivity of the second-generation founders and not on either the founding environment or the first-generation founders. This was because, Ellis and colleagues argued, entrepreneurial knowledge was tacit and could only be passed on through direct interaction with potential founders. Overall then, the authors showed, in line with the parent–progeny approach, that the founders of start-ups were influenced by the founders of firms where they were employed before starting their own firms. In addition, according to Ellis et al. (2017), the study supported their agency-based transmission view and the adjoining revision they proposed in imprinting theory, which suggested that the persistence of founding imprints occurred not because of inertia or path dependence, but rather due to "inheritance" by successive organizational generations—at least in the case of the entrepreneurial knowledge or proclivity that was examined in their research.

Survival Strategies: Resources, Routines and Dynamic Capabilities

After a close interaction with (business) history at the outset, namely in terms of deriving theory from historical cases (see Chapters 2 and 8, this volume), strategy research turned toward quantitative data and "static" theoretical modeling—a trend that only started being reversed during the 1990s with "dynamic" models gaining more traction (Ghemawat 2016). Similar to the ecological research program, these more dynamic approaches in strategy scholarship focus on understanding organizational success and survival, conceptualized by the latter as "sustainable competitive advantage". However, ecology and strategy differ in one fundamental aspect, in particular when taking into account the concerns of strategy consultants and practitioners, as noted succinctly by Ghemawat (2016: 738–39): "The practical problem with such ecological explanations, and the theories of imprinting that underlie them, is that they leave little or no room for managerial action, at least once an organization has been founded—nor, indeed, for strategy".

There were some early attempts to bring strategy back while accepting the findings of the organizational ecology literature. Thus, Aldrich and Auster (1986), for instance, suggested strategies for addressing the dual liabilities of "aging and bigness" and "newness and smallness" (p. 167). They namely suggested that the former "emulate" or "exploit" the "smaller and younger organizations continually being created all around them" (p. 195). But this, rather fatalistically, further limits the latter's options, hence the title of their paper: "Even Dwarfs Started Small". Historians, and in particular, the oft-mentioned Alfred Chandler, also pointed to the crucial role of managers—though they focused on managerial action in the past rather than the present.

It Pays to Be Early: First Movers

As mentioned (Chapter 3, this volume), Chandler's early work on the origins of the multidivisional organization, or M-form (Chandler 1962), has been included among the foundational texts of management and organization theory. In addition, the same book has been credited with developing one of the early models in the strategy literature: "structure follows strategy". In his subsequent work, Chandler (1977) focused on the crucial role of the "visible hand" in the creation and ultimate superiority of American capitalism. It is on this basis, and in comparing the US with the British and German cases, that he developed a model which included the "past" as a determinant for the longevity of certain companies since the second industrial revolution of the late nineteenth and early twentieth centuries. This model is probably most clearly presented in *Scale and Scope* (Chandler 1990: 34–36), where he argued that those who were the first to make "the three interrelated sets of investments in production, distribution, and management" "acquired powerful competitive advantages"—investments that ensured an ongoing superiority of these "first movers" over possible "latecomers" or "challengers", leading to "little turnover among the leaders". In his comparison of the US with developments in Germany and the UK, he related in particular the latter's lack of competitiveness in many of the relevant industries of the second industrial revolution to the failure of companies to invest in the necessary managerial hierarchies. And he also attributed the struggles of leading US companies since the 1970s to their unrelated diversification, since his model required the "managerial organization" as a success factor to be industry-specific (Chandler 1990).

Chandler's views on the importance of history in determining long-run competitive advantage found some support in the work of the economist Steven Klepper. While focusing on technology and industry rather than company evolution, he sketched a similar past-dependent model that also pointed to the advantages of "early entrants"—mainly due to their ability to leverage their experience in product development and production (e.g. Klepper 1996; Klepper and Simons 2000; see Mowery 2015 for a critical analysis and comparison of Klepper's and Chandler's views). Nevertheless, the universalistic claims of Chandler's model were subsequently criticized by other historians, namely those who had studied the UK and German cases. His portrayal of the origins of large-scale corporate and managerial capitalism in the US was also challenged by several management scholars (see, for details, Chapter 12, this volume). And transaction cost economists even questioned the central role of managers by pointing to the lasting and—in particular during more recent periods—growing importance of market-based transactions—a development they characterized as the "vanishing hand" (e.g. Langlois 2003). It was therefore ultimately left to mainstream strategy scholars to find ways to restore "managerial action"—as postulated by Ghemawat (2016).

Managing the Past: History as a "Resource"

The first of the research programs that placed the past into a pivotal position as part of strategic action is the so-called resource-based view (RBV). Its origins are usually attributed to Edith Penrose's (1959) *Theory of the Growth of the Firm*, another book considered a management "classic" today (see Musson forthcoming for an overview of her life and work as well as the book's reception). Penrose (1959: 5) pointed to two historically conditioned factors, i.e. "the crucial role of the firm's 'inherited' resources" and "the experience of management", which, in "a truly 'dynamic' interacting process" both enable and limit the growth of the firm. Thus, the past has a very explicit part in her theoretical model both with respect to resources and management (see Penrose 1959: Ch. V). Moreover, she used a historical case study of the Hercules Powder Company to illustrate her theory, though apparently due to space constraints, it was ultimately published separately (Penrose 1960). In contrast, Wernerfelt (1984), who is widely credited with introducing RBV into strategy, remains largely mute on the importance of history or the past for a firm's resource position—though he does link it to first mover advantages and the experience curve. He also highlights, somewhat prophetically, "the practical difficulties involved in identifying resources" as compared to products (p. 180).

In the article that came to define RBV more than others, Barney (1991: 107–108) explicitly included history in the definition of what makes resources "inimitable"—and hence contributes to firm heterogeneity and, ultimately, "sustained competitive advantage". Thus, he "assert[ed] that not only are firms intrinsically historical and social entities, but that their ability to acquire and exploit some resources depends upon their place in time and space". In doing so, Barney explicitly refuted the mainstream strategy literature at the time, which accorded no relevance to firms' unique histories. Instead he pointed to different research programs, notably imprinting and path dependence—with reference to, among others, Stinchcombe (1965) and David (1985), which were also "recognizing the importance of history" (Barney 1991: 107; see also Chapter 10, this volume). As to the evidence for the "history-dependent nature" of many resources, Barney referred to "the case analyses that have dominated teaching and research for so long in the field of strategic management", while admitting that "the systematic study of the impact of history on firm performance is in its infancy" (Barney 1991: 108).

While RBV became hugely popular among strategy scholars (Ghemawat 2016), its empirical study was hampered by the difficulty "to operationalize and measure resources and capabilities that are specialized, unique, and idiosyncratic for each firm in the context of large sample studies" (Hitt, Gimeno and Hoskisson 1998: 12)—the kind of methodological approach which remained the mainstay of strategy research. One study that did combine quantitative methods with historical data in testing RBV was conducted by Maijoor and Witteloostuijn (1996) on the Dutch audit industry. However, they extended RBV from the firm to the strategic group and industry level and could only confirm rent-producing resources for the last two, notably in the form of labor market restrictions by the larger firms and government regulation. Case studies remained rare—and even rarer those that looked at how "history" contributed to the constitution of the imperfect imitability of these resources. Hitt and colleagues (1998: 14–15) reported on three "richer empirical studies" relating to RBV, though only one of them— a study of the bearings industry—referred to Barney's framework and discussed the historical origins of firm idiosyncrasies, while combining them with "core competency" and "organizational capability" (Collis 1991). The study did cover a longer period, but still relied mainly on retrospective interviews. And the author operationalized history mainly as "administrative heritage", i.e. "the organizational constraints on strategic choice" (p. 52).

As time went by, history, if not completely ignored, was actually increasingly perceived as a problem rather than a "resource". Partly responsible for this shift was probably a widely cited article that aimed to combine RBV with neo-institutionalism (Oliver 1997). While recognizing the value contribution of resources "rooted in history and culture of firms", that same rootedness, according to the author, "also increases their likelihood of being perpetuated without question" (p. 702), ultimately turning firms into "captives of their own history" (p. 700)—a reasoning that can also be found among studies examining routines and capabilities (see later). This has been challenged more recently by those considering history a rhetorical construct and a manageable resource that could be put to strategic use for generating an advantage over competitors. Standing in opposition to various approaches discussed previously, such as imprinting and path dependence, for Suddaby, Foster and Quinn Trank (2010: 160), for example, rhetorical history "views firm history as a deliberate and strategic construction—an organizational resource designed to confer identity, motivate commitment, and frame action amongst organizational stakeholders". Accordingly, rhetorical history is not emergent but deliberate, and as a "strategic resource" it can confer "legitimacy" and "identity" and can be facilitative in "strategic change" (p. 165; see also Chapter 12, this volume).

Change Is Back: From Routines to Dynamic Capabilities

Thus, while RBV gathered a significant following among strategy scholars, history, which had played an important part in the early theorizing (especially Penrose 1959), fell largely by the wayside—or was seen as a burden rather than an asset. Similar to what happened in strategy-as-practice (Chapter 8, this volume), preferences in terms of data and research methods also contributed to sidelining historical approaches. More importantly, the perception of history was indicative of a broader theoretical challenge faced by RBV, namely, to allow for organizational change and adaptation in increasingly unpredictable and fast-changing environments. The answer was found in a new theoretical framework, "dynamic capabilities", which seems to have become even more popular than RBV.

The origins of this idea ultimately go back to another classic, *An Evolutionary Theory of Economic Change* by Richard Nelson and Sidney Winter (1982). While addressing the same question about survival as the ecological research program, they looked for the answers not at the population level but within organizations, focusing on "routines" as their key building blocks—with organizational routines widely "defined as repetitive, recognizable patterns of interdependent actions, carried out by multiple actors" (Feldman and Pentland 2003: 95). While operating at a different level of analysis than organizational ecology, the theorized mechanism(s) and outcomes were largely the same in that routines were mainly designed for stability and therefore largely inert with limited adaptability. And it was left to markets to select the "superior" routines (Nelson and Winter 1982). History was once again a powerful factor driving inertia and lock-in. This was criticized by Feldman and Pentland (2003: 115), who aimed to remove that burden of history and make endogenous change more feasible by reasserting the role of agency namely through what they, drawing on Latour, referred to as the "performative aspect" of organizational routines in addition to the largely abstract, schematic "ostensive" one. Their revised theory of routines prompted an important and still expanding research program (see, e.g. Howard-Grenville et al. 2016) which had little use for historical data—not surprising, given the now well-known research preferences among (process) organization scholars (see also Chapter 8, this volume). It had even less room for past dependence in terms of theorizing—especially since it would have brought back the dreaded inertia.

The concept of routines—in combination with insights from organizational economics—made their way into strategy research as a building block of what came to be referred to as dynamic capabilities, which were also intended to address the challenge of the widely observed and theorized inertia (see, for a comparison between this capabilities perspective and the earlier-mentioned process-oriented "practice perspective", Parmigiani and Howard-Grenville 2011). And within the strategy discipline, dynamic capabilities ultimately became the dominant research program (see, for recent overviews, Wilden, Devinney and Dowling 2016; Helfat 2017; Teece and Leih 2018). There are multiple definitions of what dynamic capabilities are and what they entail. The foundational text by Teece and Pisano (1994: 553) posited "that the competitive advantage of firms stems from dynamic capabilities rooted in high performance routines operating inside the firm, embedded in the firm's processes, and conditioned by its history". This shows how this novel "approach"—as the authors characterized it at the time—is drawing on and combining a number of different perspectives, including the notion of "routines". However, the erstwhile "approach" became increasingly considered a "theory" and a more recent definition described dynamic capability as "the capacity of an organization to purposefully create, extend, and modify its resource base" (Helfat et al. 2007: 4). Not only had the notion of "resources" replaced reference to "routines", there was no longer any explicit link with competitive advantage or performance—admittedly the main concern of strategy research, probably because empirically and causally connecting the two had proved largely elusive.

More relevant in the context of this chapter is the importance accorded to history in the original formulation of dynamic capabilities. Thus, while Teece and Pisano (1994) focused on flexibility and change, emphasizing "the key role of strategic management in appropriately adapting, integrating, and re-configuring internal and external organizational skills, resources, and functional competences toward changing environment" (p. 538), they also made explicit reference to path dependence and stressed that "a firm's previous investments and its repertoire of routines (its 'history') constrains its future behavior" (p. 547). However, as the theory was being developed, references to history and the constraints it imposed dwindled. Thus, Eisenhardt and Martin (2000: 1114) turned "the unique histories of firms" into an element of flexibility by arguing that the resulting path dependence is best understood as "learning mecha-nisms [which] guide the evolution of dynamic capabilities"—though they are overall rather skeptical about the ability of firms to change in "high velocity" environments. And in a later article, Teece (2007) himself no longer made reference to "history", though he continued to highlight the constraining influence of path dependencies. As a way to address these, he suggested that "the enterprise frees itself of certain routines [and] con-straints," namely by "jettisoning 'dead' or dying assets" (p. 1333).

This, however, was easier said than done, as some of the few avail-able historical case studies of organizations faced with radical techno-logical change demonstrated (Tripsas and Gavetti 2000; Danneels 2011). In both cases, inertia trumped dynamic capabilities resulting in these companies ultimately going out of business—though the authors of both studies attributed this failure mainly to managerial cognition. In theoreti-cal terms, this suggests that they saw managerial agency as more pow-erful than historical conditioning or path dependence, since managers apparently could have overcome the latter had they recognized and acted on the challenges early and decisively enough (see also Augier and Teece 2009). This created an additional direction for work on dynamic capa-bilities; examining their interaction with cognition (see, for an overview, Eggers and Kaplan 2013), which was much easier to research—and theo-rize—with the traditional sources and methods of organizational studies than the "unique histories of firms" mentioned previously.

There has been a recent attempt to revive the attention to history (Sud-daby, Coraiola, Harvey and Foster 2020)—though with an understand-ing of history that is very different from its past-dependent nature in the earlier manifestations of the dynamic capabilities research program. This attempt comes from a similar group of authors, who had previously pointed to the possibility for organizations to use history as a strate-gic resource (see earlier). Building on that work, they argued "that the capacity to manage perceptions of the past, in the present, for the future, is a critical cognitive capacity that underpins the micro-foundation of any dynamic capability", since it "informs a firm's ability to successfully enact changes needed to adapt to disruptive technology". This argument ticks all the boxes of current research on dynamic capabilities, including the role of cognition and managerial agency, and also addresses current concerns about "disruption". Overall, this view of the possible, positive "uses of the past" is diametrically opposed to the past dependence and resulting inertia, theorized—and tested empirically—by the research pro-grams summarized in this and the previous chapter, including the early manifestations of dynamic capabilities. Whether it holds up to empirical research remains to be seen.

A Way Out? Combining Imprinting and History Dependence in Co-evolution

Thus, to put it somewhat simplistically, the ecological research program sees survival as a population-level process of selection in a changing environment, whereas strategy scholars looking at routines, resources and dynamic capabilities grant organizations varying degrees of room for adaptation to that environment—an adaptation increasingly seen as constrained less by original choices, i.e. "history", and more by contemporaneous internal impediments linked in particular to managerial cognition. Situated somewhere in between the two is the relatively recent research program on co-evolution, developed as an attempt to bridge adaptation vs. selection views on organization–environment relationships and organizational change.

An example for such a view is the Red Queen theory discussed earlier, which essentially depicted an ongoing co-evolutionary process between firm-level adaptive behavior and population-level competitive and selection pressures. But co-evolution has gained broader traction as a perspective in itself. Its core idea has been that there are reciprocal causal influences unfolding over time across multiple levels, such as between organizations and organizational populations. Adaptive actions at one level take place within the context of and with effects on competitive and selection processes at a higher level. As Lewin and Volberda (1999: 526) summarize, "change can be recursive and need not be an outcome of either managerial adaptation or environmental selection but rather the joint outcome of managerial intentionality and environmental effects". Cross-level influences may involve and drive macro-level evolution, as in the interactions between organizations or organizational forms and their environments, i.e. populations, communities or societies. Co-evolution may also occur at the micro level, as organizations serve as a selection environment which shapes strategy by linking external and internal possibilities of competitive action (see e.g. Burgelman 1994).

Lewin and Volberda (1999: 526–528) have included "path and history dependence" as one of the main properties of co-evolution, invoking ideas of imprinting and historical legacies by referring to the influence of origins of organizational populations or forms as well as the past experiences of individual organizations (see also Lewin, Long and Carroll 1999). They have also stressed that the study of co-evolution would need to cover long spans of time and attend to the historical context of organizations and their environments. Not all of the research on co-evolution has heeded these assertions. As the following examples will show, some have done so by considering historical influences on co-evolutionary processes. But there have also been studies which have paid less attention to the influences of the past. Instead, they have taken the historical context into account to show its effects and/or—similar to those discussed in Chapter 9, this volume—as a setting to demonstrate or illustrate how co-evolutionary processes operate.

In an early study Kieser (1989) examined the transition in manufacturing from medieval craft guilds to putting-out systems and factories with specific reference to Germany. He explicitly drew upon a co-evolution perspective, suggesting that this transition occurred within a context of society-level cultural evolution involving greater acceptance of profit-making as a legitimate motive. This meant that selection mechanisms were evolving—a shift also driven by those with economic interests. Alongside the new forms of organization, labor and capital markets were developing too. According to Kieser (1989: 543), primacy should not be given to any one of the levels he identified: worldviews, institutions and human behavior. Instead, he suggested considering "all three of them and [paying] special attention to reciprocal selection processes". Emphasizing historical effects, he also asserted that the "new forms of organization incorporated or built upon the guild shops" (Kieser 1989: 548). That the latter were outcompeted he attributed to their core characteristics based on religious and security concerns, which hampered innovativeness and reduced their survival chances in an environment where selection criteria had been altered.

Pertaining to more recent history, Carney and Gedajlovic (2002) developed a co-evolution framework to show that Chinese family business groups (FBGs) in Southeast Asia emerged and were shaped in the post–World War II environment as they replaced colonial-era trading firms. The shift could happen, the authors argued, because the latter, given their "path dependencies", were unable to adapt to the emergent context. While opportune for business development due to the retreat of colonial firms, the environment where the Chinese FBGs emerged was also characterized by adverse conditions, in particular strong nationalism—and an associated discrimination of foreigners—in the newly independent Southeast Asian countries. The core features of FBGs, such as family ownership and management, tight control and diversification, hence reflected these uncertain conditions. These characteristics have persisted, since, after the 1980s, FBGs were able to improve their relations with government authorities and to garner greater status because of the contributions they were seen to be making to economic development. Moreover, not only were FBGs instrumental in generating a pro-business outlook on the part of governments but also, the argument went, they contributed to the persistence of existing societal-level institutional structures, such as the limited development of financial institutions.

In their study of the international luxury fashion industry, Djelic and Ainamo (1999: 622) likewise argued that in broad terms change had been "one of coevolution, where environmental transformation and organizational change have fed upon each other through time". Their research, based on three firms, one each from France, Italy and the US, also showed, however, that within a "globally" evolving industry, organizational evolution toward what looked like a common "network form" involved variation across the three countries. According to the authors, this was because the evolution of organizational forms occurred in each setting in a "path-dependent" manner, conditioned by "historical and institutional legacies". Similarly, in a study on the paper industry Lamberg and Laurila (2005) sought to demonstrate how organizational forms were shaped by and co-evolved with their national institutional setting. Focusing on Finnish firms in comparison to those from the US, they showed that the dominant organizational form, which was characterized by various combinations of state and cooperative or dispersed ownership that emerged in Finland after World War II, benefited from the standing that the industry had gained historically and the resulting state support. At the same time, Finnish firms based on this form could continue to influence state authorities and thus benefited from various financial and educational advantages which helped them develop their technological capabilities. The authors argued that the capabilities that were developed based on an historical legacy and in interaction with their institutional environment led to change at the international level, in that Finnish firms overtook their US competitors, which did not enjoy similar advantages, as they had developed in a different societal context.

In addition to this type of study, there have been others which, as already mentioned, while making some reference to the influence of history, have been more concerned with how co-evolutionary processes unfolded in the early stages of particular industries and how these processes could be studied through historical analyses. An example is the narrative account of the formative period of the American film industry between 1895 and 1920 by Jones (2001), which aimed to "provide insights into co-evolutionary processes" (p. 938). Nevertheless, she also demonstrated that the career backgrounds of founders influenced not only the practices pursued by their firms but also the early development of the industry. Moreover, technology-oriented firms, which helped shape the first phase of development, had difficulties in adapting to the shift in the competitive environment after the industry entered into the second phase following the advent of firms that were content-oriented. Another notable example where a main focus has been to advocate the use of historical data and analysis in co-evolution research is Murmann's (2013) study on the first 60 or so years of the synthetic dye industry. His main thesis was that despite the initial supremacy of British and French firms, German firms came to dominate the industry before World War I due to the ways in which the industry and the academic discipline of chemistry co-evolved in Germany.

Conclusion

Apart from the various issues that they raise with respect to the effects of history, the research programs summarized in this chapter basically answer a similar question, i.e. why certain organizational forms or organizations thrive over particular periods of time but often find it difficult to survive in rapidly changing environments. Their answer depends on how seriously they take history as part of their theorizing. The rich literature on organizational ecology does take history very seriously. The theoretical models and constructs it has developed—and empirically tested, often with historical data—suggest that when environments change, organizational forms are brought down by the weight of history; they succumb because of the structural inertia and other past-dependent factors that served them well during times of stability.

The various models developed within the strategy discipline recognize the positive role of the past embedded in organizational routines and resources, which give certain organizations a competitive advantage over others. And they also recognize the inertia befalling these organizations—due to those same resources and routines—in "high velocity" and "turbulent" environments. But because of a focus on managerial agency, they are loath to accept the outcomes researched and theorized by the ecologists—striving instead to theoretically lighten or remove the burden history turns into when things change. One recent approach even argues that managers might be able to use a constructed history to address these changes. But while becoming ever more detailed and sophisticated theoretically, such history-less dynamics have yet to find more support in empirical work, with many case studies actually reasserting the constraints imposed by the past.

The co-evolution research program offers a more dynamic, less one-sided perspective on the interplay of environmental selection and agentic adaptation, but poses its own challenges in terms of the historical evidence necessary to document this theoretically enticing model.

References

Agarwal, R., Sarkar, M. and Echambadi, R. (2002) "The conditioning effect of time on firm survival: An industry life cycle approach," *Academy of Management Journal*, 45(5): 971–994.

Aldrich, H. and Auster, E. R. (1986) "Even dwarfs started small: Liabilities of age and size and their strategic implications," *Research in Organizational Behavior*, 8: 165–198.

Amburgey, T. L., Kelly, D. and Barnett, W. P. (1993) "Resetting the clock: The dynamics of organizational change and failure," *Administrative Science Quarterly*, 38(1): 51–73.

Augier, M. and Teece, D. J. (2009) "Dynamic capabilities and the role of managers in business strategy and economic performance," *Organization Science*, 20(2): 410–421.

Barnett, W. P. and Hansen, M. T. (1996) "The Red Queen in organizational evolution," *Strategic Management Journal*, 17(Summer): 139–157.

Barnett, W. P. and McKendrick, D. G. (2004) "Why are some organizations more competitive than others? Evidence from a changing global market," *Administrative Science Quarterly*, 49(4): 535–571.

Barnett, W. P. and Pontikes, E. G. (2005) "The Red Queen: History-dependent competition among organizations," *Research in Organizational Behavior*, 26: 351–371.

Barnett, W. P. and Sorenson, O. (2002) "The Red Queen in organizational creation and development," *Industrial and Corporate Change*, 11(2): 289–325.

Barney, J. B. (1991) "Firm resources and sustained competitive advantage," *Journal of Management*, 17(1): 99–120.

Baum, J. A. C. and Shipilov, A. V. (2006) "Ecological approaches to organizations," in S. R. Clegg, C. Hardy, T. Lawrence and W. R. Nord (eds), *The Sage Handbook of Organization Studies*, 2nd edn, London: Sage, pp. 55–110.

Burgelman, R. A. (1994) "Fading memories: A process theory of strategic business exit in dynamic environments," *Administrative Science Quarterly*, 39(1): 24–56.

Carney, M. and Gedajlovic, E. (2002) "The co-evolution of institutional environments and organizational strategies: The rise of family business groups in the ASEAN region," *Organization Studies*, 23(1): 1–29.

Carroll, G. R. and Delacroix, J. (1982) "Organizational mortality in the newspaper industries of Argentina and Ireland: An ecological approach," *Administrative Science Quarterly*, 27(2): 169–198.

Carroll, G. R. and Hannan, M. T. (1989) "Density delay in the evolution of organizational populations: A model and five empirical tests," *Administrative Science Quarterly*, 34(3): 411–430.

Carroll, G. R. and Hannan, M. T. (2000) *The Demography of Corporations and Industries*, Princeton, NJ: Princeton University Press.

Carroll, L. (1896) *Through the Looking Glass and What Alice Found There*, London: Macmillan.

Chandler, A. D. Jr. (1962) *Strategy and Structure: Chapters in the History of the Industrial Enterprise*, Cambridge, MA: MIT Press.

Chandler, A. D. Jr. (1977) *The Visible Hand: The Managerial Revolution in American Business*, Cambridge, MA: The Belknap Press of Harvard University Press.

Chandler, A. D. Jr. (1990) *Scale and Scope: The Dynamics of Industrial Capitalism*, Cambridge, MA: The Belknap Press of Harvard University Press.

Collis, D. J. (1991) "A resource-based analysis of global competition: The case of the bearings industry," *Strategic Management Journal*, 12(Special issue): 49–68.

Danneels, E. (2011) "Trying to become a different type of company: Dynamic capabilities at Smith Corona," *Strategic Management Journal*, 32(1): 1–31.

David, P. A. (1985) "Clio and the economics of QWERTY," *American Economic Review*, 75(2): 332–337.

Djelic, M.-L. and Ainamo, A. (1999) "The coevolution of new organizational forms in the fashion industry: A historical and comparative study of France, Italy, and the United States," *Organization Science*, 10(5): 622–637.

Dobrev, S. D. and Gotsopoulos, A. (2010) "Legitimacy vacuum, structural imprinting, and the first mover disadvantage," *Academy of Management Journal*, 53(5): 1153–1174.

Dobrev, S. D., Kim, T.-Y. and Carroll, G. R. (2003) "Shifting gears, shifting niches: Organizational inertia and change in the evolution of the U.S. automobile industry, 1885–1981," *Organization Science*, 14(3): 264–282.

Eggers, J. P. and Kaplan, S. (2013) "Cognition and capabilities: A multi-level perspective," *Academy of Management Annals*, 7(1): 295–340.

Eisenhardt, K. M. and Martin, J. A. (2000) "Dynamic capabilities: What are they?" *Strategic Management Journal*, 21(10–11): 1105–1121.

Ellis, S., Aharonson, B. S., Drori, I. and Shapira, Z. (2017) "Imprinting through inheritance: A multi-genealogical study of entrepreneurial proclivity," *Academy of Management Journal*, 60(2): 500–522.

Feldman, M. S. and Pentland, B. T. (2003) "Reconceptualizing organizational routines as a source of flexibility and change," *Administrative Science Quarterly*, 48: 94–118.

Ghemawat, P. (2016) "Evolving ideas about business strategy," *Business History Review*, 90(4): 727–749.

Greve, H. R. and Rao, H. (2006) "If it doesn't kill you: Learning from ecological competition," *Advances in Strategic Management*, 23: 243–271.

Hannan, M. T. (1997) "Inertia, density and the structure of organizational populations: Entries in European automobile industries, 1886–1981," *Organization Studies*, 18(2): 193–228.

Hannan, M. T., Baron, J. N., Hsu, G. and Koçak, Ö. (2006) "Organizational identities and the hazard of change," *Industrial and Corporate Change*, 15(5): 755–784.

Hannan, M. T. and Freeman, J. (1977) "The population ecology of organizations," *American Journal of Sociology*, 82(5): 929–964.

Hannan, M. T. and Freeman, J. (1984) "Structural inertia and organizational change," *American Sociological Review*, 49(2): 149–164.

Hannan, M. T., Pólos, L. and Carroll, G. R. (2007) *Logics of Organization Theory: Audiences, Codes, and Ecologies*, Princeton, NJ: Princeton University Press.

Helfat, C. E. (ed) (2017) *The SMS Blackwell Handbook of Organizational Capabilities*, Oxford: Blackwell.

Helfat, C. E., Finkelstein, S., Mitchell, W., Peteraf, M., Singh, H., Teece, D. and Winter, S. G. (2007) *Dynamic Capabilities: Understanding Strategic Change in Organizations*, London: Wiley.

Hitt, M. A., Gimeno, J. and Hoskisson, R. E. (1998) "Current and future research methods in strategic management," *Organizational Research Methods*, 1(1): 6–44.

Howard-Grenville, J., Rerup, C., Langley, A. and Tsoukas, H. (eds) (2016) *Organizational Routines: How They Are Created, Maintained, and Changed*, Oxford: Oxford University Press.

Jones, C. (2001) "Co-evolution of entrepreneurial careers, institutional rules and competitive dynamics in American film, 1895–1920," *Organization Studies*, 22(6): 911–944.

Kelly, D. and Amburgey, T. L. (1991) "Organizational inertia and momentum: A dynamic model of strategic change," *Academy of Management Journal*, 34(3): 591–612.

Kieser, A. (1989) "Organizational, institutional, and societal evolution: Medieval craft guilds and the genesis of formal organizations," *Administrative Science Quarterly*, 34(4): 540–564.

Klepper, S. (1996) "Entry, exit, growth, and innovation over the product life cycle," *American Economic Review*, 86(3): 562–583.

Klepper, S. and Simons, K. L. (2000) "Dominance by birthright: Entry of prior radio producers and competitive ramifications in the U.S. television receiver industry," *Strategic Management Journal*, 21(10–11): 997–1016.

Lamberg, J.-A. and Laurila, J. (2005) "Materializing the societal effect: Organizational forms and changing patterns of dominance in the paper industry," *Organization Studies*, 26(12): 1809–1830.

Lange, D., Boivie, S. and Henderson, A. D. (2009) "The parenting paradox: How multibusiness diversifiers endorse disruptive technologies while their corporate children struggle," *Academy of Management Journal*, 52(1): 179–198.

Langlois, R. N. (2003) "The vanishing hand: The changing dynamics of industrial capitalism," *Industrial and Corporate Change*, 12(2): 351–385.

Le Mens, G., Hannan, M. T. and Pólos, L. (2011) "Founding conditions, learning, and organizational life chances: Age dependence revisited," *Administrative Science Quarterly*, 56(1): 95–126.

Le Mens, G., Hannan, M. T. and Pólos, L. (2015a) "Age-related structural inertia: A distance-based approach," *Organization Science*, 26(3): 756–773.

Le Mens, G., Hannan, M. T. and Pólos, L. (2015b) "Organizational obsolescence, drifting tastes, and age dependence in organizational life chances," *Organization Science*, 26(2): 550–570.

Levitt, B. and March, J. G. (1988) "Organizational learning," *Annual Review of Sociology*, 14: 319–340.

Lewin, A. Y., Long, C. P. and Carroll, T. N. (1999) "The coevolution of new organizational forms," *Organization Science*, 10(5): 535–550.

Lewin, A. Y. and Volberda, H. W. (1999) "Prolegomena on coevolution: A framework for research on strategy and new organizational forms," *Organization Science*, 10(5): 519–534.

Maijoor, S. and van Witteloostuijn, A. (1996) "An empirical test of the resource-based theory: Strategic regulation in the Dutch audit industry," *Strategic Management Journal*, 17(7): 549–569.

Mowery, D. C. (2015) "Steven Klepper and business history," *Industrial and Corporate Change*, 24(4): 755–768.

Murmann, J. P. (2013) "The coevolution of industries and important features of their environments," *Organization Science*, 24(1): 58–78.

Musson, D. (forthcoming) "The life and work of Edith Penrose: Appreciating the classics in temporal and historical perspective," in J. Reinecke, R. Suddaby, A. Langley and H. Tsoukas (eds), *Time, Temporality, and History in Process Organization Studies*, Oxford: Oxford University Press.

Nelson, R. R. and Winter, S. G. (1982) *An Evolutionary Theory of Economic Change*, Cambridge, MA: The Belknap Press of Harvard University Press.

Oliver, C. (1997) "Sustainable competitive advantage: Combining institutional and resource-based views," *Strategic Management Journal*, 18(9): 697–713.

Parmigiani, A. and Howard-Grenville, J. (2011) "Routines revisited: Exploring the capabilities and practice perspectives," *Academy of Management Annals*, 5(1): 413–453.

Penrose, E. T. (1959) *The Theory of the Growth of the Firm*, New York: Wiley.

Penrose, E. T. (1960) "The growth of the firm—A case study: The Hercules Powder Company," *Business History Review*, 34(1): 1–23.

Phillips, D. J. (2002) "A genealogical approach to organizational life chances: The parent-progeny Transfer among Silicon Valley law firms, 1946–1996," *Administrative Science Quarterly*, 47(3): 474–506.

Singh, J. V. and Lumsden, C. J. (1990) "Theory and research in organizational ecology," *Annual Review of Sociology*, 16: 161–195.

Stinchcombe, A. L. (1965) "Social structure and organizations," in J. G. March (ed), *Handbook of Organizations*, Chicago, IL: Rand McNally, pp. 142–193.

Suddaby, R., Coraiola, D., Harvey, C. and Foster, W. (2020) "History and the micro-foundations of dynamic capabilities," *Strategic Management Journal*, 41(3): 530–556.

Suddaby, R., Foster, W. M. and Quinn Trank, C. (2010) "Rhetorical history as a source of competitive advantage," *Advances in Strategic Management*, 27: 147–173.

Swaminathan, A. (1996) "Environmental conditions at founding and organizational mortality: A trial-by-fire model," *Academy of Management Journal*, 39(5): 1350–1377.

Teece, D. J. (2007) "Explicating dynamic capabilities: The nature and microfoundations of (sustainable) enterprise performance," *Strategic Management Journal*, 28(13): 1319–1350.

Teece, D. J. and Leih, S. (eds) (2018) *The Oxford Handbook of Dynamic Capabilities*, Oxford: Oxford University Press. (Published online since 2015.)

Teece, D. J. and Pisano, G. (1994) "The dynamic capabilities of firms: An introduction," *Industrial and Corporate Change*, 3(3): 537–556.

Tripsas, M. and Gavetti, G. (2000) "Capabilities, cognition, and inertia: Evidence from digital imaging," *Strategic Management Journal*, 21(10–11): 1147–1161.

Tucker, D. J., Singh, J. V. and Meinhard, A. G. (1990) "Founding characteristics, imprinting, and organizational change," in J. V. Singh (ed), *Organizational Evolution: New Directions*, Newbury Park, CA: Sage, pp. 182–200.

Wernerfelt, B. (1984) "A resource-based view of the firm," *Strategic Management Journal*, 5(2): 171–180.

Wilden, R., Devinney, T. M. and Dowling, G. R. (2016) "The architecture of dynamic capability research: Identifying the building blocks of a configurational approach," *Academy of Management Annals*, 10(1): 997–1076.

12 Not a Conclusion
Multiple Ways Forward

Introduction

The concluding chapter of the book has a dual purpose. First, it will summarize—very briefly—the main findings of all the preceding chapters, highlighting in particular the modifications and additions that were made to the earlier article (Kipping and Üsdiken 2014). This summary of the main thrusts of the book will provide the backdrop for the second, more forward looking and in many ways more important part of this conclusion: a purposeful glimpse into what may be next for both "history *of* management" and "history *in* management"—purposeful in the sense that it will not only outline broad avenues for future work but, drawing on recent exemplary research, also make specific suggestions for how to move along these avenues faster and further.

Hence, the main part of this conclusion will present and critically discuss three directions that might provide opportunities for not only continuing and expanding what has been done since the 1980s but for taking history even more seriously and more fully integrating its insights and approaches into the mainstream of management research—beyond its current use as evidence for developing, testing and modifying theory or "history *to* theory", on the one hand, and with the past as a building block in theoretical models or "history *in* theory", on the other. The focus on these three directions is not meant to dismiss or preclude additional ways forward. However, the ones presented here are those that emerge most prominently from the review of past and current efforts in this book—with the presence of exemplary research suggesting that there is an underlying dynamic and a reasonable chance for further development and ultimate success.

The first of these directions concerns history itself, and in particular business and management history. At the moment, there seems little hope for a sustained and sustainable interaction with mainstream management scholarship. But there are a few—very few—promising examples, which might yet lead to historians contributing more actively to management and organization studies. Second, there is an emerging research program called "uses of the past" which draws in part on insights from neo-institutional research on legitimacy and in part on memory as well as museum studies. But rather than providing data for theory testing or drivers for theoretical models, here the "past" and how it is employed in the present are the *object* of study. Finally, there is what the 2014 article called "historical cognizance", an approach where history in addition to data and driver also is seen as a kind of boundary condition, with scholars making their theorizing more contingent on context, in this case historical context. This might ultimately offer an avenue leading away from the predominantly scientistic and timeless ambitions of mainstream management scholarship—ambitions, which originally prompted Mayer N. Zald, Alfred Kieser and others to call for "more history".

Main Findings in Brief—Very Brief

This book originated as an extension and expansion of an article in the *Academy of Management Annals* (Kipping and Üsdiken 2014). It notably added context in Part I by providing (a) an overview of the development of both history and business and management as pursuits in research—and teaching, as well as their respective establishment and recognition as "sciences"; and (b) a systematic survey of history-related publications in various top management journals—showing how these took one of two main directions: examining the history *of* management as a practice or, more so, academic discipline or, alternatively, using history *in* mainstream management research as evidence in theory building/testing or as an element of the theoretical model itself. In Part II, the book then elaborated on the history *of* management, drawing on a much larger literature comprising articles—also outside the top journals, books and contributions to edited volumes. Chapters in this part traced the overall progression of both the history of management and of management thought since the early twentieth century and its evolving relationship with mainstream management research. Last not least, Part III looked at history *in* management, covering similar research programs as the 2014 article, though both more extensively and with an updated body of literature. Most importantly, while maintaining the crucial distinction between "history *to* theory" and "history *in* theory", it adopted the predominant methodological approaches, qualitative or quantitative, as a second dimension. This choice enabled a sharper distinction between the different research programs—despite a not insignificant number of studies using both methods. Figure 12.1 provides a summary resulting from these revised distinctions based on the framework introduced in Chapter 4, showing the research programs discussed in the book, with the main ones indicated in bold.

Overall, what this book shows is a sharp contrast between the development of history *of* management and history *in* management. The former

History-Theory Relationship

Methodology		History *to* Theory	History *in* Theory
	Qualitative	**Old institutionalism**; **neo-institutionalism**; **institutional logics**; process organization studies; strategy-making	**Path dependence**; resource-based view; dynamic capabilities; co-evolution
	Quantitative	**Organizational ecology**; **institutional ecology**; categories; organizational economics; resource dependence	**Imprinting; organizational ecology**

Figure 12.1 History, theory and methodology

had an earlier start, shortly after the turn of the twentieth century, and enjoyed a moment in the sun, when it was among the first professional divisions to be created by the Academy of Management (AoM) in 1971. But with their almost entirely descriptive accounts that focused on the management pioneers and presented a needs-driven progressive evolution of management theory and practice, history of management and management thought became marginalized as the scientistic turn that management research took gained pace in the 1970s and the 1980s. When becoming rapidly excluded from the extant and the burgeoning new journals, management historians did not change but persisted with their "classic" or "orthodox" views. Rare attempts at critical and alternative approaches such as labor process theorizing have quickly shed their historical dimension or, like work drawing on Foucault and Latour, continue to remain at the gates of mainstream management research (see Chapters 6 and 7, this volume). As a result, management history is today largely invisible among both historians and management scholars and so is its journal—though there have been some ongoing attempts to revive both (see later).

For history *in* management the picture is a very different one. The journal survey in Chapter 4 and the detailed examination of the various research programs in Part III of the book confirmed even more clearly what the

2014 article had already suggested: That at least since the 1980s history had taken a more important place than was widely known or acknowledged within mainstream management research both in the form of evidence ("history *to* theory") and as an integral part of theoretical models ("history *in* theory"). And its importance has grown further and faster over recent years, in particular during the 2010s. Whether this expansion of history in management is in response to the previously mentioned and later calls for "more history", even a "historic turn", is difficult to gauge. The early start suggests otherwise. One could also speculate that the opposite is true, that these calls were just an explicit expression of a broader malaise with the overly scientistic approach that had been taking hold within management scholarship since the 1960s and that those looking for alternatives took action on their own. This would be supported by the increase in qualitative research more generally (Üsdiken 2014).

Whatever the reason, history is right there in some of the main research programs in management and organization studies—and it is growing, whereas management history seems to be withering. But the history that there is has had to play by the rules of management research: It is transformed into "data" that can be analyzed with established methods—and in certain research programs, such as process organization studies or strategy-as-practice, these established and well-honed methods have made it difficult for history to deploy all the obvious potential it has to address their central questions. Or it is put—as a kind of stylized past—into the straitjacket of theoretical models claiming universal applicability without being allowed to deploy its strength, which are geared more toward singularity, serendipity and contextualization. Not to dismiss anything that history *to* and *in* theory have been able to achieve so far—and can and should continue to achieve— but the question is what it would look like if history as history—rather than as data or some "past"—could be integrated into management and organization studies. The studies reviewed and examined for this book suggest three main avenues for taking history more seriously—each of them with their strengths and weaknesses.

No Hope in History—Well, Maybe a Little

As noted in Chapter 2, management and business have found very limited interest among the vast majority of historians. Even within the now fashionable "history of capitalism" entrepreneurs and managers are largely absent and so are, for the most part, firms. And if included, they are usually painted in broad, often negative brush strokes—not necessarily surprising, given the origins of the history of capitalism in what used to be called "labor history". And while this work has found some interest and recognition within the broader academic community—clear from the prizes and nominations received by books like *Empire of Cotton* (Beckert

2014), it has done little to spark debates or additional research within management studies (see for the reactions of others, e.g. Parry 2016).

Management History as a division of AoM survives, but it commands little interest, and probably even less respect, both among management scholars and among historians. And the *Journal of Management History* (JMH), founded in 1995 as a way to provide more publishing opportunities, has a tenuous existence. Whether a recent and ongoing effort succeeds to turn the Management History Division into a meeting point for those subscribing to the "historic turn" and a vehicle for promoting a deeper exchange and possible integration between history and management and organization studies remains to be seen. The *Management & Organizational History* (MOH) journal was founded in 2006 explicitly with such a purpose but has yet to reach sufficient status to attract this kind of scholarship on a more consistent basis.

Business history seems to offer another avenue—or even venue—for a "closer union between organizational and historical research" (Maclean, Harvey and Clegg 2016: 609). The same authors who advocated such a union to management scholars in this *Academy of Management Review* article published a companion piece in the *Business History Review*, where they encouraged business historians to seek a "more extensive engagement with organization theory" (Maclean, Harvey and Clegg 2017: 457; see also Chapter 3, this volume). The extent to which business historians are likely to follow these exhortations is uncertain, if not doubtful. While they have debated the issue at many of their conferences and in a number of papers and special issues (e.g. Godelier 2009; Kobrak and Schneider 2011), the reaction has often been critical, if not outrightly negative. This reaction might be driven by a fear of being reduced to the role of "unearthing the raw materials for the social scientists who alone explain [. . .] human life in a 'scientific manner'" (Breisach 2007: 1) or, even worse, losing their identity—as "niche" as it might be.

And they are right to be weary based on the example of economic historians who since the 1960s, first in the US, started to embrace the mathematics and theory-driven turn of economics, leading to what has been called "cliometrics" or "new economic history" (for an early optimistic overview, see Cochran 1969). In hindsight, that optimism seems to not have been warranted, neither intellectually nor institutionally, since these cliometricians were increasingly out of synch with their fellow historians, many of whom took the postmodern or cultural turn (Chapter 2, this volume). Neither could they live up to the ever more exacting mathematical and modeling standards of mainstream economics. Today, a growing number of the remaining economic historians have come to recognize *The Poverty of Clio* (Boldizzoni 2011). This includes some of the earliest proponents of "new" economic history like Deirdre McCloskey (e.g. 1978), who has since returned to more traditional narrative accounts in a series of three books on the bourgeoisie, ultimately arguing that "ideas, not capital or institutions, enriched the world" (McCloskey 2016). Thus, business historians wanting to be more respected by or interact with management scholars should probably not heed calls for a "new business history" issued by some (e.g. de Jong, Higgins and van Driel 2015; for a critique see Decker, Kipping and Wadhwani 2015)—especially since mainstream management journals, mainly in Europe but increasingly also in the US, have become more accepting of qualitative approaches in general over the past few decades (Üsdiken 2014; see also Yates 2014).

However, business history does remain an example for the possible—though yet largely unfulfilled—promise of combining historical research and broader, more theoretically grounded insights. Thus, two fundamental texts for the discipline, Chandler's *Strategy and Structure* (1962) and *The Visible Hand* (1977), are also considered "classics" within management and organization studies. Research on the subject of the former, the multidivisional form of organization, or M-form, however, was taken further almost exclusively by management scholars (see Chapter 3, this volume). And when these scholars contradicted or modified Chandler's views, business historians showed little, if any, reaction. Thus, when Freeland (2001) revisited one of the original cases, General Motors, based on in-depth research in historical archives, and questioned Chandler's interpretation regarding the crucial role of competition and complexity—pointing instead to an ongoing power struggle between top and middle management, business historians remained largely mute—possibly because of a lack of interest in the author's more theoretical concerns. Nor did they pick up the trail when Whittington and Mayer (2000) extended the original comparative studies at the Harvard Business School (HBS) for France, Germany and the UK until the late twentieth century with the explicit aim to provoke a debate of how to interpret the persistence of the multidivisional structure. Instead, business historians extended Chandler's original work in both geographic and sectoral dimensions, albeit with limited theoretical ambitions.

The same reluctance to engage in broader, theory-driven or even theory-conscious debates marked the reactions of business historians to extensions and critiques of Chandler's other path-breaking study, *The Visible Hand* (Chandler 1977), which had examined the rise of large-scale managerial corporations in the US. For the business history discipline, this was probably the more formative of his books and prompted many replica studies elsewhere, especially regarding the pioneering role of the railways (for an overview see John 1997). However, the subsequent extension of his universalist model of corporate growth and success based on technology-driven *Scale and Scope* (Chandler 1990) to the British and German cases met with doubts and outright rejection from business historians who had examined these countries (see, e.g. Cassis 1997), while others also started questioning its validity for the US itself (see especially Scranton 1997). It should not come as a surprise that these internal challenges to Chandlerian orthodoxy were almost exclusively based on in-depth empirical research, usually case studies, rather than more theoretical reasoning.

In contrast, business historians proved largely indifferent toward more fundamental, theoretically grounded challenges to Chandler's account emanating from a number of management scholars. Thus, in a comparative study Dobbin (1994), for instance, examined railroad policies in the US, UK and France and highlighted their role not as a model for large-scale corporations, as Chandler had done, but as indicative of the political culture in these countries. This culture, so Dobbin argued, and, more concretely, the specific policies geared toward the railroads shaped the subsequent "industrial ideology" in each country: (a) market mechanisms in the US, regardless of their possibly negative impact on smaller firms and start-ups; (b) a preference for exactly those smaller firms in the UK; and (c) a belief in the superiority of centralization and bureaucratic state control in France. While this offered an alternative *historical* explanation for the different national models identified by Chandler (1990), namely "competitive" (US), "personal" (UK) and "cooperative" (Germany) capitalism, it was never discussed by business historians.

Neither were two other books that took even more direct aim at Chandler's view of the emergence and development of big business in the US. Instead of the latter's technology- and market-driven causality, they offered, simplistically put, a "power logic". Thus, in *Socializing Capital* Roy (1997) relied on an institutional framework to question what he characterized as Chandler's "efficiency theory". Drawing on census and stock market data, he demonstrated the absence of a clear causal relationship between capital intensity and productivity, on the one hand, and growth and profitability, on the other. Even more importantly, based on the analysis of secondary data, he located the emergence of the industrial corporation with its "visible hand" of management not in the private sector, but in a combination of an organizational form created by the government to compensate for the lack of private capital in the construction and operation of early transportation infrastructure such as canals and the powerful financial institutions that came to be collectively known as "Wall Street" but had originally traded government securities. It was only later that they came to fund the creation and expansion of the large private corporations.

But while Roy (1997), as one prominent business historian pointed out in her review of the book (Wilkins 1998: 1532), "recounts a familiar narrative with a nonstandard vocabulary, a new set of insights on the growth in the use of the corporate form, and a message that challenges 'efficiency' arguments with those of power relationships", his work did not provoke much of a response, let alone a debate, from others in the discipline. The same is true for Perrow (2002) who, like Roy (1997), argued that "power" was key for the rise of big business in the US, and in particular the power of managers, shareholders and investment bankers. Unlike their European counterparts, they did not have to contend with a strong state or an established nobility—and therefore managed to coopt the legislative and even the judicial branch of government. For Perrow (2002), similar to Chandler and Dobbin (see earlier), the railroads were where it all started in terms of the dominance of private over public ownership, a lack of regulation and national rather than regional networks. These choices then shaped the subsequent industrial development of the country as a whole: "The railroads' twisting historical path [. . .] made the modern multidivisional multiproduct corporation possible" (Perrow 2002: 183). Another well-known business historian called *Organizing America* "an extremely important book" (Levenstein 2004: 661), closing her review by stating: "Its analysis is a very direct challenge to each of the major streams in contemporary business history: Chandlerian institutionalism, mainstream economic history and cultural history" (p. 663). Sounds like this should have warranted a more sustained reaction from those being challenged. But it did not get one either.

In sum, while there were opportunities for business historians to engage with management scholarship, notably around some of the discipline's early and ongoing research questions such as the emergence and evolution of large-scale managerial corporations, not much has happened. So, what would be the way forward here? First, as noted, there needs to be a willingness to engage with ongoing debates within management and organization studies, or even simply to respond to challenges regarding some of the core questions within business history emanating from scholars outside their own discipline—not easy, it seems, with most apparently content to live on their own Galapagos-like island. Second, to move beyond the apparently dreaded role of supplying input for others (see earlier), business historians should be prepared to generalize and theorize their own findings to some extent. What gave Chandler such a prominent position within management and organization studies was exactly that: his willingness and ability to draw some general, as he seemed to believe, universal insights from his in-depth company and industry studies—even if some of them were subsequently questioned and challenged by others, which is the fundamental mechanism of scholarship. At the very least, business historians wanting to interact with management researchers should be prepared to learn some of the latter's language and engage with their relevant conceptual frameworks.

The number of those willing and able to do this seems to be growing, though it remains small overall and there is quite a range in terms of the depth of engagement—all of them viable and commendable. At the deep end, one can find somebody like Dan Wadhwani, who has been among the business historians working hardest to establish a mutually beneficial connection between both disciplines (see especially Bucheli and Wadhwani 2014). And he has achieved the same in some of his own research, including a recent article showing how savings banks in the nineteenth-century US emerged as an organizational field in response to poverty (Wadhwani 2018). In the middle, there is, for instance, JoAnne Yates who has a kind of dual identity: as a highly respected business historian based on her work on information technology and as the co-author of impactful articles in top management journals using concepts such as "genres"—though not always based on historical evidence (e.g. Yates, Orlikowski and Okamura 1999). At the somewhat shallower end, there is a recent volume edited by Dan Raff and Phil Scranton (2016) that uses the notion of "routines" to tie together a wide range of historical case studies that recount how new enterprises, new formal initiatives within firms or new means of accomplishing old tasks came into being. Others could and should follow these examples of how to successfully combine historical research and management and organization studies.

Third, and possibly most fundamentally, if management and business historians do want to be taken seriously and contribute to management research in their own right rather than as suppliers of "raw material", they should make their data and methods more explicit. Just to stress, they do have a methodology—its creation was part of the Rankean "revolution" in the nineteenth century (see Chapter 2, this volume), but it is not easily identifiable for outsiders—a no-no for management researchers and their need of following natural science standards. But it should be possible to overcome this challenge, in particular since some of the core elements of the classic approaches in historical research are familiar to management scholars, though not always with the same terminology (see, for details and examples, Kipping, Wadhwani and Bucheli 2014):

1. *Source criticism*, which is a way to address the biases in any given data—crucially important when, as usual in historical studies, only limited and uneven evidence is available—which in most cases is also skewed in favor of those most powerful in any given context. But the same, if not worse, biases also affect retrospective interviews (e.g. Golden 1992), a mainstay data source for most qualitative research in management—and also widely used in so-called oral history in particular to give voice to the less privileged.

2. *Triangulation*, which is an important way to address the disparity of the different, usually incomplete, sources and increase the validity of findings. This approach is also widely applied in management and organization studies, where it is used more broadly, often by combining qualitative and quantitative data and methods or by having several researchers examine and analyze the data independently and then comparing and reconciling the results. The latter is less common among historians, since they tend to work alone—but who is stopping them from collaborating with each other or management scholars?

3. *Hermeneutics*, which refers to both the need to contextualize the various sources and, even more importantly, to reinterpret sources and findings in light of additional evidence until a point when its interpretation no longer requires modification. This is reminiscent of what is called "grounded theorizing" within management research. While now used in widely different ways (Suddaby 2006; Walsh et al. 2015), in its essence it refers to an iterative process that derives meaningful categories from the data collected, which helps address the core concern(s) of the research project—with iteration continuing until reaching a point of saturation. While historians should probably be careful of using the "grounded theory" term, they could definitely describe their own similar hermeneutic approach more explicitly.

These are just the basic methodological tools available to historians—though they are quite fundamental ones. There are many other, more specific approaches to conduct historical research in a way that makes it accessible to management scholars and publishable in management journals. Their choice depends on the underlying research program and the particular question(s) asked. Take the case of process research on both organizations and strategy, which this book has identified as one of the most promising areas for more history in management. This can be done based on multiple ways of collecting and analyzing data, including both qualitative and quantitative methods (for an overview and examples, see Kipping and Lamberg 2017). A particularly promising approach is so-called "process tracing", which is widely used in the social sciences to establish causal mechanisms and "contextualized explanation" in qualitative cases (see especially George and Bennett 2005: Ch. 10; Welch et al. 2011; Beach 2017). Well suited to address historical questions (Mahoney 2015; see also Mahoney, Kimball and Koivu 2009), it needs to go beyond "a purely historical account that *implies or asserts* a causal sequence" (George and Bennett 2005: 225; emphasis added). To do so requires exploring the links between different recorded events to develop a single narrative and explain this narrative "by making reference to existing theories, generalities and known patterns" (Welch et al. 2011: 749). A good example for its application within management scholarship is the study by David, Sine and Haveman (2013), which examined the role of institutional entrepreneurs in the legitimation of the "professional form" of management consulting in the post–World War II period based on—mainly secondary—historical sources.

History in the Present: Uses of the Past

While the engagement of management and business historians with core concerns and theories in management and organization studies is at best an emergent reality, the notion that history can be considered and examined as a manageable "resource" has created a significant following in a short time among a group of management scholars and a few historians. While some have pointed to earlier roots of the suggestion that organizations can make and have been making "strategic use of the past" (Wadhwani et al. 2018), the corresponding research developed largely as a response to calls for more history in management (Chapter 3, this volume) and in particular since the advent of the twenty-first century. An early example outlining the contours of this approach can be found in a special issue of a journal focusing on organizational change edited by Carroll (2002). Thus, in his introduction Carroll (2002: 557) identified the main concern of the special issue as being the "strategic appropriation of the past" and "how current circumstances influence the very presentation of the past". In their contribution to this special issue, Gioia, Corley and Fabbri (2002: 622) endorsed this view, namely by suggesting that "history must be treated as malleable—subtly but significantly open to revisions that make it conform to current needs and perceptions".

Subsequently, Suddaby, Foster and Quinn Trank (2010: 160) further elaborated on these ideas, proposing the notion of "rhetorical history", which described, in Carroll's (2002) terms, "how actors within organizations engage in the 'strategic appropriation of the past' ". Positioning themselves in opposition to various other historical approaches within management research, such as imprinting, path dependence and dynamic capabilities, discussed in Chapters 10 and 11 (this volume), the authors argued that rhetorical history "views firm history as a deliberate and strategic construction—an organizational resource designed to confer identity, motivate commitment, and frame action amongst organizational stakeholders" (Suddaby et al. 2010: 160). Accordingly, rhetorical history is, in Mintzbergian terminology, not emergent but deliberate. And as a "strategic resource", it can confer "legitimacy" and "identity" as well as being facilitative in "strategic change" (Suddaby et al. 2010: 165).

Scholars embracing this approach have proposed, for example, a model of organizational change where change is viewed as more likely if history is not deemed a constraint but rather as being susceptible to managerial agency through interpretation and the construction of narratives (Suddaby and Foster 2017; see also Gioia et al. 2002). History construed in this manner could, it is also argued, serve as a resource for generating advantages over competitors—as they illustrate in another article with reference to the Canadian donut chain Tim Hortons, which systematically appropriated national-level historical symbols by drawing on the earlier hockey career of its eponymous founder (Foster et al. 2011). Going even further, according to Foster et al. (2017: 1176), "the success of an organization is [. . .] dependent on the ability of its managers to skillfully develop historical narratives that create a strategic advantage" (see also, more generally, Suddaby et al. 2020). The view that history may be used interpretively also led to the construal of remembering and memory as equally being subject to reinterpretation and reconstruction (Rowlinson et al. 2014). Thus, for Suddaby, Foster and Quinn Trank (2016: 298), "organizational remembering" referred to how "an organization's history is made relevant to a group by contextualizing past events in the present through memory and recollection".

Accordingly, organizations could be viewed as mnemonic communities whereby collective memory serves, for example, as a basis of organizational identity, as shown by Anteby and Molnár (2012) in a study on Snecma, a French aeronautics firm. Based on archival material—mainly the internal bulletin of the firm, spanning a period of about 50 years, the study examined the "official history" of the firm, which the authors considered the "rhetorical expression" of collective memory, defined as "a reconstruction of the past that adapts images of ancient facts to present beliefs" (Anteby and Molnár 2012: 517). The main theme to emerge from the study was that the firm's "national" identity was maintained over this long period through "repeated forgetting", that is, by omitting or neutralizing events in the firm's history that were not congruent with this particular aspect of the firm's identity. Hence, by reconstructing the history and the collective memory of an organization, rhetorical history can also serve as a mechanism for "identity work" geared toward creating communal identification with the organization for its significant stakeholders. Notably though—and differently from the role accorded by Suddaby et al. (2010: 149) to the "powerful" in strategically "designing" rhetorical history—Suddaby et al. (2016) do acknowledge that there could also be "emergent" remembering at lower levels in the organization. Nevertheless, they believe that any divergences that might exist as a result will eventually "merge into a powerful shared historical narrative of a mnemonic community" (Suddaby et al. 2016: 311).

The foregoing theoretical conjectures notwithstanding, the "uses of the past" perspective has fallen short in empirical research, with a significant part coming from studies on organizational identity. A relatively early example was Brunninge's (2009) presentation of vignettes from his case studies on two long-established Swedish firms, the vehicle manufacturer Scania and Handelsbanken. Focusing on strategy, Brunninge pointed to instances where history was used, in his terms, in "moral" or "ideological" ways or not used at all in demonstrating, respectively, continuity with past actions or in legitimizing a break from the past. Much of the subsequent empirical work was published in management history journals, including the earlier-mentioned study on Tim Hortons by Foster et al. (2011), which was based entirely on secondary sources. An example of archive-based research is the article by Smith and Simeone (2017), which aimed at "historicizing", or in organization theory terms, adding a contingency dimension to the use of rhetorical history by showing how the London headquarters of the Hudson's Bay Company (HBC)—one of the oldest firms in the world, turned to using this long history as an "asset" around World War I to confront challenges from political unrest and the development of social democracy in Britain and Canada (Smith and Simeone 2017: 335).

As noted previously, some of the research on identity dynamics has complemented the "uses of the past" literature. Indeed, even before the latter approach became more visible, Ravasi and Schultz (2006), in a study mainly concerned with the interrelationships between organizational culture and identity, pointed to how an organization's history, or "cultural heritage", could be brought in and reinterpreted during initiatives to reconstruct the identity of an organization in view of external identity threats. Based on a study of Bang & Olufsen, a Danish manufacturer of audio-visual systems, the authors claimed that organizational culture served as a context for "sense-making" and a basis for "sense-giving" by providing cues for a reassessment of the key attributes of the organization "through a retrospective rationalization of the past". Importantly, they stressed that "whether these interpretations were actually 'true' [was] beside the point" (Ravasi and Schultz 2006: 451, 452). What mattered was that these connections with "history" facilitated a reconstruction of the organization's identity.

Along similar lines, Schultz and Hernes (2013: 2) specifically addressed the question of how the past is "evoked" in organizational identity reconstruction in a study that examined two such managerially led occasions in 2000–2001 and 2005–2007 at the LEGO Group, a Danish toy manufacturer. They took an "ongoing temporal perspective" based on "process thinking" whereby "organizations are seen as in a continuous state of creation, emergence, and becoming while being shaped by a *changing past*, and future ambitions" (Schultz and Hernes 2013: 1; emphasis added). For Schultz and Hernes, identity was constructed from past experiences and through memory. The study showed that the two reconstruction occasions in the LEGO Group differed in their time horizon for the future, which then had parallels in the time periods in which past identity claims were sought. In the short-term-oriented first occasion, clues were found in the recent past, whereas in the longer-term horizon of the second initiative, history was traced back to much earlier stages in the development of the firm, namely, the time of founding in the 1930s and then the 1950s. The authors also suggested that the differences in the extent to which textual, material and oral memory were used and in the ways they were combined were a source of variation in the "scope" and the "depth" of identity reconstruction.

Despite gaining some popularity lately, the "uses of the past" approach has not remained without criticism. Critiques have mainly centered on two issues, one related to the question of authenticity—or the links with the historical record—and the other to the degree of agency attributed to management in "molding" history. With respect to the former, Hatch and Schultz (2017), for example, in a study of the Danish brewer

Carlsberg, highlighted the role that expectations of and the quest for authenticity played in two occasions of what they referred to as "organizational historicizing" processes. And touching upon the question of managerial agency, they noted that their research challenged "the assumption that those in power have the unquestionable ability to use history to support their own intentions" pointing to a "more-nuanced idea that anyone who wishes to use history needs to authenticate the intended historical content in the eyes of those on whose acceptance of its uses they depend" (Hatch and Schultz 2017: 689–690). Based on these findings they also suggested that "forgetting" could not be assumed to persist, as history always has the potential to be discovered.

In a study of digitalization at the British museum from 1970 onward, Blagoev, Felten and Kahn (2018) stressed the influence of the materiality of past objects on what could be "made" of history. In their view, while the past might be open to interpretation, material objects from the past have a "stickiness", which could constrain or indeed direct processes of remembering, sense-making and the course of actions that could be selected. To develop this argument and with a view to reconciling objectivist and subjectivist approaches to history, they drew upon the notion of "affordances", which was defined as "potentials for action that depend on both the material properties of objects and the ability of actors to perceive and use them" (Blagoev et al. 2018: 1758). Based on the analysis of archives, published documents and a few interviews, they did find that recourse to the historical principles of the museum enabled the construction of "affordances" to make use of the new material technology, i.e. the computer. Yet at the same time, as the authors put it, "the past mattered in a second way, namely as a material reality inherited from previous times [meaning: paper-based technologies] that constrained and oriented *how* actors enacted digitization" (Blagoev et al. 2018: 1776; emphasis in original).

In a similarly motivated study, Ravasi, Rindova and Stigliani (2019) addressed the question of how "material memory" was used in the construction and the maintenance of organizational identity and in shaping organizational action by examining four corporate museums. Most notably, they concluded that, much like the notion of "categorical imperative" which has been associated with audience expectations in the categorization literature (see Chapter 9, this volume), organizations encounter a "historical imperative". For Ravasi and his colleagues, this historical imperative necessitates, because of the "burden of history", that organizational action is based not only on current concerns but that it is "historically informed" as well.

With respect to the agency attributed to managers in using the past, one of the early studies mentioned earlier was already hesitant about the assumption that "single actors can fully control how groups of people conceive history" (Brunninge 2009: 13). Yet the author also remarked that "the studies cited earlier render empirical evidence that conceptions of history can be purposefully influenced", foreshadowing the direction that the uses of the past approach took since. More recent work has returned to a more critical stance, though. Thus, quite a few of the papers in a special issue on the "Uses of the Past in Organization Studies" (see Wadhwani et al. 2018) have questioned the "hypermuscular" image of managers (Lubinski 2018) who are viewed as having the ability to shape history "almost as they wish" (Blagoev et al. 2018: 1758). Common to all these studies is the view that the capability of actors to "make" history may actually be constrained in various ways and not remain under the full control of organizations and their management (Zundel, Holt and Popp 2016). As Lubinski (2018: 1787) has argued, for example, "in their attempt to highlight the strategic use of history and its constructed nature, some rhetorical history scholars overemphasize the power of managers in controlling the narrative and *persuading* their audiences" (emphasis in original). Instead, she pointed to the need to "contextualize" the purportedly interpretive reconstructions of history by considering the reception and involvement of different audiences in the construction process. There is also a need, Lubinski suggested, to consider the recall of prior dormant histories and not only the influence of texts but also social practices—such as forms of recruitment, which she exemplified through an archival study on the claims of joint Aryan roots by German firms in colonial India during the period from 1890s to the beginning of World War II.

In their contribution to the special issue Cailluet, Gorge and Özçağlar-Toulouse (2018) showed how managers may be constrained in the use of founder figures as historical assets due to the influence of and the struggles generated by various internal and external "stakeholders". Studying Abbé Pierre, the founder in 1949 of Emmaus, a charity established in France, they argued that he had turned into a "public good" appropriated by various parties—including a competing charity, which not only complicated Emmaus's claims to his legacy but also led to tensions within the organization when doing so. Likewise, Ybema (2014: 499) viewed the uses of the past approach of authors like Suddaby et al. (2016) as consensus-based (see earlier) and thus as "premised upon the assumption that history is used to produce and promote historical continuity and collective identity". Advocating a more conflictual view instead, while at the same time adhering to the broad interpretive thrust of the uses of the past approach, Ybema (2014) aimed at showing through a comparison of a historian's account and his own ethnographic study on the Dutch newspaper *de Volkskrant* how the past could be invoked in politically motivated ways to promote identity change and to thwart competing views.

Taken together, these critical studies appear to be leading to a more tempered view which recognizes, as Lubinski (2018) suggested, that the uses of the past are "socially embedded" (see Wadhwani et al. 2018). Debates will probably be ongoing, as more empirical research is likely to question some of the "strong" assumptions made in the earlier, mostly theoretically based literature. This, as the next section will show, is not necessarily a bad thing, in that history might have a broader—and in some ways unique—role of imposing certain contingencies and boundary conditions on some of the overly universalist theoretical claims in management and organization studies.

Toward "Historical Cognizance": Contextualized Theorizing

Thus, the two possible avenues for bringing history and management closer together discussed so far both have their limitations in terms of how far reaching they can be. Most historians seem clearly reluctant to engage more deeply with the theoretical concerns of management scholars—and aren't even responding to the challenges to their own research questions raised by the latter. And while the "uses of the past" have some promise as a research program, especially as empirical work progresses, some of its assumptions remain questionable—meaning its appeal will probably remain limited to certain issues such as organizational identity and corporate legitimacy. To take history more seriously, as has been claimed by a growing number of scholars within management and organization studies itself (see Chapters 1 and 3, this volume), more is needed.

To understand what is required, a good starting point is the distinction between "Chandlerism" and "Chandlerian" introduced by Richard Whittington and his co-authors to frame their extension of the original Harvard studies on the expansion and persistence of the multidivisional organizational structure, or M-form (Whittington, Mayer and Curto 1999; Whittington and Mayer 2000; see earlier). This is a particularly good starting point, because Chandler's (1962) original study is still considered a classic by management scholars, while also being a foundational text for business historians and has, moreover, been seen nostalgically by many as reflective of a time when the desired union between the two still existed (see earlier; also Kipping and Üsdiken 2008). The point here— and the merit of the discussion by Whittington and colleagues—is that the reception of and reaction to Chandler's claims are indicative of two "extremes": On the one hand, there are the "universalists"—represented, in their view, by Chandler himself and what they call "Chandlerism"— with "the imperialism of their generalizations and the unacknowledged simplification of their prescriptions". On the other hand, one can find the "contextualists", representing what they characterize as a Chandlerian position, who "counsel caution and point to the real complexities of practice" (Whittington and Mayer 2000: 43)—with the previously mentioned empirically based rejection of the universalist claims by Chandler's (1990) *Scale and Scope* a good illustration. What should also be noted is that Whittington and Mayer (2000: 32–33) largely dismiss postmodernism, which has been one of the motivators of the more recent calls for the "historic turn" in management and organization studies, namely for those relating it to a much broader "cultural turn" in the social sciences (see especially Clark and Rowlinson 2004; for a critique Kipping and Üsdiken 2015).

Whittington and Mayer (2000: 43) also point to a way out of this quagmire by combining "the leverage of generalization and the checks of contextualism". Based notably on Mouzelis (1995), they see this more as an ongoing process in terms of being "reflective and adaptable about which tools work best, where and when", suggesting in particular that "[t]he boundaries of any general framework need constantly to be probed and tested". But such an approach also works for achieving a truer union between historians' quest for detail and context and the drive of management researchers toward a theoretical contribution, often emulating the natural sciences in their claims for universality—claims that had in large part motivated the original calls for "more history" by Zald, Kieser and others (see Chapter 3, this volume). The review of the extant history *in* management literature in Kipping and Üsdiken (2014) had identified a growing number of examples for such contextualized theorizing, referred to as "historical cognizance"—writings where theories were not seen as universally applicable but subject to boundary conditions derived from particular historical contexts.

In terms of the broad characteristics of the studies displaying such historical cognizance, it should not come as a surprise that, given the need to provide sufficient detail on contexts and the resulting boundary conditions, they are often published in book form—though, more recently, they can increasingly be found as articles in sociology and even top management journals. Neither is it very surprising that, with respect to the classifications applied in this volume, most of these kinds of publications use qualitative historical data and methods or, sometimes, a mix of qualitative and quantitative evidence to develop, modify or test theories—theories that are, at least initially, seen to be contingent on the contexts from which they were derived. Historical cognizance are rarer within history *in* theory studies, probably because it would seem counterproductive to make theoretical models, even those incorporating the past, contingent from the outset—though there are some suggestions, for instance, in the imprinting literature, that organizations might be more susceptible to be imprinted in certain contexts rather than others or during specific periods in their life cycle rather than only at the origin (Marquis and Tilcsik 2013). The theories on organizational path dependence might also move into that direction by suggesting that "not only the emergence of path dependence but also the escape from an organizational path is a highly contextual affair" (Sydow, Schreyögg and Koch forthcoming). Lastly, and again somewhat logically, these historically cognizant studies tend to cluster around a number of topics where there has been sustained interest from both historians and management scholars—with the latter often, but not always, drawing on the empirical work of the former. Following are some examples (for more details and additional publications, see Kipping and Üsdiken 2014: 562–571).

Cognizant vs. Universalist: Big Business in the US

This topic has already been discussed earlier, mainly as an illustration for the unwillingness of most business historians to engage in debates with the evidence and arguments brought forward by a number of management scholars. But it is also an example for the fine line dividing predominantly universalist from more historically cognizant approaches. Thus, while generalizing the origins and evolution of big business in the US in his earlier research, Chandler (1962, 1977) took into account context, namely the changing natures of technology and markets as well as organizations. It is only when he later extended this work to the British and German cases (Chandler 1990) that he turned the US example into a kind of universal yardstick against which he measured the development of business in the other two countries—and found them more or less wanting. For the multidivisional structure, it was Oliver Williamson (1971) who established a very explicit and generic hypothesis postulating the M-form's superior efficiency—as compared to the preceding unitary, or U-form, lending itself to quantification and causal testing that never achieved clear results though, with more recent research by Whittington et al. as well as Freeland going back to a more contextualized approach pointing, respectively, to the influence of national differences and changes in the power balance between top and middle managers over time (see earlier).

Another example that shows how historical cognizance is a matter of degree rather than an absolute is the work by Dobbin and Dowd on how public policy affected business strategies and competition in the early Massachusetts railroad industry. In a first article (Dobbin and Dowd 1997) mentioned previously (see Chapter 9, this volume), they tested the predictions of the density dependence model of organizational ecology, finding that these only held when changes in policy regimes were taken into account. In a second article based on the same data (Dobbin and Dowd 2000), they looked at competition in the industry in an even more contextualized and complex way, highlighting the impact of anti-trust legislation adopted in 1897 and showing how the preceding "cooperative" model was followed by a finance one—due to another contextual factor, a banking industry promoting "friendly" mergers. In a kind of counterfactual analysis, they contrasted the latter with the also possible "predatory" model, where larger competitors would have driven the smaller ones into bankruptcy and acquired them. This difference of degree in the level of historical cognizance might also have to do with where these articles were published, the first in a top management journal, the second in a sociological one. Another scholar working at the borderline between sociology and management studies who has numerous historically cogni-zant publications to his name is Neil Fligstein. These include an empirical test of various theoretical explanations for the expansion of the M-form (Fligstein 1985) and a deeply contextualized account of the evolution of what he called "conceptions of control" in US corporations since the late nineteenth century (Fligstein 1990).

From Comparisons to Cognizance: "Management" Goes Global

Another topic with some examples for contextualized theorizing is the global expansion of management knowledge and the agents/actors pro-moting this expansion—a topic that has drawn attention from both his-torians and management scholars (for a brief review, see Kipping and Üsdiken 2008). Like in the case of big business in the US (see earlier), they have mostly done so independently from each other, with the former usually very light on theory and the latter often rather overtheorized. There are nevertheless some examples for work that could be character-ized as historically cognizant. The fact that much of this work is not only historical—how else would you look at expansion—but also—implicitly or explicitly—comparative has generally prompted a greater sensitiv-ity to contextual factors. Yet again, with some exceptions, little of this research has found its way into top management journals, and most of the publications are books.

Among the pioneering studies for the international diffusion of ideas is the book by Eleanor Westney (1987), which looked at how modernizing Meiji Japan (1868–1912) imported organizational models for the police from France, the postal service from England and the press from several Western examples. Westney discarded both universalist theories about development and industrialization in latecomer nations as well as idio-syncratic explanations based in cultural specificities. Instead, she laid out a theoretical model that contextualized these organizational changes in broader societal trends, interacting in a dynamic way between moderni-zation and tradition, while also looking beyond the Meiji era to earlier and subsequent periods. Another influential example is the comparative study on the development and diffusion of three *Models of Management* (scientific management, human relations and the vaguely Chandlerian "structural analysis") by Guillén (1994)—a study that has been discussed more extensively earlier as promoting a novel, unorthodox view on the history of management (Chapter 7, this volume). It is worth mention-ing again here, because it explicitly tried to combine "some theoretically meaningful causal conclusions about the ways in which organizational change takes place that could be applicable beyond the four countries included in this study", with attention to the country-specific "condi-tions" and "configurations of institutional factors" (Guillén 1994: 266–267).

And then there is the literature on what has been generally referred to as "Americanization", the diffusion of US technology and management models to parts of Europe and Asia in the immediate post–World War II period. Numerous studies have covered this topic, usually published in the forms of monographs or edited volumes. Collectively, they demonstrate the benefits of comparative research for identifying the role of specific historical contexts in terms of applying or developing more bounded theories (see also Djelic 2008). Thus, while most of these studies draw on theories that highlight the influence of "isomorphic" forces emanating from the US, not surprising given its economic and military power at the time, they also stress the influence of the recipient countries in each of these cases. Djelic (1998), for instance, pointed to the role of differently constituted "modernizing elites" in the German, French and Italian cases she studied. Kipping and Bjarnar (1998) highlighted the importance of certain corporations as well as business associations in and across Europe as "active importers"—a notion they borrowed from Lillrank's (1995) work on the transfer of management innovations from Japan since the late 1970s. And Zeitlin and Herrigel (2000) saw companies and industries as "reworking" technologies and ideas from the US—to a different extent in different places. Focusing on the introduction of the US human relations model, two separate case studies on Turkey (Üsdiken 2004) and Israel (Frenkel 2008) showed at an even more micro level how historical contingencies shaped the specific processes of initial, but ultimately unsuccessful, resistance and subsequent linguistic adoption and practical adaptation. There seems to be significant potential for similar future studies examining other periods when certain countries became increasingly powerful economically—initially Japan and, more recently, China, so as to compare them with Americanization and theorize the underlying processes in a bounded, historically cognizant way.

The various actors/agents involved in these diffusion processes, in particular business schools and management consultants, as well as, to a somewhat lesser extent, the business media, have also been researched quite extensively both in terms of their role in these processes and their own development over time. Probably even more so than in the diffusion studies, this research has ranged from very descriptive historical accounts to rather strongly theorized analyses often based on some variant of neo-institutional theory—with initially the German and then the US influence widely seen as formative (for a fairly comprehensive account drawing on a large share of this literature see Engwall, Kipping and Üsdiken 2016). Overall, publications are skewed, like before, toward books and with few articles in top journals. And once again, international comparisons of developments over time seem to favor historical cognizance. To give but one example, in a comparative study of the management education fields in France, Spain, Italy and Turkey after World War II, Kipping, Üsdiken and Puig (2004: 105) showed "varied outcomes", both between the countries and within, with respect to different programs, despite strong isomorphic influences from the US—a heterogeneity that they attributed to "pressures from the broader educational context and traces of the past". In addition to being an example for contextualized theorization, this study is an interesting—and rare—combination of what this book has called history *to* theory (nested institutional fields) and history *in* theory (past dependence).

Cognizance in the Mainstream: Institutional Logics and Beyond

Much of the work that displayed some form of historical cognizance or contextualized theorizing summarized earlier was outside the mainstream of management research. In many respects, it was closer to history *of* management than to history *in* management, though a number of publications did refer to neo-institutional theory, in particular DiMaggio and Powell's (1983) widely known work on coercive, normative and mimetic isomorphism. Its distance from the mainstream was also visible in the fact that it was mostly published in book form or in lower ranked journals. The difficulty of maneuvering between historical specificity, while operating in an academic community requiring quasi-natural science "laws" is illustrated well by an ecological study into the origins of the film industry in the US between 1893 and 1920 (Mezias and Boyle 2005). Thus, while the authors recognized that "the specific historical events that occurred during the emergence of the American film industry are unique", they also characterized their case as "representative" and asserted that it was selected "to ensure that the results would be applicable outside the setting of the emerging US film industry" (p. 29–30). Nevertheless, there are a few examples of research that is squarely within the mainstream and has been published in the top journals while being historically cognizant.

With respect to institutional logics, from the outset, part of that literature drew on historical data to examine shifts of the dominant logics over time or to explain their coexistence within a given organizational field—though always with a view to generate or test generalizable, universal theoretical models. But history not only provided evidence, it also came to be seen as a "meta-theoretical" principle (Thornton, Ocasio and Lounsbury 2012), since it affected institutions as well their organizational outcomes. An example for this kind of dual historical contingency are a number of studies on the US higher education publishing field between 1958 and 1990, drawing on quantitative historical data and interviews. A first study showed how the dominant logics in each of the two periods identified, editorial and market, affected executive succession. Organizational structure and firm size were significant antecedents of executive succession when the editorial logic prevailed, whereas under the market logic, the acquisition strategy of firms and competition were likely to be more influential in top executive change (Thornton and Ocasio 1999). In two subsequent studies on the same industry, Thornton provided further evidence on the contingent effects of these historical periods and their dominant logics. The extent of competition, for example, was likely to increase the risk for firms to become acquired in the period when the market logic was prevalent (Thornton 2001). Likewise, competition had a positive impact on divisionalization under the market logic, whereas that was not the case when the editorial logic prevailed (Thornton 2002).

Another study that draws upon the idea of institutional logics and makes the role of history explicit, while not being grounded itself in historical data, is the work on the downsizing of manufacturing firms in Spain during the second half of the 1990s by Greenwood et al. (2010) discussed earlier (Chapter 10, this volume). Rather than identifying a succession of institutional logics, the authors pointed to their multiplicity, highlighting the importance of "regional state" and "family" logics with in an overall dominant market logic. And they saw both of these subsidiary logics and the significant influence they had on the heterogeneity of organizational outcomes as "contingent on history" (p. 535).

There are a few other examples of historically cognizant theorizing. An early—and telling—one is a purely quantitative study examining how a regulatory shift toward managed competition in the hospital and thrift sectors in California influenced both domain change and chief executive officer (CEO) succession and how these then affected financial performance (Haveman, Russo and Meyer 2001). What matters here is the authors' explicit recognition of the contrast between the "typically ahistorical" nature of such longitudinal studies that are based on an ambition to test "time-invariant" theories and their own findings, which showed that "environmental punctuations partition the history of an industry into *periods during which different causal processes operate*" (p. 270; emphasis added). In other words, they require contextualized theorizing and historical cognizance.

Another example, and in many ways an ideal template for historically cognizant management research, is an article by Haveman, Habinek and Goodman (2012) on entrepreneurship in the magazine publishing industry in the US from the mid-eighteenth to the mid-nineteenth centuries, aiming to "craft a historically sensitive model of entrepreneurship linking individual actors to the evolving social structures" (p. 585). The study combined quantitative analyses of data drawn from secondary as well as primary sources with, given space constraints, a fairly in-depth historical account. It showed that those founding these magazines had a clearly different "social position"—in terms of "occupation, education and geographic location"—in the second half of the eighteenth century as compared to the mid-nineteenth century. What makes this such an exemplary publication is not only the underlying historical research but the explicit support by the authors for "grounding studies of entrepreneurship in historical context" (p. 585), as well as their recognition that this historical context may "set important scope conditions on any theory of entrepreneurship" (p. 617). Their article is also important because it deals with a topic, entrepreneurship, where historical research used to be influential, before being drowned out by trait-based studies relying on cross-sectional data—with business historians recently trying to reclaim lost territory (e.g. Wadhwani and Jones 2014). It could therefore become a fruitful arena to build that "closer union" between historical and management research.

This Is the End . . . Not Really, Since There Is More to Come

What this book, even more so than the article (Kipping and Üsdiken 2014), has shown is the magnitude of history, broadly defined, that can be found in management research—as data to develop, test and modify theory and as a driver or moderator in theoretical models. So, based both on the journal articles survey and the in-depth review of the various research programs, history *in* management has definitely gone mainstream from the 1980s onward and even more so since the 2010s. While developing earlier, research on the history *of* management and of management thought, which this book has also examined in some detail, was hardly ever mainstream and definitely became increasingly marginalized since the 1970s when much of management scholarship had embraced sceintization—though this did not, and it bears repeating, impede the growing use of history for theory testing and the incorporation of history into theoretical models.

Since the development of history *to* and history *in* theory was only incipient and somewhat hidden, it also did not impede Mayer N. Zald and Alfred Kieser in the early 1990s to launch their calls for "more history" in management and organization studies and many others to follow suit with the notion of a—widely repeated, yet diversely understood— "historic turn" becoming a kind of rallying cry. As this book has also documented, discussions and writings about what should be done and how have grown significantly since then, possibly more so than actual empirical work, in directions that have not been explored or only partially explored thus far. For instance, the novel notion of "uses of the past", embedded in neo-institutional ideas about rhetoric and legitimacy, until very recently was almost entirely theoretically driven and has generated very few empirical studies. And as the book has also shown, there are research programs where there is significant unrealized potential, namely in process studies on organizations and strategy; imprinting; and around the notions of routines, resources and dynamic capabilities in strategy. Here, progress has often been held back by methodological issues, with management scholars being unfamiliar with how to analyze historical sources, namely archival records, and historians being unaccustomed to making their approach explicit and reluctant to generalize for their specific case(s). But it should be possible to overcome these gaps and realize more of the available potential if both parties are willing to dialogue and work together.

Last not least, the in-depth review of the many research programs in management and organization studies also identified a limited number of publications that had gone further than the vast majority of others by not only using history but by taking it *really* seriously. Based on solid empirical research, they recognized history as a boundary condition or contingency for their theories, suggesting that theories were not necessarily and always universal but depended on context, and specifically historical context. The extent to which these studies took such a position varied, but they all were what the earlier article and this book have characterized as "historically cognizant", thereby not only giving a new quality to history within theorizing in management and organization studies but also taking a step away from the still widespread scientistic approaches that had so irked Zald and Kieser as well as many others. That is an important step, and the hope is that more mainstream management scholars might be ready to take similar steps sooner rather than later.

References

Anteby, M. and Molnár, V. (2012) "Collective memory meets organizational identity: Remembering to forget in a firm's rhetorical history," *Academy of Management Journal*, 55(3): 515–540.

Beach, D. (2017) "Process-tracing methods in social science," in *Oxford Research Encyclopedia Politics*, Oxford University Press, doi:10.1093/acrefore/9780190228637.013.176.

Beckert, S. (2014) *Empire of Cotton: A Global History*, New York: Alfred A. Knopf.

Blagoev, B., Felten, S. and Kahn, R. (2018) "The career of a catalogue: Organizational memory, materiality and the dual nature of the past at the British Museum (1970-today)," *Organization Studies*, 39(12): 1757–1783.

Boldizzoni, F. (2011) *The Poverty of Clio: Resurrecting Economic History*, Princeton, NJ: Princeton University Press.

Breisach, E. (2007) *Historiography: Ancient, Medieval, and Modern*, 3rd edn, Chicago, IL: The University of Chicago Press.

Brunninge, O. (2009) "Using history in organizations: How managers make purposeful reference to history in strategy processes," *Journal of Organizational Change Management*, 22(1): 8–26.

Bucheli, M. and Wadhwani, R. D. (eds) (2014) *Organizations in Time: History, Theory, Methods*, Oxford: Oxford University Press.

Cailluet, L., Gorge, H. and Özçağlar-Toulouse, N. (2018) " 'Do not expect me to stay quiet': Challenges in managing a historical strategic resource," *Organization Studies*, 39(12): 1811–1835.

Carroll, C. E. (2002) "Introduction," *Journal of Organizational Change Management*, 15(6): 556–562.

Cassis, Y. (1997) *Big Business: The European Experiences in the Twentieth Century*, Oxford: Oxford University Press.

Chandler, A. D. Jr. (1962) *Strategy and Structure: Chapters in the History of the Industrial Enterprise*, Cambridge, MA: MIT Press.

Chandler, A. D. Jr. (1977) *The Visible Hand: The Managerial Revolution in American Business*, Cambridge, MA: The Belknap Press of Harvard University Press.

Chandler, A. D. Jr. (1990) *Scale and Scope: The Dynamics of Industrial Capitalism*, Cambridge, MA: The Belknap Press of Harvard University Press.

Clark, P. and Rowlinson, M. (2004) "The treatment of history in organization studies: Toward an 'historic turn'?" *Business History*, 46(3): 331–352.

Cochran, T. C. (1969) "Economic history, old and new," *American Historical Review*, 74(5): 1561–1572.

David, R. J., Sine, W. D., Haveman, H. A. (2013) "Seizing opportunity in emerging fields: How institutional entrepreneurs legitimated the professional form of management consulting," *Organization Science*, 24(2): 356–377.

Decker, S., Kipping, M. and Wadhwani, R. D. (2015) "New business histories! Plurality in business history research methods," *Business History*, 57(1): 30–40.

de Jong, A., Higgins, D. M. and van Driel, H. (2015) "Towards a new business history?" *Business History*, 57(1): 5–29.

DiMaggio, P. J. and Powell, W. W. (1983) "The iron cage revisited: Collective rationality and institutional isomorphism in organizational fields," *American Sociological Review*, 48(2): 147–160.

Djelic, M.-L. (1998) *Exporting the American Model: The Postwar Transformation of European Business*, Oxford: Oxford University Press.

Djelic, M.-L. (2008) "Sociological studies of diffusion: Is history relevant?" *Socio-Economic Review*, 6(3): 538–557.

Dobbin, F. (1994) *Forging Industrial Policy: The United States, Britain and France in the Railway Age*, New York: Cambridge University Press.

Dobbin, F. and Dowd, T. J. (1997) "How policy shapes competition: Early railroad foundings in Massachusetts," *Administrative Science Quarterly*, 42(3): 501–529.

Dobbin, F. and Dowd, T. J. (2000) "The market that antitrust built: Public policy, private coercion, and railroad acquisitions, 1825 to 1922," *American Sociological Review*, 65(5): 631–657.

Engwall, L., Kipping, M. and Üsdiken, B. (2016) *Defining Management: Business Schools, Consultants, Media*, New York: Routledge.

Fligstein, N. (1985) "The spread of the multidivisional form among large firms, 1919–1979," *American Sociological Review*, 50(3): 377–391.

Fligstein, N. (1990) *The Transformation of Corporate Control*, Cambridge, MA: Harvard University Press.

Foster, W. M., Coraiola, D. M., Suddaby, R., Kroezen, J. and Chandler, D. (2017) "The strategic use of historical narratives: A theoretical framework," *Business History*, 59(8): 1176–1200.

Foster, W. M., Suddaby, R., Minkus, A. and Wiebe, E. (2011) "History as social memory assets: The example of Tim Hortons," *Management & Organizational History*, 6(1): 101–120.

Freeland, R. F. (2001) *The Struggle for Control of the Modern Corporation: Organizational Change at General Motors, 1924–1970*, Cambridge: Cambridge University Press.

Frenkel, M. (2008) "The Americanization of the antimanagerialist alternative in Israel: How foreign experts retheorized and disarmed workers' participation in management, 1950–1970," *International Studies of Management & Organization*, 38(4): 17–37.

George, A. L. and Bennett, A. (2005) *Case Studies and Theory Development in the Social Sciences*, Cambridge, MA: MIT Press.

Gioia, D. A., Corley, K. G. and Fabbri, T. (2002) "Revisiting the past (while thinking in the future perfect tense)," *Journal of Organizational Change Management*, 15(6): 622–634.

Godelier, E. (2009) "History, a useful 'science' for management? From polemics to controversies," *Enterprise & Society*, 10(4): 791–807.

Golden, B. R. (1992) "The past is the present—Or is it? The use of retrospective accounts as indicators of past strategy," *Academy of Management Journal*, 35(4): 848–860.

Greenwood, R., Díaz, A. M., Li, S. X. and Lorente, J. C. (2010) "The multiplicity of institutional logics and the heterogeneity of organizational responses," *Organization Science*, 21(2): 521–539.

Guillén, M. (1994) *Models of Management: Work, Authority and Organization in a Comparative Perspective*, Chicago, IL: University of Chicago Press.

Hatch, M. J. and Schultz, M. (2017) "Toward a theory of using history authentically: Historicizing in the Carlsberg Group," *Administrative Science Quarterly*, 62(4): 657–697.

Haveman, H. A., Habinek, J. and Goodman, L. A. (2012) "How entrepreneurship evolves: The founders of new magazines in America, 1741–1860," *Administrative Science Quarterly*, 57(4): 585–624.

Haveman, H. A., Russo, M. V. and Meyer, A. D. (2001) "Organizational environments in flux: The impact of regulatory punctuations on organizational domains, CEO succession, and performance," *Organization Science*, 12(3): 253–273.

John, R. R. (1997) "Elaborations, revisions, dissents: Alfred D. Chandler Jr.'s, *The Visible Hand* after twenty years," *Business History Review*, 71(2): 151–200.

Kipping, M. and Bjarnar, O. (eds) (1998) *The Americanisation of European Business: The Marshall Plan and the Transfer of US Management Models*, London: Routledge.

Kipping, M. and Lamberg, J.-A. (2017) "History in process organization studies: What, why and how," in A. Langley and H. Tsoukas (eds), *Sage Handbook of Process Organization Studies*, Thousand Oaks, CA: Sage, pp. 303–320.

Kipping, M. and Üsdiken, B. (2008) "Business history and management studies," in G. Jones and J. Zeitlin (eds), *The Oxford Handbook of Business History*, Oxford: Oxford University Press, pp. 96–119.

Kipping, M. and Üsdiken, B. (2014) "History in organization and management theory: More than meets the eye," *Academy of Management Annals*, 8(1): 535–588.

Kipping, M. and Üsdiken, B. (2015) "Turning how and where? The potential for history in management and organization studies," in P. G. McLaren et al. (eds),

The Routledge Companion to Management History, New York: Routledge, pp. 372–379.

Kipping, M., Üsdiken, B. and Puig, N. (2004) "Imitation, tension, and hybridization: Multiple 'Americanizations' of management education in Mediterranean Europe," *Journal of Management Inquiry*, 13(2): 98–108.

Kipping, M., Wadhwani, R. D. and Bucheli, M. (2014) "Analyzing and interpreting historical sources: A basic methodology," in M. Bucheli and R. D. Wadhwani (eds), *Organizations in Time: History, Theory, Methods*, Oxford: Oxford University Press, pp. 305–329.

Kobrak, C. and Schneider, A. (2011) "Varieties of business history: Subject and methods for the twenty-first century," *Business History*, 53(3): 401–424.

Levenstein, M. C. (2004) "Book review: Organizing America: Wealth, power, and the origins of corporate capitalism," *Business History*, 46(4): 661–663.

Lillrank, P. (1995) "The transfer or management innovations from Japan," *Organization Studies*, 16(6): 971–989.

Lubinski, C. (2018) "From 'history as told' to 'history as experienced': Contextualizing the uses of the past," *Organization Studies*, 39(12): 1785–1809.

Maclean, M., Harvey, C. and Clegg, S. (2016) "Conceptualizing historical organization studies," *Academy of Management Review*, 41(4): 609–632.

Maclean, M., Harvey, C. and Clegg, S. (2017) "Organization theory in business and management history: Present status and future prospects," *Business History Review*, 91(3): 457–481.

Mahoney, J. (2015) "Process tracing and historical explanation," *Security Studies*, 24: 200–218.

Mahoney, J., Kimball, E. and Koivu, K. L. (2009) "The logic of historical explanation in the social sciences," *Comparative Political Studies*, 42(1): 114–146.

Marquis, C. and Tilcsik, A. (2013) "Imprinting: Toward a multilevel theory," *Academy of Management Annals*, 7(1): 193–243.

McCloskey, D. (1978) "The achievements of the Cliometric School," *Journal of Economic History*, 38(1): 13–28.

McCloskey, D. (2016) *Bourgeois Equality: How Ideas, Not Capital or Institutions, Enriched the World*, Chicago, IL: The University of Chicago Press.

Mezias, S. J. and Boyle, E. (2005) "Blind trust: Market control, legal environments, and the dynamics of competitive intensity in the early American film industry, 1893–1920," *Administrative Science Quarterly*, 50(1): 1–34.

Mouzelis, N. (1995) *Sociological Theory: What Went Wrong? Diagnosis and Remedies*, London: Routledge.

Parry, M. (2016) "Shackles and dollars: Historians and economists clash over slavery," *The Chronicle of Higher Education*, 8 December.

Perrow, C. (2002) *Organizing America: Wealth, Power, and the Origins of Corporate Capitalism*, Princeton, NJ: Princeton University Press.

Raff, D. M. G. and Scranton, P. (2016) *The Emergence of Routines: Entrepreneurship, Organization, and Business History*, New York: Oxford University Press.

Ravasi, D., Rindova, V. and Stigliani, I. (2019) "History, material memory and the temporality of identity construction," *Academy of Management Journal*, 62(5): 1523–1555.

Ravasi, D. and Schultz, M. (2006) "Responding to organizational identity threats: Exploring the role of organizational culture," *Academy of Management Journal*, 49(3): 433–458.

Rowlinson, M., Casey, A., Hansen, P. H. and Mills, A. J. (2014) "Narratives and memory in organizations," *Organization*, 21(4): 441–446.

Roy, W. G. (1997) *Socializing Capital: The Rise of the Large Industrial Corporation in America*, Princeton, NJ: Princeton University Press.

Schultz, M. and Hernes, T. (2013) "A temporal perspective on organizational identity," *Organization Science*, 24(1): 1–21.

Scranton, P. (1997) *Endless Novelty: Specialty Production and American Industrialization, 1865–1925*, Princeton, NJ: Princeton University Press.

Smith, A. and Simeone, D. (2017) "Learning to use the past: The development of a rhetorical history strategy by the London headquarters of the Hudson's Bay Company," *Management & Organizational History*, 12(4): 334–356.

Suddaby, R. (2006) "What grounded theory is not," *Academy of Management Journal*, 49(4): 633–642.

Suddaby, R., Coraiola, D., Harvey, C. and Foster, W. (2020) "History and the micro-foundations of dynamic capabilities," *Strategic Management Journal*, 41(3): 530–556.

Suddaby, R. and Foster, W. M. (2017) "History and organizational change," *Journal of Management*, 43(1): 19–38.

Suddaby, R., Foster, W. M. and Quinn Trank, C. (2010) "Rhetorical history as a source of competitive advantage," *Advances in Strategic Management*, 27: 147–173.

Suddaby, R., Foster, W. M. and Quinn Trank, C. (2016) "Remembering: Rhetorical history as identity work," in M. G. Pratt, M. Schultz, B. E. Ashforth and D. Ravasi (eds), *The Oxford Handbook of Organizational Identity*, Oxford: Oxford University Press, pp. 297–316.

Sydow, J., Schreyögg, G. and Koch, J. (forthcoming) "On the theory of organizational path dependence: Clarifications, replies to objections, and extensions," *Academy of Management Review*.

Thornton, P. H. (2001) "Personal versus market logics of control: A historically contingent theory of the risk of acquisition," *Organization Science*, 12(3): 294–311.

Thornton, P. H. (2002) "The rise of the corporation in a craft industry: Conflict and conformity in institutional logics," *Academy of Management Journal*, 45(1): 81–101.

Thornton, P. H. and Ocasio, W. (1999) "Institutional logics and the historical contingency of power in organizations: Executive succession in the higher education publishing industry, 1958–1990," *American Journal of Sociology*, 105(3): 801–843.

Thornton, P. H., Ocasio, W. and Lounsbury, M. (2012) *The Institutional Logics Perspective: A New Approach to Culture, Structure and Process*, Oxford: Oxford University Press.

Üsdiken, B. (2004) "Exporting managerial knowledge to the outpost: Penetration of 'human relations' into Turkish Academia, 1950–1965," *Management Learning*, 35(3): 255–270.

Üsdiken, B. (2014) "Centres and peripheries: Research styles and publication patterns in 'top' US journals and their European alternatives, 1960–2010," *Journal of Management Studies*, 51(5): 764–789.

Wadhwani, R. D. (2018) "Poverty's monument: Social problems and organizational field emergence in historical perspective," *Journal of Management Studies*, 55(3): 545–577.

Wadhwani, R. D. and Jones, G. (2014) "Schumpeter's plea: Historical reasoning in entrepreneurship theory and research," in M. Bucheli and R. D. Wadhwani (eds), *Organizations in Time: History, Theory, Methods*, Oxford: Oxford University Press, pp. 192–216.

Wadhwani, R. D., Suddaby, R., Mordhurst, M. and Popp, A. (2018) "Introduction to the Special Issue—History as organizing: Uses of the past in organization studies," *Organization Studies*, 39(12): 1663–1683.

Walsh, I., Holton, J. A., Bailyn, L., Fernandez, W., Levina, N. and Glaser, B. (2015) "What grounded theory is . . . A critically reflective conversation among scholars," *Organizational Research Methods*, 18(4): 581–599.

Welch, C., Piekkari, R., Plakoyiannaki, E. and Paavilainen-Mäntymäki, E. (2011) "Theorising from case studies: Towards a pluralist future for international business research," *Journal of International Business Studies*, 42(5): 740–762.

Westney, D. E. (1987) *Imitation and Innovation: The Transfer of Western Organizational Patterns to Meiji Japan*, Cambridge, MA: Harvard University Press.

Whittington, R. and Mayer, M. (2000) *The European Corporation: Strategy, Structure, and Social Science*, Oxford: Oxford University Press.

Whittington, R., Mayer, M. and Curto, F. (1999) "Chandlerism in post-war Europe: Strategic and structural change in France, Germany and the UK, 1950–1993," *Industrial and Corporate Change*, 8(3): 519–551.

Wilkins, M. (1998) "Review: Socializing capital: The rise of the large industrial corporation in America by William G. Roy," *The Journal of American History*, 84(4): 1531–1532.

Williamson, O. E. (1971) "The multidivisional hypothesis," in R. Marris and A. Wood (eds), *The Corporate Economy: Growth, Competition, and Innovative Potential*, London: Macmillan, pp. 343–386.

Yates, J. (2014) "Understanding historical Methods in organization studies," in M. Bucheli and R. D. Wadhwani (eds), *Organizations in Time: History, Theory, Methods*, Oxford: Oxford University Press, pp. 265–283.

Yates, J., Orlikowski, W. J. and Okamura, K. (1999) "Explicit and implicit structuring of Genres: Electronic communication in a Japanese R&D Organization," *Organization Science*, 10(1): 83–103.

Ybema, S. (2014) "The invention of transitions: History as a symbolic site for discursive struggles over organizational change," *Organization*, (4): 495–513.

Zeitlin, J. and Herrigel, G. (eds) (2000) *Americanization and Its Limits: Reworking US Technology and Management in Post-War Europe and Japan*, Oxford: Oxford University Press.

Zundel, M., Holt, R. and Popp, A. (2016) "Using history in the creation of organizational identity," *Management & Organizational History*, 11(2): 211–235.

Index

Printed in the United States
By Bookmasters